Living Goddess Spirituality

A Feminine Divine Priestessing Handbook

B. Melusine Mihaltses

ISBN#978-0-9851384-7-9
Publisher: Feminine Divine Works
Schertz, Texas 78154-0114, U.S.A
©B. Melusine Mihaltses
Year: 2012

Living Goddess Spirituality

A Feminine Divine Priestessing Handbook.
B. Melusine Mihaltses

ISBN#978-0-9851384-7-9
Publisher: Feminine Divine Works
Schertz, Texas 78154-0114, U.S.A
©B. Melusine Mihaltses
Year: 2012

Living Goddess Spirituality,
A Feminine Divine Priestessing Handbook© 2012 by B. Melusine Mihaltses.
Published by

Feminine Divine Works
P.O.Box 114
Schertz, Texas 78154-0114
Femininedivineworks@gmail.com

Library of Congress Cataloging- in- Publication Data
Mihaltses, B. Melusine, 1970-
        Living Goddess Spirituality, A Feminine Divine Priestessing Handbook

            1.Goddess Mythology, 2. Women studies 3.Spirituality, 4. Feminism 5. Paganism, I. title

Includes bibliographical references
ISBN: 978-0-9851384-7-9
LCCN: 2012950223

Although the author and publisher have made every effort to ensure accuracy and completeness of information contained in this book. We assume no responsibility for errors, inaccuracies, omissions, or any inconsistency herein. Any slights of people, places, or organizations are Unintentional.

First edition
First printing, 2012
Cover Art: B. Melusine Mihaltses
All Interior Art, Photos and Illustration: B. Melusine Mihaltses

Printed and bound in the United States of America.

ISBN: 978-0-9851384-7-9
LCCN: 2012950223

Living Goddess Spirituality, A Feminine Divine Priestessing Handbook
By B. Melusine Mihaltses

ISBN: 978-0-9851384-7-9
LCCN: 2012950223

Living Goddess Spirituality

A Feminine Divine Priestessing Handbook
B. Melusine Mihaltses

****

Other Books By B. Melusine Mihaltses

***

"Gathering For Goddess,
A Complete Manual for
Priestessing Women's Circles"

***

"Goddess Grimoire Journal,
A Collection of
Simple Prose and Spells"

Dedication

This book is dedicated to my Foremothers,
To all those women who bravely paved the way for my rights,
and the freedoms I fully embrace and enjoy now as a woman.
The rights to invoke and exalt "Her" openly and
The rights to reclaim ancestral lineage and practices, I owe to you.
Our gender stands on thy shoulders now, Thank you.
May we continue to exemplify your strength and passions.

You who fought and continues to fiercely fight;
Your battles and wounds
have not been in vain and you are not forgotten…
Invoking your strength, we take on this battle, move forward
and continue to exalt, Goddess.

Thank you.

****To all who walk the ancient path of the Goddess****

LIVING GODDESS SPIRITUALITY TABLE OF CONTENTS

CONTENTS

PREFACE

Author of Women Spirituality and Goddess Mythologies, B. Melusine Mihaltses continues on her path of empowering women to delve more into their matriarchal ancestral lineage.

In her third published book, **"Living Goddess Spirituality, a Feminine Divine Priestessing Handbook,"** she presents twelve more deities from vastly different pantheons for women to connect with and garner much wisdom.

These various faces of the Sacred Feminine piercing our modern realms from ancient times are pertinent and relatable to a contemporary women's life. And learning of these ancient deities opens us up to seeing glimmers of our own divine selves as we transcend time and space to connect with her immortal energies in monthly gatherings.

Similar to her first book, **"Gathering for Goddess,"** B. Melusine Mihaltses brings you yet another jam-packed clearly organized, well-structured book with monthly Goddess lessons, chant sheets, artistic images, workshop activity suggestions, meditations, incantations, spells and rituals. Everything you'll need to establish a group or personal Goddess spiritual practice is found within these pages.

The Sacred Goddesses featured in this Priestessing handbook are:

The Welsh Mare Goddess of Forgiveness and Compassion **Rhiannon.**
The Chinese Creatrix Goddess of Order and Peace, **Nu-Kua.**
The Hindu Warrior Goddess, **Durga**
The Japanese Goddess of Laughter and Dance, **Uzume**
The Canaanite Matriarchal Goddess, **Asherah**
The Welsh Flower Goddess of our Awakenings, **Blodeuwedd**
The Sumerian Goddess of Women's Liberation, **Lilith**
The Voodoo Lwa and Protectress of women and children, **Dantor**
(Erzulie-Dantor), also referred to as, The Black Madonna.
The Norse Goddess of Sacrifice and Peace, **Sif**
The Hindu Goddess of Beauty & Abundance, **Lakshmi**
The Slavic Crone Goddess of Death and Rebirth, **Baba Yaga**
The Egyptian Goddess of Justice and Truth, **Ma'at**

And as a Bonus; A chapter dedicated for Priestessing, Blessing and formulating a Women's Goddess Group is included.

Whether you intend to use **"Living Goddess Spirituality"** as a personal study manual or incorporate it into a Women's Goddess study group. You will find it to be an invaluable resource in your libraries and a unique Pagan reference book to consistently consult throughout the years.

INTRODUCTION

The number of archeological evidence and anthropological research over the years have unquestionably proven that ancient civilization was not only polytheistic but it also saw the Divine as Feminine; venerating her and her Matriarchal attributes alongside the masculine. When we delve and examine pre-Christian, ancient Judaic, Babylonian, Canaanite, Sumerian religions (to name just a few) and indigenous spiritual practices of the Chinese and Japanese, Native Americans, the Egyptian and Hindu cultures, we are awakened to a plethora of diverse sacred faces of the Divine Feminine.

The fact that every single culture in history has exalted and venerated Goddess, the Sacred Feminine, has already been established as truth, yet in recent years, with the rise of monotheistic religions, the Sacred Feminine has been brutally replaced by a single male, full authoritative God, up in the sky. The consequences and damaging ramifications of this has done more than change the course of religious history, it has been instrumental in directly altering women's place in society and altering our role in modern day religious rites. Where women, in pre-biblical times, had been prime candidates to priestess for the Sacred Feminine in ancient religious and cultural rites, now they were forbidden and relegated to more passive, silenced positions. It is my belief that replacing Gods and Goddesses with one Male God has contributed to demoting women within the human race. For in a rising popular religion, that proselytized women as being created from man's rib or women being inherently evil by being the cause of man's fall from God's grace, it severely changes the status of our gender. The stories that we (consciously and unconsciously) continually tell ourselves (and one another) are passed down from generation to generation and these become our sacred myths. And these myths become what we base our entire religious and societal structures on. Thus, if in our collective auric stories we have painted one group of people in a false, weak, negative light you can see how that would have a damaging effect, not only on the group itself, but also, sadly on the whole, for, when one part of the pie is damaged the other half is also adversely effected. A table cannot stand balanced, the way it's meant to stand with one leg devalued and damaged; its purpose and authenticity is compromised.

As is evident in our disintegrating modern world today, where women, mothers and children, both in the U.S.A. and abroad, still struggle to assert their fundamental human rights; our world and how we coexist in it, peacefully, is greatly challenged. When you have a predominance of male politicians, trying to legislate women's bodies and reproductive issues, and the rise of the sex slave trade, and the predominance of violence towards women and children, and the existence of countries that still behead and gruesomely execute women for the most absurd reasons like; not being "properly" dressed, reading the "wrong" book, speaking up or fighting off a rapist or abuser, **it is clear "Mother," "Wombmyn," is not being honored.** Despite the evidence that we all come from the womb, from Mother, somehow this great significance has gotten lost in our collective modern consciousness. Women and the Sacred Feminine has been tragically replaced by a power over, authoritative male God in the sky for far too long, and this has had a tragically negative influence on the treatment, value and basic civil liberties for our gender across the globe.

Our Divine titles from ancient times, our Priestess crowns, our societal value, were stripped as new tales, new myths, were spread and these new monotheistic views were established as the ruling power. As a result, women, our ancestresses, could no longer be sustained and viewed as divine mothers, as was the case before the rise of patriarchy, through these monotheistic, male dominated, religions. When a society exalts a single male God, deliberately removing the Feminine (aka his wife/ mother / daughter) we have negatively shifted the power in our society and created a grossly damaging war against our gender by removing her from her rightful place as Goddess.

Part of my mission in life has been to unearth and reclaim all those numerous, forgotten ancient Goddess myths and folklores from various cultures and bring to light the value from these revealing, significant tales. Part of my mission in life has been to resurrect the balance of the scale by refocusing on the sacred feminine and re-establishing **"Her"** back to her rightful place as Goddess and hopefully as a result, give back to women their value, their self-esteem and their forgotten power. Part of my work has been researching through numerous modern and indigenous cultures, elements of the sacred Feminine, where she might've been hidden, patriarchally altered or simply forgotten. It is my belief that our gender has much to gain when we emancipate ourselves from patriarchal tenets and monotheistic religions that only seemed to serve to oppress, control and strip women of our power and any value in society. It is my belief that at the very least women being cognizant of these underlying, largely influential issues that we can begin to shift the scale to create healing and balance in our world. Reclaiming our lost, forgotten heritage, our Women mysteries, ancient sacred rites and Goddess myths are the gateway to reclaiming our power and parts of our hidden, forgotten Divine selves.

Researching ancient Goddesses from various different cultures and connecting with their myths and archetypal energy has always been a great passion of mine. I love experimenting and seeing how these numerous Feminine deities and their immortal presence can empower and positively influence modern day women. I find their presence in a women's spiritual life can bring monumental growth, cathartic discoveries and transformative healing and her presence is just as powerful and needed today, as it was in ancient times. As we head towards this shift in collective consciousness, as the Mayans and many other cultures have prophesied, we will see a rise in the Feminine Divine Awakening and a return to Goddess Consciousness, to bring balance to our Universe. On a very mundane level, if you don't believe me just look at this past election and the political issues that were intimately connected with women. And take a look at how women's vote directly influenced the end result of this 2012 election. For the first time in our history we had a record number of women running for Congress in 2012 and in 2013 the 113th Congress will have at least **81** Females in the House of Representatives, and 20 women sitting in the Senate. These are the highest numbers ever recorded in the history of Congress and hopefully a sign of things to come.... There is an awakening to Female Consciousness and I'd like to think that we are all doing our part in adding to it.

In closing I would like to leave you with this quote by Goddess Scholar and beloved bard and poet, Patricia Monaghan, who was always an inspiration to my work....

The most important fact about Goddesses, it seems to me,
is that they are invariably connected to Polytheism.
Put another way; there is no monotheistic religion based on Goddess.
Not a single Goddess appears without friends, companions, lovers, children.
The presence of the Goddess demands other Goddesses and Gods, as well.
This is comforting to me, for in my vision of the world redeemed,
the world made whole, I yearn for connection, not separation.
Throughout human history, gods have banished the Goddess,
demanding that we hold no other gods before them.
But the Goddess did not respond in kind.
In the religion that honors her, "she" had welcomed –even embraced – the other...
Patricia Monaghan

LIVING GODDESS SPIRITUALITY

DECEMBER
Welsh Mare Goddess of the Moon   **Rhiannon**   Justice or StarTarot card
Forgiveness, Steadfastness, Sacrifices, Survival, Trusting in Justice, Truth

JANUARY
Chinese Goddess of Creation   **Nu-Kua**   Empress Tarot card
Mother of Humanity, Creation and Order amidst Chaos, The Saviouress andCreatrix

FEBRUARY
Hindu Goddess of War and Transformation **Durga**   Tower Tarot card
The Wild One, Empowered Woman, Warrior, Fighter of Demons, Saviouress, Woman's Autonomy

MARCH
Japanese Goddess of Merriment   **Uzume**   Chariot Tarot card
Maiden Goddess of Merriment. Delights in her body, in nature and ecstatic dancing. Burlesque dancer,
Eradicating darkness with laughter. Springtime, Physicality, Shakti, our Body and Personal Dance

APRIL
Canaanite Matriarchal Goddess   **Asherah**   High Priestess Tarot card
Ancient Fertility Mother archetype, Tree Goddess, Nature and Pagan origins, Sovereingty & Divine Mother

MAY
Welsh Flower Goddess of Awakenings   **Blodeuwedd**   Devil Tarot card/7 of Sword
Maiden Flower Goddess of Shadows, Taboos, Hidden Dark Subconscious, Awakening, Transformations.
The gifts of the Owl. Betrayals, Beauty, Passions and Love

JUNE
Sumerian Goddess of Liberation   **Lilith**   Magician Tarot card
Freedom, Pleasure, Sexual Aggression and Liberation, The First Feminist. Refusal to submit or be
oppressed. Anger and Retribution. Awakener to injustice and gender inequality

JULY
African Lwa, Saint of Protection   **Dantor/Black Madonna**   Strength Tarot card
Revolutionist, Dagger Queen, Protective Mother, Fierce Defender of Children and Woman, Courage inspirer

AUGUST
Norse Harvest Goddess   **Sif**   Hanged Man Tarot card
Sacrifice, Harvest FertilityDeity, upholder of Family and Community, Harmony Creator, Peace maker

SEPTEMBER
Hindu Goddess of Wealth and Beauty   **Sri Lakshmi**   Queen Of Pentacle Tarot card
Feminine beauty and power. The gift of abundance, prosperity, creativity & luxuries, The Wife and Queen

OCTOBER
Russian Slavic Goddess of Fright   **Baba Yaga**   Hermit Tarot card
The Hag, the Dark side of the Goddess, Nature Mysterious, valuing the ugly, confronting our biggest Fears,
Our primordial wise Grandmother, The Crone. The Dark season

NOVEMBER
Egyptian Goddess of Truth   **Ma'at**   Judgment Tarot card
Looking deep in our Hearts to face our Truth, the afterlife, Judgment, Death's hall, life review, confronting
our Death and Judgment. Weighing our hearts and deeds on Her sacred scale

The Roles And Significant Lessons
These Goddesses Offer To Us As Women.

Rhiannon

Rhiannon is a symbol of steadfastness and forgiveness. She teaches us the importance and cathartic powers of releasing the chains of the past and allowing forgiveness to heal our hearts when tragedy has ensued. She presents great strength and unwavering faith in the face of adversity, prejudices and injustices.

Nu-Kua

Nu-Kua is the power of creation and order. She presents to us the strength to dive into chaos and make sense out of it. Calamitous events do not destroy her but rather gives her an opportunity to display her strength and great powers to formulate order and peace.

Durga

Durga is the ferocious tiger. When presented with demons and threats to her world, she fights. And she not only fights but takes great pleasure in the actual blood spewing battle. She is anger manifested and employed into action. This anger is not held within to self-destruct your soul, no, she uses that anger as a vehicle of action for her victory while defeating those who are trying to destroy her.

Uzume

Uzume is boldness and merriment all contained and reflected in the physical body. She presents to us the power and magick our beautiful physical body is capable of displaying. The power of laughter and our personal life transformative dance is represented in her.

Asherah

Asherah is the embodiment of the mother archetype and reflects our beauty, fertility, sovereignty and staying power as women. She displays the beauty in nature. She will ask you to embrace the elements of Trees and your natural environment as reflection of the Divine and more importantly, reflections of your womanhood.

Blodeuwedd

Blodeuwedd is the awakened one. She knows all too well the two realms of night and day, of shadow and wakefulness. She is the encased beautiful flower who becomes the free flying, night owl. She is the one who reflect the dichotomy our gender so often is subjected to; that of living in two realms, that of needing to be awake and alert as the owl, in a world that would rather contain us as simply beautiful, voiceless flowers.

Lilith

Lilith is the adamant voice that will not be victimized, oppressed nor play by patriarchal rules. She is autonomy and freedom and will not succumb to societal pressures no matter what names are flung at her. You can call her demon, bitch, cunt, dyke, witch, monster, whatever... but she WILL remain whole and authentically true to herself, for she will not lay herself down for anyone. She will not subordinate herself for man's pathetic, sick ideologies and she soars in flight with her autonomous woman power intact throughout the ages because of it. She is brazen pleasure seeker, whole unto herself and epitomizes woman's sexual liberation and a powerful representation of Feminism.

Dantor

Dantor is the spirit of the revolutionist who incites our courage to stand for what is right and just. She is the Mother who defends at all cost her offspring. She is the protectress and defender of women and children and will wield her machete and daggers to go into battle when the only way to be emancipated is to finally fight back.

Sif

Sif is the sacrificial one, who has her eyes on the bigger picture and not the individual. She is the one who seeks to formulate peace and harmony among her tribe and will often offer herself up in sacrifice for the greater good of all. She willing surrenders parts of herself for the protection and greater good of her family. With her, we are made aware of our role within our community and the sacrifices sometimes required of us for peace, harmony and prosperity. She is the golden Harvest that must be pruned in order for greater prosperity to eventually ensue.

Sri Lakshmi

Sri Lakshmi represents our feminine beauty, fecundity and prosperity. She enters our realm at the Harvest to make us aware of our many riches and our potential to maintain and manifest even more. She is the Harvest itself with its great beauty and palpable ripeness and she beckons you to embrace with gratitude the gifts of abundance.

Baba Yaga

Baba Yaga inaugurates the Dark season, when all around you is barren or appears to be preparing to die, as it settles and enters into the deep earth to compost itself. She stands to represent that which is frightening and unknown, as the start of the winter months often brings a tangible fear of what the weather may become and if our harvest will last throughout the next four months. She is the wise crone that in appearance (with her bony hunchback, wild silver hair and long warty nose) is a frightening sight. Yet, she is meant to dare you to take a daunting step towards growth and transformation by initially first confronting her. All that we fear but must confront is represented in the hag and she comes into our realm to challenge and build up our courage.

Ma'at

Ma'at is cosmic law and truth. She is the power of final judgment and she beckons you to take an honest look at your whole life now before it's too late. She invites you to closely inspect your heart to unearth what weights it down and offers you the cathartic gift of an unburdened soul.

"My primary relationship is with myself –
all others are mirrors of it. As I learn to love myself,
I automatically receive the love and appreciation that I desire from others.
If I am committed to myself and to living my truth,
I will attract others with equal commitment…"
Shakti Gawain, from Reflections in the Night.

AS A PAGAN, I CHOOSE GODDESS!

Why solely Goddess? I can hear most devoted Pagans and Wiccans asking this question, concern that perhaps I am spiritually deficient and not properly balanced in my religious practice or simply failing to understand long standing Wiccan traditions. I can assure you, I am not, but perhaps it's best if I start from the beginning.

As far back as I can remember, quite early on in my Spiritual path, it was Goddess who called me. I grew up in a very eclectic, occult honoring household and was privy, from an early age, to an array of spiritual traditions and practices. I was also always encouraged to follow my heart and intuition and thus when Goddess called, I was not dismissive but rather receptive and welcoming.

I remember in my youth seeing and feeling Goddess in almost everything I personally encountered and yet, that reality did not match with the one being offered to me by mainstream society. Even at this young tender age, I saw the Feminine Divine in various aspects of nature; flowers trees, rivers, the stars and the Moon and I could spend hours, days really, enamored by "Her," not realizing I was already worshipping Goddess. Yet, it appeared that would prove to be more challenging than expected, as all around me there were images of the masculine being forced upon me, almost demanding that I relinquish my love of Goddess, less I would be deemed as (*oh dear…*) "strange."

Growing up, it appeared as if the masculine was being championed as the hero, the great divine, worthy of our complete sole reverence. In subtle and yet blatantly obvious ways for me, men appeared to have all the authority and what they deemed as power. Their portrayals in the movies and television shows then and in news forecast, radio and sports, seemed, to this young maiden, over amplified, and I won't even get into the mundane, daily experiences that supported this perspective like; school proceedings and the neighborhood playground. I felt a consistent bombardment of images tooting and championing the masculine as the only true heir of our exaltation and divine veneration, for it was men who became presidents of our great country, it was men who became admired and feared dictators and rulers in other faraway lands and folktales. It was men who became wealthy and powerful as CEOs and business moguls, it was man who would always become Pope for the Vatican in Rome and it was man, who as Jesus Christ, was (to the over populous Christians) God. It was a chubby man who was adored during Christmas time for his ability to climb down our chimney to bring us gifts and toys in the cold winter and it was men who appeared to have all sorts of accolades and respect, while women, it seemed, at this time in the 1970's, had to fight, and fight hard, for every single measly piece of recognition. These were the false tales being presented to me as a young girl. This was my exterior experience and perspective at the time and it certainly clashed with my inner world and the deep rooted feelings I was nursing for the Feminine Divine. As a young girl, it appeared to me the media proselytized that man was everything and he could do no wrong, as all of his follies were excused and blamed on this gender's enigmatic divine stereotype. The masculine was being exalted and everything connected to the masculine had great power, even God was a man (according to most mainstream religions I initially encountered) and I inherently saw that belief as having a grander impact on our human consciousness than first realized. As a result, there was even a point in my own youth, where in my confusion and ignorance, I started to dress and behave more boyishly, believing this was the only way I could even come close to elevating my gender to equal status footing. While it was perfectly fine to experiment in this way in my household, it did not go over too well outside of my home environment.

It was the 1970s and I was privy to witness the global conscious awakening for gender equality and the rise of Feminism....but this was merely the inception of a long journey and a vicious battle with patriarchy that would continue for many more years to come. It was the male that appeared to have power, but from where I stood, from my heart center, from my spirit, it was women/"womyn"/"wombmyn" who deserved it. For quite early on I saw her Creatrix powers, her nurturance, strength and love and yet, her voracious qualities....qualities that for a modern day woman, was deemed as bitchy, manly, mental, horrifying, unladylike, and quite often, degraded by society as a whole, for seemingly being so "unfeminine-divine" and far from powerful, but to my young eyes, this could not be further from the truth.

Despite the messages I was being fed by society, messages that conflicted with my mother's teachings, I intuitively felt there was a lot more to this male propaganda and subjugation of women. Quite early on, I distinctly noted the coercion of male energy as it was being exalted, sold, and championed and I remember feeling it seemed so irrelevant to me as a girl. I could not surrender nor connect with this venerated male energy, it felt so foreign to me, and as the years went by it felt more and more inappropriate, almost damaging to my core. I noted how unfair it seemed that God(s) derived so much adoration and respect, while women and images of the Goddess were barely being discussed and almost concealed. And I began to have the impression that they were being purposefully hidden from the world and I wondered why.....

Angels, female saints, the immaculate Virgin Mary, the controversial Mary Magdalene and the numerous female deities presented to me in various mythologies, and researched folklore, held my attention. It did not take much for me to intimately connect with Artemis and Athena, more so than Zeus or Hermes. I found myself able to connect with the Virgin Mary and the numerous other women mentioned in the bible much more than the male Christ archetype. The more I researched this initially fragile ideology, the more I began to tap into something so powerful that I could intuitively see why it was being concealed. There is great power for women inherently found in the Goddess and at a very early age this knowledge was gifted to me... A woman who connects with Goddess, connect with a most vital, ancient, powerful inner part of herself and she is awakened. It is this awakened state that is so empowering to women and downright frightening and dangerous to a patriarchal society.

I noticed that the more I chose to focus on female energy the more important it became and the more I realize its great value to my own personal growth and self-esteem. As the years progressed I made the significant connection that linked our gender's self-esteem, wellbeing and self- worth, inherently intertwined in our spiritual choices and our religious beliefs. The more I had focused on male energy and the God, the less I was feeding myself and the more it was tearing away at my core -negatively affecting a vital ancient part of myself. Focusing on the Feminine Divine had more relevance for me as a woman, imparting significant spiritual growth, helping me connect with my inner power and strengthening my magick in ways I had not anticipated. The more I delved into the Sacred Feminine, the more I unearthed my own spark of divinity and, something I had not anticipated but, quite miraculously, my own self- worth and self- esteem increased the more I learned the truth of "Her" Divine existence.

In Goddess, I discovered that the energy we deemed as "male" and "female" was inherently contained in "Her", for she contains **all** and thus, my own personal spiritual practice was not lacking at all. Just as we human beings exemplify both male and female characteristics at various times in our lives, there are many deities in countless pantheons throughout the ages that exemplify, respectively both "male" and "female" energy. For me, there has never been a need to seek specific male energy within a male God, for I have always been able to easily tap into this type of energy, when necessary, in the immortal Goddesses of ancient time. Just as you may have a very feminine (womanly) expression of Goddess in Aphrodite, Lakshmi, or Hathor, you will also find the fiercely aggressive (male like -And I only label it as such because it is what most will comprehend as male...) energy of Morrighan, Medea, Baba Yaga or Kali and the cerebral energy of Athena etc... And thus I learned that balance, perhaps, is not best defined as "male" and "female," but rather as an assortment of varying opposing energies. If we pause and look at ourselves closer we will find this is true for us humans, as it is for divine archetypes and the Goddess.

When I am in need of a specific energy in my Spiritual practice, whether it is deemed by our society as "male" or "female," I look to Goddess to fulfill this need, for she invariably always reveals her infinite connection to **all**. And as a "Wombmyn," I simply understand her language and her manifestations best.

So, when faced with perplexing grimaces and the question, why Goddess....? My answer is, why not? Mainstream religion and society continues to put all of their veneration unto one male God, why would it seem incomprehensible to do the same, only now with the Feminine Divine, the Goddess? The acceptable claim by many Christians is that God contains all, both male and female, so why not call this all-encompassing deity, **Goddess**? It certainly fits the bill best in my humblest opinion but I suppose claiming it as masculine, fairs better in a patriarchal society in which women are to never to realize their full potential as Divine beings, or so they hope.

In this day and age when it appears patriarchy is still very much alive, oppressing, killing, silencing and destroying our gender all across the globe, it would seem Goddess holds the key to our gender's resurrection and empowerment and yes.... balance. Balance, because in the face of patriarchy **nothing** is balanced and it almost requires the "drastic measures" (a labeled so often deemed by others) of embracing the Goddess. In this patriarchal world we live in, the male will always be exalted and God will always have center stage for mainstream society, as Wiccans, we needn't worry about that, but it is Goddess, who is so often shrouded in mystery, fervently concealed and sadly forgotten. And it is "She" who most requires and deserves our veneration. Learning about God(s) and their many purposeful attributes is not a difficult thing to do, for the God archetypes are always in plain sight, championed and plenty has been written about them. Yet, it is women and all of her great complexities and many mysteries that, to this day, continue to **be** unknown as we move forward and try to unearth all of her sacred rites, multiple aspects and "Her-story." It is women and her worship that has been concealed, undervalued and hidden throughout the years and it is precisely this quest and intuitive knowledge that personally led me to this path of self-discovery and empowerment.

"She" has been hidden long enough and we don't know nearly enough as we should regarding Goddess and our Divine lineage. It is woman and the Feminine Divine that needs to be exalted because SHE IS everywhere; though we try to conceal her, put a blanket over her to dismiss and ignore, try to out- shout her and silence her... it is Goddess that permeates everything around us, including our very earth. It is the female that has always and ever shall be; The Mother, Creatrix, the source of ALL and it is from Mother that we have the Gods. The fact that in our patriarchal society man is venerate, first and for most, does not change this monumental detail, that sacred Mother, the Divine Feminine, birth us all. And in fact, the blatant disregard and disrespect for women, the Mother and the Feminine Divine is manifesting a vile, self -sabotaging, corrupt society that is negatively impacting everyone upon this earth.

Why Goddess? Why not??? To disregard my gender and the Feminine Divine is to reject my own self, and it is fundamentally detrimental to my own personal growth. Goddess is the source of all and yet, in my humblest opinion, "She" doesn't get enough accolades. The sacred Feminine and all of Womankind deserve more credit and respect than has been expressed in recent years and as women it is up to us to be "Her" biggest advocates and liberate ourselves from patriarchal practices and thus, be our own best proponents. The time has come to return home, to return to source and honor the Sacred Feminine for this is the truest way to achieve balance after a harsh millennium under patriarchy, only then can we all (both male and female) find balance and healing.

"Imagine a Woman who names her own Gods.
A woman who imagines the Divine
in her image and likeness,
who designs a personal Spirituality
to inform her daily life..." Patricia Lynn Reilly

Hail to the Goddess and all Blessings to her Daughters and Priestesses!!!

CHAPTER ONE

Rhiannon

"...The most beautiful people we have known are those who have known defeat, known suffering, known struggles, known loss and have found their way out of the depths. These persons have an appreciation, a sensitivity, and an understanding of life that fills them with compassion, gentleness, and a deep loving concern. Beautiful people do not just happen. .."

Elisabeth Kubler-Ross

"I forgive, I release, I move forward, I send love, I send light, I am all-right..."

B. Melusine Mihaltses

RHIANNON

RHIANNON

" Forgiveness is the cleansing fire that burns away old regrets and resentments ..."
Jonathan Lockwood Huie

RHIANNON ALTAR SET UP
OUR ALTAR

Altar cloth : *A white or silver colored altar cloth is best at this time of year. If you wish to be creative, you may also incorporate an equestrian altar cloth with images of horses. She is known as a Lunar Goddess, and so, an altar cloth with symbols of the moon would also be a nice touch.*

Image: *The image of the Welsh Goddess, Rhiannon, can be featured in the center of your altar but if you can't obtain one, you may also use a simple statue of a Horse. I have a lovely, silver colored, horse sculpture that I often feel inspired to place on my altar to Rhiannon.*

Always present on the altar;
A silver pentacle, a cast iron cauldron, drums, speaking stick, wand, athame, elemental representations…..

Air: *feather bundles, angel wings, bird, eagle or owl statuaries. Bell &, chimes, Incense type sticks, cones, charcoal brisket and fine powdered herbs; frankincense , myrrh.*
Fire: *pillar candles, glass enclosed candles in yellow, gold, white*
Water: *Small glass bowl with Water and or chalice with Champagne, Cranberry Juice or Red wine.*
Earth: *At this time of the year I like to use bare branches and create a beautiful center piece of these long, arm-like branches. A small dish of soil or dry herbs can also be used*

Other items pertinent to this particular gathering
An Image of the Sun
Representation of the Moon
A figurine of a Horse
A photo or image of the Badger
Tarot cards

Sacred objects from members:
Notes:

MONTH AND THE SEASON

December

The twelfth month of the Gregorian calendar, December, arrives bringing the gifts of numerous festivities and holidays from Christmas, to Hanukkah, Kwanzaa, Wassailing, to Yule, Modranicht (*Mothernight)* and the Winter Solstice. It seems the ancient Pagan traditions of our ancestors have quite subtly infiltrated the celebration and practices of numerous other religions. It probably received its name from the Latin word *"Decem"* meaning "Ten" as it was considered the tenth month of the Roman calendar. Astrologically, Sagittarius (the Archer) which is ruled by generous, benevolent Jupiter (Nov.21 –Dec. 20), influences the energy of the month.

December, for most people, is unquestionably a very busy time of the year. For me personally, the month becomes a blur that goes by entirely too quickly. At a time when our ancestors probably spent a great deal of time indoors, less active, more introspective and when all of nature (even the critters of the land) seem to join in this customary retreat and hibernation, it would seem logical for us to do the same. Yet, this time of year finds many of us harried, stressed, overbooked with activities and little time to withdraw from the world.

Some parts of the world are knee deep in snow with cold weather and quite appropriately one popular name for the Full moon this month is, "Full Cold Moon". It was also known as "Longest night Moon" a reference to the longest night of the year, on the Winter Solstice (December 20-21st). Despite the cold encouraging us to stay cozily indoors and less active, the energy levels outdoor, at this time of year, seems highly charged, split and very festive.

With the inundation of commercial advertisements and storewide sales beckoning you to shop till you drop and everyone appearing to be in such a rush to get things done and get to their appointed destinations, our environment feels far from meditative and reflective. It's easy to get swept into this swirling of fast paced holiday energy, despite what our own bodies and spirit might prefer at this time of year. Perhaps the holiday decorations everywhere, the sparkling lights, tinsels and mistletoe, the trees and the landscape of glistening white snow, covering some parts of our Earth like a blanket, can beckon us to slow down and embrace the festive atmosphere. Such imagery can sometimes touch upon our most nostalgic, tender memories in its beauty. It can also bring unexpected healing to our spirit, to be amidst this wintry canvas.

December brings the Winter Solstice, which inaugurates the rebirth of our brightest star, the Sun. On the longest night of the year, when our ancestors braved the cold of the darkest night, The Goddess gives birth to her child (the bright Sun) and thus to a special part of her own self. We honor the infant born at this time of year and the healing afforded to all of us with the sun's arrival. It is a perfect time to tap into our inner child and view the world through childlike eyes, with curiosity, freshness, hope and a sense of new perspective.

The old calendar year is coming to an end and we are in the midst of celebrating the birth of the new. The much welcomed sunlight begins to grow in strength, bringing much hope for the subsequent arrival of Spring. When you are in the dead of Winter and the lack of daylight is playing havoc on your emotional and physical health, the sun's arrival is something indeed to be celebrated.

We have much reason to celebrate the growing light as it points to yet another turn of the sacred wheel. This month we will endeavor to connect with the Welsh, Mare Goddess of compassion and forgiveness, Rhiannon.

All Monthly intro text taken from author's first book,
"Gathering for Goddess, A Complete Manual for Priestessing Women's Circles"

RHIANNON GODDESS LESSON

Rhiannon is the Beautiful Lunar Goddess in Welsh mythology, who later becomes known as a Fairy Queen. Her name literally translates as, *"Divine Queen"* and she was known to have a beautiful singing voice. She is most popularly known as the Welsh Mare Goddess, sometimes depicted as a beautiful long haired woman dressed in gold, ridding her white mare sidesaddle and sometimes she is depicted as the horse itself. She is closely linked with fertility, freedom, creativity and maternal concerns, typical attributes of a Lunar deity, but she was also protector of horses, animals and the stable.

As the horse was a very important, sacred animal to ancient cultures and held a great deal of esteem and veneration, there are a number of Goddesses all closely associated with horses, like Rhiannon. In Celtic mythology there is the Goddess Epona, who had a great cult following there and when she was brought over to Rome, they named her Rigantona or Rig Antonia which translates as, *"Great Queen."* For the Irish she was known as Macha and for the Gaulic, Edain.

According to one of her folklores, Rhiannon was being pressured to follow her family vows and marry an older God who was more suited to their Divine family lineage, but she refused. Instead she sought after a mortal prince by the name of Pwyll (also known in English as Paul).

In Welsh mythology there was often an enchanted small mound in various distinct sacred areas on the land, known as a "tor" and it was believed to be a portal for the Divine to interact and sometimes even enchant mortals. One day, the handsome mortal prince, Pwyll, found himself standing on one of these very sacred mounds. His accompanying entourage saw him and fearing the legendary tales warned him not to stay but quite unexpectedly, while standing there, he witnessed a beautiful white mare, galloping quickly right passed him. A woman with long tresses, dressed in gold, rode on this white horse and he instinctively was captivated. The next day he decided to try his luck again and see if, perchance, he can actually catch up with this beautiful maiden.

The next day, he approached the same "tor" and waited well prepared. Within minutes she appeared again, only this time she galloped even faster and his attempt to catch up with her failed miserably. On the third day, he was more determined than ever to catch up with this fast paced white mare but when, defeated and out of breath, he failed again, he finally just called out to her in desperation to wait and please stop. To his surprise, she did and when they met, eye to eye, they were immediately enamored with one another. He asked her what she was doing there and her answer was simply that she was there to acquire his love. From the very first day he saw her, he admitted, she indeed had acquired his devotion. Rhiannon then tells him to return to the same sacred mound, a year and a day later, and promises him that if he does, they will be married on that day. And so a year and a day later, the mortal prince returns to the same "tor" to claim his beautiful Lunar Goddess as his bride and future Queen.

As promised by the Goddess, their beautiful marriage ceremony took place that very day, in the enchanted forest, with all of nature supporting their union, all except for one very angry ex-suitor. The old, resentful man she had been promised to in marriage made unwarranted scandalous advances to the new bride and in her effort not to draw too much attention to the situation and ruin their special wedding ceremony; she converted the harasser into a badger. She then placed the badger into a sack and tossed it into the ocean, but the bag became undone and he managed to sneak himself back into the Prince's entourage as they were heading back home. Later on in this tale, this would prove to be a most dreadful calculating occurrence, as he vowed to have his revenge for being rejected by the Goddess.

Soon after the wedding, the mortal prince and his new bride returned to his kingdom where she was greeted as a stranger with much suspicion surrounding her qualifications as a Queen, for she was not like them. She was a Lunar Goddess, of divine lineage and now she was among humans. They did not easily embrace her and she quickly became the subject of many rumors, gossips and distant mistreatment. Finding fault with her at every bend, they wondered why after a few years of marriage she had not provided a proper heir, with a baby. By the third year of marriage Rhiannon finally did give birth to a beautiful baby boy and the entire kingdom seemed overjoyed with their celebrations.

As was the custom back then, the Queen had several attendants especially with a newborn. The attendants were all required to help in keeping a close watch over the baby while the new mother would catch up with her sleep and recuperate from the strenuous birthing experience. On one particular night, as Rhiannon slept, in confident that the baby was well cared for, all six maid attendant inexplicably fell asleep simultaneously and it was then that her beloved newborn was kidnapped. When all her maid attendants woke up and, to their mortified surprise, could not locate the royal baby, they feared their own fate and knew they would be executed for child neglect. In their desperation to save their own lives they immediately sought to blamed the Queen, Rhiannon, who was already subject to much suspicion and prejudice. Frantically, they located and killed a nearby puppy, smeared its blood and bones across the slumbering Queen and prepared to plot and accuse Rhiannon of the unthinkable. They accused her of eating her own child in a moment of insanity. All in the kingdom already disliked Rhiannon for her unusual Divine blood lineage and so it was not a particularly demanding task to convince everyone that indeed the Queen had gone mad and done this horrific act.

Being totally traumatized by this horrific crime, both she and her husband reacted in the way that most people would react to traumatic news regarding their own child. Rhiannon started to question herself and traumatized and guilt-ridden she blamed herself, while her husband didn't know who to believe. He too was traumatized and could not defend his wife but he neither wanted to divorce nor have his wife executed. He beseeched the courts to spare her life and rule for clemency. He implored the courts to have mercy and find another form of punishment besides the death sentence she was expected to receive for such a heinous crime.

In the end, they allowed her to live and stipulated her punishment would be to forever greet all visitors to the kingdom with the sad, horrific tale of the death of her son and then she was to offer them her back, as a mare, and carry them all the way into the castle. Most people who heard her story did not take advantage of her offer to ride on her back but many came from far and wide to hear her tell this very ghastly personal story.

One day, a couple with a young child arrived at the entryway and as Rhiannon had done for the last seven years, she resigned herself to tell the sad tale once more and then offer her back to carry them into the castle. When she finished telling her story, she looked into the young boy's eyes and noted a familiarity within his gaze; it stunned her to the bones. He was the spitting image of her husband, the King Pwyll and it was in that very moment that the old couple admitted they had found her baby seven years ago, abandoned in a field, and since they had no children of their own, they raised him as if he was their very own. They now believed him to be the King and Queen's royal son. Immediately the news spread of the young boy's return and when pressed, the maid attendants from that horrid fateful night finally confessed to what they had done. Later, it was revealed that the badger, Rhiannon's resentful old suitor, had kidnapped the child that night, seven years ago while everyone slept.

When the story spread quickly of this injustice and Rhiannon's innocence, they quickly restored her to her throne and re-embraced her as their Queen. She was more loved and respected than ever before because she had endured so much unjust pain and suffering in this entire cruel misunderstanding and yet, she exemplified such strength and dignity in the way she handled herself and the way she accepted her wrongful punishment for the last seven years.

Despite the horrific accusations and the loss of her child for seven years, she remained steadfast in her truth, believing one day the real story would be revealed and justice would prevail. The Goddess impressed the people of her land even further when she expressed great compassion and forgiveness to those who had placed her in such a dreadful position with their false accusations. She understood full well why her maid attendants did what they did and, despite the great loss and pain it caused her, she extended boundless compassion, understanding and forgiveness to her accusers in the end. This is the gift of this Welsh Lunar Goddess, for she teaches us to remain steadfast in the face of great chaos and crisis and above all, she exemplifies the healing gift of forgiveness and compassion.

RHIANNON MUSING

Rhiannon is a Goddess of truth and integrity and the strong belief that justice will prevail no matter what. There seems to be hints of the Justice deity, Themis, in this Goddess but more than anything, while working with this deity, I was most struck by her similarities to Goddesses like Kwan Yin, the Virgin Mary and Corn Mother, Selu, in her ability to withstand so much sadness and heartache and yet, be able to trust that in the end, everything would work itself out. There is an aspect of Rhiannon that wholly exemplifies the cathartic gift of compassion and the power of forgiveness, for despite everything that she was put though, she was able to look into the heart of the situation, face the truth and move on. In her ability to endure the loss of her newborn and then survive with dignity, the cruel accusations that she had eaten and killed her very own son is demonstrative of a Goddess who knows great inner strength. She exemplifies the art of holding onto ones truth in the mist of horrific chaos and calamities.

Throughout her myths she appears misunderstood and always going against the grain by exclusively following her heart. From the moment she refused to marry her family's first choice for a husband, to her unwelcomed arrival in her mate's mortal realm and kingdom. She follows her heart despite surrounding pressures and great discomfort in her life and yet, she display great faith that all will work itself out. In this case she appears to consistently refuse to play the role of victim and is continually illustrating for us inner strength and steadfastness.

These attributes; strength and steadfastness, are closely linked to her totem animal, the mare, for indeed horses are powerful, strong, grounded animals that exemplify stamina, loyalty, devotion and an uncanny ability to overcome obstacles. The Horse is also a warrior spirit; safeguarding its master. A lover of freedom and travel, the horse is, most interestingly, faithful to its master at all cost. And these are transferable qualities palpable in the Goddess Rhiannon. It is these very significant attributes that we see revealed to us in her myths.

Personally, I think for those of us who have been wronged in our lives or erroneously accused of things that go so against our very nature. Rhiannon can offer us solace and is quite a powerful message to help us sojourn to inner healing. This is Goddess work! She invites you to step back into your own power and not necessarily fight fire with fire, nor get entangled in "he said, she said" games but rather move passed beyond the drama and trust that the truth will eventually prevail. Now this is easier said than done and it takes a great deal of patience, maturity and divine wisdom to be able to rise above certain situations and release negative events in our lives, like she so illustrated for us in her myths. In meditating on Rhiannon, I contemplate on those who are victims of gossip and lies; whether it's in a scholastic environment, religious, labor or residential community, it is an excruciating thing to have to deal with and our natural inclination might be to fight back with our own set of nasty lies and rumors or worse... but Rhiannon opens the door to yet another way of handling the situation, one where you will not lose your heart and soul in the battlefield.

With her, I also contemplate on those who at this very moment are incarcerated and are wrongly accused of crimes they could not have possibly committed but... because of gender or race or social status or any of the other ridiculous prejudicial reasons, except for the facts, must endure our flawed judicial system. Rhiannon is not very well received by her husband's kingdom, they hold prejudice views against her, right from the start and it's clear no matter what she does or doesn't do, she will not have a chance to have a fair trial. And sadly this tragedy happens too often on so many different levels in our own lives. The unfairness of judgment exercised, simply based on something other than the facts is routine in our modern day society and it is wrong... Yet, on every level from job applications, politics, to popularity contest in schools and Universities, to actual crime investigations, people are subject to unproven accusations that can negatively, destroy lives.

Rhiannon does not allow herself to be destroyed by the horrific loss of her son nor by the damaging, erroneous accusations that she was entangled in, instead she anchors herself in the truth. She accepts her punishment and remains strong, knowing that the Universe will always return to balance after periods of chaos... and truth, no matter how long it may take, will always prevail.

"Only what is true will remain because what is true doesn't need anybody to believe it..." Don Miguel Ruiz

There is great wisdom, maturity and trust that we so often fail to have naturally within us, but with Rhiannon as our guide, we can begin to consciously practice these attributes and tap into those helpful traits, applying them to our own personal lives. She gives us the strength when strength is needed... and she helps us to stand in our truth amidst chaos and insurmountable crisis.

RHIANNON GODDESS GATHERING DAY

PURPOSE: To connect with the energy of the mare Goddess, Rhiannon and commemorate the sabbat of Winter Solstice.

CHECK INS: We gather around the Circle and introduce ourselves to one another, while also voicing our feelings on this month and our hope for the upcoming season.

CHANTING WORKSHOPS: *(see song textsheet included)*

DRUMMING: A drumming musical CD track will be played, to give participants a chance to connect and ground to this very moment. They are invited to find a comfortable seat or stand and add movement, however they are most inspired by the drumming.

AGREEMENTS: We go around the circle reading a few lines each, of our Group Agreements and add any new ones that seem necessary. Agreements are signed and submitted in confidence.

CHECK INS: Consider for a moment the Goddess Rhiannon as a mare. Reflect meditatively on her image, found in the Goddess Oracle or Goddess tarot or any other image you have available and begin to invoke her by stating aloud the images we see in her.

LEARNING ABOUT THE GODDESS RHIANNON
Learning of Rhiannon's attributes, tales, her lineage and myths

GODDESS WORKSHOP
WORKSHOP I.
The Justice or Star Tarot card. Exploring its meaning and how it relates to the Goddess Rhiannon
WORKSHOP II.
Connecting with the Horse as sacred totem and unearthing its deep lesson for us as women.
WORKSHOP III.
Exploring Wales and Welsh history and culture by viewing photos, books, slides or a movie to get a better understanding of her home and Welsh landscape.
WORKSHOP IV.
A Badger was responsible for inaugurating the devastation that manifested for Rhiannon, what are some myths and folklore connected with the badger? We will explore the Badger's mystical meaning for the Goddess.
WORKSHOP V.
Spell workings to stop or prevent gossipers. Crafting, to rectify and protect victims of gossipers. A clearing out negativity spell or mantra.
WORKSHOP VI.
Since it is the sabbat of the Solstice we will craft a plaster or paper-mache, Sun, to use on our altar to remind us of the power of the growing Sun at this time of the year.
WORKSHOP VII.
Meditation offering. Documenting in our journals our trance work journey and unique experience.

I was inspired to work with Horse Medicine after having a dream in which I saw a Silver young Colt, grooming itself in a nearby neighbor's front yard. This was also near the time of a Sagittarius New Moon. My journey to the Welsh Mare Goddess, Rhiannon, was clearly asserting itself now in my dreams and I wanted to share its energy with my sisters.

Attributes of Horse Medicine

1. Faithfulness
2. Stamina
3. Endurance
4. Wild powerful Energy
5. Physical prowess
6. Very Friendly, cooperative
7. Adventuresome
8. Friendship or group alliance
9. Appeal and persuasiveness
10. Wildness
11. Trustworthiness
12. A great aid to Overcoming obstacles
13. All kinds of travel... Physical & Spiritual Journeying
14. Considered a Valuable Spirit Guide
15. Human Companionship
16. Herbivore
17. Needs little sleep; can help one get a lot done.
18. Effectively helps direct your energy
19. Powerful ally
20. Helps create positive alliance, friendships
21. Horse Goddesses often were Solar and Lunar and
22. Represented Complete life cycles; birth death, rebirth
23. Used in numerous human work situations and wars
24. Horses are very loyal animals,
25. Upholding honesty, trust, dignity, self-respect
26. Introduced to the Native Americans by the Spaniards
27. Shamans believed horse to be valuable spirit guides to travel through different realms, especially related to helping the soul travel from life to death.
28. Aids astral travels.
29. A very Social animal
30. The male will leave the herd when mature,
31. The female, usually stays with the mother, according to one source.
32. Invites you to let people in your life like family, friends, colleagues,
33. Associated with Swiftness, Attribute of Speed in our workings as they can be very fast. Riding a horse, one literally felt like flying...
34. An animal often associated with wind because it allowed people to explore and find freedom from there localities
35. Horse has always been an ally and of tremendous service to humanity

36. **HORSE MEDICINE:** It asks you to consider where you are restricted? Where do you crave more freedom? Awaken and discover your own freedom and power.

37. **ASSOCIATED WITH NUMEROUS DEITIES**
    a. Like the Norse God Odin,
    b. Indian /Hindu, Sun God, Surya
    c. Greek Sun God Apollo's chariots
    d. Kwan yin was symbolize by a white horse
    e. Vishnu's final incarnation is believed to be a white horse
    f. Greek huntress Artemis
    g. Middle Eastern Goddess, Anahit rode a chariot of Horses
    h. Roman and Celtic Goddess Epona, Macha, Edain, Rigatonia etc..
    i. Welsh Goddess, Rhiannon

RHIANNON GODDESS GATHERING RITUAL

PURPOSE: Connecting with the Welsh mare Goddess, Rhiannon, honoring the season and reclaiming our inner truths.

Smudging & Anointing: with our special Blessing Oil made of Rue and Rosemary oil

WELCOMING; one another with Love and gratitude. Incense of sandalwood and frankincense or a smudge of Sage and copal will burn by the entrance of our ritual space.

INTENT SPOKEN: Today we honor the Goddess, Rhiannon and welcome the light of truth.

CIRCLE CASTING

From Sister to Sister and hand to hand,

this Sacred circle is now cast...

We now stand between the realms

on hallowed space our feet do dwell...

The circle is cast!

Blessed Be!

ELEMENTAL INVOCATIONS

From the South, we call the sacred Element of Fire

Hail to the Red mare of Fire, come through, from thy Southern realm. Come, the Sun's charioteer with thy fierce impetuous speed, moving, shaking, shifting us to our desired destiny.
Hail and Welcome Fire!!!!

From the West, we call the sacred Element of Water

Hail to the Blue mare of Water. Come through, from thy Western realm. You bring the healing through your lunar seeds and awaken the tears of compassion. Come allow us to ebb and flow in your cathartic gifts and abstractions. **Hail and Welcome, Water!!!!**

From the North, we call the sacred Element of Earth

Hail to the Brown mare of the solid earth, come through, from thy Northern realm, affirming our existence, supporting our human form. We feel you in our bodies, encaser of our flesh and soul. **Hail and Welcome, Earth!!!!**

From the East, we call the sacred Element of Air

Hail to the White mare of the Ether, come through, from thy Eastern realm. Bring shifts to innovations, stirring winds of inspiration and the vision to fly to new terrains.
Hail and Welcome, Air!!!!

GODDESS INVOCATION

Mare Goddess, Rhiannon

Hail to you almighty one,

Steadfast Queen,

Holding her Grouund,

Teaching us of true power

Wherever She is found.

Come Rhiannon,

We honor you my dear,

Forgving Mother of Pwyll,

We invoke you here,

Hail and Welcome!!!

CHANT: *"Mother, Mother I call you"*

MEDITATION, TRANCE AND RAISING ENERGY *(with cone of Power or with Drumming)*

SPELL WORKING

In complete darkness, we will gather around the circle, holding our unlit, charged pillar candles. Participants are invited to be still and meditative.... Reflect on a time when you were accused of something that was untrue. Calmly reflect on false accusations or statements you've heard others say about you...Negate it now! One by one around the circle we will stated aloud the opposite, for example; *"I speak truth", "I do my best", "I never did that," "I do not cheat," "I am loving and honest,"* etc... Whatever you were accused of, state now aloud the opposite and light your candle as you recite this rhyme...

"Light of the Sun, Rhiannon Blessed,
With this flame, I endure the darkness..."

One by one, light your candles as we now state aloud what false accusations and statements we relinquish & eradicate. When all candles are lit, together we will cap spell with this incantations;

As the mare is steadfast
and gallups away,
so shall all lies
burn with the light of day.
So Mote it be!

CHANT: *"We are opening up to Sweet Surrender"*

Final Check Ins

DEVOKING GODDESS

Immortal Welsh Goddess,
Thank you for your presense here today,
We bid thee Rhiannon,
Receive our gratitude,
Return to your enchanted realm,
In peace,
As we bid thee adieu.
Hail and Farewell Rhiannon!!!

CHANT: *"We all come from the Goddess"*

DEVOKING ELEMENTS

Hail to the White mare of the Ether, You came when called to guard our space and lent your gifts of Air today. We send our gratitude, as we bid thee adieu.
Hail and Farewell Air, to you!!!

Hail to the Brown mare of the solid earth, You came when called to guard our space and lent your gifts of Earth today. We send our gratitude, as we bid thee adieu.
Hail and Farewell Earth, to you!!!

Hail to the Blue mare of Water. You came when called to guard our space and lent your gifts of Water today. We send our gratitude, as we bid thee adieu.
Hail and Farewell Water, to you!!!

Hail to the Red mare of Fire, You came when called to guard our space and lent your gifts of fire today. We send our gratitude, as we bid thee adieu.
Hail and Farewell Fire, to you!!!

CHANT: *"The earth, the air, the fire, the water, return, return, return return...."*

OPENING CIRCLE

"The Circle is open but unbroken may the peace of the Goddess be ever in our heart, merry meet and merry part and merry meet again...."

*****TRADITIONAL POTLUCK TO FOLLOW*

RHIANNON MEDITATION

Find a comfortable place to sit or lie down and take a nice deep breath. Hold it for two counts then release. Again breathe, as this is the easiest way to charge and revitalize your lungs. Now exhale letting go of all concerns and stressors in your day. (pause)

We start this journey on a large open field. A few months ago this place was a cool green meadow and you recall the brightness of the grass on the ground and the surrounding trees then. But now with winter finally approaching, you sense the change amidst the cool breeze and the ground has lost its verdant hue, in its place is a thin layer of frost. Before you, up ahead, there appears to be a circle on the ground and it is slightly elevated, as if the critters of the land, or some other entity, has marked this space as a sort of special important stage. Carefully approach this mound with reverence, for in Welsh mythology, it is considered a "tor" and it holds great power.

As you get closer to the "tor" notice how quiet and still the earth and your surrounding appears now. There is a hush…. the kind of sacred hush one experiences after the first snowfall of the season. It is so quiet and still, that the only thing you can hear are your footsteps on the crunchy frost, as you finally approach the" tor."

Take a deep breath and as you do, step upon this sacred mound (pause). All of a sudden you hear the galloping of horses rustling quickly nearby. The earth beneath your feet strongly vibrates with the weight of their gallop. It is indisputably the sound of horses but no horse can be seen anywhere near you. The sound of the galloping almost goes right through you and within minutes it is no longer detectable (pause). Minutes later the sound returns once more, even stronger, much like an ocean wave and the earth beneath your feet again rattles and vibrates with every step. You look around to search for the horses but your eyes cannot detect anything even remotely resembling a horse. Again the galloping ends just as quickly as it had started and you are left dizzy and dumbfounded, wondering how you can hear this galloping and yet not see anything for miles. The earth once more begins to quiver and shake right under your feet and undeniably the galloping is felt even stronger than before, only now you can tell there is one sole horse. Close your eyes, breathe, and allow your third eye to engage to this metaphysical experience at this present moment. (pause)

With your third eye look around and see if you can detect where this horse is….. (pause) Fiercer than before, the earth shakes and vibrates and the galloping begins once more. This time however, with your third eye engaged, you see the source of the galloping. It is the white mare of Rhiannon, the fastest horse around. Swiftly it passes right through you, so rapidly it went almost undetectable again. Now that you've seen her with your third eye, running past you, call her…it is the only way she will slow down and stop for you. (pause).

As you say her name, the "tor" under your feet vibrates once more, and as if her name was the magick key to this enchanted spot, it opens from under your feet and swallows you down, down into the earth, down into a spiral. Down you go, deep in the earth, deeper to journey even further to her realm… (pause)

Take a moment to re-orient yourself to this new environment, here under the dark earth. Look around now, make note of your surroundings and how you feel. The vibrant image of the glittering Goddess, Rhiannon on her white mare, still fresh on your mind, you look for signs of her here, but instead you begin to detect whispers. Lots of tiny little whispers...as if the earth's soil surrounding you had living blabbering mouths and a clan of earth folks with much to say. The whispers get louder and you begin to notice movement and shadows in the distance. The whispers are experienced so intensely they almost begin to make you dizzy.

You hear this collection of whispers, numerous whispers of different voices, indistinguishable, you can't quite decipher what or who is the source because there are so many but slowly you begin to realize the whispers are all about you. To your surprise you hear they are talking about you. Down here in this dark place someone among the many is accusing you of something horrible...and they are all voicing an opinion about this. Do they even know who you are? Yet, you hear all the whisper as they continue to talk about you. See if you can focus and narrow in on at least in one particular voice, at least one... to hear exactly what is being said? What are they accusing you of doing? Pause and open your auditory senses and listen carefully... make note of what you are accused of.... (pause)

Notice how all the other voices go to the waste side now, as you focus on that one particular voice. Everyone else slowly fades into the background while that one voice you have distinguished, comes in clearer. Listen... (pause).the accusations are so incessant and so strong you almost believe them to be true...you almost absorbed them as part of your truth but just as this person with their accusations gets closer to you, you intuitively clutch your heart chakra for it feels the daggers being thrown at you...

Both your hands reach upon your chest and firmly press there to feel your own heartbeat, life force and your vitality. It is so warm. Notice how your hands begin to feel so much warmer in contrast to the cold bitterness coming from the accuser. Feel your hands upon your chest now, feel this warmth get even hotter. Feel your heart chakra get scorching....feel your hands almost melt within your heart, feel it actually sinking in now.

Your hands are now sinking into your chest where the sensation only gets warmer... let your hands now explore your chest cavity and see if you can detect something inside. You will feel around and find something that calls you to take it out, (pause)...it is a mirror.

A special mirror in your heart chakra needs to be unearthed and at this moment in your life you are required to pull it out of your chest and utilize it. Take it out now and use it, turn the mirror to the accuser and all the voices of accusations and let the mirror become your shield now. (pause) Place it in front of you and let it block the negativity coming your way from this accuser.... Hold the mirror there before you, reflecting outwardly, so that whatever accusations, negativity or lies are being said can now be deflected.

The mirror that came from deep within your heart is your protective shield now. Watch as it slowly silences the accuser and the whispers.... Slowly they diminish and the whispers begin to dissipate and silence takes over. (pause) When you are ready and feel totally safe, lower your mirror shield, take a deep breath and place this mirror to the ground. Take a few steps to survey the area and make sure they have all left, no one remains to accuse you of anything. (pause)

In this instance you feel the earth begin to vibrate again and the familiar galloping sound reappears but it is not coming from the earth it is coming from the mirror. The shield mirror you were holding is the only thing vibrating now and from this mirror sprouts the Goddess Rhiannon. She appears to console you and guide you back to restore your true authentic self, for after battling such demons as lies and gossip our souls sometimes finds itself embattled and weakened. She is here to remind you of what is real and what has been false. Rhiannon will guide you to your dignity and inner strength. Take this moment now to talk with Rhiannon. She is quite sympathetic to our journey and plight as women. Share with her the struggles of your darkest hours. Tell her what you've been accused of and what you have endured, as you too tried to remain steadfast. (pause)

When you are ready, mount her white mare with her, put your hands around her Divine waistline and prepare to ascend towards the sun. Up you both go. You will journey with her upwards now, as you go up, feel your mind traveling upward. Make sure to breathe and exhale as you traverse and navigate towards the light outside of the earth's core. Come forward on her white mare, you travel now, as she guides you to where this journey began on the sacred "tor." (pause)

Humbly give your gratitude to the Goddess and say your final goodbyes to Rhiannon now, as she too bids you adieu. Watch her as she fiercely gallops away into the mist. When you are ready, take a deep breath and begin to walk towards my voice. Walk away from the magickal "tor" and don't look back. Continue to follow my voice and breathe. Exhale and breathe again. Follow my voice as I count from five to one, backwards, and when I reach one, please return to this room... to this time and space. Five, four, three, breathe and exhale, two and one.... Welcome back!

******Take a moment to journal your experiences from this meditation, in particular make note of any messages given to you by the Goddess...*

RHIANNON INVOCATIONS

Lunar Goddess, Rhiannon my Dear,
Blessed beauty, whose melody I hear,
Dressed in glitter upon your fast mare.
You show us how much, our gender can bare.

Rejected the known,
to embrace your Prince Pwyel,
Left to join his Kingdom,
Believing all would be well,

For three years as his bride,
as a stranger to his land
As the outsider you would be greeted,
but a baby would soon be at hand.

Your blessed son was born,
cared for by all the maids,
But the unthinkable happened
On this particular day...

Asleep they failed to watch him
He vanished in mid-air,
And shocked, these maidens feared
The punishment they would bare.

And so in fear they plotted,
On You they smeared puppy's blood
Shocked beyond reason
the accusations came in floods.

Your traumatized husband,
Didn't know what to believe,
But begged that they may offer you clemency.

Rhiannon as punishment,
Required to act like a mare,
At the entrance of the King's Castle
Forced to tell your horrific tale.

You would offer to carry them
As they rode on your mare back,
For seven long years
You performed this painful task.

Until that day,
When three people appeared,
a husband, a wife
And a boy of seven years.

(con't...)
You told your sad tale
And looked this young boy in his eyes.
All learned that day,
He was your son and he was alive.

The Kingdom rejoiced
And the Goddess Re-embraced,
Exalted and respected,
For all the wrong she faced.

She forgave her accusers,
Despite all she withstood
With compassionate and dignity,
Rhiannon understood.

Dearest Goddess of the Mare
How you stood your ground,
The truth would prevail
And your innocence would be found

Your strength and steadfastness
We champion today
Hail to you Rhiannon,
We invoke you on this day!!!!

RHIANNON RITUAL INVOCATION

Mare Goddess, Rhiannon
Hail to you almighty one,
Steadfast Queen,
Holding her Grouund,
Teaching us of true power
Wherever She is found.
Come Rhiannon,
We honor you my dear,
Forgving Mother of Pwyll,
We invoke you here,
Hail and Welcome!!!

SPELLS

SPELL FOR CLEARING & FORGIVENESS

I forgive, I release,
Sever ties that swallowed me,
Let the past be far removed,
So that all within me is smooth.

Lightly ease all doubt and pain,
As the moon each day now wanes,
Feel my heart grow wings to fly,
I transcend this moment in time.

No experience will label me,
Those who hurt me, I release,
From my anger and my pain,
I rise with new eyes
To meet each new day.

Give my soul
A chance to breathe,
A chance to love,
A chance to be...

I am more than these past tales,
I will rise,
where yesterday I failed.

I rewrite the book of my life,
Liberated from the hurt,
I fly..fly.. fly...

GOSSIP REMEDY

Tongue that cuts,
meant to pierce a soul,
Hurt intangible
but deeply cold
> Gossip Lies
> Viciously told
> Bullies victimizing
> dragging me low

With this spell,
I call to cease
All the Falsities told of me
> Mirrors planted
> that they may see,
> Feel the hurt they tried inflicting

Rise above
With shield on guard,
Gossip and hate
I banish you far....

SPELLS

SPELL FOR STRIFE

The light of the sun return, return
Bring back the healing lost by strife
The light return upon this flame
As spells are cast tonight

I rise above the conflict,
Unearth my inner strength
Call forth the light within me
And tap into it at full length.

Speak words to call the Goddess
Scry gently into her light
And ask her for her blessings
To rise above all strife.

This spell bound round and it shall be
These things or better to protect me.

By the power of three, time three,
So mote it be!!!

MIRROR BOX HEX REVERSAL

This mirror box I bless tonight,
To be my Magick Tool,
To be my means of protection,
And guard me from evil fools.

Send back any negativity,
Reflect it to its source,
The person who has wished me ill,
Will soon feel much remorse.

I place herein the culprit,
The one who's caused me grief.
Bind their way of evil,
Forbid them from reaching me.

Until I have released them,
Herein this mirror they'll stay,
To feel the full force of their nature,
And the evil, they tried to create.

In the name of Themis, Maman Brigitte
And Skadhi,
In the name of Oya, Ma'at
And Hekate,
Guide your Priestess
And surround me with your shield,
Deliver a punishment,
That will allow me to heal.

It is done!!! It is done!!! It is done!!!

RHIANNON GODDESS GATHERING CHANT TEXT SHEET

BEGINNING CHANT
The Earth is a Woman
And she shall Rises, by Z. Budapest

LISTEN TO MY HEART SONG *by Susun Weed*
Listen, Listen, Listen to my heart Song
Listen, Listen, Listen to my heart Song
I will never forget you
I will never forsake you
I will never forget you,
I will never Forsake you .....

RHIANNON *by T. Thorn Coyle From music CD, Reclaiming, Second Chants*
Rhiannon carry us,
Rhiannon carry us,
Rhiannon carry us over over.
Crossing the threshold from
Sleeping to waking from
Birthing to dying and over...

FREE THE HEART *by Starhawk and Reclaiming community, from music CD, Reclaiming, Second Chants*
Free the heart and let it go
What we reap is what we sow...

LET IT IN, LET IT FLOW *by Marie Summerwood*
Let it in, Let it flow
Round and Round we Go
Weaving the Web of Women,
Let it in, Let it flow
Round and Round we Go
Weaving the web of life...

WE ARE A CIRCLE *by Rick Hamouris*
We are a Circle, within a Circle, with no Beginning and never ending....
You hear us Sing, You hear us Cry,
Now hear us Call you, Spirits of Earth and Sky
Within our Hearts, there goes a spark
Love and Desire, a burning Fire...
We are a Circle, within a Circle, with no Beginning and never ending....
Within our blood, within our tears,
There lies the offering, of living water...
Take our fears, take our pain
Take the Darkness, into the Earth again,
**
The Circle closes, between the Worlds
To mark the Sacred Space,
Where we come face to face...
We are a Circle, within a Circle, with no Beginning and never ending....

ELEMENTAL SONG
Earth my Body,
Water my Blood,
Air my breath
and Fire my Spirit.... unknown

CLOSING CHANT
by Victor Anderson, song from Elaine Silver's Music CD; Faerie Goddess
By the Earth that is her Body
By the Air that is her Breath
By the Fire that is her bright Spirit
By the Living waters of her womb
May the Peace of the Goddess
Be forever in our Hearts
The circle is open but unbroken
Merry Meet and merry Part
The circle is open but unbroken
Merry Meet and merry Part *(continue from the beginning)*

CHAPTER TWO

Nu-Kua

"You need Chaos in your Soul to give birth to a Dancing Star..." Friedrich Nietzsche

NU-KUA

NU-KUA

"In chaos, there is fertility" Anais Nin

NU-KUA ALTAR SET UP

Altar cloth: a white altar cloth is suggested but you may also use dark green to symbolize her Creatrix fertile gifts. Textile with images of dragons or serpents is ideal but also altar cloths decorated with special Chinese letterings.

Image: a photo, art image or Statue of the beautiful Chinese Goddess, a mermaid/melusine or half serpented woman is ideal to place on your altar as representative of Nu kua.

Always present on the altar;
A cast iron cauldron, drums, speaking stick, a silver pentacle, athame, elemental representations.....

Air: Bow & Arrow, Smudge wands, Incense type sticks, cones, charcoal brisket and fine powdered herbs Mugwort, Vervain, Sage, Orange blossoms.
Fire: candle, glass enclosed candles or pillars in white, silver, yellow or gold
Water: Chalice or small glass bowl with Water
Earth: Plants, lots of Greenery and fresh flowers. Also incorporate a small dish of soil and or herbs, like mugwort and sage. You may also include animal symbolisms.

Other items pertinent to this particular gathering
Air drying Clay
Felt fabric and human shaped poppets
Needle and thread
A bowl of mixed enchanted dry herbs
Colored stones
Pens and markers
Snake or dragon scupltures
Glass Bowl of water
Human figurine waxen images, various colors
Goddess Oracle or tarot cards

Sacred objects from members:
Notes:

MONTH & SEASON

January

The Full moon this month is known as the Old Moon, it is also sometimes called Wolf Moon by the Native Americans who traditionally gave the thirteen full moons in a year, various reflective names. Wolves would often be heard howling in the distance at this time of the year and thus, those who were attuned to the earth, and its cycles, gave the full moon, of this month, its appropriate title. Also interesting to note, the Saxon name for January is *"Wulf-monath"* which translates as wolf month.

The weather was extremely cold in some parts of the world and thus sometimes January's full moon was also called, the Cold Moon by various tribes. This month is ruled by the astrological sign of, Capricorn. Known as the goat, it is ruled by authoritative, prudent, restrictive, Saturn (Dec 20th-Jan 20th) and its energy can be felt subtly during this month.

The first month of the Julian and Gregorian calendar, January, probably derives its name from the ancient Roman Goddess, Jana or her husband, the two faced God-Janus. Together, they were believed to rule doorways and gateways, which were considered a very sacred realm. January, being the first month in our modern day calendar year, is a good example of those precious, yet mysterious gateways. In January, we stand at the threshold of a new calendar year, while bidding adieu to the old. Most might see this as a time of new beginnings, renewed hope and thus a time to make vows and New Year's resolutions. It is not surprising then, to hear of gym memberships escalating to record breaking heights at this time of the year.

With the temperatures, in some parts of the world, still very frigid outdoors, we spend most of our time indoors and thus another common theme for January is the hearth, home and handmade crafts. Before modern technology, the cold Winter forced many to slow down and retreat into their abode and the only form of entertainment was to be created within close families. The home and the creations of handmade crafts, games, storytelling and the Bardic arts, naturally became almost crucial to ones general happiness and wellbeing during the dark wintry season.

This month, we might also find ourselves recovering from all the frenetic holiday activities of the previous month by slowing down and hibernating. It can also be a time of the unexpected slumps, and let downs, after all those highly charged festivities from the previous month. The highs of excessive shopping, partying and family gatherings are over now and we are left with a return to the mundane. It is not surprising that this month, may also find us combing through our finances, as we try to settle debts incurred from the holidays and we endeavor to start the year off with a clean slate.

Although it may feel like, after January first, there is a halt to celebrations, it can also be a time of much needed respite and a perfect time to gather up our energy for the next stage in life.

Often, works of divination at this time are appropriate to foretell what the new calendar year will bring. With the start of a new year it appears that brainstorming, fantasizing and goal commitments are the common theme for all. It is the perfect time to take advantage of the powers found in starting anew, purging and rebuilding, making goals and following them through. It is never too late to make a better choice in life and January gives us an opportunity to exercise this philosophy.

This month we will connect with the Chinese Goddess of humanity, Nu-Kua, who will help us unearth peace, creativity and order in our lives.

All Monthly intro text taken from author's first book,
"Gathering for Goddess, A Complete Manual for Priestessing Women's Circles"

NU-KUA GODDESS LESSON

Nukua, also known as Nu Wa, Nugua, Nu-Gua, Nu Kwa, Nu Kua Shih, Nu Hsi, is the foremother of Humanity in Ancient Chinese mythology.

Nu-Kua is a primordial Chinese Goddess connected with the creation of Humanity and Civilization. She is a half dragon, serpent bodied Goddess, sometimes appearing almost like a melusine or a mermaid due to her half creature and half divine makeup and yet, sometimes depicted in contemporary Chinese art as a beautiful woman. She is also associated with the sky, the heavens, waters, the moon and the earth. She is often depicted as a divine woman with her lower body resembling a snake or a Dragon's tail but she was a known shape-shifter, like many primeval ancient deities. She is worshipped as a fertility Goddess and a patroness of marriages and childbirth. Nu-Kua is the beloved Goddess of Order and Creation, a benevolent matriarchal deity associated with teaching humanity about agriculture, dam building and irrigation and even introducing the art of whistling. She is attributed for inventing the *shenghuang,* a reed-pipe musical wind instrument and the vertical bamboo flute, known as *xiao.* Nu-Kua is a Goddess who helps restore order and clarity amidst chaos and disarray and as many of her Chinese myths will reveal, this matriarchal deity is also venerated as the savioress of the earth and its inhabitants.

What is most interesting to note is that in a culture that has a plethora of male deities and in its contemporary state, so often appearing to be downright patriarchal, here is an ancient female deity, in its midst, held in the highest regard, as the supreme mother of humanity. This Goddess called on me as the perfect deity to present at the start of this book which endeavors to present a more feminist, Dianic style of Wiccan, Neo-Pagan worship. Nu-Kua's most prominent myths greatly resonated with me in their obvious exaltation and positive depiction of our gender.

While in Christianity, and many other mainstream religions, humanities birth is attributed to a single male God and women are depicted as secondary or as a lesser form of man, in ancient Chinese writings a vastly different depiction can be, thankfully, unearthed.

Nu-Kua's name frequently appears in early records of the Hans Dynasty, most notably the ancient texts of *"Huainanzi,"* but also text from the Warring State era, like the *"Shanhaijing"* and the *"Tianwen"* in *"Chuci."* Interesting to note, in the *Tianwen,* her actual insides are credited for nursing and birthing ten spirits that would later spread across the earth's wilderness and become humanity, of course that is only one obscured version of her myth.

According to the ancient text of the second century CE, found in *"Fengsu Tongyi"* (*Popular Customs and Traditions*) Nu-Kua is the foremother and creator of humanity. The early myths explain Chinese cosmology by introducing the belief that in the beginning of time there was simply a cosmic egg. There was chaos, nothing formed; no earth, no sky, no star, no moon, no boundaries set... nothing... just an egg. And in this cosmic egg was a microcosm of chaos and within this contained chaos, a sleeping giant named P'an Ku dwelled, in a tiny embryonic state.

The first part of his name, "P'an", means "coil up" and "Gu" or "Ku", the second part of his name, refers to "antiquity." Thus this divine being was the old or antiquity curled up, encapsulated in this cosmic egg and it held the promise of our earth's creation, according to Chinese cosmology.

As the years went by, the giant P'an Ku grew and grew within this cosmic egg. He slept, as various myths reveals, for 18,000 years and as he slept he grew bigger and bigger. The sacred egg also grew and expanded to accommodate the growing giant. Amidst this chaos of light and darkness, jumbled and crammed inside this encapsulating egg, the Giant slept, until one day the deafening sounds of chaos woke him up. He stretched out his enormous muscular physical form and the egg, unable to support his out-stretching limbs, cracked and shattered open. Everything that, up until that point, had been held together inside this cosmic egg was now released, surrendered to the nothingness of the formless Universe. All darkness and the light that had been held pinched and strangled by it, was now released with the Giant's birth. All the fragments of light united as they levitated and rose up to create the sky and all the essence of darkness fell down, creating the earth. The giant who was, according to some scholars, around thirty thousand miles large, watched as light and darkness separated before him. He saw the fragments of the shattered egg rise up to create parts of the moon, the sun and the stars. He witnessed the Universe forming itself, as light created the sky and the darkness sunk, creating the earth. And in his fear that the sky would fall unto the earth and chaos would return if they would collapse into each other again, he decided to hold up the sky and hold down the earth to keep them separated. P'an Ku took it upon himself, as the only living being, to banish chaos and preserve order with the sky and the earth separated.

For centuries the giant, P'an Ku held up the sky with his strong muscular form but he then began to age and inevitably grew fatigued. Slowly, he began to lose his strength according to some folklorist. As he got older he started to get weaker and weaker and, exhausted, this impaired his ability to continue holding the sky upward. Eventually the giant died. Now some scholars claim he had held the sky up, long enough, probably over ten thousand years as some sources claim. And being confident that his mission to maintain the sky and earth separated had been accomplished, he then gave himself permission to release it and expire.

Regardless, P'an Ku's exhaustive mission was accomplished but he could not live forever. His death, however, brought about a number of important gifts to the earth. According to Chinese mythology, P'an Ku's body served to become the mountains, the hills and the land. His tangled long hair and beard became the trees and the bushes. His remaining teeth and pieces of his bones sunk down into the earth to become precious metals, gems and minerals. Chinese myths claim that the precious gemstone of Jade, which is highly regarded in Chinese culture, manifested from P'an Ku's decaying bone marrow. His blood flowed as streams and rivers while his veins became the arteries of the earth. His semen became pearls, his sweat and final tears became rain droplets and dew. And P'an Ku's voice became thunder while his very last breath became the winds and the puffy clouds in the sky. In this way, the giant P'anKu was indeed the traditional sacrificial entity whose death created the lush, colorful, fertile earth. This was documented in the third century CE, in "Wuyun Linianji" (*A Chronicle of the Five Circles of Time,*) a compiled book from the Three Kingdoms era.

We must note that P'an Ku is well-regarded and considered one of the *"Three Divine Sovereigns,"* the earliest divine beings highly venerated in ancient Chinese mythology. He is accompanied in this honor by Nu-Kua and Shennong (the Divine Farmer) although other variations include Fu Xi. P'an Ku is first mentioned in the Three Kingdom era and his myths can be found in ancient text of the third century CE; *Sanwu Liji, "Historical Records of the Three Sovereign Divinities and the Five Gods."* He was described in some text as being a giant with a cat's head and his trunk, like that of a serpent. The people of the Henan Province in Central China viewed P'an Ku as divine protector of humanity and executor of the earth. They believed he had horns, as it was a common belief all primordial divine beings in ancient times had horns. He is also depicted with a Dragon's head in the *Wuyun Linianji.*

In some myths P'an Ku is associated with earth-quakes by the people in the Gansu Province of Northwestern China. Here there was a lore that connected him to an ox. In this myth P'an Ku would hold up the heavens but he required additional help keeping the earth below from sinking. It was then that P'an Ku crafted an ox from clay mixed with his own saliva and he breathes life into it and assigns it the duty to maintain the earth. At this time, P'an Ku also crafted a divine rooster to help keep watch over the ox's important duty. Keeping the earth from sinking proved to be too arduous a job for the ox and one day he wanted to take a break and nap. The rooster however, would not let the ox rest, as it firmly upheld P'an Ku's commands and this angered the divine ox. In his anger he shook the earth on his back three times and this explains early earthquakes in ancient Chinese lore.

P'an Ku is still venerated today in many of his temples found in Henan, Guandong, Jiangxi, Zhejiang provinces and the Guangxi Zhuand regions. Henan Province holds his most famous temple on mount P'an Ku and many from distant lands sojourn to gather on his feast day, celebrated on March 3rd of the Lunar calendar.

When P'an Ku eventually expired he left the earth as a beautiful oasis and it was perfect but no one inhabited it, according to most myths. Then from across the sky slithered the half Dragon Goddess, named Nu-Kua. Her birth or origins are unmentioned and unknown, we simply are told that she roamed the heavens and upon P'an Ku's death she descended to find his divine body spread across the earth below. She marveled at the great beauty of the earth and what P'an Ku had accomplished and yet, she felt a twinge of sadness in her isolation and inability to share this great world with anyone. Of course, later we will address another version of this myth where Nu-Kua is not alone at this pivotal time in the myth, but rather, paired with her older brother. But I digress, in her sadness at finding herself alone, Nu-Kua sat by the river banks, where she picked up the accumulating yellow clay and began to shape it into a ball and then into an image like hers, only with legs. She continued to gather the yellow clay and formed numerous human beings in her image to keep her company and banish her loneliness but they were inanimated and they simply stood there as rows upon rows of tiny human clay figurines. She longingly picked one of them up and placed her divine breath upon it. Remarkably the clay statue became animated with her vital breath of life upon it. It gave her great joy to see her statue creations come to life and she derived great pleasure in their laughter as well. She decided to animate all of her clay creations and then started crafting more beings; both male and females.

As time went on, the Goddess Nu-Kua began to get tired and overwhelmed at the thought of how many humans she would have to sculpt by her hands, with the yellow clay, in order to fully populate the earth. She looked at the arched reed near the river (although most myths state she took a cord or a rope) and she dipped it in the mud to complete the human race. Wherever a dripping of the mud fell on the ground, a new animated human being emerged. In this Chinese myth we have an explanation for the two distinct types of people on the earth. Those that are noble and rich were descendants of Nu-Kua's initial hand crafted yellow clay human being and those who were poor peasants were the descendants of the human figures she crafted afterwards with the rope's mud droplets. A rather prejudicial, harsh way of looking at things but revealing that for the Chinese, there are only two types of people; the rich and the poor, those divinely touched and sculpted by the Goddess herself and those that came later as a result of her fatigue, via the mud droplets.

Yet there are other versions to Nu-Kua's myth to consider. There is even a tale that holds an uncanny resemblance to Genesis in the Old Testament of the bible. In this Chinese tale, Nu-Kua is not just attributed for birthing humanity, but for creating all of the creatures upon the earth. The myth claims that on the first day she created chickens and on the second day, she crafted dogs. Then it goes on to state that on the third day she made sheep and then pigs on the fourth day. On day five she created cows and on the sixth day she made horses. Finally on the seventh day she created humanity from the yellow clay by the banks of the river.

The Goddess Nu-Kua resembles the Greek Goddess Gaia in her primordial matriarchal Creatrix abilities. Both are ancient deities credited for populating the earth with its inhabitants. It is also interesting to note another tale linked with Nu-Kua and the seeds of similarities it holds to many other deities from various cultures. Quite often with primordial Goddesses there is a connection between their creation, bloodline and their consorts. With Nu-Kua there is one version of her myth that alludes to her sexual connection to her brother, who becomes her husband, Fu-Xi. And there is some ambiguous concern or guilt she wrestled with concerning procreation with her brother, according to some interpretations of these Chinese old folklores, which is why she begins to impart to humanity the importance of marrying, birthing children and admonishes the practice of incest.

In the ancient Chinese text, *"Duyizhi"* (*A Treatise on Strange Beings and Things*) by Tang dynasty writer, Li Rong (ca.846-974CE) we have a different tale of the Goddess Nu-Kua connecting her to a partner. According to this Chinese folklore, Nu-Kua was initially not alone on the earth after P'an Ku's death. She was accompanied by her older brother and they lived on the mountain of Kunlun. In this myth they desired each other and wanted to procreate and fill the earth with their children but the shame and guilt of incest caused them much apprehension and distress. Together the siblings prayed to the heavens asking for direction and a clear sign that would grant them permission to unite and procreate. They began to divine by numerous interesting means, for example; the Goddess would run down the mountain and if her brother could catch her, then they were ordained to be married. Another way of divining involved threading a needle successfully from a long distance and yet another test was if the smoke from a fire would gather and unite, then that was a sign that they indeed had divine permission to marry. Although they were given clearance to unite as husband and wife, according to these various myths, the shame was too much for Nu-Kua. As a result, she gathered and weaved grass into a fan to cover her face and thus, this is the Chinese explanation why traditionally brides hold up fans during their nuptial ceremonies.

Her consort Fu-Xi resembles Nu-Kua in his half dragon, half human appearance and when they are depicted together sometimes their Dragon tails are actually intertwined to show their deep intrinsic partnership. He is seen in artistic depictions holding a square to represent the heavens, although some sources say he holds a representation of the round sun, while she often holds a compass in her hands to represent earth or the moon. Together they unify the heavens and the earth.

Fu-Xi is a Chinese God who imparts to humanity the gifts of tending to ones flock, hunting and the art of fishing with a net. He was also known to be a music teacher, inventor of musical instruments and a song composer of a melody known as "Jia Bian." He was credited for the eight tiagrams/diagrams, the Ba Gua, which helped develop the Chinese form of divination known as the, I-Ching. He taught humanity to barbecue food and is attributed for inventing the calendar, matrimony dowries and written characters for documenting life events, instead of the traditional knots on a cord. Fu-Xi also made copper coins and manufactured many tools and objects from metal. While Nu-Kua's main myths always seem to present her alone or single, it is interesting to also make note of who she was inevitably paired with in Chinese Mythology. Writings, particularly in the Hans Dynasty, refer to Nu-Kua and Fu-Xi as the parents of Humanity and the first of the San Huang people. Nu-Kua is also highly revered by the Miao people.

Some folklore reveals that Nu-Kua did not want to spend eternity tending to her clay human figures. And she did not want to continue laboriously hand crafting mud or clay beings. It was becoming much too tedious for her to craft daily and tend to the earth's population. Thus, she taught humanity the importance of joining male and female, ying and yang, to procreate, self-populate and maintain the human race upon the great earth. In this way, Nu-Kua expressed a desire to equip humanity with all the tools they needed to thrive and succeed upon the earth on their own, without her constant watchful eyes. It gave her great joy and satisfaction to empower humanity in this manner and it allowed her to simply enjoy their existence.

Nu-Kua's name itself can be looked at for further insight as some suggest the Goddess contained both male and female essence. The first part of her name "Nu" is translated as "first male" while the second part, "Kua" or "Kwa" denotes a "first female." Perhaps revealing that in this Goddess we see the "ying" and the "yang" uniting and the very first male and female embodied.

HOW SHE BECAME SAVIORESS OF THE WORLD

The earliest mention of the collapsed pillars of the heaven and Nu-Kua saving the earth is found in the early Chinese writing of the "Tianwen." She is also mentioned in the Lunheng (*Critical Essays, written by Wang Chong*, ca. 27-100CE) and"Bu Shiji Sanhuang Benji" (*Biographies of the Three Divine Sovereigns: A Supplement to the Historical records,*" Tang dynasty). According to the text of this period, one day a quarrel ensued between a few of the most powerful deities in Chinese mythology, the details of what they were arguing about are lost to us but according to folklore the quarrel turned into a huge vicious battle. Included in this battle was the Water God named Gong-Gong and the God Zhuanxu (also known as, Zhurong, Di Ku or Shengnong). Some sources refer to Gong-Gong, also known as Kaghui, as a monster so we can only assume he was quite powerful and volatile in Chinese mythology. As the story elucidates Gong-Gong became angered when he feared he was losing the battle and in his volatile anger he proceeded to whack his head against one of the sustaining sacred Pillars of the sky, which was known as Mount Buzhou (meaning, "not full"). Needless to say this resulted in the imbalance and tilting of the sky towards the northwest and consequently the shifting of the earth's axis. With one pillar off course the existing pillars collapsed and the sky could no longer cover the earth. And the earth was said to be unable to hold all things. The "*Huainanzi*" text, however, states that initially all four pillars collapsed but this challenges other sources. Nevertheless, the Chinese nine sacred regions of the world were exposed and in severe jeopardy. Gong-Gong's thoughtless explosive act inaugurated much devastation upon the earth, as it set a chain reaction to numerous catastrophic events. Floods and roaring fires ensued, as well as the strange manifestations of man eating beasts spreading across the earth, threatening humanities existence. The earth was badly plagued with insurmountable chaos and devastation at this time.

The Chinese Goddess, Nu-Kua came to rescue humanity during these monumental calamitous times. Some tales claim she used her very own body, as a half dragon deity, to seal up the torn parts of the sky and this helped stop the flooding that was permeating the various realms. She was also believed to have gathered the ashes of the reeds to help stop this flooding. To this day, some parts of China worship Nu-Kua in an annual Water Splashing Festival that honors her as the one who saved ancient China from the cataclysmic floods. She is a Goddess attributed for the seasons and the rain falling where it is most needed upon the earth.

A more popular myth reveals that Nu-Kua gathered colored rocks (some sources say seven different rocks, others say five) and she melted these colored stones and used them to patch and mend the various holes in the sky that were causing the flooding. She managed to stop the flooding in this manner but the sky could not be fully fixed and remained slightly tilted. This folklore explains the earth's unusual tilted axis and why the sun, the moon and the stars move northwest, while the river in China is said to flow southeast into the Pacific Ocean.

The beloved Goddess Nu-Kua is highly venerated for rescuing humanity and restoring the balance of the earth during this catastrophic time. The earth's cardinal points fell out of alignment when the monster God, Gong-Gong, banged his head on one of the pillars of the sky. Her myths reveal that she helped support the compromised four corners of the sky by utilizing the four cut legs of the sacred giant tortoise and replacing the pillars with these cut turtle legs. She confronted and killed the Black Dragon that was one of the creatures causing much havoc on the earth. Eventually Nu-Kua pacified the numerous hideous creatures that were devouring human being and because of this she became a Goddess recognized for introducing animal domestication. There is another myth that tells of her taming a treacherous giant named King-of-Oxen, at another time, by jamming a rope through his nose. This miraculously allowed her to tame him, as well as many other wild animals she encountered, according to Chinese legends.

When the earth was restored to her peaceful state, Nu-Kua, without seeking accolades, humbly departed to the heavens, where some believe she remains today. Some claim she rode to the heavens seated on a chariot of six winged dragons and yet other creative depictions reveal she was carried off by a thundering chariot containing two winged dragons and two green hornless dragons. A special mattress is reputed to be under her as she travels on her chariot while holding her sacred compass. White dragons are before her and a flying snake is visibly behind her and she is said to be surrounded by the most celestial gilded clouds. Clearly, references of this Goddess in ancient Chinese literature idealize her with much respect and grand adoration and she continues to be worshipped today, especially among women.

Nu-Kua's worship continues in Shexian County and Hebei Province. There is a great Temple dedicated to her, named *"The Palace of Empress Nuwa"* and from February 15th till March 18th, in the Lunar Calendar, festivities take place to honor the Divine mother and great grandmother of humanity. March 15th is notated as Nu-Kua's birthday and thus, this day takes on great significance for the Chinese. She is exalted with singing and dancing on this day, in the hopes that she will bless her worshippers with fertility, good health, happiness, safety and blessing on marriages and children. *"The Temple of Human Ancestors,"* also known as *"Renzu Temple"* or *"Tomb of Tai Hao,"* found in Huaiyang County, Henan Province, celebrates the God Fu-Xi, along with the Goddess Nu-Kua, for a month long. From February 2nd till March 3rd in the Lunar Calendar, women offer the Goddess dances like the *"danhualan"* or the *"danjungtiao."* These are ancient ritual dances for the Goddess Nu-Kua, performed solely by women. At the Renzu Temple, contemporary worshippers might burn incense, paper money, paper architectural buildings to represent ancestral dwellings and offer handmade shoes, lovingly dedicated and ritualistically burned to Nu-Kua.

Clearly Nu-Kua is a beloved Chinese deity that exemplifies women's creative powers and her innate ability to manifest peace and order out of chaos and calamitous situations. For feminist Wiccans, she is a beautiful symbol of matriarchal energy, attributed for humanities birth, and our gender unearths a great source of empowerment in this beloved highly venerated ancient Goddess.

MUSING ON NU-KUA,
CHAOS & ORDER AND THE NEED FOR POLYTHEISM

"Chaos is what we've lost touched with. This is why it is given a bad name.
It is feared by the dominant archetype of our world, which is Ego, which clenches because its existence is defined in terms of control..." Terence McKenna

As an artist and a mother of three boys and numerous household critters, Nu-Kua is a Goddess that I can easily identify with. Even as I write this and research this highly revered Chinese Goddess I feel her energy, for as mothers we are always called upon to find order amidst chaos.

My home is often subjected to the challenge of maintaining itself organized, most days it suffers from a topsy-turvy-itist, laundry piles waiting annoyed by the laundry machines, piles of animated shoes by the entry doorway, dirty dishes gracing our kitchen sink, various children's toys scattered about with every step one tries to take in our home and yet, I am required to thrive and somehow find order amidst this chaos, as well as facilitate my loved ones to do the same. It is in these moments that I sense some of Nu-Kua's important attributes and I am able to connect with this ability to confidently get organized and get things done despite the less than ideal situations and challenges.

Yes, I feel her necessary presence in my life and her great importance for my own sanity and sense of accomplishment. There are things that, as a womyn, I must do, things related to my own personal well-being that sometimes differ and conflict with the things I must do as a mother. Finding time to connect with my spirit, commune with my inner voice, write, paint, meditate and be in stillness feeds my wellbeing as a womyn but goes in complete opposition sometimes to being a mom of rambunctious little ones. Needless to say, finding a moment of serenity and quietude in our household is somewhat challenging but even amidst this tenacious obstacle it is indeed achieved and I do manage to find those important moments to cultivate inner peace and order.

There is a beauty and order I must create for myself daily amidst chaos and disarray (whether it's physical or mental) and yet, I am also required to create it for others by providing an environment that is safe, clean and conducive to raising healthy children. There are things of beauty and expressiveness that, as an artist, I am passionately obliged to create for my own happiness and wellbeing, just as I imagine the Goddess Nu-Kua felt as she created that first yellow clay human figure. It made her feel good to create this being in her beautiful image (the mother archetype must create). It also helped her feel less lonely and it made perfect sense to add this, almost necessary, finishing touch to a world that seemed incomplete without it.

As a matriarchal Goddess I find Nu-Kua fascinating, even more fascinating is her part in a cosmology that differs so greatly from what mainstream religion would have you believe. Her role in cosmology greatly contrast the tales found in Genesis, a tale most

53

mainstream religions wholeheartedly accept and believe. Here in this ancient Chinese tale, explaining humanity's birth and the earth's creation, is an empowering tale for our gender, certainly much more empowering than the crippling, degrading explanation of a male god creating man and then creating a woman from the rib of that man. There is no sense of equality in that myth, dare I say, there is no sense of true Divine love in humanity's manifestation in those tales in the bible. There is an obvious perverse domination and distasteful hierarchy that serves only to disempower one gender and thus harm one half of the human race. When you compare the two tales; one deems a male god creating humanity in his image and that was Adam. Then a female was formed by taking of this man's rib. Inherent in this biblical tale is the potentiality for massive injustices, obvious discrimination and a subordinate view of women, a downright cruel view, clothed in divine reasoning, why women should be deemed as the lesser human than man.

Herein this ancient Chinese tale is an explanation of humanity's birth filled with the potentiality for gender equality. We have a loving Goddess, composed of both creature and divine essence, for she is part dragon (a sacred ancient serpent) and part human and she hails from the heavens. She embodies the sacredness of the earth and the sky and yet also the waters and fire in her savioress and creatrix abilities. And she lovingly creates humanity out of sheer love, desiring someone to share the great beauty of the earth - the earth that had been created and passionately maintained by one who was birthed and formed inside of chaos in the sacred cosmic egg, the giant P'an Ku. And after maintaining the sky above and successfully keeping the earth and the sky separated, an act that he does for fear of the destruction of something he finds so precious; our earth, he then finally grows weary and old and dies. He is the sacrifice so commonly recurring in many ancient mythologies regarding humanity and the earth's existence across numerous prominent cultures. It is not from a place of soveignty or a great self-imposed power that the giant creates and sustains the earth but from a place of love. Something beautiful is before him and P'an ku does not want to see it destroyed; he was after all birthed from its essence. The creation of the universe and humanity is thus beautifully shared by both genders, both male and female, and by all really, for less not forget
Nu-Kua is half beast and P'an Ku is a giant, sometimes also depicted as half beast as well. And thus this cosmology includes everyone as being part of the creation of this Universe, not just one male deity as we so often see in other mainstream religions. It is not one person, nor one ruler, not one god who is attributed for creating the earth and the human race, it is a combination of many who left their divine imprint on us and because of this we are many, in respectively different sizes, colors, shapes, gender, different life paths and titles. We are not one type of people, we are many and this diversity is mirrored for us in this cosmology much more so than in the one presented to us in Christianity. It is this noted fine detail that purports polytheism vs. monotheism.

I must say that here is where the study and connection to the Chinese Goddess Nu-Kua has been the most impactful for me and where I may stray from some established Pagan, Christian and Non-Christian viewpoints. There are many who discovered Paganism after years being indoctrinated into other monotheistic religions and this obstinate belief in *"the One"* has a way of lingering rather subtly into newly adopted religious and spiritual practices. This *"one deity"* concept seeps into our culture's prejudicial practices and seeps into the fibers of our so called melting pot that seems to only want to lump everyone into the same mold, whether that mold is Christianity, Paganism or Americanism etc.. It seems to feed the *"oneness monster"* that is so often threatened and intimidated by anything that stands out in its difference and its eccentricities. I think the rise of monotheism has brought about a wave of unconscious and conscious prejudicial harm and I can see that issue harboring in many aspects of our lives.

The problem with our nation's intolerance for differences becomes most apparent when we see the epidemic of bullying taking place in schools now a day. From an early age children are indoctrinated into this perverse practice of tearing down and degrading anything or anyone that appears different or dares to assert itself as unique. And the evil of this world is not in our differences, the evil in this world is in our inability to embrace, respect and seek understanding of differences. No... it's much easier to bully people into submission to assimilate, abandon their culture, race, belief, sexual orientation and succumb to social pressures. It's much easier to manipulate, beat down with alienation someone until they question their very own self -worth and whole purpose to exist... that's the world we've become, a world that fears the unknown, the different, and does not seek to conquer its fear with knowledge but rather, feed it with hate and prejudice and false assumptions.

I think Polytheism supports diversity and honors differences and reveres unconventionalities and this has magnanimously more far reaching implications than we can fathom –it extends into all human and civil rights matters.

I, personally, do not like to impose a "oneness" belief tenet in my spiritual practice; advocating for Polytheism and opting for diversity and great respect and embracing of all cultures. We are indeed all human beings composed of spirit and matter and most cultural myths do unify us as being divinely manifested, but we all come from different parts of the world, with different cultural myths aligned to our ancestral genetic makeup and that's a great thing!!! It is not something to shake off or be admonished for. The Gods of our ancestors are just as indispensably important as the Gods of this new found land and neither needs to be placed on a pedestal at the expense of the other. While some mainstream religions set out to eradicate any cultural religious allegiance people may have, with numerous violent crusades, wars, persecutions and persistent missionaries, a belief in Polytheism renders these practices unnecessary and almost tragic. We have much to learn from one another but the "oneness" concept found in monotheism purports that there is only one way, one culture, one supreme race and one being and one God and one religion, leaving little room for anything else. It is these consistently narrow definitions in our world that are at the root of all forms of prejudice.

We pride ourselves in being a melting a pot of various races and cultures but the operative word is melting pot because you are expected to melt away what makes you, you, and blend into the vanilla-ness of the "ruled over." It allows for the "one" to have full authority to declare what should and shouldn't be accepted. It is irrespective of people's various cultural, ancestral differences and it begs one to assimilate and assimilation is disregard for one's uniqueness and history. Assimilation is the one thing that has destroyed so many beautiful ancient cultures and religions and yet, assimilation, is almost required to herd the sheep, control and manipulate the masses. We are a nation intolerant of differences as if differences can and would destroy the very fibers of our nation and yet, difference are not what causes strife and wars, it is our intolerance and prejudice, which is rooted in ignorance, that creates wars and devastations, it is our insistence that everyone be ruled by the *"one theory."*

Diversity is a positive thing only when we respect and embrace our differences. I think the problem in our society is that a lot of people want to glaze over it and not respectfully acknowledge differences of race, religion, sexuality, culture and class and deceptively lump everyone under preordained stereotypes or categories and if you don't fit that societal criteria you get ostracized. This has the stench of monotheism because we are not so easily classified as the same but to someone who sees this as positive trait, this is a gloriously divine human attribute to be celebrated not a reason to persecute, dominate or destroy. These differences, while they appear like societal chaos, are in fact that sacred kaleidoscopic beauty of our very human divine nature which upon closer inspection has perfect order.

NU-KUA GODDESS GATHERING DAY

Purpose: To create harmony, clarity and order out of Chaos. To connect with the Chinese Goddess, Nu-Kua and re-organize, re-strategize, re-motivate ourselves after the long chaotic holiday season. To create peace and assess what needs clearing to prepare ourselves for the new calendar year.

Check Ins: We gather around the Circle and introduce ourselves to one another, while also voicing our feelings on this month and our hope for the upcoming season.

Chants: Together we will join our voices to sing some commonly known Pagan chants, as well as new ones offered on the Chant sheet in the hand outs (see the last page of this chapter). Singing aloud is a wonderful way to raise energy effortlessly and it also sometimes helps in creating harmonious bonds.

Our Agreements bylaws and Pertinent group discussion... We go around the circle of women, reading a few lines each of our "Group Agreements" and add any new ones that seem necessary. Agreements are signed and submitted in confidence.

Drumming Grounding: A drumming musical CD track will be played, to give participants a chance to connect and ground to this very moment. Women are invited to find a comfortable seat or stand and add movement if they wish.

Conjuring Goddess via her Image: A photo image, Goddess oracle card or scuplture image of the Chinese Goddess will be shared around the circle, as each woman present will reflect on the image and state aloud what attributes and Divine messages need expression.

Lecture on the Chinese Goddess, Nu-Kua
Her myth and various folklores, her attributes and relevance for us today.

GODDESS WORKSHOPS
WORKSHOP I
Clay working, crafting and enchanting a clay figurine

WORKSHOP II
Herbal Human Poppets made of felt fabric and dry herbs

WORKSHOP III
Fertility Magick; a discussion on ancient and modern day spells for fertility

WORKSHOP IV
Discussion on Chaos magick and how to strategize order in our lives

WORKSHOP V
Crafting with natural Stones

WORKSHOP VI
Snake, serpent and dragon as personal totem.Their folklore and power of transformation.

NU-KUA GODDESS GATHERING RITUAL

Purpose: To commemorate the start of the new calendar year. To honor the Goddess Nu-Kua and manifest clarity, harmony, motivation and self blessings for us.

Smudging Asperge
Anointing & Welcoming

INTENT DECLARED: We gather here to welcome the new calendar year and give praise and honor to the Chinese Goddess of Peace and Harmony, Nu-Kua.

CIRCLE CASTING
(very tenderly, a light bell/chime around)
Goddesses, Ancestresses,
Spirits of old,
Hearken now,
Our Circle hold,

Circle around to keep us safe,
Evil at bay, far from our gate,
Truth and Love invited here,
Spirits and Gods,
We draw you near.

Contain and preserve,
The energy we create,
By will and word
This Circle is made!

ELEMENTAL INVOCATION
AIR
Hail Guardian of the watchtowers of the East, ye powers of Air. The realm of our feathered friends, whispers murmured by the gentle breeze, place of vision and conceptions, we invoke you to guard and hold our sacred space today. Join us in our rites, **Hail and welcome Air!!!**
FIRE
Hail Guardian of the watchtowers of the South, ye powers of Fire. Realm of thy fiery passions, boiling, brewing from within our soul, extending to our working hands that creates and expresses with great passion, we invoke your fiery energy to guard and hold our sacred space today. Join us in our rites, **Hail and welcome Fire!!!**
WATER
Hail Guardian of the watchtowers of the West, ye powers of Water. Realm of the healing waters that quenches our thirst, our potted plants and our expansive landscapes. Source of our heavenly rain that serves to provide divine waters to all of humanity, we invoke your cathartic waters to heal us and our earth. Guard and hold our sacred space today as we invoke you here. Join us in our rites, **Hail and welcome Water!!!**
EARTH
Hail Guardian of the watchtowers of the North, ye powers of Earth. Realm of our dark fertile labyrinths held within our bones. Place of regeneration and transformation, we invoke your grounding powers to guard and hold our sacred space today. Join us in our rites,
Hail and welcome, Earth!!!

CHANT: *"Do you remember, when God was a woman"*

GODDESS INVOCATION
MEDITATION, TRANCE & RAISING ENERGY *(Drums, dance, cone of Power)*

SPELL WORKING I

At the start of the calendar year it appears to be a perfect time to sort though our lives and get ourselves organized. Our first working involves colored stones, the kind we envisioned Nu Kua using to save the earth from those floods. Around the circle, these stones will be passed along, with permanent markers. Each participant is asked to write one goal on each stone. Later these stones will be scattered around haphazardly on the floor of our ritual space, where we will be required to search and re-find & reclaim these goals.

SPELL WORKING II

We will enchant aloud 4-5 different herbs with our wish for the new calendar year. When all have done this, we will then place these herbs in our small human-formed poppets and sew it as a self-blessing tool of magick. While holding up our individual poppet state aloud around the circle;

"This is me, Healthy and Strong
Thriving with energy
Singing my song...."

Afterwards we will begin our search for the colored stones while singing...
CHANT: *"We are opening up in Sweet Surrender..."*

Final Checks
DEVOKING GODDESS

DEVOKING ELEMENTS
EARTH

I send my thanks to the Guardians of the watchtowers of the north, to the powers of earth. Its dark fertile labyrinth making its gifts known to us throughout our rites. Your presence was felt here today as you guarded our sacred space. Receive our thanks as we bid thee farewell. In peace may you return to your realm. Thank you.

Hail and Farewell Earth!!!
WATER

I send my thanks to the Guardians of the watchtowers of the West, to the powers of Water. To the rain and healing waters that quenches our needs, your gifts known to us in these rites. Received our thanks as we bid thee farewell. In peace may you return to your realm. Thank you.

Hail and Farewell Water!!!
FIRE

I send my thanks to the Guardians of the watchtowers of the South, to the powers of Fire. Heart of great passion, hands that create, your fiery gifts were tasted upon today. Received our thanks as we bid thee farewell. In peace may you return to your realm. Thank you.

Hail and Farewell Fire!!!
AIR

I send my thanks to the Guardians of the watchtowers of the East, to the powers of Air. Murmuring breezes that announces our inaugurations, your gentle winds were experience today. Received our thanks as we bid thee farewell. In peace may you return to your realm. Thank you.

Hail and Farewell Air!!!

CHANT: *"We all come from the Goddess"*

OPENING CIRCLE

Our Circle is open but never unbroken,
may the love and peace of the Goddess
rest forever in our hearts,
Merry meet, merry part
and merry meet again....

CAKES AND ALES/POTLUCK FEASTING

RESTORING PEACE AMIDST CHAOS,
NU-KUA MEDITATION

I invite you to find a comfortable position. You may sit or lie down and take this moment to connect with your body, mind and spirit. Take a deep breath now. Exhale and with this next inhalation, feel the weight of your eyelids as they begin to close to relish in this sacred moment. Let yourself sink deep down with each breath and relax.

In your mind's eye, I invite you now to bring your attention up to the sky. Look up and gaze upon the cerulean blue infinite heavens, it is almost like an ocean above your head. Study the numerous cotton white, gauzy patterns stretching across this azure sky and make note of the numerous sculpted white clouds. Breathe in this peaceful panorama and allow serenity to imbue every cell of your body now. Continue to gaze lazily at this landscape above your head.

The ocean blue sky is beautiful and elicits such a peaceful energy. You are so transfixed and absorbed in its beauty that you fail to realize something has changed right before your eyes. On the far left corner of this panoramic celestial scene is a noticeable tear. There is an open perforation in the sky. The sky has a small tear, as if a lion's claw has punctured the celestial canvas, creating a striking gash upon its hue and compromising its seamlessness. From this growing slash you shockingly notice something seeping through the ruptured sky. Look very closely at this unsuspecting wound upon the fabric of the heavens and see if you can make note, what is seeping through it. Continue to study and observe what is seeping through the tear of the sky. You might make note of its color, texture, any accompanying objects, creatures or people oozing in with this fluid. Take a good look at what is seeping and make note of the volume and the negative effects this is having on your peace. What is this suspicious fluid corrupting your heavenly azure landscape and altering the serenity you had just tasted? Make note of what you see now in the sky; is it translucent rain water, is it black sleek oil, is it mud or blood? Take a closer look and note the color and the consistency of this cosmic fluid. What is seeping through the cracks of this idyllic façade? What is altering your otherwise peaceful state of being?

Now if you can, please bring your attention to the earth below you and the ground that is right under your feet. Below the once intact beautiful sky everything was in its proper place and all was perfect. Yet here now, in this instance, there is a newly discovered tear upon the fabric of our infinite sky which could potentially jeopardize all that is below its monumental canvas. Take a deep breath now and know that you are safe throughout this journey. The images that appear in this meditation are yours to create and will only appear with your permission and you are fully safe in this process. You have full control throughout this meditation to participate in as little or as much as you feel comfortable in choosing. This is your transcendent journey and no matter what images may appear you are safe throughout this process.

Make note of how you are feeling now in contrast to the beginning of this journey and notice the energy shifts taking place. The energy might begin to feel uncomfortable and chaotic all of a sudden but the frenzy convolution gets worse as you noticed the Pillars, holding up the sky, are starting to also tear and disintegrate. Everything seems out of order now, unnatural and far from serene. Make note if you can what is altering the foundations of your world at this moment. Make note for yourself in this meditation what is compromising the foundation of your world by wounding these sacred upstanding pillars. Remember as you are guided in this meditation you are safe and protected throughout. Breathe please.

This is your opportunity to connect with the Matriarchal Chinese Goddess of Order and Harmony, Nu-Kua. This is your chance to tap into her gifts of manifesting order and peace, out of cataclysmic chaos. At this very moment in this meditation, with the once intact, picturesque blue sky now torn, you will see a glimpse into what is potentially causing distress and chaos in your own personal life. And with the addition of witnessing the sacred pillars of the earth also damaged, you are witnessing a crisis; a representation of a potentially real crisis in your own personal life. Take this opportunity now in this meditation to connect and invoke the Chinese Goddess, Nu-Kua, for she is equipped with the skills you will need to thrive and make sense out of this chaos. She has proven herself to be humanities best ally and defender and in this meditation she will bless you with her equivalent gift.

In your mind's eye see now the celestial ray of light that transports the Goddess, Nu-Kua to your presence. She quickly directs your attention to the pathway behind you, a road made of loose pebbles and colored stones. She instructs you to gather several colored stones and melt them in her golden warm light. You take into your hands as many stones as you can carry and offer them to her to melt. In her warm light the stones begin to soften and melt, the way putty or a sculptor's clay would, in human hands. Nu-Kua invites you to take these melted stones and ride with her to the top of the torn sky to mend and patch this perforation upon the sky. Quickly you join her and place the melted stones on the heavenly gash and just as quickly the sky is restored and healed whole.

Then Nu-Kua asks you, what do you think can mend those pillars and stop them from disintegrating. Nu-Kua wishes to know what you personally think can bring order to your realm now. She offers you a long scroll of rice paper and she invites you to take this moment to contemplate the chaos that has ensued and consider what will ease and bring back order and harmony. With quill in hand, the Goddess, Nu-Kua invites you to write on this long scroll of parchment paper, what action is required of you now to bring peace and harmony to your realm.

Take a deep breath and allow yourself this moment to quietly brainstorm and consider realistic what will help your situation. This is your very own personal resolution and it is uniquely yours. The Goddess, Nu-Kua has provided this time and sacred space for you to carefully scrutinize the disturbance to your peace and invites you to observe the chaos in your life and its negative effect in your world. You have this moment to consider what methodical course of action is required of you now to mend the foundation and sacred pillars of your life. Write down on the long scroll of parchment paper, what will mend the chaos in your life, what will restore those important foundational pillars back to health in your realm? (Pause)

When you have finished writing on your scroll, approach the Goddess and present it to her. (Pause) She looks at your handwritten words and quickly leads you to the pillars where she instructs you to wrap the torn edges of the pillars with your paper scroll. Gingerly wrap the wounded pillars like you would a sprained ankle, she says. Wrap the pillars with your healing words found in your resolution upon this scroll of parchment paper. You begin to wrap the pillars with your paper, going around and around until they are completely covered. Magickally, right before your eyes the pillars become whole again; appearing brand new once more. All begins to feel calm and serene once more, as the sun begins to shine brightly and the infinite ocean blue sky appears seamless once more.

You take this moment to thank the Matriarchal Goddess for her help in restoring peace and harmony again to your realm. Listen carefully as she whispers the final words of counsel to you, before she departs into the heavens. Take one final look at this peaceful exquisite panorama as you admire the sky you helped restore and the pillars of the earth, which hold the sky, are now strongly healed, as good as new. Take a deep breath and exhale any last remaining concerns. Take another deep healing breath and with it, feel it renew and revitalize your lungs. Inhale and let your breath restore your hope for order and serenity in your life from this day forward.

Make note of the air around you now and the gentle breeze caressing your skin as it picks up speed. Feel this refreshing air gently brush up against your skin as it begins to stir and awaken you gently back to this time and space. Let the air tickle your face, your eyes, your ears, as you become more aware of my voice now. Allow yourself to become more aware of your physical body, as the gentle breeze in this meditation begins to bring your attention to your physical form. Feel the breeze rustle your hair. Feel this same breeze enter and invigorate your breathing, through your nostrils. Feel this rejuvenating breeze awaken your lung's regenerative full capacity, as you begin to take livelier, deeper breaths. Feel this animated breeze now nudge you to quicken your pace and begin walking, begin walking towards my voice as we come to the end of our journey. Follow my voice as I begin counting backwards from ten to one. Safely and calmly you will draw nearer as we transition back to this time and space, back to this room, back to my voice, back to your physical form, back to this space. Ten, nine, eight, breathe deeply. Seven, six, five, four, breathe and exhale. Three, two, one... welcome back! Please join us in the circle as we talk together and share our trance experience.

INVOCATION

NU-KUA
Slithering ancient Goddess,
Slither from thy sky home.
Cross the Giant P'an Ku,
To the fertile Earth below.

Crafting,
with thy delicate touch
Each clay formed
with hope in thy clutch.

Hope for companionship,
And the human race,
Beauty, P'an Ku created,
Mirrored in each human's face

Multiplying each miracle,
Breathe life to form each soul,
Divine Nu-Kua, with your gifts,
Our earth is now made whole.

Saviouress of China,
Holding all of earth's seams,
Apocalyptic remedy,
You were the earth's vaccine.

Oh, ancient Mother,
Who formed us in thy clay,
Dear Beloved Nu-Kua,
We honor you in our rites today.

SPELLS

MEDITATION

I take a pause from daily life,
To contemplate
And gain insight.
To watch the flame
And hear my breath
To soothe away,
Unnerving stress.

Remind myself,
Of where I've been,
Awaken the Goddess
That lies within.

Connect to who I really am,
All powerful, Creatrix
Priestess,
"Wombmyn".

As daughter of the Sacred Moon.
I work my spell,
With rhyme and tune.

And learn the depths,
Found in my soul,
The ancient Ones,
From long ago.

And with this chant,
I re-connect,
To "She" who rules,
The elements.

Goddess from above, below
And all around
"She" who wears the sacred crown.
I call you to this time and space,
Awaken in me,
the Divine's inner face.

NU-KUA GODDESS GATHERING CHANT TEXT SHEET

WE ALL COME FROM THE GODDESS
We all come from the Goddess
And to her we shall return,
Like a Drop of Rain,
Flowing to the Ocean *By Z. Budapest*

SWEET SURRENDER
We are opening up,
in sweet surrender,
to the luminance
Love light of the one, (Repeat)
        We are opening ….We are Opening (z2X) *by Gladys Gray*

DREAM WEAVERS
Dreaming, Weaving
We are the Magick weavers,
As above so below,
Within us and without,
 We are the dream weaver.

We are the weavers, we are the woven ones
We are the dreamers, we are the dream.
By Michelle Mays from her music CD, "FireLeap, a Collection of Chants."

WE ARE THE POWER *by Starhawk*
We are the Power in everyone,
We are the dance of the Moon and the Sun
We are the Hope that will not hide,
We are the turning of the tide.

SNAKE WOMAN
Snake woman, Beginning again,
Shaping, changing,
Renewing her skin

Snake woman, Shedding her skin,
Shaping, changing,
Renewing, again.

The spiral of life keeps changing
It spins and turns rearranging.

For everything there is a season,
For everything there is a reason.
By Michelle Mays from her music CD, "FireLeap, a Collection of Chants."

ELEMENTAL INVITATION, by B.Melusine Mihaltses
East of the Winds,
That stirs and inspire,
Come Eagle's gift
Guard and hold me like this.
        Fire with your spark
        Passion's in my heart
        Come with the Jaguar
        In this circle stand on guard.
Hail to you Waters,
Realm of all tears,
Womb of all wommin,
Come approach my dear…
        Earth that transforms,
Making Visions to form,
Realm of my seedlings,
Guard our space as we're born…..
        Earth, Air, Fire, Water,
        I am the Witches' daughter….(Goddess daughter etc…) raise energy!

<u>CHAPTER THREE</u>

DURGA

"In every crisis there is a message —crisis are nature's way of forcing change- breaking down old structures, loosen negative habits so that something new and better can take their place..."
Susan Taylor

<u>DURGA</u>

DURGA

"You have to leave the city of your comfort and go into the wilderness of your intuition, what you will discover will be wonderful... what you'll discover is your true self..." Alan Alda

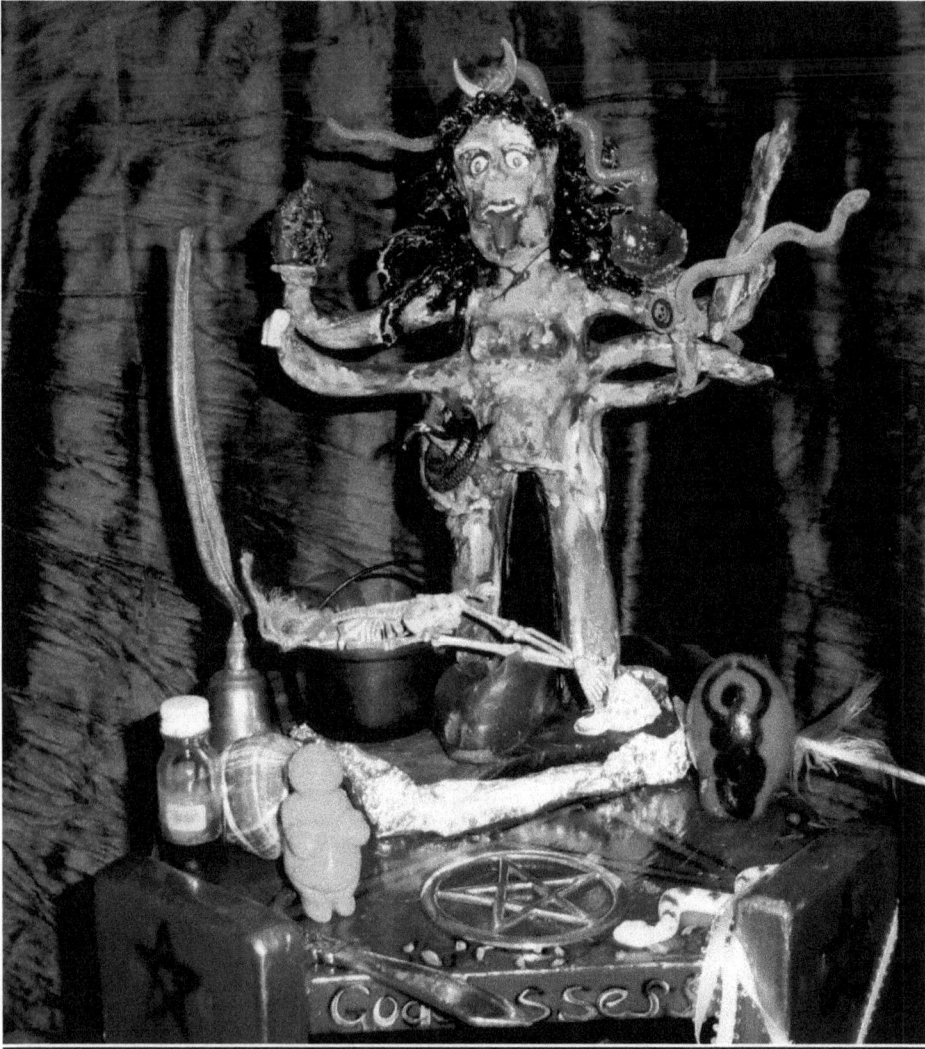

DURGA ALTAR SET UP

Altar cloth : _Red, which is a power symbol of blood and victory for the Hindu Goddess, Durga, is the most obvious choice of color for her altar cloth. Black may also be used or crossed under the red._

Image: _The image of the multi armed, Hindu Goddess, Durga or images of Kali are acceptable for her altar. And because Durga is often connected with the tiger or lion she rides on during battle, it is also a good idea to display the statuary or photo image of a Tiger/Lion._

_Always present on the altar__;_
A silver pentacle, a cast iron cauldron, drums, speaking stick, wand, athame, elemental representations.....

Air: _feather bundles, angel wings, bird, eagle or owl statuaries. Bell &, chimes, Incense type sticks, cones, charcoal brisket and fine powdered herbs; frankincense , myrrh._

_Fire__: pillar candles, glass enclosed candles in red and black_

Water: _Small glass bowl with Water and or chalice with Champagne, Cranberry Juice or Red wine._

Earth: _Offer as many green plants or cut bright flowers you can to represent earth. Red Roses with thorns are a nice touch. A small dish of soil or dry herbs can also be used._

Other items pertinent to this particular gathering

Daggers, Swords, Athame
Scythe, conch, shield
Skulls, bones
Dark red beverage
Statuary of a lion or tiger
Tarot cards
Blood representation; could be menstrual or simply beet juice

Sacred objects from members:
Notes:

MONTH & SEASON

February

According to the Farmer's Almanac, Snow moon and Hunger moon are just some of the many names for this month's Full moon. For our ancestors, this time of the year may have seemed dangerous, as the crops harvested, canned and pruned back in the Fall (and meant to last all winter long) might be dwindling and coming to an end. And in some parts of the world at this time of year, nothing can grow on the cold frigid land and the best you can do is hope that Spring does not delay and that your food supply will last you till then.

February's full moon is also commonly known as Quickening moon because at this time of year the core of the earth appears to be quickening and new life seems to be on the edge, underneath, patiently waiting to be born. There is a quickening towards longer hours of daylight, as the sun grows in strength. Some might begin to plant seeds indoors in preparation for Spring. Many pregnant animals now are also feeling the fluttering of their unborn within their wombs and soon, in the Spring, they too will be born. The sabbat of Imbolc, which means "in the belly," is a reference to this magickal moment in nature and the precious cycle of our Mother Earth. Many Pagans, at the start of the month, celebrate this ancient Celtic sabbat that honors the new precious life, and the seedlings, nursing in the womb and belly of the Earth, awaiting to be born in the Spring. On a spiritual level, both figuratively and literally, this is a time of incubation and gestation, as we prepare for what will transpire in the coming Spring.

February is known as the shortest month of our calendar year. It probably received its name from the ancient purification festival, *"Februa,"* derived from the Latin word, *"Februare"*, which means "to purify." Indeed February can be seen as a perfect time to purify our land, our homes, our families and ourselves, in preparation for the coming of Spring. Perhaps it is this reason why the Full Moon of this month was also sometimes refered to as the Chaste Moon.

Numerous Pagans, at this time of year, go through Craft and Coven initiations and elect to dedicate or rededicate themselves to their spiritual practice. As this time of year resembles our Pagan ancestor's new year, there are some that refer to it as the true Wiccan New year. It is also considered the start of the season of the Maiden and the astrological sign for this month is water bearer, Aquarius, ruled by Uranus (Jan 21-Feb 20).

Throughout all of nature we are now looking for early signs of Spring's impeding arrival- birds chirping, thawed soil, the first flower buds. Today, the sight of a groundhog inaugurates much hope and excitement in the U.S.A. as we rely on this tradition to foretell if Spring will come early. In ancient time, however, Celtic myths reveal that initially our ancestors searched for a slithering snake (who represented the Goddess Brigit) that would come out of the mountain and slithered down to announce Springs arrival. February also has many of us celebrating the great, fire festival of the Chinese New Years, with fireworks and festive processions. By mid- month we are honoring old Presidents in the U.S.A., but also celebrating our own romantic relationships with Valentine's Day. It seems so appropriate that on the coldest month of the year, we have what is, traditionally, known as a warm-hearted, romantic holiday, called Valentine's day -named after the legendary Celtic patron, St. Valentine.

Beneath the seemingly cold, barren, hard Earth there are great stirrings, that we will only be privy to see when the weather begins to get warmer. It is thus a time of magickal transformations, as the Earth begins to thaw and slowly transform itself into the lush, fertile, oasis for Spring. We call upon the warrior Goddesses of major transformation this month, the Hindu Goddess, Durga.

All Monthly intro text taken from author's first book, "Gathering for Goddess, A Complete Manual for Priestessing Women's Circles"

DURGA GODDESS LESSON

"I must not fear. Fear is the mind killer; fear is the little death that brings total obliteration. I will face my fears. I will permit it to pass over me and through me. And when it has gone pass, I will turn the inner eye to see its path where the fear has gone, there will be nothing, only I will remain..."

Frank Herbert, Dune, Bene Gesserit, Litany against Fear.

DURGA

Durga is one of the most beloved and widely embraced Hindu Goddesses. She is often considered the supreme Goddess (Mahadevi) and a Universal Mother credited for protecting the world from demons in Hindu religion and Mythology. She is the warrior Goddess who combats anything that threatens the stability of the cosmos and is devoted to fighting the evil and negativity afflicting the world. Her numerous aspects and incarnations make her one of the most multi-dimensional deities and by far one of the most intriguing.

Most of what we know today about Durga and her worship can be extrapolated from the puranas, the agamas (ancient Hindu texts) and the ancient Vedic text of around 4th century A.D. The Yajur Veda, Vajasaneyi Samhita, Taittareya and the Devi-Mahatmya all reveal a great deal about this well esteemed Goddess. We know that, although her worship can be traced to the 4th century B.C.E. and during the Harappan period, her worship became more prevalent after the 6th century. There are several puranas (sacred text) ranging from the third and fifteenth century, that mention her and several are even dedicated exclusively to her. The Devibhagavatan is one such purana, as well as the very similar, Durgasaptasti, better known as the Devi-Mahatmya. This seventh century text dedicated to Durga can be found in the Markandeyapurana also known as Chandi Mahatmya. It is one of the most highly recognized and venerated text to Durga and it is even often used as a mantra dedicated to the Goddess. There are also many Hymns like the Narayanistuti, which describes Durga as the mother of all creations and the physical embodiment of the earth. The Aparajitstotra Hymn praises Durga for her unconquerable abilities to defeat the demons; Sumbha and Nisumbha. Further research into this Goddess reveals there is no other deity among the vast impressive Hindu pantheon that comes close to exemplifying all that Durga does.

Her name is often translated as *"a Fort"* or *"One who is unreachable"* or *"difficult to know."* Sanskrit interprets her name as *"invincible"* and already these combined translations of her name begin to paint a perfect picture of this ancient deity. Some scholars believe the name Durga is actually an abbreviation for Durgatinashini, which translates as, *"the one who eliminates suffering"* and this definition probably describes this Goddess best. It is interesting to note that **"Du"**represents the four devils; poverty, suffering, famine, evil habits, while the **"r"** represents diseases and the **"ga"** in her name represents, destroyer of sins, injustices, cruelty, laziness. **Source from kalikraft.com*

Durga protects mankind from misery and evil by destroying the demons known to man as selfishness, jealousy, prejudice, hatred, anger, and most of all, ego. Some of her incarnations are known as Kali, Bhagvati, Ambika, Lalita, Gauri, Kandalini,

Kaushiki, Chamunda, Parvati, Java, Rajeswari, to name a few. Sometimes she is referred to as "Triyambake" meaning, Three eyes. Her left eye is representative of "desire," connected to the Moon. Her right eye is "action," connected to the Sun and the middle or center eye is "knowledge," linked with Fire. (*www.Hinduism .Com, KOAUSA .org/ gods/goddess Durga*)

Durga has numerous Feminine cosmic powers and aspects and I will mention a few of her most known aspects here. She is known as Kali (power of eternity and infinite night) and as Tara (void and night of anger). She is Chinnamasta (sacrifice and night of courage) and Kamalatmika (perfect happiness, night of paradise). Durga is also known as Dhumavati (deprivation and night of frustration) and as Tripura Bhairavi (death and the night of destiny) as well as Matangi (domination and night of illusion).

As her numerous myths, found in the sacred Hindu text, will reveal, Durga is the defender and protector of the Universe. She is slayer of numerous demons like; Sumbha, Nisumbha, Raktabija and Mahisura and she is the one who eradicates all the demons that plague humanity, represented in ego, lust, hatred, jealousy and greed.

The Goddess Durga is the embodied strength of the Gods. The Hindu Scriptures note she was born from the assemblage of all the angered and infuriated male deities who had gathered on one fated night to express their collective rage. Long ago there was a demon who was threatening to destroy the world and because this demon appeared to be succeeding in his venomous endeavor, it angered the Hindu pantheon. The story begins with the sly, demon Mahisa (Mahishasura). He was born to a Goddess who bestowed on him great powers. One day his mother approached the creator God, Brahma, and asked him to make her son immortal but the God refused, believing every man that is born must eventually meet his own death. Mahisa, trying to outsmart Brahma, asked, *"Then, let me meet my death in the sole hands of a woman."* He secretly thought, surely this would render him immortal, for what woman could possibly defeat this powerful demon to death? Women in India at this point in time, just didn't engage in wars and battles. Unsuspecting Brahma agreed to the wish and granted Mahisa his desire, never considering the consequences of his action. Soon thereafter Mahisa, believing he would live forever, gathered an army of demons and marched to the capital of heaven, the home of the Gods, known as Amarapur, to make his demands and claim the heavens for himself as Lord of all the worlds. On the turf of the Gods a horrific battle thus began between the King of Heaven, Indra, his league of Gods and the army of demons, led by Mahisa. This terrible battle would last for hundreds of years, according to Hindu writings.

Eventually, the Hindu pantheon of Gods was defeated, angered, and hopeless they were removed from their home by the demon Mahisa. They did not know how to reclaim their sacred realm and overthrow Mahisa and his Demon army and they felt disheartened. Desperate, the Gods consulted Brahma but when he realized his part in this disaster, since it was he who granted the demon his wish, he suggested they all consult Lord Shiva. Then utterly frustrated and hopeless after speaking with Lord Shiva, together they traveled to Lord Vishnu to see what he might have to say about the situation. The three fuming Gods; Vishnu, Shiva and Brahma were beside themselves in complete rage that they would lose their sacred abode to the deceitful demon, Mahisa. The more they talked about it, the more their anger grew and grew until it literally created a piercing bright light that first emanated from their mouths and grew brighter, until the form of a women's body, brighter than a million suns, appeared before them. As they expressed their anger it spilled forth, creating a powerful energy and this energy transformed itself into the great Goddess, Durga.

According to Hindu scriptures, Durga's body was formed by these male Gods. They also equipped her with copies of their own powerful weapons. Hindu scriptures state her face was fashioned by the light of the God Shiva. Durga's ten arms were formed by the light of Lord Vishnu, while her feet were formed by Lord Brahma. Her beautiful long hair came from the light of Yama, the God of Death; although some text claims it was Brahma who created her hair. From the King of Gods, Indra, her waist was formed. Her breasts were created by the Moon God, Somanath, while her toes were created by the light of the Sun God, Surya. Varun, God of the Oceans, gifted her with her legs and thighs and her swaying hips came from the light of the God of the earth, Bhoodev. It was the light of Prajapati, the Lord of creatures, that created her teeth and the light of the Fire God, Agni, is credited for manifesting her three eyes. Her ears were fashioned by the light of Vayu, the God of the Winds and the two Sandhyas, known as sunrise and sunset, created her eyebrows. *(source; www.dollsforindia.com)* It is clear Durga embodies the sacred Hindu Gods with every fiber of her being and she is their great anger and fury personified.

Upon her magnificent birth, Durga was gifted with the most treasured weapon possessions and many other powerful tools from these Gods, all in an effort to equip her with the necessary tools for victory in battle. Lord Shiva surrendered a Trident to her and Lord Vishnu presented her with a discus. Her spear was given to her by the God Agni and Vayu gave her the arrows. The Thunderbolt was given to her by the King of the Gods, Indra, as well as his white skinned elephant. The God Varuna gave her the sacred conch and a noose she would later use on Mahisa. Yama surrendered his sword and shield to the Goddess. From Vishwakarma, Durga received the axe and armor, while the God of the mountains, Himavat, gave to her, jewels and the magnificent Lion/Tiger as her sacred vehicle. Many other Gods bedecked her with numerous other gifts and weapons to arm her for full battle with the demon, Mahisa. *(source;www.dollsforindia.com)* There are also many variations to this tale as can be expected with ancient myths. Some, for example, claim it was Brahmna who bestowed to her the bow and arrow.

Although she was created by the Hindu male deities, the Goddess Durga is fully autonomous, never requiring their direct aid in battle and never producing male helpers, instead opting to manifest female, bloodthirsty, helpers in battles, like Kali. Her ravenous female helpers are known as "Matrikas," which interestingly enough means, mother. Durga does indeed fight for her male creators when invoked and she defends them without their assistance, one of the only deities in Hindu mythology who can boast this attribute. She also does not lend her (Sakti/Shakti) powers to the Gods, unlike many other Hindu Goddesses but she is known to seize their powers and their fires for battles. And their inner strength is quite often surrendered to her freely. Vishnu for example is made to sleep and is rendered powerless and helpless in her presence. She causes him to be unconscious and he is thus disempowered in her presence. In this aspect she is Mahamaya, the supreme creator of illusion and the one who puts powerful spells that even Gods, like Vishnu, cannot escape. She bestows the Yoganidra (meditation and deep sleep) the power of sleep, cosmic slumber unto Vishnu at the inception of the Universe according to some text.

This brings us to her connection with the God Vishnu. Durga is personified Maya, also recognized as the mysteries power of Lord Vishnu. Some texts refer to her as the female version of Lord Vishnu, because of her recognized ability to create, sustain and destroy the world and yet, repeat the sacred cycle numerous times. She intervenes on a grand cosmic scale to rid the world of anything that threatens its balance and equilibrium. She becomes not only a sheroe/saviouress of the Universe but also a personal saviouress for her children and devotees. Durga is known to come to the aid of her worshippers during times of great calamity. She is personified power and strength and when invoked by her devotees, she proves to be most helpful in battling both inner and outer demons. Forest fires, imprisonment, robberies, attacks, executions and even threats from wild animals also fall under her protective domain.

The Great Mother Goddess, Durga, personifies Maya, that which deludes individuals into thinking they are the center of the universe. Maya is ego, individualism, personal identity and a delusion according to Hindu tenet. Yet creation and delusion fall under this domain and are under her jurisdiction. She is known by many names and each name describes an attribute or prominent role she plays. As Raktadanta, she is the one with red teeth. As Sataksi she is the one with one hundred eyes. As Bhima, she is the terrible one and as Simhavahini, she is the rider of Lions. One of Durga's epitet is "Mardini" the slayer of the demon Mahisa (Mahishasura).

As Durga's infamous myth continues on, upon her birth she was immediately dressed in the weapons of the Gods and sent to the Vindhya Mountains where she would meet and confront the demon, Mahisa. She is known in this aspect as Mahisasura-mardini. The demon, upon hearing of this brilliant beautiful mysterious woman arriving at the sacred mountain was smitten and he sent a personal message to the Goddess, that he had every intention to claim her as his bride, since he was now the Lord of the Worlds, but Durga had other intentions. *"I can only marry a man who can defeat me in battle,"* she said to him and he took this as an invitation for battle. He brought his army of demons with him to claim her and what ensued was a horrific, catastrophic battle that is forever memorialized in the sacred Hindu text.

Upon meeting the beautiful Battle Queen, the demon was greeted with a proper introduction to his destined killer but he didn't believe it to be so. Durga reminded him of the wish Brahma had granted to him and with great confident, she engaged him in battle. Mahisa was a known shape shifter and when he saw how great Durga's strength was, he changed himself into his true form, a black buffalo and charged at her but he was of no threat to the great multi-armed Goddess who was riding her fierce lion and wielding her multitude of arms with commanding weapons. She relished in the bloody battle as if it was a game for her (Lila aspect). The gruesome harsh battle continued with no end in sight and Mahisa was astounded at Durga's great strength. Many demons died by her hands and despite Mahisa's numerous animal shape shiftings, he could not defeat the Great Durga. In one version of the story, Durga pins him down with her trident and kills him but in another version of the story Mahisa, desperate to be the victor, cast a spell to make every droplet of his blood spilled on the ground, manifest into new fiercer demons. In this way, his army would only multiply and grow in power with every drop of his spilt blood on the earth. The Goddess Durga, for a temporary moment, found herself overwhelmed by the sheer multitude of demons springing to life and in her rage and supreme powers she manifested the Blue/Black bloodthirsty Goddess, Kali from her brow. She would then become the embodied manifestation of Durga's wrath and great fury. Kali thus, sprang forth from Durga's furrowed brow and with her long darting, magnificent tongue, she immediately began lapping up every droplet of blood preventing it from spilling onto the ground, lessening the volume of demons on the battlefield. With Kali, Mahisa and his army of demons were finally defeated by the Goddess.

This aspect of Durga, ferociously helped defeat the demon Mahisa and restored harmony and dharma upon the earth once more but it was not the only time Durga battled demons with her fierce bloodthirsty helper, Kali, by her side. There is another tale of Durga fighting the Demon brothers; Sumbha and Nisumbha and their generals; Canda, Munda and Raktabija. These demon brothers drove the Gods out of heaven and again, Durga comes to their aid, in her form as Mahatmaya (mother Goddess). The Devi-Mahatmya text reveals it was the demon, Raktabija, whose spilt blood on the earth continued to birth even more demons and it was Kali who emerged from an aspect of Durga as Kaushiki, to lick up this blood, again, preventing any more blood to fall on the earth. Ultimately Kali swallows Raktabija whole and thus the battle against the myriads of demons is won once again.

Durga is described as exceptionally beautiful but her beauty lacks its normal function according to Hindu text, for it is an exquisite beauty that is not meant to attract a spouse but rather to lure her victims into fierce battles. And while it was most common to depict women in relation to men, as daughters, sisters, mothers, wives, lovers, Durga's appearance breaks with these conventionalities. She is depicted autonomously and without significant reference to a consort. She simply is and stands on her own in the bloody battlefield fighting without the aid of male Gods. There is no man coming to her rescue but on the contrary, it is Durga who is invoked to come to man's rescue. It is interesting that while she is worshipped as a Matriarchal Goddess who cares and protects the world and her children, Durga's image in these early writings is quite the contrary. She quintessentially appears as a maiden, unwilling to marry any of her numerous embattled suitors and she appears to take great pleasure in her freedom and her ability to defeat any man who thinks he might be worthy of her hand in marriage.

"In many respects Durga violates the model of the Hindu woman.
She is not submissive; she is not subordinate to a male deity,
she does not fulfill household duties and she excels at what is
traditionally a male function, fighting in battle.
As an independent warrior who can hold her own
against any male on the battlefield,
she reverses the normal role for females
and therefore stands outside of normal society..."

Page 97 -Hindu Goddesses, Visions of the Divine Feminine in the Hindu Religious Tradition, by David R. Kinsley, University of California Press, Berkeley and Los Angeles California, 1988

In one of her festivals, held during the Autumnal Harvest, she is worshipped as the returning daughter, not as the Mother. And here we start to see a resemblance to that other highly venerated daughter archetypal energy, the Greek Maiden, the Goddess Persephone.

A closer look at this fierce Goddess and how she is portrayed both in Hindu art and ancient writings reveals a wild ferociousness unlike any other Hindu deity ever seen. She is a warrior Goddess who delights in the flesh and blood of the battlefield, as well as on her offering altars. It was customary to petition the Goddess Durga with offerings of flesh meat, alcohol and blood sacrifices in ancient times. There are still hidden, far away parts of this world that continue to worship her in this manner. It becomes clear that she is a power that stands outside of what we deem as normal and civilized. One look at Kali, Durga's most well-known aspect, will convince you of this, as this aspect of hers appears, wild, primal, dark, untamable, violently bloodthirsty, gruesome and strong beyond belief but this is just proof of Durga's very well known, liminal nature.

Durga was known as Vindhyavasini (she who dwells in the mountains) and Tribal people on the outskirts of civilization, like the Sabaras, venerated her and held her up to high esteem, offering flesh and blood sacrifices. It is for this reason why one may conclude that her worship originates with non-Aryan or pre-Aryan people, for the Aryan would have considered this type of worship unthinkable as they viewed wine, flesh meat and blood as pollutants to religious rites. In the Devi-Mahatmya her devotees are even encouraged to offer their own flesh and blood as offering to the Goddess Durga.

When we consider the harsh terrains of the Himalayas and the Vyndhya mountains and its geographical location, outside and far away from civilization and city centers, we begin to understand Durga in a different context. Also keep in mind the frightening, hostile appearance of tribal people and how they would've been viewed by Aryan society, yet this is where Durga's worship manifested and flourished most. She has a liminal nature that almost requires her worship to take place outside of understood civilized edifices and confinements. This is what makes Durga's presence only found when we step outside of orthodoxies. She can only be understood in this way.

Durga is often depicted dressed in the color red, which symbolizes both death and birth, our blood, action, war and the victor in battle. She appears standing next to or ridding a tiger/lion to denote her supreme powers, although it may also denote her ability to control and have power over others. She is also sometimes depicted riding a Buffalo, representing her defeat of the Buffalo-demon, Mahisa. The Goddess is often depicted with a multitude of arms; sometimes, four, eight, ten, eighteen, or even twenty arms. Each hand from her arm always holds a significant weapon, the various tools necessary to combat the numerous kinds of evil that plague humanity. Displayed in her many hands are the Trident, Bow and Arrow, sword, discuss, mace, spear, rosary (mala beads), bell, conch and wine-cup, to name just a few of her most common Divine tools.

The conch shell she carries is used as a musical instrument to make the primordial sound of creation, "aum." The bow and arrow represents the energy of the thunderbolt. The lotus, also known as Pankaja and born of mud, is a symbol of steadfastness amidst the evil and obstacles of the world. The sword represents knowledge and the discus, which she spins on her finger, represents the unfailing weapon that destroys evil. The Trident or trishul, a gift from Shiva (Siva) represents three qualities; Satwa (inactivity), Rajas (activities), and Tamas (non-activity). As fighter of evil, negativity and injustices, she stands in "Abhay Mudra" to guarantee freedom of fear.

In a more domesticated role, there is an aspect of Durga as the wife of Shiva, she is known as Parvati. In the "Skana Purana" she is the demon that threatens the world, Lord Shiva calls on the Goddess Parvati, who then becomes Durga herself, fighting this demon also named Durga. Seems confusing but it is important to note that when Parvati endeavors to fight this demon she sheds her outer sheath and it is thus the great warrior Goddess Durga that arises.

Durga was also connected to Lord Shiva in yet another aspect, as the Goddess Sati. As Sati, she was the first born daughter of King Daksha. From an early age Sati showed exemplary devotion to the God Shiva and thus, upon learning of her great devotion to him, Lord Shiva sought to have her as his bride. The King however, did not approve of such a match for his daughter but despite his disapproval the two got married. Later the story reveals the eventual demise of Shiva's beloved bride. After the union, the King arranged for his daughter, a Yagna, which is a kind of penance ceremony in which offerings were made to a fire deity. Lord Shiva was not invited to this event but he attended it anyway and was subjected to a multitude of grave insults and humiliation by the King. His daughter was so distraught by the entire incident that she sacrificed herself within the sacrificial altar fires. The grief-stricken, enraged Shiva picked up the body of his deceased beloved and there commenced his violent dance of destruction upon the earth, known as the Tandava. The witnessing Gods were frightened as the earth shook as a result of this powerful dance. The only thing that finally pacified Shiva was Vishnu's successful attempt to cut up Sati's body, while being held up by Shiva, into little pieces that were scattered about the earth. When the last piece of Sati's fragmented body fell, Lord Shiva was placated and now it is believed the land known as Shaktipeeth holds her scattered sacrificial body parts. This was one know aspect of the Goddess Durga as wife to Lord Shiva.

There are also three important elements Durga illustrates; Sakti, Moksa and Prakrti.

Sakti/Shakti: It is the creative, powerful force of the Divine. It is the underlying power or source of the Gods. Sakti is different from the term **Tejas,** which is understood as the energy or fire of the Gods.

Moksa: In this element, she is protectress of the cosmos and destroyer of demons. Created by the male gods, she acts on their behalf and defends them, as well as transcends them. She restores harmony in the cosmos. She births, destroys and rebirths again in continuous sacred cycles.

Prakrti: In this element she is the actual physical world. Durga is the embodiment of the earth, and the rhythm of the Universe. Durga sustains and protects the world and its inhabitants. As **"Sakambhari"** she provides the world with food and sustenance from her very own body and this is very reminiscent of the indigenous Goddess of the Americas; Selu/Corn Mother but also resembles the Greek Goddess Demeter and the primordial Goddess, Gaia, as an actual embodiment of the earth.

Durga is the personification of knowledge, memory and wisdom in this aspect she is Aparavidya (knowledge of secular Sciences). As Paravidya, she is linked with higher knowledge concerning spiritual matters. She is Tamasi (darkness) and she is the great delusion as Mahamoha. She descends from time to time to defend the earth, the Gods and humanity and restore the earth's harmony; in this way she resembles the Chinese Goddess, Nu Kua, who was also creatress and saviouress of ancient China.

FESTIVALS

There are numerous Festivals associated with the Goddess Durga and her worship but there are two that are universally, well known; the Navaratra (Durga Puja) and the Dasara. It is also important to note that her worship in the North of India varies from the South.

Durga Puja is her annual festival held for nine days near the Autumnal harvest, it is also known as Navaratra. This festival is held during the lunar month of Asvin and it is a splendor to behold. During the Durga Puja she is often depicted with four other deities considered her children; Sarsawati, Lakshmi, Ganesa, Karttikeya. Other texts, however, reveal she is the mother of Jyoti as well. The altars for Durga during the Navaratra festival are often elaborate with numerous offerings and larger than life images of the multi-armed Goddess, made out of Clay but also many other interesting materials like fibers and food. Durga's many appellations are commemorated for each of the nine days of Durga Puja, they are listed below.

HER NINE APPELLATIONS, mentioned in the Devi Kavacha of the Chadipatha scriptures...

1.Shailaputri, This word means daughter (Putri), daughter of the mountains (Shaila). She is worshipped on the first day of the festival and she embodies Brahma, Vishnu and Shiva. She rides a bowl and carries a trident and a Lotus in her two hands. Also known as Parvati, Sati, Hemavati, daughter of the Hemava/Himalayan.

2.Brahmacharini, (meaning unmarried) In her second form as mother goddess she is worshipped on the second day of the Navaratra festival. Her name means one who practices devout austerity. This was Parvati during her period of great devotion waiting for Lord Shiva to recognize her as his destined bride. She holds a rosary on her right hand and water utensil or a Kumbha, which is a water pot, in her left hand. She is blissfully happy and peaceful and is the way to emancipation. She bestows prosperity and grace upon all her devotees who worship her. This aspect of Durga is the holder of knowledge and wisdom and Divine grace is gifted to us in her presence.

3.Chandraghanta, The third form of the Goddess and worshipped on the third day of the festival, she brings peace, tranquility and prosperity in the life of those who invoke her. She has a Chandra or half Moon on her forehead in the shape of a bell. This form of Durga is depicted with ten hands, each holding a powerful weapon and three eyes. She is a disciple of bravery and possesses great strength to fight in the battle against demons. She is giver of knowledge and bliss.

4.Kusumanda, (Kushumanda) The fourth form of the Goddess, worshipped on the fourth day. "Ku" means a little, "ushma" means warmth, and means the cosmic egg. In this form she is considered the creator of the universe and she holds weapons in her eight hands and a rosary and she rides the lion/tiger.

5.Skondamata, (Skanda mata) Her name means the mother of Skanda. Notice similarity to the Norse Giantess named Skadi. In Hindu mythology, Skanda was the son of Lord Shiva and Parvati, He was a commander in chief of the Gods, to fight the demon. In this appellation, she is worshipped on the fifth day, accompanied by Lord Skanda, in his infant form. She has a bright complexion and she sits on a Lotus. She is depicted with four arms and three eyes while holding a Lotus in her hands.

6.Katyayani, The sixth form, worshipped on the six day of the festival. She is an avatar of Durga. There was once a sage named Kata or Katyayan, who had a son named Katya and according to one legend, Kata, prayed for a daughter like a Goddess and his wish was granted when Katyayani was born as an avatar of Durga.

7.Kaalratri, Her name represents the enemy of darkness and ignorance. She is the seventh form of Durga, worshipped on the seventh day of the Navaratra festival. She is dark skinned, disheveled hair, in a fearless posture and wearing a necklace, flashing around her neck. She has three eyes, flames from her breath and her vehicle is a donkey. On her upper left hand she holds a thorn like weapon, made of iron. She is also known as, Shubhamkari, the one who does good. She resembles Kali in her midnight hue and she holds a sparkling sword in her right hand, ready for battle.

8.Maha Gauri, her name means "Fair." She is exalted and worshipped on the eighth day of the Navaratra festival. The sins of the pass, present and future get washed away and purified in her presence. She is intelligent, peaceful and calm. She wears white clothes and displays four arms while riding a bull. Her right lower hand holds a trident.

Her left upper hand holds a damaru. She expresses unfailing and fruitful attributes for her devotees.

9.Siddhidatri, The name means the giver of siddhis (magical or spiritual powers to control the self and others and the forces of nature) This is Durga in her ninth form and the most powerful form. She is worshipped on the ninth day of the Navaratra Harvest festival where she exemplifies supernatural healing powers. She has four arms, holding a club, a lotus and a conch shell. She is always happy. She rides on a lion/tiger as her sacred vehicle, displaying great powers and she blesses the entire Universe.

Durga's second festival, held after the Navaratra, is the Dasara, which is much more connected to military feats and the impactful influence of the powerful Goddess, Durga and her ability to bless military weapons and grant victory in the battlefield to her worshippers. She is exalted as Abita, Ambika or Aparajita, as the one who blesses the military and its soldiers but she is also directly connected with the fruitfulness of the Harvest as we will see in her other Festival.

Returning to Durga Puja, it is celebrated during the lunar month of Asvin, which coincides with the Autumnal Harvest in North India. During this festival, Durga is the power inherent in all vegetation. Nine different plants are bundled together, they create a Navapattrika, which is a bundle of different plants worshipped and venerated as the Goddess herself. Durga is associated with the successful growing, fertile crops. She is the sacred crops and frequently, as an offering, worshippers will bring to her altars, sugar cane juice and sesame seed oil. Durga in this aspect is unquestionably connected to the fecundity of crops. There is also another ritual during this festival in which a priest takes five grains, scattered firmly on the dough, rice wheat and barley, the burghii, also known as "mas." The sesame is placed on the dough as the priest says the invocation that alludes to the Goddess actually being these grains.

> *"Om, you are the rice, Om, you are the life,*
> *you are the life of the Gods, you are our life, you are our internal life,*
> *you are long life, you give life, Om, the Sun with his rays*
> *gives you the milk of life and Varuna nourishes you with water..."*

pg 111-112 Hindu Goddesses, Visions of the Divine Feminine in the Hindu Religious Tradition, by David R. Kinsley, University of California Press, Berkeley and Los Angeles California, 1988

Durga is the power of life which the Gods utilize to achieve immortality. She is the one who appeases the hunger of the world and protects her worshippers from the numerous demons plaguing society. At these Festivals, blood sacrifices are common and an intrinsic part of the ceremonies to reenact her ancient myths, connected to the buffalo demon and the blood that was shed. Goats and sheep are also sacrificed and sometimes, to quench Durga's thirst for blood, worshippers would even sacrifice their own blood as offerings to her. This was done to replenish her powers, to invigorate the Goddess and give her back life force, now contained in the form of blood and animal sacrifices. Blood was seen as a recharger and re-awakener needed to refuel the strength of the mighty protectress Goddess.

The interdependence of human sexuality with fertility and the success of harvest crops are evident in the worship and rituals of many different cultures and this extends to India as well. Particularly, when such a wild, primal powerful deity, like the one who lives outside of the boundaries of civilizations, is propitiated, one can expect an intense experience. It is to be expected, that Durga's worship might take on a boisterous, wild, rambunctiously liberating and even pleasurable undertone. It would not be unlikely to see couples, copulate in the field of India, just like in many other cultures during this time of the year, believing that their copulation and the spilt secretion of their lovemaking would result in a more prosperous harvest. This is a form of giving back vitality and energy to the spirit underlining the crops. Semen and sexual fluids were believed to have great fertilizing powers, powers that were necessary to fertilize the field and manifest a prosperous harvest.

However, in North India, we are privy to an alternate approach to her worship. It was almost compulsory for girls to be married at an early age, and as was expected they would leave their family to join their husband's clan. This was not a transition most found easy, quite the contrary, young brides would suffer much separation anxiety during those early honeymoon years of marriage. In Bengal however, daughters were allowed to happily return to their home villages once a year during Durga Puja and this was often a highly emotionally charged event for young brides, who were probably deeply missing their home and family of origins. This returning home theme is why Durga herself is sometimes perceived as the returning daughter, during this Harvest festival. Many chants sung during the Durga Puja Festival support this belief. Songs with the theme of welcoming back, farewells and the difficult life of a daughter, when she is in her husband's home (in contrast to her loving parent's home) are a prevalent theme. In these documented songs Durga is identify with the Goddess Parvati, wife of Shiva, daughter of Himalaya and his wife Mena and she is the perpetual sacred daughter returning home before having to sadly depart once more.

Many worshippers during this festival view Durga as the beloved daughter returning home and it's a very intimate experience, as worshippers' commune and connect with their beloved Goddess. A clay image of the multi-armed Goddess is often found on her altar and it is worshipped as the Goddess herself. Worshippers caress affectionately and highly venerate the image of their beloved Goddess as if she indeed is an intimate family member. She is depicted triumphing over a powerful demon but many worshippers in this part of the world simply see her as – sacred Daughter, returning home for her annual Autumnal visit. It is also a time when worshipper will consider the returning daughter, Durga, as an actual family member and lavish onto her all the love, attention and adoration to her image. It seems almost as if their Goddess becomes Persephone, returning home to help the crops grow and to share her powers of fecundity upon the land. Worshippers then take on the role of the archetypal Mother, like Demeter. *"We become the mothers that are welcoming back the daughter, the Persephone, during this festival..."* And when this festival comes to a close, everyone prepares to bid her adieu at the waters, the sacred daughter, Durga is bid adieu. This returning daughter archetype in this Autumnal Harvest festival will often find women gathering around the representative images of Durga; weeping, mourning, crying as an expression of the melancholy they feel over the daughter preparing to leave and her inevitable departure during the Dark season.

In the South there is a vastly contrasting approach to the worship of this great Goddess in the Navaratra Festival. There is a wild, untamable, almost sexual tension that is highlighted between Durga and the buffalo demon, Mahisa. A Buffalo is sometimes sacrificed on the altar to Durga and blood is significantly featured during ceremonial rites to represent the blood many shed in battle with the Goddess. This demon is viewed as her suitor and her potential future husband that she ultimately engages in battle, defeats and refuses to submit to. Her untamable sexual energy is indisputably dangerous and almost deadly to any man who dares to approach her. There is an implication that one must submit to Durga before engaging in any safe sexual encounter with her. Mahisa loses the battle and is unable to do so but other myths reveal that Lord Shiva becomes her consort, yet, this is only as the aspect of Parvati and Sati. Durga is a fatal threat to those who try to conquer her or approach her sexually. In the South, Durga Puja festival gives more credence to Durga's role as a determined, fierce independent and untamable deity, whose origins are found among tribal people, in the far off distant mountains. Her worship in these festivals, in the south, are considerably more wild, free and more ecstatic than in the North.

In conclusion, it is important to note the slight difference in her worship, for in Northern Indian tradition, Durga is viewed more prominently as the gentle young bride or daughter, in need of family tenderness and adoration. She is viewed as the returning daughter, while in the south; she is seen as wild, untamable, strong independent, unmarried Goddess, delighting in her liminal aspect.

Arjuna's Hymn to Devi
Bhishma Parva 23: 4-16

This Hymn follows after the Bhagavad Gita in the Mahabharata. Lord Arjuna prays to Durga after being instructed by Lord Krishna to pray to Durga for Victory over his enemies. It is offered as a reflection of her gifts.

Prayer to Durga

"I bowed to you, O foremost of Siddhas, O Noble One, that dwells in the Forest of Mandara, O Virgin, O Kali, O wife of Kapala! O you of a black and tawny hue."

"I bow to you, O beneficent Kali, I bow to you, O Maha-kali, o wrathful One. I bow to you, O Tara, (the savior) the great boon bestowing one."

"O Durga! Great Being, the fierce bestower of victory! O personification of victory, O you that bears a banner of peacock plumes, O one and decked with every ornament."

"O you that wields an awful spear, beholder of sword and shield, O you that were born as the younger sister of the chief of cow–herds, O eldest sibling, born in the family of the cow-herd, Nanda.!"

"O you who are always fond of buffalo's blood, born of Kusika's clan, dressed in yellow robes, having assuming the face of a wolf you devoured the Asuras! I bow to you who are fond of battles!"

"O Uma! O Sakambhari! O you that are white in hue and also black! O slayer of the Asura Kaitabha! O yellow-eyed one! O you that see everything! O you of eyes that have the color of smoke, I bow to you!"

"You are the Vedas, the Srutis and the greatest virtue! You are propitious to Brahmana engaged in sacrifice. You are all knowing, you are ever present in the sacred abodes erected to you in cities of Jamvudwipa, I bow to you!"

"You are the knowledge of the highest truth among sciences and you are that sleep of creatures from which there is no waking. O mother of Skanda, possessor of the six highest attributes of Divinity, O Durga, that dwells in the most inaccessible regions."

"You are called Swaha and Swadha and the subtle divisions of time such as Kala and Kashta. You are the Goddess of Knowledge; Saraswati, and the mother of the Vedas and the personification of Vedanta."

"With inner mind purified, I praise you O great Goddess, let victory always attend me through your grace on the field of battle."

"In inaccessible regions, where there is fear, in places of difficulty, in the abodes of your worshippers, and in the nether regions (Patala), you always dwell. And in battle you always defeat the Danavas."

"You are the unconsciousness, the sleep, the illusion, the modesty, the beauty of all creatures. You are the twilight, and the radiant light of day! You are Savitri, and you are the mother of all creation."

"You are contentment, development, fortitude and light. You increase the radiance of the Sun and the Moon. You are the prosperity of those that prosper. The Siddhas and the Charanas behold you in deep contemplation!"

www.srimatham.com/storage/docs/arjunas-hymn-to-durga

DURGA MANTRA:

"Om Dum Durgayei, Namaha..."

Om and Salutations to that Feminine energy which protects from all manner of negative influence and for which dum, is the seed.

DURGA GODDESS GATHERING DAY

Purpose: To welcome and exalt the warrior Goddess, Durga; she who helps us fight and eradicate the self-destructing demons that plague our lives. To connect with her fires of transformations on this sabbat of Imbolc. To unearth her fires from within, to welcome she who victoriously slays our inner demons and liberates us from their grip.

Check Ins: We gather around the Circle and introduce ourselves to one another, while also voicing our feelings on this month and our hope for the upcoming season.

Chants: Together we will join our voices to sing some commonly known Pagan chants, as well as new ones offered on the Chant sheet in the hand outs (see the last page of this chapter). Singing aloud is a wonderful way to raise energy effortlessly and it also sometimes helps in creating harmonious bonds.

Our Agreements bylaws and Pertinent group discussion... We go around the circle of women, reading a few lines each of our "Group Agreements" and add any new ones that seem necessary. Agreements are signed and submitted in confidence.

Drumming Grounding: A drumming musical CD track will be played, to give participants a chance to connect and ground to this very moment. Women are invited to find a comfortable seat or stand and add movement if they wish.

Conjuring Goddess via her Image: Using a photo image, sculpture, Goddess oracle card or other image of the Goddess will be shared around the circle, as each woman present will reflect on the image and state aloud what attributes or Divine messages need expression.

Lecture on the Hindu Goddess, Durga
Her myth and various folklores, her attributes and relevance for us today.

GODDESS WORKSHOPS
WORKSHOP I
Recognizing and Facing our personal demons.

WORKSHOP II
The powerful tools of the dagger, scythe & sword. Employing these tools in our workings.

WORKSHOP III
Exploring her Liminal aspect, how do we tap into the Wild one?

WORKSHOP IV
Today's radical feminist, Warrior archetype. How has Feminism changed through out the ages?

WORKSHOP V
Protection and Hexing politics and practices.

WORKSHOP VI
Living autonomously, unearthing independence...

WORKSHOP VII
Employing Mudras and Mantras to our Spirituality.

DURGA GODDESS GATHERING RITUAL

Purpose: To welcome and exalt the warrior Goddess, Durga; she who helps us fight and eradicate the self -destructing demons that plague our lives. To connect with her fires of Transformations on this sabbat of Imbolc. To unearth her fires from within, to welcome she who victoriously slays our inner demons and liberates us from their grip.

Smudging Asperge
Anointing & Welcoming: Heavy trance drumming or Hindi mantras can be played in the background throughout the ritual.

INTENT DECLARED: Today we will gather to honor and connect with the multi-armed Goddess, Durga and victoriously identify & slay our demons.

CIRCLES CASTING*(with Sword or athame)*
With Sword, I conjure this magick sphere,
Outside of space,
Outside of fear,
For love is all that shields us here,
Bright lights to quell,
The baneful and weird.

Upon this Sphere,
This Circle is cast,
Keep evil at bay,
Let kind spirits pass.

No more a room,
But your Holy Space,
To worship and invoke,
Your essence and grace.

Container, Preserver,
All within thee,
This circle is cast,
SO MOTE IT BE!

QUARTER CALLING

AIR
Welcome element of **Air**, Sacred Guardian of the **East**,
From the realm of the East, I call the sacred Element of Air. Air; that swishing of the breeze we feel at thy feet as she dances, the warriors dance, wielding her swords and daggers freely. Cutting all that needs severing, making space for new atmospheres to breathe. Hail to you Air, come to this ritual space may we feel your sacred energy. Hail and Welcome!!!

FIRE
Welcomed element of **Fire**, Sacred Guardian of the **South,**
From the realm of the South, I call the sacred Element of Fire. Fire, the incinerator, burning away what needs to be transformed, from these burning embers sacred ashes are formed. Burning heat of catapulting action, I welcome you in this ritual space today. Hail and Welcome!!!

WATER
Welcomed element of **Water**, Sacred Guardian of the **West**,
From the realm of the West, I call the sacred Element of Water.Water's gift; from invincible tides, from Oceans that can move mountains on high. From Oceans that can swallow up its choice of lives. Water's power from her tides that destroy and births since the beginning of time. Ebb and flow to this ritual today, may we feel your sacred presence as it sways within. Hail and Welcome!!!

EARTH
Welcomed element of **Earth**, Sacred Guardian of the **North**,
From the realm of the North, I call the sacred Element of Earth. Earth that holds me solidly, firmly planting my soul and feet. Grounding me to this moment in time, fertile earth support me and mine. I welcome the dark moist, rich soil, supporter of every single creative toil. Come earth's energy, be here now. Hail and Welcome!!!

CHANT: *"Eight Bead Chant"*

GODDESS INVOCATION

MEDITATION, TRANCE & RAISING ENERGY *(Drums, dance, cone of Power)*

SPELL WORKING
The priestess will ask, **"What blocks you and your success? What are the demons you must fight and engage in war with?"** Identifying who or what are the demons in your personal life and severing them from your life by burning it in her fires,
by first stabbing with your dagger then burning it.
Light your candle now and reflect quietly,
while soothing music plays in the background and
allow a meditative moment to contemplate on what blocks you now?

CHANTING: MANTRA 108x CONTINUOUSLY:
"Om Dum Durgayei, Namaha"

Slips of paper will be passed around the circle, as everyone will have a chance
to write down the demons/blocks/hidden issues that presented themselves through this mantra and light their candle.
Every participant will share one of her demons; give it a grand exotic name
and then place the dagger through the paper,
before setting it ablaze in the communal cauldron. While reciting:

"Ye Demons known to me as_____,
I recognize and name you,
And stab you with my sword,
I burn you here now with Durga's might
until you are no more..."

Chant: *"Mother of Darkness, Mother of Light"*

Final Check ins
DEVOKING GODDESS

DEVOKING QUARTERS
Sacred element of **Earth**, Guardian of the **North**,
Thank you for guarding our rites today
In peace ye came when called
In peace depart with our gratitude,
Hail and farewell!!!

Sacred element of **Water**, Guardian of the **West**,
Thank you for guarding our rites today
In peace ye came when called
In peace depart with our gratitude,
Hail and farewell!!!

Sacred element of **Fire,** Guardian of the **South,**
Thank you for guarding our rites today
In peace ye came when called
In peace depart with our gratitude,
Hail and farewell!!!

Sacred element of **Air,** Guardian of the **East,**
Thank you for guarding our rites today
In peace ye came when called
In peace depart with our gratitude,
Hail and farewell!!!

DEVOKING CHANT
Chanting: The Earth, the Air, the Fire, the Water, return, return, return, return...

OPENING CIRCLE:
Our Circle is open but never unbroken,
may the love and peace of the Goddess
rest forever in our hearts,
Merry meet, merry part
and merry meet again....

POTLUCK FEASTING

DURGA MUSING

I think probably one of the most fascinating attributes that the Hindu Goddess, Durga conveys to our gender is the power of an independent, autonomous woman and the expression of the wild uninhibited, unbridled, confident Wombmyn.

Here is a Goddess who, according to Hindu cosmology, was created by the collected wrath and anger of the male Gods. Behold, here is a Goddess who embodies not just anger and rage but the fierce action and courage required to express that anger. This is Durga! She exists in this universe solely, without the need for male support or love or protection or permission from them. She is autonomous and whole unto herself and that is part of her lure and beauty. Her strength and powers are unmatched and unrestrained and she breaks, utterly demolishes, any stereotypical images connected to our gender. These images might seem savage like, primal and monstrous, especially to those who would rather keep us pristine, quiet, predictable and obedient but she won't let herself be defiled in this way.

We looked to her, to help fight our inner and outer demons and thus, she becomes our Divine protectress. These demons might be associated with the many demands and expectations from the world at large but also can be connected with our own personal and ethereal negative indoctrinations of our gender. We looked to her to strengthen us with the ability to face our numerous conscious and unconscious hindrances and face the many ways demons manifest themselves in our lives. She enters our realm that we may touch upon her powerfully fierce, liminal qualities, the ones that often guarantee victory when facing the insurmountable. The Goddess Durga, as well as her helper Kali Ma, are ferocious, exceptionally potent female deities that can help us awaken suppressed, yet very much needed, parts of ourselves. Collectively they are indispensable deities and archetypes that every modern woman would benefit from connecting with, especially as we continue to fight for women's rights and equality.

On a personal, more intimate level, Durga can help us find the courage to take bold action in our daily lives, when we are most prone to deny, hide, or be complacent to the most mundane of situations that can have catastrophic implications for our future. A perfect example would be someone who is continuously being harassed at work or is being mistreated and undervalued but opts to deny this daily occurrence and makes up excuses, preferring to maintain the status quo, until one day, she gets fired and replaced by a more aggressive candidate. Another example would be in the case of the abused wife or girlfriend who, while subjected to numerous forms of physical and mental abuse, might make excuses and ignore the daily danger signs until one day she ends up in the hospital emergency room.

Durga awakens the thirst for blood, freedom and victory and sets aflame our inner warrior Goddess. There is no doubt in her presence, only fearlessness and drive. She demands that you treat yourself with self-respect and love. I have found her to be indispensable during those chaotic moments in my life when confronted with shocking adversaries and an overwhelming work load. The multi armed Hindu Goddess has a way of blessing you with the *"I can do this and then some..."* attitude, which leaves you wondering in the end what were you so hesitant about at the start of your journey.

Honor Durga and you unearth and honor a deep, forgotten part of yourself that initially might shock but will surely liberate you to your true potential and power.

CHAKRA MEDITATION

1st ROOT CHAKRA

We begin this Chakra healing meditation by first bringing our focus to our Root Chakra, located down below near our tail bone. Think upon where the Serpent neatly snugged is coiled up in your Kundalini region, the base of your spine. In your mind's eye now see a crimson red apple, an apple like the one we imagine Snow White received from the Old Crone in the famous, beloved Childhood fairy tale. Or better still; envision a red rose with all of its numerous veiny petals and the passion it often connotes. Notice this deep red color and now think upon our blood and how similar its color is to this apple and this crimson red rose.

Consider when we bleed; whether pricked by a needle, slashed by a kitchen knife or through the dark crimson blood of our monthly menstruation as women. See this pool of dark redness, lulling you back and forth into a trance, and allow your mind to delve into this deep red color. See this red now at the base of your spine, flowing back and forth like a Cabernet Sauvignon swishing in a contained large chalice... back and forth it swishes, reminding you of your vitality, reminding you of your life force... reminding you of your passion and your sacred womanhood. Life to death, death to rebirth.... Blood, crimson red blood.... this red is located in your Root chakra. It symbolizes life, the roots of your personal tree, the veins that transport vitality to your very being. Open yourself up to its power at this moment. This is the gateway of the earth. It is the sacred gateway to your very birth and existence... Honor this Root Chakra now.

2nd SACRAL CHAKRA

At this time I invite you to hold in the palm of your hands a tangerine... hold a bright ripe orange fruit, ready to be personally tasted by you. First however, before peeling it, notice the texture of this Orange in your hands. Notice its slight grainy skin and the vibrancy of its hue. Now, look down on the ground, by your feet, and see if you can spot the same hue on the fallen Autumnal leaves. Take a moment to trace with your mind's eye the many times the color orange asserts its presence in your life right now. What else do you see in this Orange hue and how does it make you feel? Continue to hold the Orange fruit, smell its spicy sweet scent and now begin to peel it. When it is peeled, hungrily place it in your mouth and taste it. Let its sweet tangy juices burst and dribble down the side of your lips, as you delight in its taste, and allow yourself to get sticky from its sweet nectar. It's okay if you get messy and it's okay to delight in its sweet taste. At this time you are being invited to tap into your aesthetic awareness, your pleasure markers and sensuality, which just might connect you to your sexuality, the realm of your Second Chakra. Bring this Orange hue, its juicy stickiness from its orgasmic spillage and its sweet scent, all to the sacred region above your genitalia. Spend a moment experiencing this vibrant hue of Orange through all of your senses while resting in your Sacral Chakra. Open yourself up to the gifts of a balanced Second Chakra as it invites you to explore your sensuality, your powers of fertility, the magick of your physical being and a balanced ego. Let it offer you its gift of optimism and creativity. It is the Gateway of the Moon, home of the self and home of your sweetness. Take a moment to honor the Sacral, Second chakra.

3rd SOLAR PLEXUS

As a child, when asked to color or paint a picture of our Sun, oftentimes we reached for the brightest Yellow crayon, or paint, to proceed to depict what we perceived to be the brightest star in our galaxy, the Sun. I invite you now to retrieve this picture you yourself might have created in your youth. Retrieve this image of the sun and allow yourself to even remember its warmth and piercing bright yellow light on a perfect summer's day. If you can, reflect on the cathartic powers of the bright yellow sun as you might have found yourself happily sunbathing on a beach or on a grassy fertile field. We are about to enter the Gateway of the Sun through our third chakra, our Solar Plexus. Consider the joy and laughter the color yellow inspires you to feel. Consider for a moment, the many positive attributes the Sun conjures in our memories; memories from our childhood, memories of running wild and free without many cares or concerns or fears. This yellow is a powerful confident hue and it spins like our very sun in your third chakra above your navel.

In your mind's eye see the Yellow Sun spinning vibrantly, awakening your self-confidence and exuding balance, strength and appropriate self-expression. See this solar yellow disk, spinning brightly above your navel area, under your chest. It is alive and this third chakra is a magnet for respect, confidence, popularity and positive recognition. Take a moment now to honor the Manipura, your known Third chakra, the Solar Plexus.

4th HEART CHAKRA

Bring your attention, if you will, to the middle of your chest. You may also wish to physically place your hands in this region. Feel the pulsation of your own heart, beating in affirmation of your fertile existence and helping you transcend to the realm of emotions, this is Anahata. This is your heart Chakra…gateway to the winds. These gentle breezes stemming from this realm will carry you now to the season of spring. See yourself amidst a grove of bright green colored trees. As is to be expected in the springtime, everything surrounding you takes on this bright, fertile green hue. The trees with their bulbous bushy green crowns, the tall blades of grass beneath your feet, the tiny leaves on a bouquet of roses, the various insects that cross your path at this time of year. They all share in this bright cathartic verdant hue, the color of your fourth Chakra. Let your eyes now wander, for a moment, as you spy numerous objects around you in this flourishing green hue. How does it make you feel? What emotions in your heart does it conjure up for you? Take this moment to see the vibrancy of this fertile green within your Heart chakra. This is the realm of unconditional love, altruism, empathy and great human compassion. As the green hue spins its doors of compassion wide open within you, see if you can detect how best to put this gift to good use in your own life. How different can your life be experienced with this chakra opened, healed and balanced? Can you offer your own self, the gift of compassion? Can you offer compassion to your perceived enemies? Take this calming moment to connect with and honor your Fourth Chakra, the Anahata; your heart.

5th THROAT CHAKRA

Now I invite you to move your energy and focus from your heart to your throat region. This is Vishuddha (the Purifier) it is the Fifth Chakra also best known as your Throat Chakra. Spend a moment here still, quietly assessing the sensations you might be feeling in this region. Does it feel healthy, moist or dry and scratchy? Is it relaxed or tense and cut off? Take a moment to quietly assess and connect with your truth expressor. In subtle ways, if you listen closely, it will reveal to you its true present state. Have you been comfortable speaking your truth and expressing your authentic self? Are you being as imaginative and freely creative as can be? This is the Gateway of time and space and I invite you now to dig… yes dig a little deeper for your answers…

You are now invited to notice the blue of the infinite sky above your head and the turquoise blue of the infinite oceans- a blue that has been since the beginning of time. Let yourself journey in this trance by this turquoise blue, a blue symbolizing the infinite Universe. And now, catch a glimpse of a blue sphere as it forms on the top of the skin over your neck region. With your mind's eye, take your hand and gently press your larynx in this area. Feel your fingers, over this blue sphere; pierce gently right through your flesh to enter your throat region. You intuit there is something wedged, blocking your throat chakra and at this very moment it is imperative you pull it out. Gently feel your fingers explore, wiggling as they search around this sacred region of your throat. You detect a small smooth pebble, the obstacle in your trust and communications. Gently, try to extract this stone from your Throat Chakra now and take this moment to inspect it. Herein this stone were all the thoughts that went unexpressed by you; all the doubts you brushed away, all that you suppressed in fear of being revealed, all the words you feared to speak, all the true emotions you kept securely locked to avoid the eyes of judgment, all the parts of you -frugally hidden away. This stone you have unearthed within may be tiny but its power to silence and sabotage has been great and today we end its reign. Rub this discovered stone within your fingers now and watch as it pulverizes in the light of day. Let its fragments and debris fall and evaporate in the air. Breathe now and with each breath allow your throat chakra to heal itself as it mends the hole that held the block, in this old stone. Breathe. Remember the blue of the infinite sky... they are within you here in this chakra. Remember the blue of the infinite waters.... They are within you here in this fifth chakra. Breathe and take this moment to honor Vishuddha, your sacred Throat Chakra.

6th PINEAL THIRD EYE CHAKRA

Bring your attention now to your Pineal gland, better known as your third eye. It is locate on your forehead between your brows. Known as Ajna, it is the realm of perception, intuition and wisdom. Here you will see with no eyes, hear with no ears, feel with no touch, journey to internal and external far off realms all through your sixth chakra. Take this moment to bring your attention to this special place now. With your eyes closed try to bring your focus to the middle of your forehead by gently crossing your closed eyes to look into this direction, between your two eyebrows. In this region, carefully search for any sign of the color indigo. Search and continue to look deeply to discern quite subtly the glow of a purple, indigo color. See this indigo color spin in a circular motion ever so gently as it transforms before your eyes into an Amethyst crystal. Continue to look deeply into the Amethyst crystal as it becomes your third eye. Open this divine third eye, blink and open it wide to see what is before you.

Now, if you will, begin to reflect on the concept of gratitude. With your open third eye, see what you are most grateful for in your life.... and let your intuitive sight now gaze on the feeling of gratitude. This sixth chakra is known as the Gateway of liberation....the place of detachment, of Universal compassion, the realm of our interconnection awareness and the freedom found in a non-dualistic view of life. Here is where your true sight originates from. Here is where self-mastery and extrasensory gifts are born. Continue to gaze with your open third eye as the purple Amethyst crystal and allow yourself to absorb it and its intuitive attributes into your Ajna chakra. This amethyst is your third eye and it sees with an exceptional acuity, far better than any physical eye can see. Take a moment to receive its personal message to you. When you are ready, prepare to shut your precious third eye close and express gratitude for all that revealed itself here today through your sixth chakra. The Gateway of liberation has freed you from illusions. We take this moment now to honor our sixth chakra, honor its intuitive attributes and the immeasurable powers of our Third Eye.

7th CROWN CHAKRA

Journey now upwards and bring your attention to the top of your head, your Crown. Feel if you will, the weight upon your head, as it sits upon your relaxed neck and shoulders. Extend your awareness now to the space above your head and feel this space lightly vibrating overhead. Like a blossom feel the top of your head now open... open, simply open in a state of receptivity. Allow your head to open like a multi petal lotus flower, becoming a sacred portal for Divine light and sacred union to take place. Here is where we are the chalice. Here is where we become one with source. Quietly observe your seventh chakra, welcoming this moment of transcendence...listening for the whispers emanating from the flecks of the streaming Divine light. You are the chalice, inviting the nectar of life.

In this trance you have journeyed through almost all of your chakras and now you have arrived at the Gateway of the Void, your Seventh chakra.This chakra is known as Sahasrara; meaning a thousand petalled. This is the realm of receptivity and union with source. Take this moment to honor this sacred realm, as you intuit the subtle vibrational energy. Inviting the light, begin to detect the sounds that birth our Universe. **Om....**Unearth the state of bliss and unity... **Om...** Connect to all things within and around you now. **Om...** Open your seventh chakra now and in this very special moment; honor yourself, honor your Crown, honor and weave the thread that connects you to this expansive Universal tapestry of humanity. Honor your part in the infinite, sacred circle of life.

Keep your Crown chakra open for a moment and welcome the Divine and Her message into this portal. When you are ready, gently close it and briefly go back and revisit all of your chakras to make sure they are now cleared, balanced and closed. If it helps, see yourself zippering or buttoning close each one of your seven chakras, as we prepare to end this meditation. We will count slowly from seven to one backwards to help us in transition back to this room, this time and space. Please take a final, deep cleansing breath as we begin to count; **seven, six.** Breathe, **five, four,** and take one more energized breath, **three**, exhale and release. Follow my voice back to this space, **two and one.** Gently stretch out and place the palm of your hands flat on the earth to help you ground better and ease you back into this room and with both hands in prayer pose, welcome, Namaste!

INVOCATIONS

DURGA

Fierce Hindu Mother,
Fighting my wounds,
Battling illusions,
Cutting them through.

Multi armed Goddess,
Wielding thy Sword,
Chopping the Demons,
Till all their blood pours.

Born of Divine Wrath,
Collected from the Gods
Piercing the darkness
Standing autonomous.

Mahisa's enemy,
Slaying all that is vile,
Awakening our woman power,
To embrace the sacred and wild.

Hail to you Durga,
Ancient Mother of my soul,
With you I gather my fragments
To embrace myself whole.

SPELLS

PROTECTION SPELL

Shield, protect me,
Round and round
Hekate's arms shield me now,

Kali, my defender,
Help me with this war,
Like Durga, please save me, Kali ,
I am yours...

Oya remind me,
I am not alone,
Let my ancestors come,
To secure me in my home

Enchantress Medea,
Beautiful and skilled,
I conjure the right love,
With my words and my will.

Surround with great powers,
This magickal spell
From this day forth,
All will go well,

By all the powers of Universal light,
Infuse this spell,
With magick and might,
I draw upon my reserve of powers,
This spell manifest now,
On this sacred hour...

It is done......

REVERSAL

Return to those
who've hurt me so,
Return their hate,
with their own cords.

Return their work
and evil deed,
Return and keep them,
far from me...

Return their spells,
Their wicked ways,
Return , exposed,
By light of day,

Return as Karma
Has final say,
Return to them,
And keep me safe!!!

GOSSIP REMEDY

Tongue that cuts,
meant to pierce a soul,
Hurt intangible
but deeply cold

Gossip Lies
Viciously told
Bullies victimizing
dragging me low

With this spell,
I call to cease
All the Falsities told of me.

Mirrors planted
that they may see,
Feel the hurt they tried inflicting

Rise above
With shield on guard,
Gossip and hate
I banish you far....

DURGA GODDESS GATHERING CHANT TEXT SHEET

AFFIRMATIONS words by Valerie Girard From Music CD, "She Changes Moving Breath"
I am a powerful woman, I am- I am a powerful woman, I am
I connect with myself in everything,I am a powerful woman, I am
      I am a passionate woman, I am, I am a passionate woman, I am
      I express myself with power and love, I am a passionate woman, I am
I am a feeling woman, I am, I am a feeling woman, I am,
I accept all the things expressing through me, I am a feeling woman, I am,
      I am a loving woman, I am, I am a loving woman, I am,
      I love myself in everyone, I am a loving woman, I am,
I am divine woman, I am I am divine woman, I am,
The Goddess is fully awake in me, I am divine woman, I am...

EIGHT BEADS CHANTS *by Carolyn Hillyer*
Girlseed
Bloodflower
(dip it)Fruitmother
Spinmother,
raise it) Midwoman
Earthcrone
Stonecrone
Bone .....

INVOKING MOTHER by B. Melusine Mihaltses
Mother, Mother, Mother, I call you,
Deep within my soul, you're stirring my womb.
Mother, Mother, Mother, Hear my Cries,
In this Sacred Circle I Call you tonight.
Light the inner Flame, as I light the candle wick,
Call your sacred name and embrace myself as Witch.
Sky-clad I approach, to Elemental thrones,
Hear me, Mother hear me, Through these words I wrote.

AWAKENING by Anne Hill, From music CD, Reclaiming, Second Chants
If I touch you, I will know you;
Though my veil be drawn , you're glowing,
In my mind and soul and body...

Mother of Darkness
Mother of Darkness,
Mother of Light,
Earth Beneath the Soul in flight,
Songs of love and Love of life,
Guide us to our heart.....

SHE'S BEEN WAITING - by *Paula Walowitz*
She's been waiting, waiting
She's been waiting so long,
She's been waiting for her children
to remember to return (repeat)
Blessed be and blessed are the Lovers of the Lady,
Blessed be and blessed are, Maiden , Mother, Crone,
Blessed be and blessed are, The ones who dance together
Blessed be and blessed are, The ones who dance alone.......

EARTH, MOON,MAGICK, by B.M.M.
In the Earth, deep within,
There is A Magick, I draw it in.
      In her Caves, in the Trees
      Hear her Heartbeat, Pulsing thru me.
When I Rise, I feel her Love
With feet Grounded, I'm soaring high above,
      In the Earth, deep within,
      There is A Magick, I draw it in
Ancient Moon, my Soul reveres
With my Singing, I call you here.
      When this flame, ignites tonight,
      Priestess dancing, Under the moonlit night....
In the Earth, deep within,
There is A Magick
I draw it in.... There is A Magick, I draw it in }3x

BONES, *By "Flight of the Hawk"*
Bones, come Dance with me,(3x rept)
Dancing in the the desert, in the desert tonight (2Xrept)
Bones, Come Sing with me, (3X rept)
Dancing in the desert, in the desert tonight (2Xrept)
Bone dance know the Shaman dance
Bone dance hear the Raven cry
Bone dance see the Ancestors,
Dancing in the desert, in the desert tonight (2xrept)
Bones, Come fly with me, (3x rept)
Dancing in the desert, in the desert tonight (2Xrept)
Bones come die with me, (3Xrept)
Dancing in the desert, in the desert tonight (2X)*back to start*

CHAPTER FOUR

Uzume

"An intention is a quality of consciousness that you bring to an action..." Gary Zukav

UZUME

UZUME

"When the heart of woman is healed, there will be a thousand years of peace ..." Prophecy

UZUME ALTAR SET UP

OUR ALTAR

Altar cloth : As a Spring-like Goddess, it is best to prepare Uzume's altar cloth in the bright greens of the season.
Image: The image of the beautiful Japanese Goddess, Uzume or images of Japanese dancers, is also appropriate for her altar. I also suggest having an image of the Sun or the Japanese Sun Goddess, Amaterasu, as she is intimately connected with Uzume's lore.
Always present on the altar;
A silver pentacle, a cast iron cauldron, drums, speaking stick, wand, athame, elemental representations.....
Air: feather bundles, angel wings, bird, eagle or owl statuaries. Bell &, chimes, Incense type sticks, cones, charcoal brisket and fine powdered herbs; frankincense , myrrh.
Fire: pillar candles, glass enclosed candles in green, gold, yellow
Water: Small glass bowl with Water and or chalice with Champagne, Cranberry Juice or Red wine.
Earth: Offer as many green plants or cut bright flowers you can to represent earth. A small dish of soil or dry herbs can also be used

Other items pertinent to this particular gathering
Monkey(figurines) as they are connected to her dance
A Japanese Fan
A large symbol of the sun
A mirror
Kimono & garter belt
Tarot Cards
Bell chimes

Sacred objects from members:
Notes:

MONTH & SEASON

March

March is the third month in the Gregorian calendar. Interestingly enough, it originally was the first month of the Roman year, known as Martius. In Rome this was not only the beginning of Spring but also the start of the military campaign season and it is therefore not surprising, the month was named after Mars, the Roman God of War, to honor this civic time. Many ancient cultures viewed the first month of Spring as the start of the year and according to scholars, it wasn't until about 450BC, when perhaps King Numa Pompillius made the change, making January the first month of the year. *(wikipedia)*

The full moon, this month, was known as Crust Moon, a reference to the crunchy crust layer of thin ice, that formed over the earth throughout the evening hours and thawed by the midday sun. It was also known as Sap Moon and Crow Moon due to the arrival of cackling crows. And because there were many rainstorms that developed at this time of year, it also garnered the name Storm Moon. According to the Farmer's Almanac, March's Full Moon was also named Worm Moon, by the Native Americans, because at this time of year, as the earth began to thaw from the long cold winter, the earth worms would rise up to the surface of the earth and announce the arrival of spring.

All around us are the very first visible signs that we have entered a new season. And in no time, Spring will make the harshness of Winter a distant memory. In some parts of the world, the snow may not have thawed on the ground and there may even be fresh snow still falling. Some days give hope for early Springs arrival, while other days, stubbornly cling to Winter. Unpredictability clearly reigns this month and although winter can still be felt, we've survived the worse of it. If we look closely we'll see, that although Winter might linger faintly, its bitterness, begins to wane.

March's astrological sign is the fish, Pisces, and it is ruled by dreamy, elusive fantasy driven, Neptune (Feb 21-march 20).

There are some important holidays for us, as wommin, to make note of. The entire month of March is considered Woman's History Month and March 8th is officially International Woman's Day. March 17th is dedicated to St. Patrick's day and Mardi Gras is also grandly celebrated during this month. Night and Day are in perfect balance on the Vernal Equinox on (March 20-21st) as most Pagans celebrate the sabbat of Ostara. To experience this phenomenon try to stand an egg (her sacred symbol) at the exact hour of the Equinox and feel the Earth's magnetic pull and current on this special day. It's quite magickal to experience this, especially when incorporated within a sabbat ritual. The season of the Maiden is fully present in March and her inquisitive, sprouting energy can be represented in the numerous symbols of Spring, including seeds.

One of my favorite names for this month's Full moon is, Seed Moon. For me this is an equally appropriate name among the many already mentioned. Traditionally, this is the time for planting seeds, whether figuratively or literally. It is an ideal time to hope and dream, plan and plant our wishes, as nature itself is supporting our very own endeavors. As we bear witness to the amazing powers of Mother nature and delight in the robin's arrival, let us plant those seedlings in the soil and be confident that they will sprout soon and manifest into a multitude of beauty, before too long. This is the season of great optimism and potential.

Witnessing nature's magical transformation inspires us to look into our own personal transformations and the work that began at Imbolc continues to transform us now.

We call upon the Maiden Goddess Uzume, to move us with Courage into this new phase in our lives, as the wheel of the sacred year turns once more.

All Monthly intro text taken from author's first book, "Gathering for Goddess, A Complete Manual for Priestessing Women's Circles"

UZUME GODDESS LESSON

UZUME

Uzume is the Japanese Goddess of Dawn, revelry and joy. She quintessentially represents the cathartic power of laughter and is also depicted in Japanese Kyogen farce- as a woman who delights in her sensuality, called Okame.

Her full name is Ame –no-Uzume no Mikoto and it is quite intriguing to note that her name is sometimes interpreted as meaning *"The Terrible Female of Heaven."* In the Shinto religion, the name Uzume is linked to a "strong, brave woman." Today you might even hear the term *"osushi,"* to refer to a Japanese woman, a modern reference to one who exemplifies Uzume herself and the attributes she blesses women with.

As a deity often associated with the springtime, Uzume is considered a patron Goddess of the Rice fields. She is also very much connected with trance drumming and Shamanic practices. And as her most popular myth will reveal, she is a Goddess of revelry and dance, more specifically ritualistic, ecstatic dancing. She is also known as the wild chaotic abandonment sometimes found amidst the powerful surge of creative energy. Uzume is embodied Shakti energy and is a Goddess often linked with early forms of Divination and psychic powers. Though often portrayed as the maiden there are some texts that suggest another aspect of hers, represented as the wise crone.

There is very limited scholarly research and information on this early Japanese deity but we can extrapolate much from the ancient writings found in the Japanese sacred texts of the Kojiiki and the Nihonghi. The Kojiiki (*The Japanese Records of Ancient Matters*), C712 C.E./712 A.D. is one of the oldest existing written record of Japanese myth, legends and historical narrative related to Japan's imperial family and its assertion of Divine connection. The Nihonghi, (*Chronicle of Japan from the Earliest Times*) AD 697 AD, also sheds a great deal of insight into Japanese mythology, its origins and the worship of deities in ancient times. In these early sacred texts, the Goddess Uzume, is known as *"The Heavenly Alarming Female"* as well as *"The Great Persuader"* and she is still very much worshipped today as a prominent Shinto deity.

Shinto comes from the Chinese word, *"Shen-tao,"* meaning the way of the Gods. It is the indigenous, native religion of Japan that quite possibly has its roots in the Animist religions of Siberia. It is an ancient religion that lacks dogma yet practices the venerations of nature, spirits, ancestors and deities (referred to as Kami) and it pre-dates Buddhism. There is a strong belief in animated and unanimated objects and it is a Polytheistic religion that venerates a myriad of superior beings and spirits, known as Kami.

Interesting and most important to note, the Japanese name for Japan is Nippon, which literally means; Sun Origin and this is a direct reference to the highest venerated deity in Japan, the Sun Goddess, Amaterasu. Shintosim is a religion whose central deity is female unlike other World religions. And the Sun Goddess, Amaterasu, is of great significance because she is attributed for birthing Japan itself. Thus Shintoism is a spiritual practice intimately connected with Japan's divine origin and its people.

The Goddess Uzume is most often associated with the Japanese Sun Goddess, Amaterasu and she is attributed for playing a big part in tricking the Goddess out of her cave and self-imposed imprisonment. In the ancient myths, it was Uzume, with her ability to raise a ruckus that helped return Amaterasu back to her rightful place in the heavens, as the Sun Goddess and restore balance upon the earth.

According to Japanese lore, the Sun Goddess, Amaterasu O-Mikami, had retreated from the world when her volatile brother, the Storm God, Susano-O-no Kami, had defiled her sacred Temple. In one of his usual uncontrollable episodes he haphazardly tossed excrement and a colt (her sacred animal) unto the weavers of her holy temple. This vicious act singlehandedly caused great distress and misfortune to Amaterasu and her Priestesses. The benevolent Sun Goddess had tried many times before to reconcile with her brother, forgive him and somehow live peacefully in the world with him but this time he had gone too far. In his violently explosive behavior he had not only defiled Amaterasu's sacred temple but also injured many and killed one of her beloved priestesses. The Sun Goddess, saddened beyond measure, reached a monumental turning point and decided she could no longer shine her light for the world in his presence. Grief stricken, she retreated into the Heavenly Rock-Cave, where she removed her brilliant light from the world and stayed hidden, refusing to come out again. The earth, as a result, stood motionless and was needless to say negatively affected by the darkness that ensued. Nothing grew upon the earth without her divine light. There was famine, chaos and much calamity without the bright power of the sun. Both mortals and Gods alike were adversely affected by this kind of indefinite Solar eclipse and they were greatly concerned about the state of the world, as the wild untamable, Susano-O-no Kami, now reigned freely. The ancient text found in the Kojiiki stated that the eight million Gods (or Kamis, as they are known in Japan) gathered to discuss a possible resolution and devise a plan to bring back the Sun Goddess. They too suffered gravely without her Divine light and the Kamis were desperate to restore balance and world order. The Japanese God, Takami-Musubi-no-Kami, called upon the council of Gods and they gathered on the Eight-sand-Bank River, in the heavens, according to Shinto lore and they began to brainstorm. The craftsman God, Ishiko-ritome-no-Kami was to build a great big mirror made out of copper, brought from the Heavenly mount Kagu and it was their hope that if Amaterasu caught a glimpse of her own Divine reflection in this sacred mirror she would enchant her own self with her brilliance and finally return to her post as the venerated Sun Goddess. The deity, Kushi-Akarutama-no-Kami was in charge of creating yet another magickal tool of enchanting distraction- sparkling jewelry. It was their hope the sparkling brilliance of these divinely crafted jewels would entice the Sun Goddess to come out further for a better look and hopefully remain out of her dark cave. Woven white cloths, made from mulberry paper, were also among the many items made and hung by the sacred trees surrounding the cave entrance all in an effort to entice the Sun Goddess. Ame-no-Mahitotsu-no-Kami crafted and offered swords, axes and tinkling bells of iron as well. The Sakaki tree from the Heavenly mount of Kagu, with its multitude of braches, was carried by the Gods. It was decorated with all the bright jewels, reflective items and finely woven cloths and streamers in an effort to lure the Goddess even further out of her cave. The God, Futotama-no-Mikoto held the sacred Sakaki tree while he began to eulogize the Sun Goddess and Ame-no-Koyane-no-Mikoto recited invocations to Amaterasu... still the Goddess would not come out of her cave.

The Spring maiden, Ame-no-Uzume-no-Mikoto then took center stage. Uzume wore a scarf made of club moss around her shoulders and a wreath. And while holding a tinkle belled crafted spear and bamboo grass and leaves, she lit the sacred bonfires before the Heavenly rock-cave. With all the Kamis surrounding the area, intensely waiting for a sign from the Sun Goddess, Uzume jumped on top of an overturned bath tub and began a silly, almost burlesque-like, dance. This wild dance was steeped in licentiousness and it stirred up the audience of tense Japanese deities. The laughter that ensued from Uzume's bawdy striptease created quite a commotion and it, unsuspectedly, also stirred Amaterasu's curiosity from behind the blocked caved. She wondered how there could be any laughter or joy upon the earth in her absence. Hearing all the laughter and frivolity, she wondered if they had forgotten her or had somehow replaced her with another deity. These gnawing, uncomfortable doubts motivated her to investigate even further and so, she proceeded to crack open the entry of her cave, just enough to get a peek at what was going on outside. Naturally when she took her first glimpse outside of the cave she caught sight of all the brilliant sparkling jewels hanging from the trees and its beauty moved her to come out even further. Then she caught sight of her own divine reflection. Needless to say she was enamored by the golden luminescence of her own reflection. The surrounding Gods seized that very moment to quickly close off the cave entrance behind her to secure Amaterasu's staying presence in the world. She then discovered that it was Uzume's dance that had inspired such a wonderfully loud, joyful noise outside of her cave. Thus, Uzume and her bawdy, sexually liberating dance is attributed for pulling the Sun Goddess out of her grief and self-imposed exile, in the same way as the old nurse maid, Baubo, in Greek Mythology, helped awaken the Grain Goddess, Demeter, from her own despondency. Just as it was Baubo's bawdy lifting of the skirt, exposing her genitalia that snapped the Greek Grain Goddess out of her depressive hopeless state, so it was the Japanese Goddess Uzume who achieved the same feat. With her licentious, frenzied dance, lifting her kimono, she roused up not only the eight million Kamis but the dark grieving earth itself. And their collective joy and laughter over what they witnessed in Uzume, eradicated the darkness and brought forth the rebirth of the great Sun, Amaterasu. It becomes clear that Uzume is a Goddess who speaks to women on the power of laughter and the unabashed joys found when one embraces their sexuality. Yet, Uzume also speaks to us about the incredibly cathartic powers found in our physical body, Shakti energy, our body's rhythm and our personal dance.

There is another tale in the ancient Japanese text found in the Kojiiki and the Nihonghi that allows us yet an additional alternative glimpse into the beloved Goddess, Uzume.

When the Sun Goddess was ready to send to earth her beloved grandson, Ninigi, the August Child, to rule the people of Japan and proselytize her divine teachings, there was conflict. The heavens were divided, as some supported Amaterasu's decision, while other Gods were not happy to see Ninigi as first Japanese emperor to establish the first Imperial family. According to the Kojiiki, as he was about to descend upon the earth he noticed something blocking his entry way. It was a huge, monstrous looking creature that was described in great detail in the ancient Japanese text. This deity blocking the pathway for Ninigi was a frightful sight. It had a nose seven hands in length and glowing fiery eyes according to text found in the Kojiiki. This being was huge in size and was fiercely intimidating to Amaterasu's divine grandchild. Desperate, Ninigi called upon the Goddess Uzume who had acquired the powerful reputation for being the one who could always be relied upon to help the Gods.

The August Child called upon the Goddess Uzume, explaining his plight and asking for her assistance in this matter. She quickly descended to the heaven and earth threshold to confront the blocking monster. With her pushed down band across her navel and her exposed pendulum bare breast she confronted the monster and asked what business he had to be there. The monster was taken aback by her nakedness and bold candor. Bewildered by her appearance he introduced himself as Saruta-Hiko-no-Oho-Kami and then inquired about her reasons for this unconventional approach. He proceeded to tell her that upon hearing the Heavenly Grandson was about to descend to the earth he wanted to make himself available to the Future First Emperor of Japan. He was there waiting for Ninigi, not as an enemy, but to offer his assistance in whichever way served the Heavenly grandchild best. Thus Uzume's bold confrontation births knowledge of Ninigi's true ally, unblocking the pathway to his destiny and becomes the vehicle for the first Imperial family to be born. Ninigi was too frightened to see for himself who or what was blocking his destiny but it was Uzume's typical bold feat that resolved the paralyzing standstill and allowed the Sun Goddess's Grandchild to take his rightful place upon the earth. Again Uzume is called upon and acts as an intermediary so that the Gods are able to take their rightful place upon the heavens and the earth.

Known as the Crossroad God, Saruta Hiko or Sarutahiko-Okami as he is sometime known, was to guide the heavenly Grandson from the plains of high heaven to the Wondrous peak of Takachiho in Hyuga, Tsukushi and then, thereafter, Saruta Hiko would leave to the river, Isuzu at Sanagata, in Ise. He was so impressed by the bold Goddess that he invited Uzume to join him in this journey and she did, becoming later on, his wife according to Japanese ancient text.

Saruta-Hiko-no-Oho-Kami, is venerated as the God of the Crossroads and he is paired with the Goddess Uzume as her consort. Together they are credited for both accompanying, the Heavenly Grandson throughout his journey to become the First Emperor of Japan and build the first Imperial family. It is this reason why Uzume and Sarutahiko are considered the ancestors of Japan's sacred Imperial family.

Consequently, Ninigi held the Goddess, Uzume with great honor for her help in facilitating his Imperial journey. She was made the founder of the Sarume Order and the patron Goddess for the ritual dancers who perform in annual Sacred Festivals. These were mostly women and their dances take on a comical appearance which is valued as divine and necessary, in most traditional Japanese religious ceremonies. At the First Fruit Festival, Japanese perform the Saru-Mahi, a monkey dance. The word Sarume actually means *"She-Monkey,"* thus, it is clear Uzume's sacred dance is a primal one, wildly connected to a monkey's movement. Many Shinto ceremonies incorporate other Uzume dances like the Nakatomi and the Imbe. These are the origins of the Kagura (a ritualistic dance-mime). Uzume's dance upon the overturned bathtub during the ancient myth related to the return of the Sun Goddess is still venerated and widely performed today in many Shinto ceremonies. These dances were often associated with early forms of medium possession, trance and shamanistic practice.

It is clear the Japanese Goddess Uzume played an important role in ancient women's lives and her significance for contemporary women needs to be highly considered. This is a sacred feminine, immortal Goddess whose spirit and energy is still very much venerated today in Shinto religious ceremonies just as it has been for hundreds of years. For those in the Goddess community, seeking to unearth, connect and worship the multitude of ways the Feminine Divine appears to us, Uzume is yet another wonderful expression of "wombmynhood" and thus, another sacred aspect of Goddess.

UZUME GODDESS GATHERING DAY

Purpose: To celebrate the Spring Maiden, to connect to our Physical bodies and experiment with a powerful form of ritual found in dance. To honor and connect with the Japanese Goddess, Uzume, to discover her sacred dances and embrace the power found in our physical bodies.

Check Ins: We gather around the Circle and introduce ourselves to one another, while also voicing our feelings on this month and our hope for the upcoming season.

Chants: Together we will join our voices to sing some commonly known Pagan chants, as well as new ones offered on the Chant sheet in the hand outs (see the last page of this chapter). Singing aloud is a wonderful way to raise energy effortlessly and it also sometimes helps in creating harmonious bonds.

Our Agreements bylaws and Pertinent group discussion... We go around the circle of women, reading a few lines each of our "Group Agreements" and add any new ones that seem necessary. Agreements are signed and submitted in confidence.

Drumming Grounding: A drumming musical CD track will be played, to give participants a chance to connect and ground to this very moment. Women are invited to find a comfortable seat or stand and add movement if they wish.

Conjuring Goddess via her Image: Using a photo image, Goddess oracle card or scuplture image of the Goddess Uzume, we will share this image around the circle, as each woman present will reflect and state aloud what attributes and Divine messages need expression.

Lecture on the Japanese Goddess, Uzume
Her myth and various folklores, her attributes and relevance for us today.

GODDESS WORKSHOPS
WORKSHOP I
Burlesque dancing; discussing its history, practice and exploration of its empowering aspect.

WORKSHOP II
Tapping into the power of our physical bodies, Shakti energy!

WORKSHOP III
Exploring the archetype of the Maiden. What does she mean to you personally?

WORKSHOP IV
Power of Friendship; writing a letter of gratitude to a beloved friend, either from your past, present or future.

WORKSHOP V
Laughter as Medicine; Experimenting with hearty belly laughs as a cone of power.

WORKSHOP VI
Yoni power, viewed in various myths and for today's modern woman.

UZUME GODDESS GATHERING RITUAL

Purpose: To celebrate the Spring Maiden, to connect to our Physical bodies and experiment with a powerful form of ritual found in dance. To honor and connect with the Japanese Goddess, Uzume, to discover her sacred dances and embrace the power found in our physical bodies.

Asperge/Anointing: Sweet scented incense will fumigate the ritual space and a Japanese fan will be used to brush away attendants as they enter the ritual. Anointing oil will be offered from sister to sister.

INTENT ANNOUNCED: We gather to commemorate the Spring season and honor the Goddess Uzume, connecting with her through our bodies.

CASTTING CIRCLE:
I circle and cast around this space,
Erect a shield to keep me safe.
In spheres of Blue and Silver and Gold,
Protection around me now takes hold....

ELEMENTAL INVOCATION
Air:
Hail and welcome to the spirit of Air, realm of the East,
Commencing here, with my breath,
I look to the East, Eagles Realm,
For clarity and vision and effortless flight,
Air, I welcome your gifts in this sabbat rite. **Hail and Welcome Air!!!!**
Fire:
Hail and welcome to the spirit of Fire, realm of the South,
Heat emanating from my Core,
Love's great passion with energy to roar.
Come awaken the drive to pursue,
Flames of thy realm, I welcome you. **Hail and Welcome Fire!!!!**
Water:
Hail and welcome to the spirit of Water, realm of the West,
Mermaids, Melusine,
Tranquil waters of Harmony,
All that aligns and fits so well,
Water's realm I call you to this spell. **Hail and Welcome Water!!!!**
Earth:
Hail and welcome to the spirit of Earth, realm of the North,
Creatrix, manifestor, upon the earth, I rise,
Welcome transformer,
You who makes our dreams alive.
All the seeds nestled in you.
All the dreams, we strive to make true.
In your realm, empowered to grow
Fertile vision now taking hold.
I call you earth, remover of fears,
Come primal strength, You are welcomed here... **Hail and Welcome Earth!!!!**

SPRING GODDESS INVOCATION
Uzume with licentious dance,
You twirled in ecstasy until **all** laughed,
You drew the Sun Goddess to step out of her cave
And see her own brilliance finally, on that day.
Unearther of her brilliance,
exposer of the truth,
You dance Sweet Spring Maiden
And today I honor you.

CHANT: *"Maiden Song"*

)O(SPELL WORKING

Ostara is the season of rebirth, spring time, the earth's axis in equal balance between night and day. In ancient times, considered the first month of the New Years for the energy is bursting with promises, hope and potentialities. We will listen to Japanese Music as we pick up and charge our personal candle. When we are ready, together we will recite these words.

I tap into source.
I connect with her powers,
manifest my dreams,
for all I see and desire.
Upon this flame,
the Sabbat is kept,
Goals are achieved
and I am blessed... *(light your candle now.)*
So mote it be!!!

Once all candles are lit, participants should gather around to witness "Dance as a form of Ritual." Every woman will have a chance to stand in the center and pantomime a kind of burlesque dance of something she hopes to achieve in the coming season. It can be a tangible or a feeling goal. When she is done, she will write what it is for all to finally see. Clapping is welcomed then.

DRUMMING CIRCLE AND DANCE

There should be a festive feel in the ritual now and if you have time you can craft floral head wreaths during this moment in the ritual, as well.

Final check ins
DEVOKING GODDESS

DEVOKING

Spirit of Earth, sacred realm of the North
We are grateful to you for guarding our rites,
Your powers of transformation felt on this night,
in peace ye arrived, in peace may you return,
return to thy realm at the sound of this bell. **Hail and farewell Earth!**

Spirit of Water, sacred realm of the West
We are grateful to you for guarding our rites,
Your powers of harmony felt on this night,
in peace ye arrived, in peace may you return,
return to thy realm at the sound of this bell. **Hail and farewell Water!**

Spirit of Fire, sacred realm of the South
We are grateful to you for guarding our rites,
Your powers of passion felt on this night,
in peace ye arrived, in peace may you return,
return to thy realm at the sound of this bell. **Hail and farewell Fire!**

Spirit of Air, sacred realm of the East
We are grateful to you for guarding our rites,
Your powers ofclarity felt on this night,
in peace ye arrived, in peace may you return,
return to thy realm at the sound of this bell. **Hail and farewell Air!**

DEVOKE CHANT: *"The earth, the air, the fire, the water, return, return, return return...."*

OPENING CIRCLE

"The Circle is open but unbroken may the peace of the Goddess be ever in our heart,
merry meet and merry part and merry meet again...."

*****Traditional potluck to follow*

UZUME MUSING

Uzume was quite a fascinating deity for me to unearth and work with. Although there isn't a whole lot of scholarly research on this Japanese deity, and her mentions in the Kojjiki and Nihonghi are minimal, her significance for women both in ancient and modern times is unquestionable. For one thing, she is intimately connected with the restoration of the Sun Goddess, Amaterasu. Her bold, unconventional actions directly facilitated the Kami's initial plans to bring Amaterasu out of her cave. It was this exact, very bold action that helped Amaterasu's divine grandson later descend to the earth to help establish the important Japanese Imperial family. Without Uzume's unconventional bold presence, Ninigi would have still remained paralyzed, hopeless, in fear and in a state of ignorance, for he did not know what stood at the threshold blocking his path, until She investigated and exposed it <u>for him</u>.

It becomes clear to me Uzume's greatest gift for women is this bold, unconventional acceptance of her physicality. She is succinctly connected with her body and its ability to function as a vehicle to birth change and enormous transformations, whether the change is from hopelessness and darkness to light (in the case of Amaterasu's restoration) or ignorance and paralysis to knowledge and action (in the case of Ninigi-no-Mikoto facing the monster God, Sarutahiko-Okami). There is a quality of freedom, vitality and joy of simply being authentic, in Uzume and her licentious dances. And this is precisely what contributes to her astounding, everlasting magick.

When we are at our lowest, facing fears, doubts, depression and the unknown, it is our bodies that are most often the first to reflect this impoverished state of mind. We become very lethargic, inactive, finding strange comfort in our laziness and our bones appear to weight more with each day that passes by. The antidote for this downward spiral of depression is action, the kind first expressed in our physicality, but most of us won't have the inkling to attempt it as a form of healing. The Japanese Goddess Uzume presents it to us. She makes it clear that the solution to stagnation, doubt, depression, hopelessness, fear and darkness is found in our body, our Shakti, it is in our body's movement. Physical movement, like dance, offers us an initial prescription to what ails many of us in moments of deep depression. It is a cathartic form of medicine and when looked at more closely it is indeed an ancient form of worshipping the Divine.

Humanity might have first discovered this in the pleasure and mind altering euphoria they derived upon first unearthing the dance of sex and this too was a form of worship in ancient time and continues to be practiced in today's day and age. It is not a far off leap to see this connection of sex to dance, especially the burlesque kind that the Goddess Uzume is most known for.

Our knowing bodies are a great source of healing; it is through our bodies that we may first become aware of imbalances in our hearts, spirit and mind and yet, it is through our bodies that we may begin to find the initial remedy to wholeness and healing. Uzume's attributes casts a light on these issues, of connecting to our bodies and delighting in its capacity to manifest positive changes in our lives. It is her bold and often unconventional actions that produce some of the most needed first steps towards healing. The power found in laughter and physical movements are her greatest gifts to us. She invites each and every one of us to gyrate, dance her burlesque, engage in her monkey dances and touch upon the divine freedom and wellbeing of simply connecting to our body.

COLOR HEALING MEDITATION FOR OUR BODIES

To begin this meditation, I invite you to sit comfortably or lie down and simply rest. Let go of your stressors and feel every cell in your body surrender to this moment in time. Take a breath and allow your body to sink into this moment with each inhalation. Breathe deeply and exhale. Exhale all the stressors from your day or week or even from the last month. Take another nice deep breath, letting your lungs expand fully and allowing your expanded lungs to fully take over the space of your chest cavity and your whole body. Release your breath and with it, release any toxins or negativity. Breathe gently, effortlessly and now exhale. Survey your body at this moment for any signs of stress or tension as you easily breathe in and out and smooth away any concerns. Continue to breathe as we begin to look more closely, with our inner eye, for any signs of physical tension or stress upon the body.

I invite you to scan and survey your whole body now with your inner eye. We will do this together, more methodically, as we experiment with color energy and its magickal usage. We will place colors to the different parts of our sacred body and offer color medicine to alter and heal those parts that need it most. We begin this meditation by first bringing our attention to the lower part of the body. Let us first examine the part of our body that holds the entire weight of our existence and is responsible for our physical journeys, our **feet**. How do they feel at this very moment? Are they relaxed and nimble or tight and bruised? Connect with your feet and toes and scan them for any tension? What color do they exude at this very moment? **See if you can offer your feet a different experience now and change the color. How does that now, make you feel in this feet region? (pause)**

Now we will bring our attention to our **knees.** Consider for a moment how you are often called to utilize your knees in the mundane world. How they bend at our request and support our physical form. How do they feel at this very moment? Can you associate a color to your knees? At this moment are your knees; red, brown white, pink, blue, green, orange or purple? Pick any color that initially comes to mind and do not worry of its accuracy. Trust your instincts and allow yourself to experiment. There is no wrong or right answer here. This is your own personal imagery and everyone will come up with their own personal assessment. **Now take a moment to see if you can alter the color in your knee region and see how it effects your physical sensation in this area. (pause)**

I invite you to take a deep breath again and connect now with your **pelvic region**, your hips. These are your majestic, womanly curves! They rumble and sway and have their own rhythmic dance at various intersections of your daily life. Notice how they feel at this very moment. Is there any tension in this area? Can they sway with ease or are they stiff and hard to move? What color would you assign to your hip region now? Is this a color you feel happy maintaining or would you like to experiment by switching the color? **Take this moment to offer your hips this color therapy. Focus on a color in your pelvic region and make note of how it changes now the sensation in your physical body. (pause)**

Now let us visit with the **belly region**, a consecrated area that is so often neglected and yet so revealing to us as women. Again please make note of how you are physically feeling in this part of your body and please, associate a color with your belly. How does it feel? Can you detect any subtle sensations in this region? Are you holding any tension or are you totally relax in this area around your stomach? **If you care to experiment with this sacred region, ask yourself what color can you offer your belly now to bring further healing to this** area? Notice how this color offering changes the sensation of your belly region. (pause)

Now I invite you to bring your attention to the middle of your chest, your **heart centered area.** Carefully and with reverence come to this region, inspect its present state and quietly search for a color you can link your heart with at this moment. Is it pink, or blue? Is it a fertile green or a dark hue like black? Is it a brilliant orange or a Queenly purple? See the color appear in your heart region and now consider how vastly different it might feel to you if you changed its present color. **Experiment and take this moment now to change the color association with your heart region. How does that make you feel? How does this color change alter and heal the physical sensations in this region? (pause)**

Now I invite you to visit with your neck, the **throat area.** Place your attention in this region and make note how your throat physically feels. Is it fatigued or energized? Is it dry and raspy or well hydrated? Take this time to search for a color you would like to assign to this region. Consider how vastly different your throat would feel now if we changed the color association. **If you will, please choose a different color to offer your throat region now and study the effects of this change. How does that make your throat region feel now? (pause)**

We have arrived to the last area of this Color therapy exercise. I invite you now to bring your attention to your **cranium,** your head or crown region. Take this moment to inspect how your head physically feels at this very moment. Is it heavy, tense or lightweight? Is it holding any tension at this moment? Ask yourself what color do you see associated to your head region. Do you see blues, yellows or maybe black? Is it white or red? Or maybe you prefer to detect another fancier color linked with your cranium. Take this time to associate a color with your head region and all its physical attributes connected with this hue. See this color vividly and if you will, offer it now a different color. **What color therapy can you offer your head region now to alter and heal it further? How does that effect the physical sensations around your crown region? (pause)**

We have traveled through seven important regions of our body to offer healing and color energy medicine to these areas. In the future you may wish to experiment further and offer this therapeutic exercise, in color magick, to other parts of your body as you see fit but for now we will end our special journey here. As we began this journey with our breath we end this mediation in the same way by breathing deeply and connecting to our breath. Take a deep breath now and again, exhale. I invite you to scan your body one last time to release any lingering tension.Breathe and with your breath offer yourself infinite physical healing and continue to breathe in your favorite colors as we transition back to this time and place. Follow my voice as it guides you back to this room. I will count backwards from seven to one and on the count of one, please open your eyes and join us back in this room for a final check-in. *Seven, six, five...continue to breathe bright colors and release with your exhalation. Four, three, almost there and two, one...Welcome back!

INVOCATION

SPRING GODDESS INVOCATION
Uzume with licentious dance,
You twirled in ecstasy
until **all** laughed,

You drew the Sun Goddess
to step out of her cave
And see her own brilliance
finally, on that day.

Unearther of her brilliance,
exposer of the truth,
You dance Sweet Spring Maiden
And today, We honor you.

UZUME INVOCATION

She swirls in ecstasy
and slithers her form,
Cackles in abandonment,
She purges dark storms.

She dances and swirls
and calls forth the light,
her body is her magick
and it's invoking the Sunlight.

She raises her skirt,
Revealing her pearls,
And shocks the spectators,
As in ecstasy, she twirls.

Awakening the shadows,
Inviting unsuspecting births
Her magick is her laughter,
As it eradicates all hurt.

She extends her arms,
With a seductive glance,
Connect with her magick,
As She invites you to dance,

Laugh in abandonment,
as your hips gyrate to her tune,
Wild and empowered,
May her magick work soon.

Goddess within,
I call you to my core
Awaken the pleasure seeker,
The bold one, guarding sacred doors...

Hail and Welcome, Goddess of Merriment....

SPELLS

INNER HEALINGS

Maladies that plague me cease to be,
Illness, sadness, loneliness flee,
Draw to me appropriate friends,
Heal, to bring loneliness to an end.

Deeper, Deeper into Zen,
Beneath the Earth where I can mend,
Going through each body of pain,
Emerge ever stronger never the same.

Shadows confronted,
No longer feared,
I face you,
I enter you,
I leave you with no tears.

And pierce thru the soil,
Shaking off all debris,
To emerge ever gifted,
Like the Goddess meant for me.

A tree, giving fruit,
Giving life, thus renewed.
Drawing my strength,
From the earth's ancestral roots

I am transformed,
Not by the world,
But by the gifts,
I embraced as a young girl,

Woman! Woman!
Shake off your shell,
And leave behind,
The wretched internal Hell.

The time is now,
To enjoy and embrace,
Thank you Goddess,
For this sacred space.

UZUME GODDESS GATHERING CHANT TEXT SHEET

ELEMENTAL INVITATION
by B.Melusine Mihaltses
East of the Winds,
That stirs and inspire,
Come Eagle's gift
Guard and hold me like this.

Fire with your spark
Passion's in my heart
Come with the Jaguar
In this circle stand on guard.

Hail to you Waters,
Realm of all tears,
Womb of all wommin,
Come approach my dear...

Earth that transforms,
Making Visions to form,
Realm of my seedlings,
Guard our space as we're born.....

Earth, Air, Fire, Water,
I am the Witches' daughter....(Goddess daughter etc...) raise energy

THE FOOL by Suzanne Sterling From music CD, Reclaiming, Second Chants
Night and stars are falling down
A wild breeze is blowing,
Earth and moon are whirling round
The fool walks through the door...

WE ARE A CIRCLE by Rick Hamouris
We are a Circle, within a Circle, with no Beginning and never ending....
You hear us Sing, You hear us Cry,
Now hear us Call you, Spirits of Earth and Sky
Within our Hearts, there goes a spark
Love and Desire, a burning Fire...
We are a Circle, within a Circle, with no Beginning and never ending...(chorus)

MAIDEN DANCING, *by B. Melusine Mihaltses*
Spiraling Dancing, Up and Down
Reaching the Center with Floral Crown
Laughing Maiden, Giggles are free
I've awaken the Maiden in me.

See me Jump, Jump, Jump,
Cross the meadow Field,
See me Fearless and Beautiful, and dancing the Wheel (rpt)

EIGHT BEADS CHANTS *by Carolyn Hillyer*
Girlseed
Bloodflower
(dip it)Fruitmother
Spinmother,
raise it) Midwoman
Earthcrone
Stonecrone

SHE'S BEEN WAITING - by *Paula Walowitz*
She's been waiting, waiting
She's been waiting so long,
She's been waiting for her children
to remember to return (repeat)
Blessed be and blessed are the Lovers of the Lady,
Blessed be and blessed are, Maiden , Mother, Crone,
Blessed be and blessed are, the ones who dance together
Blessed be and blessed are, the ones who dance alone......

CHAPTER FIVE

Asherah

"To be without trees would, in the most literal way, is to be without our roots..."Richard Mabey, Beechcombings

"The creation of a thousand forests is in One acorn..." Ralph Waldo Emerson

ASHERAH

ASHERAH

"Two trees, a portion of your soul has been entwined with mine. A gentle kind of togetherness, while separately we stand. As two trees deeply rooted in separate plots of ground, while their topmost branches come together, forming a miracle of lace against the heavens..." Janet Mills-
The Power of Women

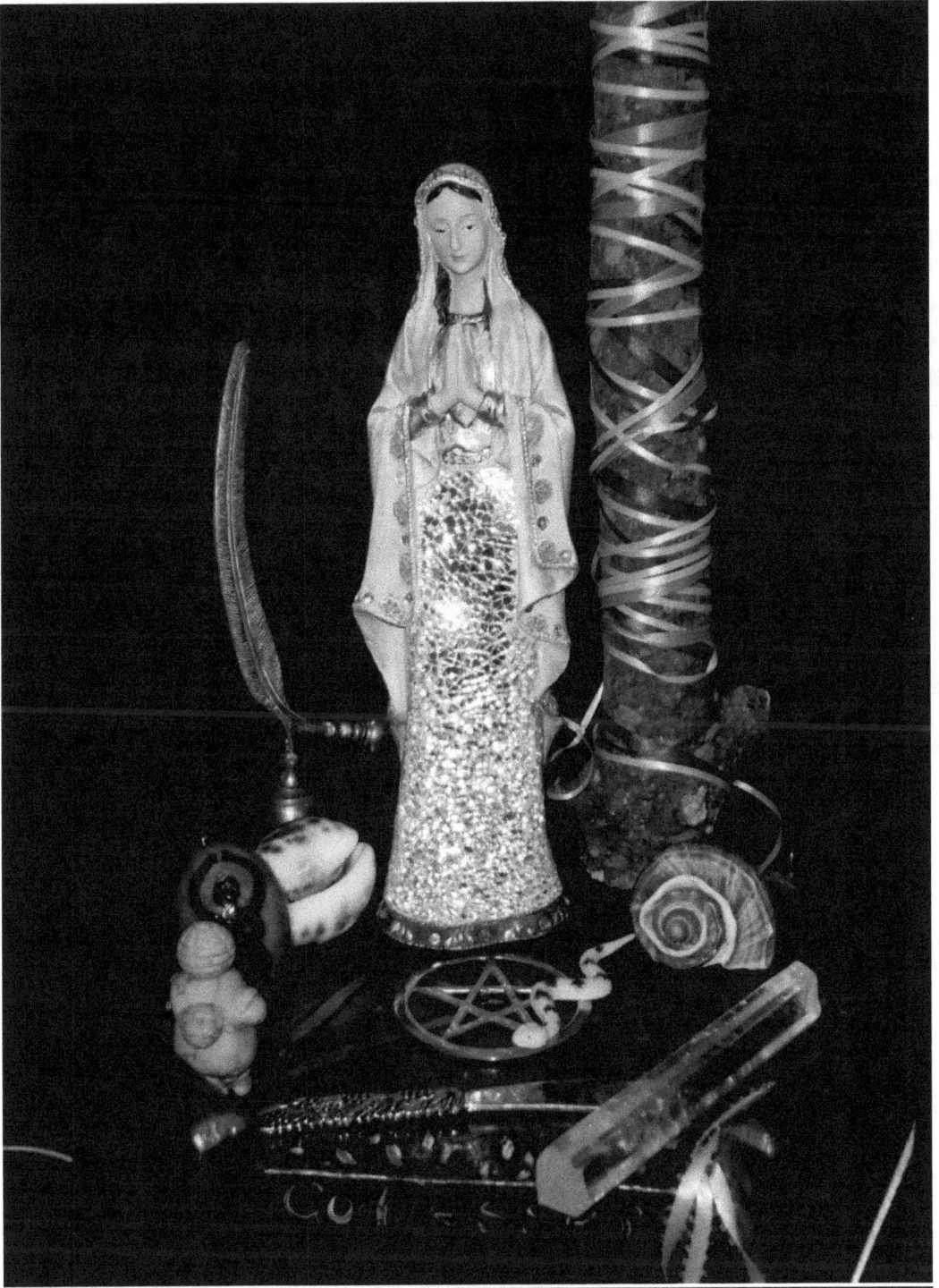

ASHERAH

"There is always music amongst the trees in the garden, but our hearts, must be very quiet to hear it..." Minnie Aumonier

ASHERAH ALTAR SET UP
OUR ALTAR

Altar cloth : *Brown and green altar cloths are suggested. We are now in the midst of Spring and it only seems logical to incorporate an altar cloth that depicts nature and spring images like; flowers, green leaves, meadow, etc... Asherah's altar cloth can also have images of trees, since; she is so often associated with trees.*

Image: *The image of the Canaanite Goddess, Asherah should be placed on the altar. Since Asherah in ancient times was often represented as a pole, it is suggested to have a large wooden pole or simply a representation of a tree on an altar to the Goddess.*

Always present on the altar;
A silver pentacle, a cast iron cauldron, drums, speaking stick, wand, athame, elemental representations.....

Air: *feather bundles, angel wings, bird, eagle or owl statuaries. Bell &, chimes, Incense type sticks, cones, charcoal brisket and fine powdered herbs; frankincense , myrrh.*
Fire: *pillar candles, glass enclosed candles in green, gold, silver and pink*
Water: *Small glass bowl with Water and or chalice with Champagne, Cranberry Juice or Red wine.*
Earth: *Incorporate lots of green fresh plants and colorful flowers and offer a small dish of soil or dry herbs, can also be used*

Other items pertinent to this particular gathering
A representation of a tree or long branches
A pole, like a Maypole with some ribbons
Symbol of a golden calf
Colorful ribbons
Tarot or Oracle deck

Sacred objects from members:
Notes:

MONTH & SEASON

April

The Astrological sign of the month is Aries, the ram, and it is ruled by Mars, (March 21-April 20). April is the fourth month of the Gregorian calendar, though originally it was known as the second month in the Roman year. It is believed that when King Numa Pompillius changed January, electing it to be the first month of the year, April thus became the fourth month. Because the Romans named their months to honor their deities it would seem likely that this month was named after the Roman Goddess of Love, Aprilis. She shares many similarities to Aphrodite, the Greek Goddess of Love, who was also known to the Romans as Venus. April, also comes from the Latin word, *"Aprilis"*, meaning "to open" and we can only assume this is a reference to the number of trees and flowers opening up and blossoming during this season. This is truly a magickal time of the year to relish the many wonders of nature, the multitude of colors beginning to sprout amidst our landscape and enjoy the milder temperatures outdoors. With gentle breezes felt throughout the month of April, it is not surprising the month's full moon is also called, Wind Moon.

If we look even further at the word April, it is derived from the Latin word *"aper"* also meaning *"boar."* The boar was considered one of Aphrodite's sacred animals, another indication of how connected this month is to the Goddesses of love; Aphrodite and Aprilis. The hare was considered another sacred animal to the Goddesses of Love and thus, it is only fitting that the Full moon of this month is sometimes known as the Hare moon. According to the Farmer's Almanac, April's full moon was also referenced as Fish Moon and Egg Moon, which can be viewed as alluding to Aphrodite's beloved food offerings and the predominance of eggs as a sacred symbol of rebirth, Spring and the Goddess.

Other names for the April Full moon are Pink Moon and Sprouting Moon, due to the numerous beautiful flowers sproutings at this time of the year. The Earth indeed, appears ripe, verdant and at the height of its powers of fertility. All around us are signs that Spring is finally here and we are showered with ancient symbols of the Goddess; the hare, eggs, chirping birds, the bright sun, blooming flowers, crafted baskets filled with goodies, colorful ribbons and bonnets, gardens with green lush landscapes. And it appears that the offspring of both humans and animals begin to make themselves better known as they come out to play more often in the warming climate.

Those seeds we planted in the previous months, now begin to sprout into small blossomings and, excitedly, we begin to see signs of hope, fruition and beauty every-where. Even in the Christian holiday of Easter, there is hope and renewal and the theme of resurrection. The value and the beauty of the Earth is also commemorated on National Earth day, also known as Arbor day, on April 22nd. This holiday that started in Nebraska in 1872 by a newspaper publisher named, Julius Sterling Morton, aimed to plant more trees and honor the earth. The first of the month is reserved for all kinds of mischievous pranks and youthful joviality, with the advent of April Fool's Day. The Maiden energy is truly exemplified right from the start of the month and reaches its zenith upon the following months.

This month, we take the time to recognize the beauty that is manifesting itself all around us, in nature & within us and we will connect with the Matriarchal deity Asherah.

All Monthly intro text taken from author's first book, "Gathering for Goddess, A Complete Manual for Priestessing Women's Circles"

ASHERAH GODDESS LESSON

We first learn about Asherah through the Ugaritic documented mythologies of the 14th century BCE but evidence of her existence can be traced three centuries before this time.

Asherah is a Pre-biblical, Canaanite Goddess whose worshipped was tenaciously found throughout various tribes in ancient times as far back as 1750 BCE. The Creatress, known as the consort of the Canaanite Chief God of the heaven's, El, and later, controversially, coalesced and addressed as the wife of Yahweh, upon Christianity's inception, her worship was unquestionably cemented in the inhabitants of this land in the far and Middle East. Some suspect that her numerous names in various regions were; Elath (meaning Goddess and the feminine aspect of the God, El), also Athirat, Atharat, Astarte, Ashtorah, Ashratum, Ashrurah. And there still exist confusion regarding her titles and attributes in various regions, as they are used interchangeably in the writings of the time. The bible also seems to indistinguishably address her as both Asherah and Ashtarte, Astarte. It is clear from archeological findings and writings of this period that Isaraelite, Perizzites, Hittites, Hivites, Jebusites, Amorites, shared in the Canaanite's love and veneration of this great mother Goddess and the cult of her son Ba'al.

In Southern Arabia she was known Atharath, in Egypt as Qudsu (meaning Holy One) and in Sumeria and Akkadia she was known as wife to the supreme chief God, Anu. There, she was more commonly known as, Ashratum, a specific name found on excavated 14th century BCE artifacts, supporting her importance in this region.

She was known as a fertility deity called upon by "cursed" barren women, as well as for agricultural blessings. She was creatress, mistress of sexual rejoicing and she who facilitated childbirth. As Qudsu, she was the revered Holy one. Asherah was considered Mother of all the Gods, princes and Kings, and as the one who suckled and nurtured both mortals and gods alike. In particular she was mother of the seventy deities in the Ugaritic pantheon, which included; Ba'al, her son, and Anath, her daughter.

As the supreme mother Deity and one of the first Goddesses worshipped and embraced by the Hebrews, who shared the land with the Canaanites, in the area of Palestine now, her worship was incised in the root of this region. At this time, numerous intermingling of marriages and religious practices was common, thus it was assumed that in marriage one naturally took on the gods of their marital partners.

In Judah, Rehoboam, the son of Naamah (an Ammonite and wife of King Solomon) marries Maacah, who helps spread the worship of Asherah in this region, as she was a known priestess of the Goddess. Another example of how the intermingling of marriages between different people of different tribes promulgated Asherah's worship is in the story of Jezebel and King Ahab. In Samaria, when the King Ahab, married Jezebel, yet another Sidonian Princess, the worship of Asherah again took center stage in this region. Jezebel ordered a more elaborate carved wood image of the Goddess (which it appears had been destroyed at an earlier date) and she had this sacred Goddess and her image placed in the center of Samaria- contributing even further to the growing popularity of this revered maternal Goddess. Another perfect example of the contribution of intermingling of tribes is found in the tales of King Solomon and his extraordinary First Temple of Jerusalem in the mid 10th century BCE, documented in the bible and the writings of the time. This temple was dedicated to the monotheistic Israelite God, Yahweh, during King Judah's reign. Although the bible states Solomon loved Yahweh, it also claims that Solomon, was easily led astray by his old age and his many wives (700 wives and 300 concubines to be exact), in his controversial idolatry and polytheistic religious practices. King Solomon married numerous wives from various nations in his effort to gain power, wealth and allegiances and naturally every one of his wives brought to their union, and consequently, their home in the temple, the worship of their respective gods. The Temple of Solomon had multiple sanctuaries and became known as the sacred place of worship but there were numerous deities from different pantheons who were being worshipped here, as this was Solomon's way of accommodating his numerous wives. In particular, he is credited for introducing the worship of Asherah to the people of Jerusalem, as his first wife (at the start of the building of the Temple) was a Sidonian princess, daughter of the Pharoah and a beloved priestess of Asherah. Clearly we see reflected here, the new religion of Yahweh being practiced among the existing and well established polytheistic religions of neighboring regions.

Solomon's father, King David, was attributed for unifying Israel and was to formulate the first house of Jerusalem for Yahweh but he was not able to complete this task and it was left up to his son to fully accomplish this ambitious feat. Most significantly, the Temple of Solomon was meant to house the treasured "Ark of the Covenant" and Mose's Ten Commandments, received on Mt. Sinai. It was Jerusalem's First temple reputed to exalt Yahweh, the tenets of this new monotheistic religion and unite Israel but this is in direct contrast to the numerous finding and writings about King Solomon's temple true function.

The temple itself shared many similarities to Pagan temples of old, in particular, its three section structure with; a Vestibule, Nave, Inner sanctuary was identical to a ninth century Pagan temple in Canaanite and Syria. King Solomon also used a Tyrian craftsman called Hiram Abif (tribe of Naphtali) to help build it, including the two distinguished Pillars made of brass, a common metal often incorporated in Pagan Temples, like the one in Hazor. It becomes quite evident that King Solomon's Grand Temple in Jerusalem, though initially built by Yahweh's command and counsel, was heavily inspired, influenced and created with Pagan polytheistic ideals.

Interesting to note, it was also documented that a King, in the land of Amorite (yet another region known for Asherah worship) was known as Abdu-Ashirta, which translates as "slave of Asherah" proof of his personal devotion to the great Goddess and an indication of her reverence and popularity in this region as well. In some of the writings, we also learn about Asherah's servant who was called, Qadesh wa-Amrur, which translates as, *"Fisherman of the Lady Asherah of the Sea."* This reveals a distinct connection this Goddess had with the Sea.

Some documents translate the name Asherah as meaning; *"She who walks on the Sea."* Her worship in the independent seaport towns of Tyre and Sidon, which were near the Mediterranean coastline, made the water's ocean a vital part of the people's wellbeing and garnered her the name, "Lady of the Sea." There are also many other indication of her strong prevalence at this time. There were towns and seaports with her name like Elath (which is one of her many titles, the female aspect to her Consort El) it was in the south gulf of Aqaba and titles like, Elath of Sidon and Asherah of Tyre that also reflect the importance of this Goddess.

DEPICTIONS OF ASHERAH

There are some conflicting mysterious stories regarding Asherah's actual appearance. In the Hebrew Bible and the writings of the time, she was depicted as an actual wood pole, set up, planted in the ground near the altars to her son, Ba'al and she was often closely linked to his popular cult following. Yet, the altars to her son did not have the same weight or meaning as the actual planted sacred pole known as the Asherah herself. She was often depicted as a tree and or groves - sometimes addressed as singular and sometimes in the plural form. Most often she is described as a sacred carved elaborate wood pole, planted firm in the earth. Some say an obelisk represented her, as well as the Pagan, modern day phallic, Maypole.

Though the harsh rainy climate of Palestine was not conducive to preserving much archeological evidence of Asherah's sacred wood pole artifacts, we do find plenty of evidence in the writings of the time on clay tablets and even within the Hebrew bible. Numerous archeological evidence of Asherah's dominance in the polytheistic worship of ancient Israel and the whole of the far and Middle East is found in the survival of a multitude of naked female figurine statues made of clay. These were small figurines with large pronounced breast, protruding bellies and the hands upholding, cupping, the breasts in a sign of nurturance. And the most fascinating discovery was that these clay figure religious artifacts, were found in archeological sites near and within residential homes, proof that Asherah was not only a Goddess revered in public, communal town rituals, but her worship extended privately and more intimately in the homes of ancient women. This was clearly indicative of a Goddess who was so revered and loved that she was worshipped in formal public rites, as well as in domestic religious practices of women at the time.

BIBLICAL EVIDENCE

Asherah is mentioned at least forty different times in the Hebrew's Bible. Several times in the Old Testament she is documented as the "Queen of heaven;" Jeremiah 44:17-21 and Jeremiah 7:17-18

"The Children gathered wood, the fathers kindled fire
and the women knead the dough to make cakes to the Queen of heaven
and to pour out drink offerings unto gods..."

An invocation to Asherah found on a 7th century BCE artifact tablet, invokes the Goddess for help with fertility and childbirth and it is believed that in the very early chapters of the Hebrew bible, (Genesis 30:10-13) we encounter Leah who actually names Zilpah's son, Asher. This is an obvious reference and namesake to the Goddess Asherah who was clearly invoked for childbirth blessings and highly venerated during this period. It also hints at the likelihood that the worship of Asherah was occurring simultaneously with other deities, including Yahweh.

The book of Judge (Judges 6:25-32) reveals yet again the worship of Asherah and the poor attempt to eradicate it by the son of the town Chieftain and devoted Priest of the Goddess -Joash the Abiezrite. In the town of Ofra, in the 12th century BCE, his son Gideo ends up destroying the town's beloved Asherah and altar to Ba'al and manages to escapes the town's persecution due to his father's prestigious position as the Priest of Asherah.

Another interesting set of passages in the Hebrew bible indicative of obstinate Pagan worship alongside Yahwenism is found in *Ezekiel 8*. The chapter begins with...

> *"...and it came to pass in the sixth year,*
> *in the sixth month in the fifth day of the month...."*

Perhaps this is the month of August, as August in Latin translates as Sextilis, the sixth month, and was considered the sixth month during Augustus Caesar's reign. This coincides with the Harvest and a time when the sun's strength was viewed as dying and waning. One can only surmise that for people who depended on the fertility of their land, this was a time when they were more intimately invested in the nature deities that would assure their land's sustainable wellbeing and thus their own livelihood.

> *Ezekiel 8:14- "Then he brought me to the door of the gate*
> *of the Lord's house, which was towards the North;*
> *and behold, there sat women weeping for Tammuz..."*

This passage reveals that the women worshipped **inside** the temple and clearly they were not worshipping Yahweh, but rather a highly venerated Pagan Sun God, Tammuz. They were described as loudly crying, mourning, wailing for Tammuz and this was viewed as normal. It was a common practice and not viewed as strange, as it was customary, at the time, to perform agricultural rites to manifest much needed rain for the land and they were doing this in the "house of Yahweh in Jerusalem." Women in their power, in ancient times, were the ones who **could** do this. Women, so closely linked to the Mother Goddess Asherah, were the ones that magickally bled once a month, connecting to the Divine Moon and evidently produced new life and gave birth. Women's power was clearly visible for ancient indigenous cultures and it is only later that it becomes perverse by patriarchy and monotheism; with lies, degradations, oppression and manipulations. And thus, at this time, women inside the holy temples actively involved in performing rituals to manifest rain, to help the crop of the land, by wailing and shedding their own tears (performing a type of sympathetic magick rite) for the Sun God Tammuz, is quite indicative of women's power at this time. It is in total contrast to what their role would develop years later at the hands of oppressive monotheistic religions. At the very least, this short passage reflects the acknowledgment, respect and power that women held as active participants in priestessing and worshipping the Gods of ancient times in Jerusalem.

> *Ezekiel 8:15- "Then said he unto me hath thou seen this, O son of man?*
> *Turn thee yet again, and thou shall see greater abominations than these..."*

> *Ezekiel 8:16- "And he brought me into the inner court of the Lord's house,*
> *and behold, between the porch and the altar,*
> *were about 5 and 20 men, with their backs towards*
> *the Temple of the Lord, and their faces towards the East;*
> *and they worshipped the Sun towards the East..."*

Again, this is reflecting the important worship of the Sun God/ the son of the Goddess, in the Temple. The Hebrew bible also reveals that women often weaved cloths for the Goddess Asherah **inside** the temple and they worked in the Holy Temples in numerous capacities, although they would essentially be described in the Hebrew bible as being temple prostitutes; a terminology also used very loosely for men employed in the temples as well. This was a debasing way to discredit women and the worship of the Goddess during a time when monotheism was trying to assert itself upon the people.

The most fascinating, controversial finding, relating the Goddess Asherah to the monotheistic God, Yahweh is discussed in *"The Biblical Archeology Review,"* Vol. 5,

No.2 (March/April 1979), pp24ff. It shares a more recent discovery, an inscription dated from the 8-9th century BCE, found at Kuntillet Ajrud, in the North East Sinai Peninsula, South of Israeli and Egyptian border and it reveals a most telling inscription on large storage jars (*pithoi*) artifacts.

"May you be blessed by Yahweh and his Asherah."

This is a most illuminating inscription and some speculate that it reveals a special relationship between the new God, Yahweh and the established ancient Pagan mother Goddess, Asherah. There was another discovery on a tomb at Khirbet -El-Qom which was noted for having a similar inscription. These discovered inscriptions and blessings like; *"Yahweh of Samaria and his Asherah"* and *"Yahweh of Tenan and his Asherah...."* and *"May Uriyahu* (a governor at the time) *be blessed by Yahweh, my guardian and by his Asherah, save him Uriyahu.."* an inscription dated from the 750-700BC *(Biblical Archeology Review, Vol. 10, No. 6 (Nov./Dec. 1984)pg. 42.)* indicates a possible connection between these two deities. And clearly the proselytized monotheistic initial views of Judaism and Christianity are highly challenged when we find these numerous findings connecting Asherah (a Pagan Goddess) to Yahweh (the new God claiming monotheism as the **only** way). Two Gods are clearly being venerated in these inscriptions and the presence of Asherah's name becomes quite intriguing, especially when we know her importance across numerous tribes in the far and Middle East.

These blessing inscriptions reveal the Goddess as Yahweh' right hand, worshipped simultaneously with the new, Hebrew God, contradicting the monotheistic claim of early Yahwenism. It is rather convoluted how Asherah is represented in the old testament of the bible. Sometimes she appears as a wood pole, sometimes as a place. In some other documents she is *"his Asherah,"* and then sometimes she is simply a sacred attribute. Some believe, this confusion was purposely created to diminish her importance and trivialize her great power and hold on the people. As one can surmise, the Bible, written exclusively by men in support of the new monotheistic, patriarchal religion, obviously fulfilled their agenda in maintaining the worship of the Feminine Divine veiled and behind the new God, named Yahweh. It helped implement and establish the supremacy of men over women. Anything that did not support their new patriarchal ideologies was omitted, altered or disregarded and purposely obscured. Yet, the great Goddess Asherah is actually mentioned forty times in the Hebrew bible, which reveals how powerful and prevalent her presence had to have been at this time in the ancient far and Middle East. The people cleaved to Asherah, and her worship, for centuries even after the introduction of Yahweh and it wasn't until threats, violent manipulations and coercions and the risk of persecution did her worship begin to slowly wane, for as always, those with physically mightier armies and political influence, sadly have the power to oppress and eradicate a mass of people as we have seen throughout history.

HER CONECTION TO TREES

In researching, unearthing, learning and connecting to this great ancient Mother Goddess, I couldn't help but notice how often she was associated with trees, groves, high mountain tops and carved wood poles. Writings of the time actually reveal that the wooden pole was more than just a symbol of the Goddess; it was revered as the Goddess herself. As a result, it had more weight and value than the very altars created for her son, Ba'al, which lay beside her. The altars were a place of offering but the carved wooden pole was viewed as the Goddess herself. And ironically enough, while the altars to Pagan gods like Ba'al were quick to be destroyed by overzealous Yahwenist, the large Asherah poles that stood next to them and Asherah's strong worship was not so quick to be pulverized nor obliterated. Her worship, as is evident from excavated artifacts and the writings of the time, lingered, permeating several regions, long after the introduction of monotheism and it appeared her tenacious worship was coalesced with that of the new Yahweh.

Throughout the Hebrew bible there are numerous references and warnings about idolatry via the tree aka Asherah. And we must also remember in Genesis, the introduction of the tale of the forbidden fruit in the esteemed Tree of Knowledge, of which Adam and Eve were reputed to have eaten from before being cast out of the Garden of Eden. All this talk about trees made me wonder why the big taboo concerning trees and what could possibly be so threatening; within the tree, nature, the moon, the sun and stars and Asherah's worship, to this new monotheistic deity coming into the foreground.

Then I began to muse on trees and how numerous cultures have important folklores related to trees. I started to take a closer look at women and how intimately similar our attributes can appear to that of actual trees but I suppose the same can be said for so much in nature divinely reflects woman; from the moon, the ocean, the yoni shaped flowers and sea shells, to the erupting cavernous volcanoes, thunder and rainstorms.

Trees give forth life, sustain life and yet, in them, we see its cycles of life, death and rebirth; as it appears fruitless, leafless in the winter and then returns to its fullness, fruitfulness and splendor in the Spring and Summer. It nurtures and sustains humanity with oxygen and its fruits and thus, since the beginning of time, humanity has relied on its existence. Sacred regenerative principles are easily palpable in trees, the same regenerative qualities in "wombmyn"/woman's biological make up. I suppose this can be quite threatening to the rise of patriarchy.

The veneration of trees has existed in numerous ancient cultures and religions since the beginning of time. In Scandinavian Norse Mythology there is the Ygdrasil tree, that connects the various nine worlds; from the underworld, axis, middle, halls of the gods, heavens etc... It is a pivotal vehicle for spiritual journeying. In Genesis, as already stated, the Tree of Knowledge had fruits that were forbidden due to its inherent ability to awaken truths and spiritual knowledge, but through the offer from Lilith (as the serpent) it brought about major shifts and an awakening to both Eve and Adam, that according to biblical scriptures changed the course of humanity forever. In Egypt there is reference to the Sycamore tree being utilized by the Goddess to feed the dead souls as they journey to the underworld. For Buddhist, it was the Bhodi tree that passed enlightenment and wisdom to the Buddha. In Jewish Mysticism, known as the practice of Kabbalah, the most hallowed tree was the Ash Tree, which connected the sacred realms. It is depicted as an upside down, inverted tree, in which the roots originate in the heavens and the branches reach down through the ethers, to the earth. The Goddess Shekhinah is believed to imbue this tree with her divine energy and light according to Cabbalistic lore. The special branches of this sacred tree are known as "emanations" or sephiroth, and there are believed to be ten, which humanity is behooved to journey and work through. Interesting to note this number ten, as the day of Ashurah (*Aashrurah, Ashurah, Aashoorah*) for Muslims it is considered the 10th day of Muharram and the word *Ashrurah* is interpreted in Arabic as "ten." According to Islamic lore, the beloved grandson of Muhammad, Husayn Bin ali, was killed by Umayyard, at the battle of Karbala (Iraq) and this day commemorates the tragedy of this event with mourning. The name Ashurah is clearly connected to the name of our venerated ancient Tree Goddess, Asherah. There are some scholars that link the ancient worship of Asherah to one of the most venerated symbols for modern day Jewish people - the menorah. The menorah resembles her sacred tree with its branches as the seven, sometimes ten, candlestick arms, holding the sacred lights so powerfully symbolic for Jews.

Women and trees share a similar embodiment of fertility and the divine, with its sacred cycle of; birth, life, death and rebirth in the outwardly appearance of fruition in the summer and spring and then the barrenness so apparent in the winter season. It is quite fascinating to consider that one of the most beloved ancient mother Goddesses, Asherah, still lives on today, right before our very eyes as a living breathing Goddess, still exemplified in the tall, sky reaching trees that surround us today. In this sense, Asherah reminds me of the primordial Greek Goddess Gaia, which seems to transcend all cultures and time and space and yet in her role as a Sea Mother Goddess, I can't help but think upon the Orisha, Yemaya. Asherah, and her tenacious worship, was deeply loved in ancient pre-biblical times, so much so that perhaps we can still see glimmers of her strong veneration being transferred and carried through in the discovery of many other nurturing mother deities. The supreme Mother Goddess archetype continues to prove itself to be an important force for all women to connect with regardless of time and place and I believe Asherah to be a most powerful immortal Goddess for modern women to invoke in their respective lives.

Hail to you Asherah!

ASHERAH GODDESS GATHERING DAY

Purpose: To invoke and connect with one of the earliest Pagan Canaanite Goddess, the matriarchal Asherah. To connect with the Goddess embodied in Nature.

Check Ins: We gather around the Circle and introduce ourselves to one another, while also voicing our feelings on this month and our hope for the upcoming season.

Chants: Together we will join our voices to sing some commonly known Pagan chants, as well as new ones offered on the Chant sheet in the hand outs (see the last page of this chapter). Singing aloud is a wonderful way to raise energy effortlessly and it also sometimes helps in creating harmonious bonds.

Our Agreements bylaws and Pertinent group discussion... We go around the circle of women, reading a few lines each of our "Group Agreements" and add any new ones that seem necessary. Agreements are signed and submitted in confidence.

Drumming Grounding: A drumming musical CD track will be played, to give participants a chance to connect and ground to this very moment. Women are invited to find a comfortable seat or stand and add movement if they wish.

Conjuring Goddess via her Image: Scrying into a photo image, Goddess oracle card or sculpture of the Goddess, Asherah, we will share around the circle her image. Each woman present will reflect on the image and state aloud what attributes and messages need expression.

Lecture on the Canaanite Goddess, Asherah
Her myth and various folklores, her attributes and relevance for us today.

GODDESS WORKSHOPS
WORKSHOP I
Exploring tree folk lore, tree of life and kabbalistic traditions

WORKSHOP II
Yoga Tree pose. Exploring this yoga pose and its health benefits

WORKSHOP III
Crafting a Wooden Wand creation and blessings it for our Spiritual practice.

WORKSHOP IV
The Empress Tarot card. Exploring its meaning.

WORKSHOP V
Crafting our own unique Menorah creation.

WORKSHOP VI
Moon cake Baking and imbuing our food with magick.

WORKSHOP VII
Earth Magick, connecting with the Earth. Working with tree energy, Gnome, faeries,

ASHERAH GODDESS GATHERING RITUAL

Purpose: To invoke and connect with one of the earliest Pagan Canaanite Goddess, the matriarchal Asherah. To connect with the Goddess embodied in Nature.

Asperge Entrance & Anointing
Intent Spoken: Today we meet to commemorate the sabbat of Beltane and give honor to the ancient Canaanite Goddess, Asherah.

Circle Casting *(with Crystal wand and words....)*
From East to West this circle is Cast,
Below, above, only good can pass.
I call upon good spirits and Gods,
To shield this circle and be our Guard.

QUARTER ELEMENTAL INVOCATION
Guardian of the **West,** ye power of **Water**, we call you,
Hail to you Waters, The realm of the Lady of the Sea,
Immortal, sustainer and nurturer
You who provides our every needs
Hail and Welcome Waters!!!

Guardian of the **North**, ye power of **Earth**, we call you,
Hail to you Earth, Realm of thy sacred Groves.
Trees of thy Divine embodiment,
Of all the sacredness that your trunk and roots hold.
Hail and Welcome Earth!!!

Guardian of the **East,** ye power of **Air,** we call you,
Hail to you Ether, Of ancestral breath
That seeps and spirals among us through the ages.
From Air of days long past,
Resurrected in our ritual whispers
And exaltations to you in modern rites...
Hail and Welcome Air!!!

Guardian of the **South**, ye power of **Fire,** we call you,
Hail to you Fire of the Crimson Blood,
That pours out in offerings to your name.
Fires from the ancient Flames,
That still burn on your sacred altar today...
Hail and Welcome Fire!!!

CHANT: "Mother, Mother I call you.."

GODDESS INVOCATION

ASHERAH INVOCATION

Asherah of the Canaanite,
Asherah Lady of the Sea,
Creatrix and Consort of El,
Sumerian Mother to all Seventy Deities.

Beloved Ugaritic Goddess,
Embraced by Hebrews of the land
In Tyre, Sidon, Samaria,
It was you they erected on the altar Stand

The Tree of Life, the Menorah,
In Groves on mountain high,
In every Tree you were exalted,
Asherah reigns all space and time.

Elath, pierce through the realms,
Qudsu, immortal One,
Right Hand and wife of Yahweh,
Queen of heaven, please now come.

As in those days of old,
I erect you by this altar,
To ask for your blessings in this rite.
 Asherah, ancient mother in this circle,
I give honor to you tonight.

Come, Lady of Magick,
Lady of Sexuality,
Come ancient Mother Goddess.
Bless me with creative fertility.

I offer you this flame
And the sweets on this plate
And the crimson flow of your traditions
In my womanhood
And thy Queen of Heaven, moon cakes.
Hail and Welcome Asherah!!!

CHANT: *"She's been waiting, waiting..."*
MEDITATION OFFERING
Ma... ma... ma...Raising Cone of Power....

)O(SPELL WORKING

As we are close to the Sabbat of Beltane, we will take this time to create a travel maypole;
decorate a thick tree branch with colorful ribbons, as we state aloud what we hope to manifest for
the coming season. Ribbons will be passed around as we sit around the circle
and together add ribbons to our personal Maypole,
a representation of the Goddesses Asherah.
There will be laughter and support as we all state, "**so mote it be,**" with each wish uttered....
When all is done, we will create a drumming circle to seal the magick!!!

DRUMMING CIRCLE AND DANCE

CHANT: "Mother I feel you under my feet..."
DEVOKING GODDESS

DEVOKE QUARTER
Hail to you **Fires,** Spirits of the **South,**
Fires from our hearts our sacrificial bloods
when called you came to guard our rites,
We thank you for your presence and bid thee good night,
Hail and Farewell Fire!!!

Hail to you **Air,** Spirits of the **East,**
Ethers of our ancestral breaths
when called you came to guard our rites,
We thank you for your presence and bid thee tonight,
Hail and Farewell Air!!!

Hail to you **Earth,** Spirits of the **North,**
In ancient trees, in realms of Divine Groves,
when call you came to guard our rites,
We thank you for your presence and bid thee good night,
Hail and Farewell Earth!!!

Hail to you **Waters**, Spirits of the **West**
immortal waves of sustaining Seas,
Goddess and nurturer of our needs
when called you came to guard our rites,
We thank you for your presence and bid thee good night
Hail and Farewell Water!!!

CHANT: *The earth, the air, the fire; the water, return, return, return, return. Below, above, the center is love; return, return, return return..."*

OPEN CIRCLE
Release ye Circle as ye was cast.
In peace and Gratitude,
the Circle is now open
From hand to hand...

*****Potluck and Cakes and Ales*

ASHERAH TREE MEDITATION

Find a comfortable spot to sit or lay down upon.... Close your eyes and let your body sink into this moment and time. Take your first deep breath and let it fill your lungs. (pause) Then release this breath and inhale one more time, realizing that with each inhalation you are clearing and regenerating your lungs. Exhale, breathe again and with each exhalation you are releasing stress and the mundane. (pause) Deep inhalation, one more time, feeling your breath coming from deep below, clearing your body of any toxins or stress as you let your breath go. Now breathe and exhale once more. Allow your body to relax and sink a little deeper with each breath. (pause)

Now I want you to imagine yourself standing before a large open field. Let your mind's eye guide you to this open, vast, expansive landscape. There is nothing in sight for miles on end. It is bright and sunny but the vast, open field before you appears empty, nothing has grown on it in a few months. Continue to study this expansive landscape, letting your mind's eye take in the picturesque sight. (pause)

Look deeply past this landscape to search for a sign of life somewhere. There seems to be nothing before you. Take a look all around you, make note of how this open, vastness makes you feel. Then take a breath and exhaled. Feel now, the weight of your feet pressing against the cold ground. Feel yourself fully alive and present on the earth. There is clearly a palpable energy surrounding you now. See if you can detect its source and simply be a witness to this electric energy. (pause) Feel the weight of the soles of your feet upon the dark soil and notice how they begin to sink a little deeper into the earth beneath you. Take a deep breath and with your breath feel your feet sinking, going deeper into the earth. Breathe. (pause) You sense the beginning of this journey now and you are ready to surrender to the earth and its gift.

Let yourself go deeper into the earth with each inhalation. Exhale, breathe and notice your whole body sinking deeper and deeper into the earth now. Breathe, surrender and exhale. Feel your body submersed fully into the earth with each breath.

Notice how the lower part of your body has already descended and disappeared into the earth's soil. With your next exhalation let the rest of your body follow through and descend even further into the earth. Breathe... (pause) With this next inhalation let your head also go within. Breathe as your head follows the rest of your body, disappearing under the soil. Continue to breathe deeply, comfortably and then exhale. (pause)

Your body is resting now in the moist, rich soil of the earth. Let your body rest quietly, peacefully relaxed, as you close your eyes and feel a mother's embrace surrounding you now. Feel the warmth of her womb surrounded by this dark soil. Feel her embracing you, nurturing you now. Allow yourself to sink ever deeper into the earth. Allow yourself to be lulled and cradled in her loving, warm embrace. Allow yourself to be held by her magick in this special moment.

The season of Spring has arrived. This is a sacred time of birth and rejuvenations, of all things renewed, of all things sprouting and seedlings latching onto their source of nurturance, in Mother Earth. You are one of her seedlings, now underneath the rich soil, held and nurtured by all of her rich elements and minerals. You lay deep in the earth, dormant, corpse-like but very much alive, awaiting for your debut and re-emergence into this world. Breathe, sinking into this moment, resting in the knowledge that you are safe. Breathe and sink ever deeper, nuzzled up comfortably against mother earth. No concerns, nor worries. You are safe in this vast, boundless dark void. You are consoled by her warmth, secure and supported by her strong presence. Breathe; resting like an embryo in her womb, you are a seed. Breathe and exhale in comfort (pause...) All of your needs are serenely met now through your mother, the earth. All your thirst is quenched and all your hunger is tended to. Breathe and release all concerns with your exhalation.

Now, see if you can begin to wiggle your toes and feel how they are starting to slowly aspire to stretch out and extend beyond where they were initially. Feel your toes now slowly elongate, like snakes, they are stretching out further, becoming like roots. And as your toes begin to stretch and dig deeper down into the earth, feel your body simultaneously begin to stretch upward. Sense your own body's need to slowly begin to stretch further upward, up towards a glimmer of light above your head, through the soil now. Feel your hands reaching upwards too, as they begin to stretch up, above your head, while you feel your toes continue to stretch downward, slithering, entangled roots, amidst the critters of the deep earth. Allow your feet to stretch further, going deeper into the earth. Your arms and your torso now begin to push through the soil up above, as you continue moving upward, piercing right through the earth, your torso moving from darkness to the light. (pause)

Breathe and with this exhalation feel your arms and torso stretch further upward, above the soil, as if it was reaching for the light of the sun. Notice your toes, which are now tree roots, firmly, intertwined, planted solidly in the earth. While your toes have tenaciously attached themselves to the core of mother earth, your torso and limbs reach up in a state of ecstasy trying to behold the light of the sun above. Your hands are still growing outward, stretching in every direction and you see your fingers becoming extended, sturdy branches, as they stretch towards the sky. Your torso continues to stand tall reaching for the sky and above your head you feel the hair on your scalp, also stretching upward, becoming tree branches and filling itself with bright, abundantly fertile green leaves, sprouting from your scalp.

Breathe and exhale, make note of how you feel at this very moment. Make note of how your toes feel, deeply rooted in mother earth. (pause) Make note of how your torso feels as it stands solidly, straight, covered in the dark bark of this sacred tree. Make note of how your fingers and your outstretched hands and arms feel, while embodying tree branches. (pause) Make note of how the crown of your scalp feels, as verdant, fertile green leaves are sprouting abundantly from your head. (pause) Breathe, exhale and make note of how your body takes in this breath and how it feels when you exhale now as this magnificent tree. Make note of how you feel as you stand as the tree, as you stand upon mother earth, firmly planted, strong and rooted as a tree. Breathe and exhale. (pause)

Down below, your toes are the roots, enmeshed in the soil that is Mother Earth. Your outstretched arms and elongated phalanges are your branches and your crown is adorned with the most beautiful fertile collection of verdant leaves. Make note of how you feel now as you stand as a tree. This is no ordinary tree; this is you, the **sacred aspect** of you, embodying a tree, embodying **Asherah**.

You stand tall and strong as you are her offspring. You are her divine conduit, you are her creation. You are her magick! You are Goddess!!! Listen as they speak of you...

> *"Oh Great and powerful Asherah,*
> *immortal and ancient Goddess,*
> *we stand to honor, exalt and embody you today.*
> *May we know you from deep within in our shared roots.*
> *May we know you as our elevated branches reach outwardly*
> *in exaltation of you. May we feel your fertile presence within our bark*
> *and solid tree trunk.... In the Spring and throughout the seasons,*
> *may we honor you, all the days of our lives"*

Hold this image of yourself as Asherah in your mind's eye for as long as you can. Then breathe and exhale. (pause) It is Springtime, there are many fertile things growing amidst nature at this time of the year. You have grown from a seedling, nestled within mother earth, to this grand, majestic divine tree, the sacred Asherah.

Bring your attention now to the crown of your head, overflowing with verdant leaves. Breathe and exhale now...Consider at this moment, what you wish to grow and give birth to in your life (pause). Take this moment to contemplate and envision what you hope to grow in this season of growth and rebirth. (pause)

When you're ready, hold out your branches and whisper this wish into the gentle passing breeze. Let your outstretched limbs sway back and forth, as you send your wish towards the sky. And then, let this wish reach down through your solid tree trunk and down through your feeding, fertile roots. (pause)

Let your wish rest there, upon the bountiful roots and then move your energy towards the center of your torso, the Asherah tree trunk. Feel this as the place where your heart begins to beat. Listen carefully as it faintly begins to make itself known. (pause) Detect now the faint, subtle heartbeat. You begin to hear the thump of your human heart now against your tree trunk torso as it corresponds to the tree's pulse and heat beat. Listen carefully to the rhythm and pulse of your heart coming from the torso of the tree trunk.... (pause) Listen to your heart beat as it gets stronger and you begin to remember your human form. Your heartbeat will serve to remind you of your human form and how this journey began. Feel your heart beat, hear it pulsating with hers and remember how this journey began.

Let your human limbs, that are branches now, revert back to being arms and fingertips and tender hands to hold your heart chakra. Feel your human legs, which were the strong roots of this Asherah, now become your two legs and human feet, once more. Feel your torso revert back to the way it was when we commenced this journey. (pause) Feel your head, adorned with the gifts of verdant leaves, now return to your own natural hair and the one you had at the start of this journey. Continue to hear the sound of your heart beat and connect with your human form once more. Return to your human body and spirit, and follow my voice as we begin to return home.

Breathe and exhale. (pause) With your inhalation feel your body once more as human. Feel your feet and your toes, now standing upon Mother Earth. Feel your legs relaxed and comfortably supporting and holding your body up. Become aware of the sensations upon your human flesh now. With each breath expand your belly over your pelvic bones. Exhale, releasing and leaving behind the memories of your tree form. Breathe, feel your breath expand your lungs now, then exhale ready to return. Feel each inhalation pass through your nose, your mouth and throat, then exhale. Breathe... feel yourself present once more as you... magically, simply you, still her offspring; whether as a tree or as a human being. You are a child of the Goddess, a child of mother earth, an extension of her Divine powers.

Breathe now and with this exhalation begin to step back into this time and place, the portal from which this journey had commenced. Follow my voice as I count from ten to one backwards and slowly help you return to this room, fully back into your body, back to this time and space. *Ten, nine, eight*, continue to breathe and release any tension as you exhale. *Seven, six, five*, become more aware of my voice and follow it. Prepare to join us once again. *Four, three*, breathe and gently sense your own body now. *Two, one*, be here now. You are welcomed back. When you are ready, open your eyes and gently stretch out your body. If you need further assistance grounding, please raise your hand and someone will make themselves available to you. Give yourself a moment to readjust to your body, this space, this room, the lights and your surroundings and when you are ready, please gently raise yourself up so that we can begin check in and share our experience as Asherah.

ASHERAH INVOCATION

Asherah of the Canaanite,
Asherah Lady of the Sea,
Creatrix and Consort of El,
Sumerian Mother to all Seventy Deities.

Beloved Ugaritic Goddess,
Embraced by Hebrews of the land
In Tyre, Sidon, Samaria,
It was you they erected on the altar Stand

The Tree of Life, the Menorah,
In Groves on mountain high,
In every Tree you were exalted,
Asherah reigns all space and time.

Elath, pierce through the realms,
Qudsu, immortal One,
Right Hand and wife of Yahweh,
Queen of heaven, please now come.

As in those days of old,
I erect you by this altar,
To ask for your blessings in this rite.
 Asherah, ancient mother in this circle,
I give honor to you tonight.

Come, Lady of Magick,
Lady of Sexuality,
Come ancient Mother Goddess.
Bless me with creative fertility.

I offer you this flame
And the sweets on this plate
And the crimson flow of your traditions
In my womanhood
And thy Queen of Heaven, moon cakes.

Hail and Welcome Asherah!!!

VENERATED TREES IN FOLKLORES

Since ancient time, trees were considered sacred and commonly worshipped by early Christians, Judaism, Muslims, Buddhist and many other Spiritual faiths. Throughout Europe, West Asia, India culture, for the Druids and today's modern Pagans Trees continue to be venerated. Trees exemplify the sacredness of the Divine as they reside in all three realms; living on the earth, as it reaches up to the sky, yet its roots are deep down within the Earth, touching upon the underworld. They link and unify all three sacred realms. Trees can also be seen as feminine in her ability to nurture, birth and sustain life. They are the embodiment of the Sacred Feminine, while also a Phallic masculine symbol with its tall standing, erect trunk.

BELOW ARE SOME TREES OF SIGNIFICANCE TO PAGANS

Oak Tree
It was believed that Druid priest and priestess would quietly listen to the rustling of the leaves of the Oak Tree to receive Divine insight. The Oak tree was considered King of all Trees. Most sacred to the Celts, it was revered by various cultures namely for its size, longevity and it notorious magickal qualities. Magickal wands made from Oak Tree were considered very powerful. It was also used in spells of protection, success and stability. Some would burn Oak leaves to purify rooms and it was believed that Acorns, gathered by women in the evening hour were valued for their powers of fertility.

Birch Tree
Lady of the wood. This tree provided gifts for spell workings of love and romantic nature.

Hazel Tree
Wands made of this tree were often noted for their protective attributes. They were also used to gain poetic inspiration, knowledge and wisdom.

Elder Tree
Was also known as Elderberry and Lady Elder and it is linked with the Pagan sabbat of Midsummer/Summer Solstice. It was sometimes used to drive out evil spirits. Special wands were made of this tree, but also reeds, musical panpipes and flutes.

Apple Tree
A Druid tree, highly connected to healing Magick and often utilized in spells related to love and romance.

Ash Tree
A sacred Druid tree, its straight grain made it excellent for magickal wands and rods. The leaves were known to provide prophetic dreams when placed underneath your pillow. It was associated with Solar Magick.

Elm Tree
Beloved Elm tree was associated with the Mother archetype, earth magick and the Goddess of the earth. It was believed to house faeries and is admired for it stability and grounding qualities. Often described as being fibrous, having tan colored wood, with a high sheen, it was valued for its resistance to splitting.

Pine Tree
Sweetest of woods, it was a tree of the Druids and was often utilize for fertility spells. One of the Chieftain trees of the Irish, it was believed to purify the home, and successfully employed in cleansing baths.

Alder tree
A Druid Tree known for its connection to the elemental powers of Air. It was utilized to make whistles.

Fir Tree
Often described as a very tall, slender tree, that grows high in mountainous terrain. It was believed to have excellent views and long distant vision. For this reason it is a tree associated with clarity and insight. It is also a tree whose cones respond to water/rain by closing and then opening with the light of the sun.

Fir Silver Tree
Known also as Birth tree because of its reputed blessings and connection with Mothers and Child birthing.

Blackthorn Tree
It was known as a Winter tree, with white flowers. Some ancient text reveal its sharp piercing thorns were often used in spells requiring to pierce waxen images.

Hawthorn Tree
Wands made from this tree were considered very powerful. It was reputed to have erotic attributes for men. Often employed in love and marriage spells, it was also known to have protective qualities. This beloved tree became associated with Beltane and May Day, a licentious Pagan holiday.

Juniper Tree
A Druid Tree reputed to give vision and insight.

Cedar Tree
Was considered the tree of life and a grounding tree often associated with the elemental powers of the Earth.

Willow Tree
Known as the Tree of Enchantments and witches aspirin, it is a tree associated with the Moon and therefore the Divine Feminine. One of the most sacred trees to the Irish, it was rumored to give eloquence and inspiration. A beloved as a wish granter, many would sit under the tree to receive its gifts and prophetic insight.

Holly Tree
It appears as white wood with invisible grain and sometimes used for sleep spells. Associated with death and rebirth, it became a symbol of Yule and the Winter Solstice

Mistletoe Tree
A Tree that grants protection, it was one of the most sacred trees for the Druids. Sometimes it was used in love spells and incense and today it is often associated with Yule and the Winter Solstice.

Yew Tree
Believed to be one of the oldest of trees, it is smooth, with wavy grain, a beautiful gold colored wood. Known to enhance magickal and psychic skills, it induced visions. It is a tree that represent the attributes of death and rebirth, it became associated with the Winter Solstice. Perhaps known as the Original Worlds Tree in Scandanavian Myths.
All parts of the tree are believed to be poisonous. It was commonly used in dagger handles, bows, barrels and placed on cemetery plots to comfort the dead.

Rowan Tree
A Druid, Sacred Tree, also known as Mountain Ash, Witchwood, Sorbid Apple.
It was a protective tree with the ability to help in locating water, metals and knowledge. Used to make rods, wands, amulets, it was considered protective against any type of enchantment. The Rowan Tree was sacred to the ancient Celtic Goddess, Brigit.

SPELLS

REDEDICATIONS
Never deserting, watch how I bloom
After much time off,
I return to you

Goddess within
Take your place on this stage,
Herein this ritual,
You are honored today.
Let thy elements inspire
What was dormant inside;
Earth, Air, Water
Fire and the Sacred Divine.

Priestess I am,
Always for you
Crafter, weaver,
Bless what I do

Witch, Enchantress
Priestess are my name,
Herein I dedicate myself
To your domain.

Crafter of Magick
Weaver of Spells,
Student of the Goddess,
Daughter of the Moon-Well.

I re-enter our temple,
Where love is ever abound
And open myself
To my Priestess Goddess crown.

I'll accept my journey,
As long as it's clear,
My calling to be
Witch and sacred seer.

I'll embrace my path,
And the positive course,
Magick emanates within me,
Like a charging life force...

Ancient bright moon, bless my path
Keep me mindful of the Spiral dance,
Strengthen my gifts, as you feed my mind,
With knowledge of magick and the Sacred Divine.

Herein, I connect
To **"She"** who is Breath
All powerful, ancient,
Wise, Full of strength.

Goddess within, take your place on this stage
Herein this ritual, You are honored today.

<u>SPELLS</u>

REGENERATION

"Regeneration"
Seed stage now quiet and still
Dark in my conscious
I'll birth you with my will,

Feed you with love
Patience and intent,
Imbued you with all
That the Goddess has sent,

When the time is right
You'll make your debut
Manifest like a dream
I once had of you,

From a tiny thought,
That dropped to my heart,
Awaiting the flame,
to give it its spark,

I create you with spirit,
With will, and my vision,
Awaiting on that day
for your magickal fruition

I ask that the Goddess,
Help makes it so,
And send my gratitude,
As this spell takes hold.

ASHERAH GODDESS GATHERING CHANT TEXT SHEET

INVOKING MOTHER CHANT, by B. Melusine Mihaltses
Mother, Mother, Mother,
I call you,
Deep within my Soul,
You're stirring my womb.
 Mother, Mother, Mother,
 hear my cries,
 In this sacred Circle,
 I call you tonight.
Light the inner flame
As I light the candle wick!
Call your sacred names
and embrace myself as Witch!
 Sky-clad I approach, to
 Elemental Thrones...
 Hear me, Mother Hear me,
 Thru these words I wrote...(rpt from beginning)
Mother, Mother, Mother,
I call you
Deep within my Soul,
You're stirring my womb.
 Mother, Mother, Mother,
 hear my cries,
 In this sacred Circle,
 I call you tonight. (con't to repeat in rdn)

ANCIENT MOTHER words by Deena MetzgerFrom Music CD, "She Changes Moving Breath"
Ancient Mother, I Hear You Calling
Ancient Mother, I Hear Your Sound
Ancient Mother, I Hear Your Laughter
Ancient Mother, I Taste Your Tears

OLD AND STRONG By Naomi Littlebear Morena From Music CD, "She Changes Moving Breath"
Old and strong she moves on and on
Can you feel the Spirit"? She is like the mountains
Old and strong she moves on and on
Can you feel the Spirit"? She is like the oceans
Old and strong she moves on and on
Can you feel the Spirit"? She is like the river
Old and strong she moves on and on
Can you feel the Spirit"? She is like the wind...

MOTHER I FEEL YOU UNDER MY FEET
Mother I feel you under my feet, Mother I feel your Heart Beat 2X
Heya Heya Heya, Heya Heya Ho 2X
Mother I hear you in the Rivers Sound, Eternal Waters going on and on 2X
Heya heya heya heya heya ho 2X
Mother I see you in when the Eagles fly, Flight of the Spirit gonna take our time 2X
Heya Heya Heya, Heya Heya Ho ......By; Unknown source

EARTH, MOON,MAGICK, by B. Melusine Mihaltses
In the Earth, deep within,
There is A Magick,, I draw it in.
 In her Caves, in the Trees
 Hear her Heartbeat, Pulsing thru me.
When I Rise, I feel her Love
With feet Grounded, I'm soaring high above,
 In the Earth, deep within,
 There is A Magick, I draw it in
Ancient Moon, my Soul reveres
With my Singing, I call you here.
 When this flame, ignites tonight,
 Priestess dancing, Under the moonlit night....
In the Earth, deep within,
There is A Magick
I draw it in....   There is A Magick, I draw it in }3x

CHAPTER SIX

Blodeuwedd

"...But he who dares not grasp the thorn should never crave the rose..." Anne Bronte

BLODEUWEDD

BLODEUWEDD

" When I adapt who I am so that others will not reject me, I am inherently rejecting myself..." unknown

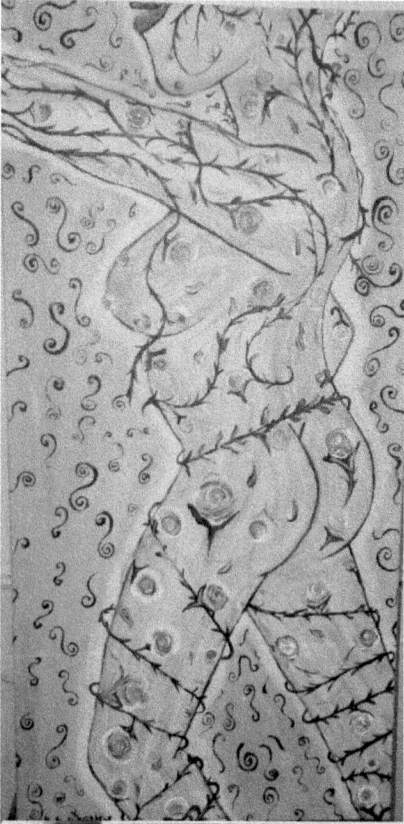

142

BLODEUWEDD ALTAR SET UP
OUR ALTAR

Altar cloth : _Rose colored or pink altar cloth is suggested. Since she is a Goddess intimately connected with flowers, you may also wish to utilize a floral fabric as your altar cloth. Brightly colored altar cloths are appropriate as well as textile with white, owl images._

Image: _The image or statue of a beautiful woman or a gorgeous single flower can be used to represent Blodeuwedd. On her altar you might consider also displaying statuary of a white owl which was so often linked to the Welsh Goddess._

Always present on the altar;
A silver pentacle, a cast iron cauldron, drums, speaking stick, wand, athame, elemental representations.....

Air: _feather bundles, angel wings, bird, eagle or owl statuaries. Bell &, chimes, Incense type sticks, cones, charcoal brisket and fine powdered herbs; frankincense , myrrh._
Fire: _pillar candles, glass enclosed candles in pinks, peaches, yellow, green_
Water: _Small glass bowl with Water and or chalice with Champagne, Cranberry Juice or Red wine._
Earth: _Incorporate lots of green fresh plants and brightly colored flowers. Create a beautiful center piece and offer a small dish of soil or dry herbs can also be used_

Other items pertinent to this particular gathering
Flowers of various kinds
Statuary of an Owl
Goddess Oracle cards or Tarot deck
Colorful papers for craft
Pen and paper
Fresh fruits

Sacred objects from members:
Notes:

MONTH AND THE SEASON

May

The Astrological sign for the month of May is the earthy sign of Taurus, the Bull. Taurus is ruled by the planet Venus (April21-May 20). Traditionally known as the planet of love, it is not surprising that the arrival of May brings the theme of love, joy, earthy pleasure and frolicking maiden energy, oozing out of the Universal auric field.

The Full moon for this month was sometimes called the Flower Moon or Fertile Moon, as these, evidently, are the predominant themes of the month. According to the Farmer's Almanac, sometimes May's Full moon is also known as the Milk moon and Corn moon as well.

May is the Fifth month in the Gregorian calendar. This month is probably named after the ancient Roman Goddess, Maia, who apparently is slightly different from the Greek Goddess with the same name. The name Maia means "mother" in Greek and as a Greek Goddess she indeed exemplified maternal attributes, as the reputed Mother of the God, Hermes. Perhaps this is why, on the second Sunday of May, we commemorate our beloved mothers with the U.S.A. holiday of Mother's Day. Even the Catholic Church honors the Feminine with Our Lady of Fatima's feast day on May 13th and, interesting to note, all of May is devoted to the blessed Virgin Mary.

However, The Roman Goddess Maia (also known as Majesta) whom this month is named after, is Goddess of Growth and Abundance and she exemplifies more of the maiden, frolicking energy, most reflective of the month. Most of the festivals during this month allude to fertility and orgiastic rites like the Floralia, held at the end of April leading right into the first week of May. It garnered the reputation for being a grand orgiastic festival to honor the Roman Goddess of Growth and Springtime, Flora.

Bona Dea (meaning Good-Goddess) was also an ancient fertility festival held in May that honored the ancient Roman goddess by the same name. The Rosalia festival, held around May 23rd, also venerated the magick of flowers and the Goddess of Fertility.

For many Pagans in the U.S.A. and abroad, this is the month to celebrate one of the four major sabbats of the witches year, Beltane. Beltane is a Celtic holy-day that honors the energy of the ancient Celtic Fire Gods, Belenus and Bel and there are numerous traditions linked to its observance. Traditionally, as part of the Beltane activities, Goddess and God or an appointed May Queen and May King, mated and became one in perfect balance. Their mating upon the earth's soil, assured the earth's abundance, healthy proliferation and fertility upon the land. This was also the time of engagements for young couples hoping to marry the following month, as it was considered lucky to marry in June, because it was believed the Roman Goddess of love and matrimony, Juno, would bestow her blessings on the union.

In May, it appears as if the Spring maiden has fully blossomed and reached the ultimate level of maturity. Some traditions view her menarche at this time of the year and celebrated her fertile, bright red blood of life. Precious seeds from the Equinox, back in March, have sprouted, lush, flowering, green and full. Her powers of creation and attraction are undeniable now, as bees and critters, of all kind, come out of hiding, drawn to her colors and scents. Now Spring is fully here and brings with it, all of her joys, light-heartedness, gentle breezes, and warmer climate. Colorful ribbons, floral wreaths, a jovial frivolity, sensuality, and a youthful spirit lingers in the air now.

We honor the maiden's arrival and this earthy, pleasure filled season, by pounding and awakening the fertile moist earth with our joyful steps, twirling and dancing around the sacred Maypole (which can be made of Ash or Birch tree but also of Cypress or Elm wood). As Pagans we celebrate Beltane, the way we believe she has been celebrated for numerous years by our ancestors. The Earth is awakened and alive and so are our physical bodies. Frolicking and lovemaking are a common theme this month. Everywhere and everyone is feeling friskier than ever, amidst the growing heat and power of the Sun.

In the spirit of the season, we call upon the Welsh Flower Goddess, Blodeuwedd, to assist us in awakening dormant shadowy parts of ourselves.

All Monthly intro text taken from author's first book,
"Gathering for Goddess, A Complete Manual for Priestessing Women's Circles"

BLODEUWEDD GODDESS LESSON

Blodeuwedd, pronounced [blow-dai-weth] is the maiden, Welsh, flower Goddess who was magickally created by two very powerful wizards. Her name is translated as "Born of Flowers" or "Flower face."

Often labeled as the Goddess of Betrayal, and one who reflects both dark and light aspects, she is known by many other titles. She is recognized as the maiden Goddess of love and beauty, a Goddess of secret lovers and the archetype of women awakening to her desires. She is sometimes viewed as the maiden part of the trinity of Welsh Goddesses, with Arianrhod, considered the Mother and Cerridwen, the Crone. Although I have also seen her classified as the Lover archetype, while Arianrhod was deemed the virgin.

Although we learn about Blodeuwedd in Robert Graves'*"The White Goddess"* We first encounter Blodeuwedd and her myths in an ancient text called *"The Mabinogion,"* of the 13th century. Some Welsh scholars, however, believe this text was in existence long before the time of Christ and throughout long standing Pagan traditions.

According to *"The Mabinogion,"* the Moon Goddess Arianrhod's second son, Llew Llaw Gyffes (or Llew as he is sometimes referred to)was cursed by his own mother due to a humiliating incident regarding his uncles and her chastity and reputation. As Arianrhod's curse stipulated, Llew was to never bear a sword or arms, he would never have a name and would never be allowed to marry a woman of this earth and this itself would preclude him of ever holding any rank or kingdom. This was a most dreadful way to assure her son's failure, for at this time in Welsh history these were the prerequisite and the only means by which a man could acquire power. The boy's crafty uncles, Math ap Mathonwy and Gwydion, however, had a plan to circumvent this powerful, wretched curse.

Map and Gwydion, who had become almost like beloved foster fathers to Llew, were two of the most powerful wizards in the land and they decided that since their nephew could not marry a real woman of the earth, they would then craft one magickally from flower blossoms. Some text state that Blodeuwedd manifested from simply three powerful blossoms but a more commonly accepted tale, confirms Graves', writings in, *"The White Goddess."* This breathtaking, beautiful woman, meant solely for Llew's pleasure, was created by layering together nine enchanted blossoms; oak, broom, meadowsweet, cockle, bean, nettle, chestnut, primrose and hawthorn. And thus, this non-human, magickal Flower woman manifested and was properly named, Flower-face, Blodeuwedd. With her as his bride, Llew (or Lugh as he was sometimes called) was able to rise to power and assert his basic privileges and civil rights as a Welsh deity. And as Blodeuwedd was created by these powerful men, one can only surmise she was breathtakingly beautiful, sexual and born fully as a grown woman. Yet it's important to note that some believed she lacked the faculties of an adult, for she was made solely to give pleasure to her husband and expected to think, act, and feel as she was dictated, never once having to unearth her own thoughts, emotions or opinions on anything. Some might say although she was unquestionably a woman, her mind and her life experiences, up to that point, were reminiscent of a child but this did not grieve anyone for many years.

Llew and his new bride lived happily for many years in their castle at, Tomen Y Mur. Blodeuwedd, who always had a pleasant disposition, had many maid attendants but very little contact with the outside world and not many opportunities to meet others. As was his custom, one day Llew left his bride alone in their castle, while visiting with his beloved Uncles in the far off distance.

During this trip away, Blodeuwedd, as always, endeavored to remain in her castle with her attendants and one day she heard the raucous sounds of people nearby the royal grounds. She looked out the window and spied several hunting hounds and a group of Hunters coming towards her direction. To her surprise this greatly excited her and the prospect of meeting new people enthralled her in ways she had not anticipated. She watched them for many hours and learned that Gronw Pebr, Lord of Penllyn, was in charge of the hunting excursion. As it was getting later into the evening, she sent one of her attendants to extend a hospitable invitation to the group for a late night dinner in her lonely abode and they gladly accepted. There are some conflicting tales that state, Lord of Penllyn actually left with his group when they were done but he later return to the castle alone to take her up on her offer for a late meal. Whichever version you accept, it is clear the two came together on this fated night and unbeknownst to both, they would be swept up in a tumultuous passionate love affair that would alter their lives forever.

According to the Welsh mythology, they talked for hours on this night and had a real soul connection. That night (and many others that followed) they gave into their strong desires for one another and surrendered to their carnal lust. They made passionate love and remained inseparable....that is until her husband's return. It grieved them terribly to think they could never be together again for they knew they belonged together. And as Blodeuwedd had a rather childlike mind and had never experienced such overwhelming emotions like desire, love and passion, she was probably beside herself. After a few days of torrid love making they decided they could not be apart and together they devised a plan to bring that to fruition by killing Llew. However, as the Sun God, he was not human and not so easy to destroy. There was a list of configurations and prerequisites before her husband could be successfully killed and Blodeuwedd had no idea what they were. She promised she would let Gronw know, as soon as she was privy to this information and the two lovers sadly prepared to say goodbye before Llew's arrival.

When Blodeuwedd's husband arrived, he noticed immediately something different about his flowered bride. She blamed it on her great love and concern for him and a gnawing worry for his life. He explained she had nothing to worry about but Blodeuwedd having ulterior motives insisted she needed to be reassured with great details. So unsuspecting Llew explained to his wife the impossible coincidences that had to be in place in order for his death to occur and gosh... were there many.

According to Welsh mythology, Lugh's death could only happen with a spear (prepared a year and a day in advance) and this would be needed to execute the final blow. Lugh continued to explain to his seemingly worried wife that there should be a thatched roof, built over a cauldron and he would need to be in a bath, by the side of the river Cynvael and somehow have one foot on the back of a deer and the other foot on the edge of the Cauldron in order for him to be successfully killed. Well, Blodeuwedd made special note of all the preposterous, overwhelming details and sent word to her lover.

Over a year passed and just as the two lovers had planned, they managed to have all the right circumstances before Gronw attacked and pierced her husband, the Sun God, to his death. However, he managed to shape-shift into an eagle and although quite injured, still managed to fly away. For Blodeuwedd and Gronw this was enough to allow them to fulfill their dream and together they took residence in the castle for quite some time as lovers.

After Llew flew away as an eagle, the Goddess and her new love felt safe enough to set up their love nest and fufill their heart's desires. And since the Sun King had abandoned his post as the ruler of Dinodia, Gronw was now the successor and ruler to both Penllyn and Dinodia.

However, Llew remained high above a tree slowly dying in his eagle form. His beloved uncles started to worry, for they had not heard from their nephew in a long time and they suspected something was wrong. It was Gwydion who one day spied an injured, sickly looking eagle, high on a tree top and after several enchanting melodies, he managed to coaxed the bird to descend for a closer look. With a swish of his wand, Gwydion unearthed his nephew in the eagle, who at this point was seriously expiring. His uncle rescues him and takes him to the best physicians in Caer Dathyl to help him fully mend and it is then that the men devise a plan for revenge and retribution.

Perhaps word quickly spread of Llews recovery for when the magician Gwydion returned to Mur-y-castle, he discovered Blodeuwedd, already trying to escape off into the mountains with her maidens. But while crossing the river Cynvael all her attendants inexplicably drowned. Blodeuwedd, alone, in the middle of the river, was then cursed by the great magician to never see the light of day and she was converted into an Owl. The myth ends when we also learn that her lover suffered a greater fate when caught by Llew Llaw Gyffes and his magician, uncles. Although Gronw, in desperation for his life, offered a number of things including his own kingdom, Llew was not impressed and wasted no time in striking his rival dead. Thus ends the tragic Welsh tale in *"The Mabinogion"* and where our initial inquisition of this great Goddess begins.

BLODEUWEDD MUSING

The Welsh Goddess Blodeuwedd had been lingering in my psyche for a few years, actually two years to be exact. I kept seeing images of her and hearing her name mentioned every now and then, even though I had no idea who this Goddess was at the time. And so I started doing some preliminary research on her, first out curiosity and then... I just stopped and turned my attention to other things in my life. The ebb and flow of my life was such that every once in a while I would have an experience or a vision that would bring her surging back into my life with intense relevance and necessity, but then, distraction would veer its ugly head. Finally, I found myself at a crossing point in my life and lo and behold found her there. She was there at this threshold, smirking at me, kind of saying, *"What took you so damn long?"* It was and is a question I still can't fully answer.

Blodeuwedd is a powerful Goddess for wommin to connect with. She is richer and so much more complex than what you might initially believe. The thought of her just being a Goddess of Betrayal does not sit well with me as there is more to this Goddess than meets the eye.

The first thing that jumps out at me in her myths is how she came to be through the element of earth via the transient, impermanence of flowers. Born of nine powerful, enchanted blossoms, she was magickally manifested by two gifted wizards. She is born and created by these men (the patriarchs in the family) solely for the purpose and pleasure of the Sun God, Llew Llaw Gyffes. She is made to be breathtakingly beautiful and sexually gratifying for Llew. She comes into being as a fully grown woman and comes into the world with no life experiences, no history, no lineage, no family, no thoughts nor emotions of her very own. Everything she is to feel, do or think, is provided for her by these men, her creators...and this for me, appears reminiscent of the modern day Stepford wives.

She appears to be created to have no desire of her own, except to please her husband and she has no existence before her manifestation; no interest or purpose besides being her husband's adored wife. And yet, because this is all she knows, she gladly accepts this way of life without any question. But lo, how one day everything changed. For in an instance, she opens up the flood gates of repressed emotions and discovers an almost undetectable buried voice of her own and it made itself known in one night...a voice she did not even know existed.... And it clamored for love and desire and engulfed her in a passion she had never known was possible. A passion so consuming and so rapturous, shockingly presented itself and quickly altered her self-image and life's purpose. Prior to the arrival of Gronw, she did know what lurked in the dark corners of her heart, yet, once this shadow and desire made itself known in her life, through this masculine catalyst, her life would never be the same.

It reminds me a little of the Abrahamic scriptural tales of Adam and Eve found in the old testament, for once Eve had tasted of the forbidden fruit offered to her by the serpent, her eyes were awakened to truths beyond what she could comprehend prior to that moment in time.   Life is never the same when we are offered knowledge and experience an inner awakening. I muse and think on an extreme level, about women who find themselves in oppressive marriages. Many wives, especially prior to the 1970s, had their own voices stiffled and some perhaps even abused so continuously, that they lose the power of their own voice, that is, until one day when something happens to awaken them to reclaim their own power. Upon unearthing that repressed inner voice, life is never the same. I think of a woman who might never have climaxed, a non-orgasmic woman, who after finally experiencing the first orgasm, is awakened to her sexual nature and her life from that point on takes on a different hue. I think of a heterosexual woman who has been comfortable in her traditional role as wife and mother and quite shockingly discovers a tiny voice from within that unearths a sexual desire for her same gender. I think of women who have committed themselves, all of their lives, to being *"good girls,"* following rules and expectations placed on them since birth and somehow, despite the loud external voices from society they have this one experience that allows them to finally break free and hear their long repressed inner desires and emotions. The common thread here is that in each one of these examples there is a discovery of a shocking, repressed emotion, an awakening to something we never suspected of housing within. This is Blodeuwedd's realm. This is her potency and great relevance to us as wommin... We quit being the pretty flower (who really has no shelf life when you think about it). The flower who lives solely for adoration, causing no conflict with patriarchy and we then awaken to our deep, inner authentic desires. And it is this desire that shifts and reshapes the landscape of the remainder of our lives.

And so, with Blodeuwedd, she is an imperative Goddess for modern day wommin to connect with, for she is more than the Flower Goddess of Betrayal, she is the Goddess of Awakenings. She is the archetype that introduces us to long repressed or unknown emotions, longings and our authentic voice. She is the Goddess who awakens us to those emotions that might have seemed foreign to us or maybe even slightly taboo. And it is not just any old awakening; it is usually a dark, deep awakening because it is something that she would never have suspected of harboring within. The discovery of such strong dark emotions, like passionate desire, can catapult us causing great upheaval in our world and can take us to a very dark place in our psyche. Just look at how this great passion and love for Gronw makes her deceitfully scheme a most horrific crime to kill her husband. Prior to unearthing these emotions she was a flower Goddess; simply pretty and bright, purely happy just being adored, and now, this was no longer satisfying. It reminds me of those in our modern world still suffering in the same scenarios, overtaken by lust and desire, engaging in extramarital affairs or addictions (drugs, alcohol, food or sexual in nature) and how these dark longing lead to dramatic, sometimes deadly, life altering experiences.

It's very interesting that in the end, Blodeuwedd was not killed but instead was converted into a nocturnal animal, the owl. A winged creature that holds so much controversy because in some indigenous cultures the owl was seen as a harbinger of death, while in others, the owl was seen as wise, all-seeing, mysterious, coolheaded, reserved, cunning and highly cerebral.

For the Greeks, the Goddess of Wisdom, Athena, was often represented by an Owl and the Sumerian Goddess, Lilith also has deep connections with this night creature. It's interesting that the beautiful, earth ruled, flower Goddess would then be given dominion over the element of air and night, as an Owl. As patriarchal punishment for her earthly sins or moral crimes of the flesh, she is sent to the realm of this controversial bird, where perhaps her mind and intellect take precedence over her flesh. She's punished by removing the earthly daylight passions, first experienced and discovered through the flesh, and it is replaced now with the cool calm, intellectual qualities of the night owl. We come to realized that Blodeuwedd is the Goddess of really two opposing realms, for as a flower Goddess she delights in the brightness of the Sunlight, yet later, as an Owl, she delight in the solitude of night.

This too reminds me of the Greek maiden Goddess Persephone, because she is a bright flower Goddess. As the Sun god's wife, and a flower bride she is in her element in the light of day but once she enters the realm of desire and all-consuming passion for her lover, she begins to descend and journey into a darker realm. And I say journey because it was a year and a day of her planning and scheming with her lover to kill her husband and I'm sure during that time an array of emotions were experienced. So this Welsh Goddess begins her journey and her descent, as a result of this initial awakening. When towards the end, she is converted into an owl; she is no longer in the light of day but rather in the nocturnal dark world. As an Owl, she is now a part of night and it reminds me of Persephone because she too ruled over two opposing realms. She also has this experience of transitioning from a fertile daylight Goddess, as Kore, belonging to her mother, then to a night Goddess and Queen of the underworld; challenged and perchance conflicted in her new role in this darker realm. She too has this familiar journey, one we can surely identify with as wommin. She too has an awakening to emotions that a maiden would never suspect from within. And she too has this experience of going from one element; daytime, sunshine, brightness, happiness even ignorance, to this other side; around this dark realm of questionable shadows. It is the confrontation of night and day, ignorance and wisdom, slumber and an awakening and both maiden deities; Persephone and Blodeuwedd, exemplify these traits for us as wommin.

I know many immediately relegate this Welsh deity simply as a Goddess of deception and lies or a deity of love and beauty and it's very easy to just pick one aspect of this deity and run with it but I personally feel this particular Goddess has a number of layers for us to study and really connect with as wommin. Blodeuwedd can be any one of us, whether in the 21st century or the first century. The inaugurated gifts, wisdom and insight that this Goddess presents to us women are timeless and invaluable for our gender.

BLODEUWEDD GODDESS GATHERING DAY

PURPOSE: To scry within the petals of a beautiful flower and see the many layers of you unfolding, manifesting, reflected in this beauty in nature. To awaken hidden parts of ourselves. To shed a light upon shadows and consider our deepest desires. Desires? What? You say you don't have any desires? Time to go deep within and unearths the hidden layers within our psyche.

Check Ins: We gather around the Circle and introduce ourselves to one another, while also voicing our feelings on this month and our hope for the upcoming season.

Chants: Together we will join our voices to sing some commonly known Pagan chants, as well as new ones offered on the Chant sheet in the hand outs (see the last page of this chapter). Singing aloud is a wonderful way to raise energy effortlessly and it also sometimes helps in creating harmonious bonds.

Our Agreements bylaws and Pertinent group discussion... We go around the circle of women, reading a few lines each of our "Group Agreements" and add any new ones that seem necessary. Agreements are signed and submitted in confidence.

Drumming Grounding: A drumming musical CD track will be played, to give participants a chance to connect and ground to this very moment. Women are invited to find a comfortable seat or stand and add movement if they wish.

Conjuring Goddess via her Image: A photo image, Goddess oracle card, flowers or scuplture image of the Goddess, Blodeuwedd, will be shared around the circle, as each woman present will reflect on the image and state aloud what attributes and Divine messages need expression.

LESSON ON THE WELSH GODDESS, BLODEUWEDD
Her myth and various folklores, her attributes and relevance for us today.

GODDESS WORKSHOP
WORKSHOP I.
Crafting a bouquet of paper flowers for an altar centerpiece

WORKSHOP II.
Looking into The Devil Tarot card. Exploring its meaning

WORKSHOP III.
Connecting with the Owl as our totem.

WORKSHOP IV.
Crafting a Floral head Circlet creation

WORKSHOP V.
Connecting with The element of the earth

WORKSHOP VI.
Creation of a small Table top Maypole with plaster of paris, flower pot and a thick branch

WORKSHOP VII.
Flower pendant clay creation

WORKSHOP VIII.
Crocheting a collection of decorative yarn flowers

WORKSHOP IX.
Collage creation using only floral pieces

WORKSHOP X.
Floral lore... Occult meaning of some flowers.

WORKSHOP XI.
Cooking with flowers and aphrodiasiatic floral creations

Exloring Blodeuwedd Aspect:

1. Have you ever experienced an all-consuming emotion that you never suspected you could possibly experience? Whether its lust, passion for someone, maybe of a different race, religion, class gender... etc, or whether it is an anger or a rage that takes you unexpectedly, or pehaps even compassion for someone you'd never consider having compassion for. You often hear of some womyn who fall in love with prison inmates and have deep compassion and unexpected love for prisoners of whom they never would've even considered feeling anything for. So when have you ever experienced an awakening of that sort.

2. Have you ever discovered a foreign strong emotion that would ultimately catapult your life? Can you explain how it has catapulted your life or how it could catapult and shift your life?

3. What would you do if you were the Goddess Blodeuwedd?

4. What animal would you feel least comfortable converting into?

5. If you could change the outcome for Blodeuwedd what would it be?

BLODEUWEDD GODDESS GATHERING RITUAL

PURPOSE: To scry within the petals of a beautiful flower and see the many layers of you unfolding. To awaken hidden parts of yourself. To shed a light upon your shadows and consider your deepest desires. Desires? What? You say you don't have any desires? Time to go deep within and unearths the hidden layers within that are you.

ASPERGE with Smidge and ANOINTING: With floral scented oil like Gardenia and Jasmine. **WELCOMING** with gentle music playing in the background for the entire ritual.

INTENT SPOKEN: To commemorate the season and awaken Blodeuwedd within ourselves, while honoring this beloved Welsh Goddess.

CIRCLE CASTING

(scatter rose petals around the perimenters of the circle as we cast the circle)

Gods and spirits circle around,
Shield us in love
Keep the profane out.
Guard and hold our sacred space
Let these petals, our circle now delineate,
We welcome the energy that maintains our shield,
Our circle is cast, our protection is sealed.
We stand between all time and space
Blessed be,
This Circle is now made!!!!

QUARTER/ELEMENTAL INVOCATIONS

Spirit of the NORTH, We honor you realm of Earth,
Transformer, Fertile Landscape. In bloom you grow and support our dreams, come show us your gifts of creation and fertility. We call you from the depths of our arms, lend us your gifts, and come near us not far. **Hail and Welcome Earth!!!!**

Spirit of the EAST, We honor you realm of Air,
We invoke your inspirational winds of change, gently stir and shift us to a positive place. We call you from the depths of our breath, lend us your gifts so that our rites are blessed. **Hail and Welcome, Air!!!!**

Spirit of the SOUTH, We honor you realm of Fire,
Passionate desires awakening from within. We invoke your immortal flames to connect us to thy sparkling vital heat. We call you from the depths of our heart, lend us your gifts, come near us not far. **Hail and Welcome, Fire!!!!**

Spirit of the WEST, We honor you realm of Water,
Our Womynhood you hold so dear, thy ebb and flow of all ecstasies and tears, oh mysteries of thy sacred moon, reflected in our blessed womb. We call you from the depths of our inner seas, lend us your gifts that we may feel your blessings. **Hail and Welcome, Water!!!!**

GODDESS INVOCATION

CHANT: *"Do you remember, when God was a woman she had many, many names"*
TRANCE & MEDITATION WIL BE OFFERED

SPELL WORKING

Women should enter the space wearing highly decorated masks, like mardi gras style. The priestess will hand every participant a rose or other bright flower with petals. Everyone will look at their respective flower in quietude for a brief moment. Consider, Blodeuwedd was born to be a flower for her husband, contemplate on her beauty and what this means to you personally.

****

With eyes half dimmed we will go around the circle, as every woman present will begin to pluck the petals of her flower as she state aloud the things that she has recently discovered about herself...For example; *"I don't like driving, or I hate the color pink,"* or, *"I hate being a mother,"* or *"I am a struggling with sobriety,"* or *"I m not sure I am in love with my spouse,"* or *"I am infatuated with a neighbor,"* etc etc...

This is about speaking **our truth** and breaking with our façades. We are undoing this perfect, pristine, silent, oppressed pretty flower and reclaiming our truth, our personal truth aloud. This might feel awkward at first but as we go around the circle it will begin to catch momentum and the energy will rise as we begin to de-petal our beautiful flower to expose it and reveal simply her stem...and our truth. The petals should be collectively placed in our cauldron. They can later be burned outside as an aromatic incense. Singing will follow this working...

DRUMMING CIRCLE: An organic Drumming Circle ensues, we may dance, move to empower and release our truth spell

CHANT: *"We all come from the Goddess..."*

Final Check in
DEVOKING GODDESS

DEVOKING ELEMENTS

Spirit of the **WEST**, We honor you realm of Water, for blessings us with your Lunar ebb and flow and the magick held in our womb. We send our gratitude for guarding and holding our sacred space, as ye came in peace, depart in peace. **Hail and Farewell, Ye realms of Water!**

Spirit of the **SOUTH**, We honor you realm of Fire, for awakening us to our inner flames. We send our gratitude for guarding and holding our sacred space, as ye came in peace, depart in peace. **Hail and Farewell, Ye realms of Fire!**

Spirit of the **EAST**, We honor you realm of Air, for enlightening us with your gentle breezes of inspirations. We send our gratitude for guarding and holding our sacred space, as ye came in peace, depart in peace. **Hail and Farewell, Ye realms of Air!**

Spirit of the **NORTH**, We honor you realm of Earth, for connecting us to our physical form and all its supportive blessings. We send our gratitude for guarding and holding our sacred space, as ye came in peace, depart in peace. **Hail and Farewell, Ye realms of Earth!**

CHANT: *"The earth, the air, the fire, the water, return, return, return return...."*

OPENING CIRCLE

"The Circle is open but unbroken may the peace of the Goddess be ever in our heart, merry meet and merry part and merry meet again...."

TRADITIONAL POTLUCK TO FOLLOW

BLODEUWEDD MEDITATION

We begin this journey by first finding a comfortable spot to sit or lie down upon and endeavoring to soothe and relax every muscle and every joint in our body. Take a deep breath and let it fill your lungs and then exhale. Breathe and let go. Let your shoulders slightly drop and become aware of your heart chakra and its continuous rhythm. Breathe and exhale. Note the unique pulse and beat of your heart and see if you can slow it down with each inhalation. Breathe. (pause) Now exhale and find yourself releasing a stream of stress, concerns and the mundane, as each breath is surrendered. Slow down your pace and feel the thumping of your heart grow slower and slower. Breathe and exhale.

I like to bring your attention from your breath now back to your heart, for this will be the portal for this meditation. So if you will, bring your focus to the center of your chest. Spend a moment in this realm; quietly examining its content. What does it long for? What pervades its veins? What secret fantasy does it hold? (pause) Slowly breathe into it, fueling it with the energy to help you see clearer. (pause) What color presents itself to you at this moment in this realm? Make note of it now and let this color become brighter and brighter in your mind's eye. (pause) Continue to study your color and begin to see it swirling, spiraling like a whirlpool, like the center of a flower. In your mind's eye see it as the bud of a precious, unique flower. Watch your color as it transforms into the petal and then fully into the flower itself. Hold this flower in the palm of your hands and while gazing upon it, make note of how it makes you feel. (pause)

Before you, appears three masked women. They are tall, elegantly dressed in exquisite satin and velvet brocade gowns, seductively wearing very elaborate feathered Mardi Gras masks. You have never seen them before and although you don't know who they are, there is a sense of familiarity and trust among them. Choose one of the women to entrust with your flower. They respectively represent the past, the present and future and therefore... consider carefully whom you will give your flower to now. One woman is wearing white, she represents the past. The woman in red represents the present and the one wearing green represents the future. Reflect now who will receive your flower and when you are ready, gently place your colored blooming flower in her hand. (pause)

The woman you've elected tenderly takes your flower and asks you to follow her and you begin to journey with her into the forest. Deep into the forest you begin to walk, with every step quickening your pace to catch up with the masked woman. Walk with her and feel your legs quickening its pace. (pause) It is beginning to get dark in the forest but you can begin to make out the form of a huge castle that is becoming clearer and clearer as you get closer to it. With a few more steps you finally arrive at the doorstep of this castle. The masked woman turns to face you and finally speaks.

"What you wish for... your secret heart's desire... what no one else knows you long for, is here, within these brick and mortared walls of this great castle. In this forest, far from civilization there is no one to judge you, no one to condemn you, no one to prevent your fantasy from fruition. I am simply the guardian of your flower. I am simply the one who has come from; either, your past, present or future, whom you entrusted to safeguard your heart throughout this journey. I bring you to this safe place to fulfill your secret fantasy. Enter through these castle doors, stay as long as you wish. Find within these walls the watered vase for this flower, that it may not wilt and die of abandonment and neglect. Quench her thirst and keep her alive, tend to your most cherished fantasy in this special moment in time...."

You take your flower, remembering what created it at the inception of this magickal journey and reflect again on your heart's secret longing. Thank your guardian, bid her adieu and enter through the doors now. In your mind's eye see your biggest, brightest fantasy come to life. Whatever that fantasy may be, whatever taboo, or secret wish, allow it now to come to fruition and unfold, in whichever way feels most enjoyable to you. Remember you are safe and this is your personal moment. Take the time to see the unfolding of your biggest desire and for this night let it be real. Play and experiment in your mind's eye with different images, colors, textures, people and props. This is your personal secret fantasy and anything you desire right now will be offered to you. Embrace and delight in this particular moment in time. Find the watered vase for your precious flower and let yourself enjoy this night to fulfill your secret fantasies. (pause) There will be a long moment of silence now, to allow you plenty of time to play, create and relish in your fantasy. (Long Pause)

(Gently ring a bell...) You have fully enjoyed yourself but now it is time to depart. You hear the faint hooting of an owl outside the castle and slowly, it begins to get louder as if it had a personal message for you. Gather your belonging now and calmly prepare yourself to leave. Remember to take your special flower from the vase and holding it in your hands, begin to walk towards the entry doors. Again you hear the owl hooting even louder now, a sign that you must depart and thus you say goodbye as you open the door to leave.

There outside, once more, is the masked woman. She greets you and gently takes the flower within her hands. Quickly she begins to walk through the forest and you follow. The hooting owl is heard flying above you as if it had more to say to you. Listen to the owl's hoot and see if you can discern the owl's special message to you regarding this night, as you continue walking with the masked woman through the forest now. (pause)

You continue to walk until you reach the exact location from where this journey had commenced. You begin to slow your pace when you catch a glimpse of the other two elaborately dressed, masked women, standing, eagerly waiting for your return. Your guardian now turns to you and gingerly hands back your special flower. Her duty as guardian of your heart has been met. She has delivered you, to and from, and now she must bid thee adieu. Take a moment to thank her in your own special way for being your guardian and for the monumental gift she has given to you. (pause)

See your flower being safely handed back to you, placed tenderly in the palm of your hands. Continue to gaze upon its beautiful petals and its bright special color and allow yourself to begin to scry into the center of its exquisiteness. Gaze into its beauty and allow yourself to get submersed in her allure. Notice every fine detail that perhaps you could not see before but now can vividly appreciate. Look at its shape; its texture, its silk feel, the curves and veins upon each petal. Detect the smell from its aphrodisiac scent and let it lulled you back to your heart. Continue to gaze at your flower. As the owl's hoot has nearly disappeared now, raise your precious flower to your heart chakra and press it there. You can begin to hear your heart beat once more. Follow your heart beat and let it lead you back to this room, to the start of this journey. Breathe and exhale and listen to your heart beat as it leads you to my voice and back to where this journey had commenced. Let it lead you back to this room. Follow my voice and return back to your body, breathe, back to this time and space. Breathe, I will count backwards from five to one to help you transition back to this space.

Five; take a deep breath and release. Four; continue to become more aware of your body in relation to this room. Three; take a breath and release any tension now. Two; start to gently wiggle your toes, fingers and pelvic, if you can. One; Welcome! Give yourself a moment to gently stretch out and ground some more, if needed. Raise one finger in the air, if you need additional help grounding and coming out of this meditation, someone will make themselves available to you to help. When you are ready, sit or stand so that we may begin a proper check in.

INVOCATIONS

BLODEUWEDD INVOCATION

In Magick's hand you came to be,
Flower Welsh Goddess
Of Love and great Beauty.
  To serve as wife
  and lover of the Sun
  To be his pleasure
  And when called, to come.
To happily exist,
For solely his joy,
To live in the light
And be alluring and coy.
  To never question
  This life We made,
  Because all was perfect...
  Until that day came.
Lugh left for a moment
To tend to his job,
Alone in our castle
For him, I did not sob...
  Instead I heard
  The longing in my soul,
  A strange, foreign stirring,
  Demanding, and taking hold.
When lo, I saw
the man of my dreams,
He far surpassed
The one I married.
  I heard a voice
  unknown to me,
  A rapturous passion,
  Fervently awakening,
My lover and I
never left the house.,
But this passion swirled my life
from within and without.
  And soon, I would do
  The unthinkable of deceit
  Kill my husband,
  To totally find myself free.
My scheme was revealed,
oh I loss everything
Including the passion to feel.
  From flower to owl,
  A nocturnal bird to flee,
  The light of the day
  Now was no longer for me.
Remaining cool
And distant, in the air,
The price, Blodeuwedd paid,
For her passionate love affair.

Cad Goddeu (Battle of the Trees)
Hanes Blodeuwedd

Pg41 from"The White Goddess" by Robert Graves©1948 by international Authors N.V.

First American amended & enlarged edition, 1966, Seventh printing 1984

Not of father, nor of mother
Was my blood, was my body,
I was spellbound by Gwydion,
Prime enchanter of the Britons,
When he formed me from nine blossoms,
Nine buds of various kind;
From primrose of the mountain,
Broom, meadow-sweet and cockle,
Together intertwined,
From the bean in its shade bearing,
A white spectral army
Of earth, of earthly kind,

When I was made of ,
the blossoms of the nettle
of the water of the ninth wave
I was spell bound by Math
Before I became immortal.

Oak , thorn and bashful chestnut-
Nine powers of nine flowers,
Nine powers in me combined,

Nine buds of plant and tree.
Long and white are my fingers
As the ninth wave of the sea....

POEMS & SPELLS

THERE SEEPS MY ESSENCE*

Seeped right out of me
All that made me,
ME
All that Fire and Passion,
The Crazies and Electricity...

All that "rised"- when you "neared" me
Lava, sweat, ecstasy.
All that eruption that swelled for you,
Silenced Volcanoes,
With no motive to move.

Seeped right out of me,
All purpose and goal,
If I failed so horribly at "Us"
Nothing's worth the fight to hold.

So my life entered
The vacant stage,
Corpse living-automatic,
Clipped wings,
surrendering to a cage.

No longer recognizable,
hanging on to faded Scents,
Denying every part of me,
slowly, there, seeps my essence....

Seeped right out of me,
Can I gather it and get "whole"?
Is it best to watch it slither away,
Pretend I don't miss, what you stole?

Seeping ALL of me,
Trying to remember, trying to regain,
Pele, Hathor, Aphrodite
And Oshun's delicious games.

Triumphantly dancing,
Shaking off what turned Black,
Rebirthing, recharging,
Refueling myself back....

THERE seeps my essence,
There in "Her" Domain.
Awakened, Rediscovered,
Ready to be Reclaimed....

A BETTER LOVE
While aspecting Blodeuwedd

In the abyss of wifehood,
Turn sadness into joy.
Turn blindness to sight,
I open up the doors
That were once closed tight.

Now doors wide open,
I make a Universal plea,
Send a good mate,
That's appropriate for me.

A better mate that's honest,
Faithful and true,
Strong, with high morals,
And sincere "I love yous"

Sexually fulfilling,
Makes money galore,
Descent and monogamous,
Good nature to the core.

Someone who will love me,
And will allow me to love him too,
Compatible and available
Sexually in tuned.

I am beautiful,
And worthy of a better love,
I am sultry, loving and fine,
Confident Sexy, Goddess am I.

Send me a love,
That's appropriate for me,
Someone to fulfill these romantic needs,

Thank you in advance,
For all that I've received,
This spell bound round,
So mote it be!

BLODEUWEDD GODDESS GATHERING CHANT TEXT

DO YOU REMEMBER
Do you remember, When God was a woman she had many, many names. (2X)
They called her Isis, Astarte, Diana, Hecate, Demeter, Kali, Innana.... *repeat*

AWAKENING by Anne Hill, From music CD, Reclaiming, Second Chants
If I touch you, I will know you;
Though my veil be drawn , you're glowing,
In my mind and soul and body...

THE FOOL by Suzanne Sterling From music CD, Reclaiming, Second Chants
Night and stars are falling down
A wild breeze is blowing,
Earth and moon are whirling round
The fool walks through the door...

EARTH, MOON,MAGICK *by B.M.M. aka B. Melusine Mihaltses*
In the Earth, deep within,
There is A Magick, I draw it in.
    In her Caves, in the Trees
    Hear her Heartbeat, Pulsing thru me.
When I Rise, I feel her Love
With feet Grounded, I'm soaring high above,
    In the Earth, deep within,
    There is A Magick, I draw it in
Ancient Moon, my Soul reveres
With my Singing, I call you here.
    When this flame, ignites tonight,
    Priestess dancing, Under the moonlit night....
In the Earth, deep within,
There is A Magick, I draw it in.... There is A Magick, I draw it in }3x

LISTEN TO MY HEART SONG *by Susun Weed*
Listen, Listen, Listen to my heart Song
Listen, Listen, Listen to my heart Song
I will never forget you
I will never forsake you
I will never forget you,
I will never Forsake you .....

SWEET SURRENDER *by Gladys Gray*
We are opening up,
in sweet surrender,
to the luminance
Love light of the one, (Repeat)
    We are opening ....We are Opening (z2X)

DON'T YOU KNOW
by Elaine Silver
Don't you know
Your body is a Temple
And Don't you know
Your Spirit is a Shrine
The other side of Fear
Is a never ending Love
Don't you know
You and I
Are both Divine

You won't know
What it means to really grow
If you don't open up
To whose inside
The other side of Fear
Is a never ending Love
Don't you know, You and I,
Are both Divine.

CHAPTER SEVEN

Lilith

"...We are all born sexual creatures, thank god. But it's a pity so many people despise and crush this natural gift..." Marilyn Monroe

LILITH

LILITH

"Don't compromise yourself. You are all you've got..." Janis Joplin

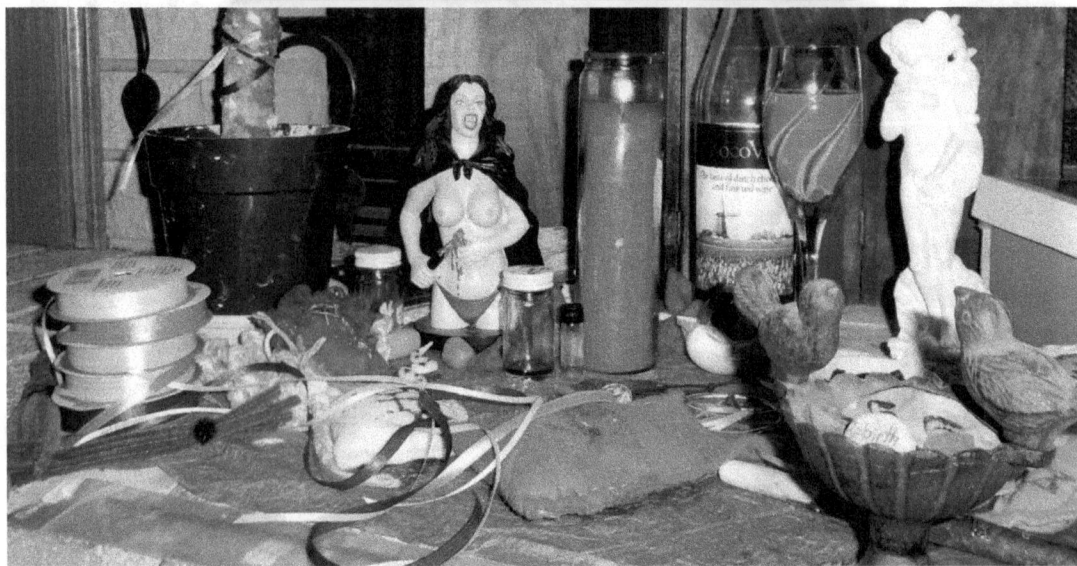

LILITH ALTAR SET UP

OUR ALTAR

Altar cloth : When I think of Lilith I am reminded of the Red Sea and thus, I like utilizing a crimson red altar cloth for her. I also like incorporating an altar cloth with images of snakes, lots of snakes as she is linked to being the serpent in the Garden of Eden.

Image: The image of a provocative woman or an enchantress, either a photo or a sculpture is fine for an altar to the Sumerian Goddess, Lilith. Snake images are also highly suggested. Gothic vampire-like statuaries are also acceptable on an altar for an ancient Goddess so often linked with the race of vampires.

Always present on the altar;
A silver pentacle, a cast iron cauldron, drums, speaking stick, wand, athame, elemental representations.....

Air: feather bundles, angel wings, bird, eagle or owl statuaries. Bell &, chimes, Incense type sticks, cones, charcoal brisket and fine powdered herbs; frankincense , myrrh.

Fire: pillar candles, glass enclosed candles in yellow, gold, white

Water: Small glass bowl with Water and or chalice with Champagne, Cranberry Juice or Red wine.

Earth: Create a beautiful center piece of lots of green plants and flower, especially red crimson roses. A small dish of soil or dry herbs can also be used

Other items pertinent to this particular gathering

Snake figurines
Owl statuary
Pen and paper
Tarot deck or oracle cards

Sacred objects from members:
Notes:

MONTH & SEASON

June

June is the sixth month in the Gregorian calendar and according to the Roman poet, Ovid, the Latin word for June was *"iuniores"* meaning *"younger one,"* alluding to the month being one that caters to the young. The Astrological sign for the month of June is Gemini, the twin. Gemini is ruled by the swift and crafty, divine messenger, Greek God of travel, science and communicator - Mercury (May 21-June 20). During this month we can see the influence of these mercurial attributes, revealing themselves quite subtly through summer.

There is one common theory attributed to the Roman poet, Ovid, that believes the month was named after the Roman Goddess Juno, who is wife of Jupiter, the Roman King of the Gods. Juno was the Goddess of marriages and the patron Goddess of all women's well-being. As a result, June became known as the traditional month of matrimonies. In ancient times, it was believed that marriages performed in June, would receive Juno's blessings for a long lasting union. This was also a respected time for all contractual agreements, and legal dealings. June, therefore appears to be a time of much celebrations with many types of unions, hand fasting, and weddings to attend. Even in today's modern age, June, remains to be the ideal, favorite month, among betrothed couples, to pledge their undying love and thus, all celebrations of merriments are common at this time of year.

Honeysuckle, strawberries and roses grew in abundance during this time of the year in some regions, therefore, the full moon in June is often referred to as Strawberry Moon or Rose Moon. It is also important to note that roses were sacred to the Deities of love and marriage and therefore it would correspond easily to one another. The Full moon of this month was also sometimes called Mead Moon, named for the fermenting drink made of honey. Honey was also sacred to the Goddess of love and marriage and it was often used in offerings to Juno, to endear her to bless nuptials and various other sacred rites. Honey has always been associated with solar sacred offerings to various deities from different pantheons, including Saraswati. This month's full moon was also sometimes known as Strong Moon due to the magnanimous, intense strength of the sun's power at this time. The daylight hours now are stretching and reaching to be at their longest, when by mid-month, we approach the sabbat of the Summer Solstice.

Interesting to note, that at this time, in the U.S.A., the patriarchal male energy is celebrated with the arrival of Father's Day on the second Sunday of June. Many of us take this opportunity to honor the men in our lives, whether they are our fathers, grandfather elders, brothers, uncles or even our own sons. We pay tribute to the role of fatherhood and those who have blessed our lives fulfilling this most auspicious role. For some Pagans, the masculine aspect of nature is venerated now, as well as, honoring the consort of the Goddess.

The waxing sun reaches its zenith and now, quite subtly, slowly it begins to shorten the days once more and this is celebrated with the Summer Solstice, also known as Litha and Midsummer. It's important to note that we are also smack in the middle of our calendar year and naturally concern ourselves with making the best of our time. Picnics, barbecues, vacations and beach outings with friend and family are common. June, more often than not, finds us enjoying the outdoors, warm bright, sunny days and numerous summer activities and we are more apt to be engaged (consciously and unconsciously) in the worship of nature and the Goddess.

This month we call upon the Sumerian ancient Goddess, Lilith and connect with her powers of autonomy and liberation.

All Monthly intro text taken from author's first book,
"Gathering for Goddess, A Complete Manual for Priestessing Women's Circles"

LILITH GODDESS LESSON

"...Once women are fee to bestow their favours and affections where they will, the whole structure of patriarchal society starts to crumble..."

The Cult of the Black Virgin," by Ean Begg, Page 137,
Chiron Publications, Wilmette, Illinois 2006

Probably one of the most controversial Pagan deities and one full of conflicting, yet intriguing mythologies, the Sumerian Goddess Lilith, is a powerful archetype for any women to unearth and work with.

Lilith today is viewed as a Goddess of the night, Goddess of Sexual Liberation, a Goddess of revenge and retribution and anger. According to a collection of ancient writings, she could not be wild and free in God's heavenly presence in the Garden of Eden and she would not subordinate herself to her spouse, Adam, and thus, she's a Goddess that represents independence among many other feminist ideals. She is the liberated Woman who does not compromise herself and she answers to no one. She is the one who embraces the pain of solitude rather than relinquish her power to any man. Lilith represents the autonomous woman who refuses to subordinate herself or lay down beneath her oppressor. She is the women who reclaims her powers and reclaims her authentic self in a world that so persistently, only wants to control and oppress her. She is the rebellious one who refuses to play societal's stereotypical roles. She is sexual liberation, delighting in her unbridled sexuality and enchanting beauty. She is flight of spirit that comes and goes as she pleases. Lilith is the opposite of the nurturing maternal Goddess, even though she is attributed for birthing a race of demonic beings, she is far from the coddling mother archetype. She is considered the shadow side of Eve, that part of her she has yet to embrace or discover, for Eve only appears to accept her limiting role as Adams' rib, created inferior to him.

We claim Lilith now as a powerful Goddess for we see her significant value and cathartic importance for modern day women, especially with the rise of Feminism, but when researching Lilith you will soon discover ancient text that reveal she was not initially viewed as a Goddess but rather as a very much feared She-Demon. Or, perhaps, as many Dianics claim, she was indeed initially a Goddess a long time ago, who was stripped of her crown and demoted with the rise of patriarchy. One will never really know. Despite limited resources, remnant scriptures, actual sacred text scattered about mentioning her numerous different names and a plethora of mixed, conflicting tales, she has survived into the 21st century, which is astounding, when you really think about it and consider that her oral traditions remained strong throughout the ages and sustained her in our auric "herstory."

Lilith has often been viewed by Wiccan Feminist as a Goddess who was simply demoted, vilified as a demon because, in a patriarchal society, that is the ultimate way to control and oppress a woman; vilify her, make such a scandalous rebellious Goddess, evil, to discourage any other woman from reclaiming her own powers or even slightly considering how vastly different her world might be, if she stood up as well. Lilith's claws or talon represents her tenacity, digging her heels, refusing to surrender her ideals. Her wings represent her freedom and her red eyes represent anger of those who tried to restrain and oppress her. She is often depicted with wings, owl talon as claws for her feet, and hairy legs, for in ancient times, a hirsute woman was considered a sign of demonic association. Suspecting that Queen of Sheba was demonic, King Solomon asked to see her legs and behold he discovered that she was indeed very hairy and this led him to conclude that she was a Lilith.

Some symbols linked to Lilith are the flower lily and the lotus as well as gemstones like the Garnet and Bloodstone. Her depictions with animals indicate that she had an affinity to wild creatures. Animals like the owl, wolves, the lion, scorpions and the serpent were accepted as her symbols and the screeching owl, a name so often used in the bible, to refer to her. The serpent in particular, was often representative of the Goddess herself. She has also been associated with harpies, sirens, mermaids, undines, nymphs and melusines, perhaps due to her close connection with water and the sea. French poet and novelist, Victor Hugo (1802-1885) even claims Lilith as Satan's eldest daughter and as a succubus, she was attributed for creating a race of vampires.

The name Lilith, which translates in the Semetic language as "Night," is also associated with the wind and the breeze. The word "Lil" or "Lilitu," meant ghost, spirit breath, wind and storm demon. What is remarkable is that the name Lilith and various derivations of her name appear throughout history in Sumerian, Kabbalistic writings and Jewish mysticism and yet, it's quite interesting that according to Kabbalah scriptures, she was the first woman God created; Lilith (night) and yet, the next woman created for Adam was consequently named Eve (again a reference to night), reaffirming a connection between woman and the night.

According to Raphael Patai, in his book, *"The Hebrew Goddess,"* he states that **Lilith or Lillu** was actually one of Four Demons, belonging to the vampire or incubi-succubae class.

Lillu and Lilitu (Lilith) believed to be a She-Demon, and **Ardat Lili** (Lilith's Hand maiden) who visited men at night to procreate offspring.

Irdu Lili (male counterpart) who visited women to also proliferate, impregnate and further expand the race of Demons.

The Goddess, Lilith was originally considered to be a part of a clan of Storm Demons, due to some confusion with the origins of her name, which sometimes refers to wind, breeze, ghost and spirit of the dead. There was also around the third Dynasty of Ur, another documented Sumerian Goddess, by a similar sounding name, Ninlil. Ninlil was a known Babylonian - Sumerian Goddess of the Wind and she was also known as the Avenging Bride, perhaps there was some confusion regarding these two feminine figures or perhaps they are one the same. Clearly the myths and attributes of Ninlil and Lilith are intriguingly similar and there is no question they crossed path at some point.

Lilith was known by many names and interestingly enough, sometimes, she was referred to in the singular form as well as in the plural. She was known as Lilin, Abito, Abizo, Amo(z)rpho, Haqash, Odam, Kephido, Ailo, Tatrota, Abniqta, Shatrina, Kalubtza, Tiltoi, Pirtsha.

By far one of the most controversial Feminine figures in ancient mythology is Lilith. There are numerous conflicting and controversial references to this ancient deity. We find references to her in Jewish mysticism; Kabbalah, the Talmudic, the Zohar, even the Bible, in Isaiah 34:14. Some early writings revealed she manifested when, on the fifth day of creation, God created the Sea creatures and she was among them. Other text, like the one found in the Zohar, claims she was a soul lodged in the Abyss that finally was called down upon, to descend, only after Yahweh had created Adam. Notice in this myth she was already present before Adam's manifestation.

In the lost Midrash Abkir, Kabbalistic writings of the 10th century, Lilith, who was also named, Pizna was actually viewed as two spirits in one. She is considered Lilith and Naamah. According to this text, Adam's beauty was so radiant and irresistible that they were both enchanted by him as he slept and they mated with him, unable to restrain themselves. Together they procreate the "plagues of mankind," the demonic race of Lilim. And the name Naamah, translates as the "**charmer**" and she is known as a high ranking demon that often accompanies Lilith. In Talmudic- Midrashic mythology, Naamah is actually depicted as a human being, a beautiful enchantress, daughter of Lamech and Zillah and sister of Tubal Cain. She is clearly a descendant of Cain and in her great beauty; she is a deadly enchantress, as sadly, all dangerously, devilish women tend to be ironically portrayed. It is believed she then becomes Noah's wife, that is according to Abba bar Kahana. However, later, in the Kabbalah she was transformed into semi-human, demonic stature and thus, an aspect or a type of Lilith.

Barely mentioned in the Bible, most of what we know today about this enigmatic female figure can be extrapolated from pre-Biblical writings, Jewish Mysticism, oral traditions passed down and documented in many scriptures, as well as Kabbalistic writings, preserved in the Midrashic, the Zohar and Talmudic works of Sages and Rabbis throughout history. Perhaps it's best to start from the beginning with one version of her birth and manifestation but as can be expected with such an ancient figure, there are numerous versions and theories related to her birth.

"The Alphabet of Ben Sira," written in German between the 8th and 10th century gives a complete narrative and description of one version of Lilith's manifestation and perhaps it came about to explain the confusing Biblical lore found in Genesis, which upon closer inspection does not make much sense. *"The Alphabet of Ben Sira"* was considered a satire but in reality it was more likely a surviving oral tradition that sustained itself through the ages to explain the existence of Adam's first wife. According to *"The Alphabet of Ben Sira,"* Lilith was the first woman created by God, not Eve. Although some authors like, Janet and Stewart Farrar in their book, *"The Witches' Goddess,"* suggests that Eve and Lilith are really one the same and thus Lilith is the shadow aspect of Eve.

> *"Truths banished to the unconscious do acquire talons –*
> *representing both our fear of them and their ability to tear away*
> *through the veils of hypocrisy and distortion*
> *with which we have tried to surround them.*
> *Only when we come to terms with them and*
> *integrate them with consciousness is their loveliness restored,*
> *so that their talons become feet again.*
> *Only when the night-owl is admitted to the sunlight*
> *can we appreciate the beauty of her plumage.*
> *Lilith the true Mother of All living, must be reacknowledge –*
> *so that She and Eve can become One again*
> *For without that One, Adam is only half man..."*
>
> *(The Witches' Goddess," Janet and Stewart Farrar page 133)*

In *"The Alphabet of Ben Sira,"* Lilith was created at the same time as Adam, on the fifth or sixth day of creation. And God had fashioned Adam from the earth and he used the same raw material to create Lilith probably before or at the exact same time. There are other conflicting works that claim that God picked up, not the clean earth as he did for Adam, but the filth and impurities or sediments from the earth to form woman and thus it was to be expected that she was to have an impure, evil spirit, this was according to some very patriarchal Talmudic writings. Clearly a poor attempt by patriarchy to pollute our entire gender right at the start of humanity by claiming woman is destined to be evil, since she was created from impure soil and sediment. There is yet another version of Lilith's manifestation which claims that she manifested not from God himself but from the spontaneous great supernal abyss and out of the power aspects of God; the Din and the Gevurah. God was believed to have ten mystical attributes, Serifot, and his lowest kinship with the realm of evil was referred to as the, *"dreg of wines"* and this is where both, Lilith and Samuel or Satan originated from, according to these early Talmudic writings.

Lilith and Adam were created equally from the earth as written in *"The Alphabet of Ben Sira."* One day Adam desiring to have sexual relations with his mate demanded that she lay down underneath him but Lilith, viewing this position as subordinate, refused. She demanded to know why she should lay beneath when they had both been created as equal. *"Why should I lower myself, surrender my power to you when we have been created equally?"* I imagine her asking. Adam would not have it any other way and neither would Lilith. A huge argument ensued and in this contemptuous, stressful, highly emotional moment, Lilith utters the unspeakable secret name of God, something that was forbidden in the Garden of Eden and she then flies away. Although, there are variant versions that reveal she actually lulled Adam to sleep, enchanted God to reveal his secret powerful name to her and then, she went ahead and uttered it to manifest the wings that would inevitably get her out of the Garden of Eden. Be that as it may, in this power struggle with Adam she uttered the unspeakable, effable name of God, which was not viewed favorably and upon doing this she grew the wings that would allowed her to flee her oppressors and escape from the Garden of Eden. And Lilith flew away from the light of God, paradise and Adam and chose the notorious Red Sea; a place scandalously known for harboring fallen angels, demons and evil spirits. There is a connection at this time between the waters and demons, especially the waters of the Red Sea and it's attraction to malign entities, evil spirits and demons. It is stated that Lilith upon the edge of the Red Sea delighted in numerous sexual relations and she fornicated and took to unbridle promiscuity; having intercourse with a multitude of demons daily and procreating a myriads of children, a race of demons called Lilim. Three days later, Adam finally begs God to bring her back to the Garden of Eden and so God sent three angels to lure and fetch her from the Red Sea. He sent the angels; Senoy, Sansenoy and Semangelof.

When the three angels arrived they found her copulating, indulging in various sexual dalliances with numerous demons and giving birth to many offspring. According to early scripture interpretations, the angels approached her and asked her to return with them to the Garden of Eden and she refused. They threatened to drown her in the Red Sea and she seemed un-moved, almost bothered by their angelic presences and demands. The angels threatened to kill off One Hundred of her very own offspring daily and she retorted she would do the same to any children born to Eve. All of these threats and the presence of these three angels was beginning to bore her and in her efforts to get rid of them, she finally agrees to not kill any future babies that have the inscribed names of the three angels, Senoy, Sansenoy and Semangel, upon them.

> *"..... Let me be for I was created in order to weaken the babes:*
> *if he is a male, I have power over him from the moment of his birth until the eighth day of*
> *his life, that is when he is circumcised and*
> *thereby protected, and if a girl, until the Twentieth day..."*
>
> Pg 224, The Hebrew Goddess by Raphael Patai,-
> Alpha Beta di Ben Sira, ed. Einstein, Otzar Midrashim, pg.47

Interestingly enough, there are other tales found in the Zohar that reveal the first humans created by God were Hemaphrodites or Androgynes, attached to each other by their backside initially. All creations were created in the image of God, according to Biblical scriptures, and thus all contained both male and female attributes, how this later changed, remains a mystery but there is a belief that Lilith was joined with the King of demons (Samuel, Satan or Ashmodai etc..) and they were created in the exact mirror image of Adam and Eve to represent the synchronicity of, as above so below. Adam and Eve were also alleged to be Hemaphrodites or Androgynes and this couple, mirrored Lilith and Samuel but I digress.

As was her custom, Lilith was known to tickle newborns (which explains why babies have these random, spontaneous smiles while they sleep) and she is credited for leading them to their deaths but in this myth she agreed to allow One Hundred of her own demon offspring to be killed daily by God and she makes an oath to not harm any babies that revealed the names of the three angels upon them. Much controversy surrounds Lilith as a SheDemon that kills and even cannibalistically devours children's blood and bones. There was no other way of explaining such horrific tragedies as stillborns and mysterious infant deaths except to blame a demoted deity and contribute to her fabricated, growing negative reputation. Stillbirths, miscarriages, children that mysteriously died in infancy and spontaneous abortions were all attributed to her. A plethora of artifacts found with incantations to her, supplicating her to keep away from newborns, supports this connection.

Returning to the tale of Lilith's manifestation from *"The Alphabet of Ben Sira,"* the angels left Lilith to live in a cave by the Red Sea and now Adam, in the Garden of Eden, required a new mate and here is where the Bible begins its tale. Adam now required a new spouse and from the hidden part of Adam, his rib, Eve was crafted by Yahweh. She was to be more obedient and subservient to Adam, always beneath him, complacent, accommodating and she was to reflect the nurturing maternal attributes that Lilith so lacked. Now here is where we get some conflicting stories because according to one tale, Lilith was matched to the King of demons, Samuel, Satan, Ashmodai, Lucifer but according to other scriptures, God, fearing these two (Lilith and Samuel) would populate the earth with a powerful breed of demons, castrated Samuel, in his effort to control their proliferation of children. And because licentious Lilith was now in need of a sexual partner, she chose to sneak back into the Garden of Eden from time to time to have relations with Adam while he slept, through nocturnal emissions. The conflicting part is that some say Lilith would inevitably return to the Garden of Eden as the Serpent and in her wrath and jealousy, would eventually lead Adam and Eve into sin, by offering them the fruit from the forbidden Tree of Knowledge. There is some text however, that reveals the Serpent was really Samuel/Satan, the King of Demons himself. Samuel, exercising retribution, since his wife was taking on Adam as her nightly lover, he felt justified in now seducing Eve in the same manner. Nonetheless, both Adam and Eve had tasted of the forbidden fruit, from the Tree of Knowledge, according to Biblical lore and as a result there immortality was taken from them. They were expelled from the Garden of Eden, as we all have learned through popular Biblical interpretations.

In his remorse and disgust, Adam vowed 130 years of celibacy and self- imposed punishment, fasting and self -denial. Both he and Eve roamed the earth during this time and according to the numerous mystical writings it was during this 130 year sojourn and because of his sin, that Lilith now had even more access to him. His very sinful nature made him vulnerable to her presence according to the writings of this time. She frequented him nightly, having sexual intercourse with him through nocturnal emissions, aka wet dreams. Eve was not spared of this either, as she too was visited nightly by the King of Demons and was impregnated daily so that she would give birth to half human and half demon, light and dark beings, just as Lilith would give birth to Adam's half demon, half human children. It is believed that through these unions between Lilith and Adam, and Samuel and Eve that the descendants of Cain, Tubal-Cain and his sister Naamah, manifested. It is also believed that when Cain, after Abel's murder, was banished by God, Lilith took him on as her lover and together they too populated the earth with the first demonic vampiric race this is according to these early Kabbalistic writings. Researching these ancient scriptures, it would appear to me that the whole of humanity is somehow connected to Lilith, Adam, Eve and Samuel as direct descendants of both human and demonic lineage.

Even older than *"The Alphabet of Ben Sira"* are the numerous artifacts found displaying Lilith's name, function and revealing how she was truly viewed in ancient time by the Sumerian people. One of the earliest mentions of Lilith is found in 2000B.C.E. on a clay tablet in which we have the Mesopotamian Epic tale of Gilgamesh, Inanna and the Huluppu (Willow) tree.

According to the Gilgamesh epic, Huluppu tree lore, the great Goddess, Queen of Heaven, Inanna, discovered the tree in the sea and brought it to her garden, planting it near the Euphrates River, where she tended to its growth and nurturance. The tree grew nice and strong and one day, lamenting that she did not have a personal throne, she saw the tree as the perfect material to make her divine throne from but when she approached the tree, she learned that it was already inhabited. There was a fierce serpent, a special serpent-dragon that could not be charmed, living at the base of this tree. She also discovered a Zu bird which had built a nest way up above, at the crown of the tree and much to her surprise, the Dark Maiden Lilith, had made her home in the trunk of this Huluppu tree. And these three obstacles sadly prevented Inanna from reclaiming her tree and thus creating her divine throne. In the tale, she calls on Gilgamesh and he's able to chop down this tree with a special Bronze axe and he saves the day by removing all the obstacles and Lilith as a result of this, abandons the tree and flies into the wilderness, the desert. Interesting to note Gilgamesh's father, a Sumerian king was known as a

Lilludemon, a reference to Lilith and her Clan of demons. This epic tale reveals Lilith's early myths and her connection to the Queen of Heaven, as she was sometimes known as Inanna's Hand-maiden and some tales reveal Lilith in "Erecht", as one who gathered men from the streets, with her beauty, to come enter the Goddess Temple for ritual sex offerings.

> *Isaiah 34:14 "The wild –cat shall meet with the jackals and the satyr shall cry to his fellow, Yea, Lilith shall repose there, and find her rest..."*

And here we have one of the only mentions of her name in the bible and it supports the Gilgamesh Huluppu tree Epic, which claims Lilith flew away to live in the desert.

In Nippur Babylonia, modern day Hilla in Iraq, there were many discovered bowl artifacts with carvings and inscriptions referring to her name. These bowls, from about 600 B.C.E., with their inscriptions, revealed how Lilith was viewed by the locals and how her myths still survived outside of academia and the scholastic researcher's domain. Sacred scriptures found in the Zohar and Talmudic writings revealed how the elite and the educated viewed Lilith and her myths but via these excavated artifacts we get a glimpse into the most precious and intimate views on this iconic female figure by the everyday people amidst their residential communities. Many of them had inscriptions, invocations with protective charms and incantations to keep Lilith away and to safeguard their offspring. In Mesopotamia and North Syria, by the eighth century B.C. E., she was clearly already known as a She-Demon in Israel. A 7th century B.C.E, clay tablet found in Northern Syria depicts her as a sphinx with an inscription...

> *"O, flyer in the darkness,*
> *Go away at once, O Lili..."*

pg 222 The Hebrew Goddess, by Raphael Patai.

There is a medieval story preserved in Hebrew and Arabic which tells of a youth who marries the daughter of Ashmodai. He later decides he wants to be free of her and gives her a *"Get"* which is a kind of letter of divorce required back then when one intended to separate from their demonic spouse. Seems strange but this tale supports the notion that demons, in ancient times, married and intermingled with humans. It is quite a curious bizarre tale and reflective of a time when the belief of Demon attachments was so prevalent. The result of this was even more enthralling. As planned, the letter is finally delivered and as documented, the daughter of Ashmodai responds to it with a kiss of death.

Rabbi Joshua Ben Perahia, and the names of other rabbis are invoked several times and found, documented on these excavated Nippur bowls. Rabbi Joshua Ben Perahia, was a first century B.C.E. sage who was believed, by the sixth century CE, to have been a powerful exorcist of demons and often called upon with regards to exorcising a Lilith. First century teacher, Rabbi Hanina stresses the importance for man not to sleep alone in his home, less Lilith gets a hold of him via nocturnal emissions, revealing she is a Goddess men should fear because, remember, it was during Adams' 130 years of solitude and self-imposed punishment that Lilith had her way with him nightly, through these nocturnal emissions. The Rabbi warns men not to sleep alone as it will invite her demonic presence and this caution for Jews still survives to this very day.

Early 14th century Kabbalist writer, Bahya ben Asheribn Halawa, (death-1340) reveals in his biblical commentaries that Lilith was one of four known Mother Demons. Lilith, Naamah, Igrath and Mahalath were the four wives of Esau's divine patron, aka Samuel, Ashmodai, Satan. These four women, each ruled their respective Tequfot (Winter Solstice, Summer Solstice, Vernal Equinox, Autumnal equinox). The writer Halawa also claims King Solomon had rule over them and they were considered his slave-women aka his Liliths, which he manipulated for his personal gains and invoked freely as needed.

Another tale reveals an encounter between the Prophet Elijah, Lilith and her Clan or band. The Prophet Elijah, saw Lilith and asked her where she was going and she boasted that she was going to the house of a woman in the middle of childbirth, Mercada daughter of Donna. *"....to give her the sleep of death and to take her child, which is being born to her, to suck its blood, and to suck the marrow of its bones and to seal its flesh..."* (Page 227 "The Hebrew Goddess" by Raphael Patai.) The prophet then recited a curse to restrain Lilith, *" with a ban from the name Yahweh, Blessed be He, be you restrained, be restrained and Be you like unto a stone....."* and she recites back and asks to be released of the restrained placed upon her and promises not to harm them. Lilith gives a list of her sacred names and her various titles, that if she is called by these names or if she sees these names in print, she will do no harm and she will be rendered powerless. These are the names she recited to him that day; Lilith, Abitar, Abiqar, Amorpho, Hakash, Odam, Kephido, Ailo, Matrota, Abnukta, Shatriha, Kali, Taltui, Kitsha.

Hayyim Vital (1543-1620) a Safed Kabbalist , explains in his writings that there was a fallen angel, known as *"the flame of the revolving sword."* This angel was sometimes referred to as a demon called Lilith and thus it would appear that Lilith and this fallen angel are regarded interchangeably and as being one the same. According to one tale in the Zohar, when Lilith first manifested she sought companionship immediately, and soaring up high she rose to attach herself to the small boy faces of the Cherubim, which she saw surrounding God's throne. When God created man, with Adam, he detached her from the Cherubim and ordered Lilith to descend to earth. Upon seeing Adam with Eve, she felt displaced and immediately sought to return to the Cherubim but by then, they knew what she was up to and barred her from heavens, banishing her to the Sea. *Which begs the question, why is she banished to the Sea? It appears that Biblical scriptures always view the sea as containing evil and water as a place for the uncontrollable, the volatile, evil spirits, and the wicked. Yet water is closely related to the Moon and therefore to Night and somehow Woman has always been linked with these realms. I find this fascinating and it conjures up all kinds of musings, but I digress.*

Visual Depictions:

Lilith has often been depicted in numerous conflicting ways. Some claim she is wind, just a breath, nonhuman in form and yet others depict her as a woman with her lower half enflamed with roaring fires. In connection with one of her totems, the Owl, she is depicted as a screeching Owl, a winged creature in nocturnal flight. She has also been portrayed as a wise calculating Serpent, with a woman's head and a snake's slithering body. As an incubus succubus and Mother of Vampires she has been depicted as an enchanting, blood thirsty vampire. During the age of Enlightenment many artist and poets, like Dante Gabriel Rossetti, romanticized her image, depicting her as an exquisite beautiful misunderstood woman. The 1889, *"La Fille de Lilith"* by Rossetti, tells her tale of retribution. Goethe includes her in *"Walpurgisnacht"* and her likeness appears in Shaw's *"Back to Methuselah"* as well as Thornton Wilder's *"The Skin of Our Teeth."* Writer, Anais Nin, dedicated the Erotic poem, *"Delta of Venus"* to Lilith and there is no question that many stories and images of Lilith have inspired many artist and writers throughout the ages. Depicted in a way that our human eyes can comprehend, an old Babylonian Terra cotta, Burney relief, remains now in a British Museum and here is a visual description of this image of her;

> *"She is slender well shaped, beautiful and nude*
> *with wings and owl feet. She stands erect on two*
> *reclining lions, which are turned away from each other*
> *and are flanked by owls. On her head she wears a cap*
> *embellished by several pairs of horns.*
> *In her hand, she holds a ring and rod combination."*

(Emil G.H. Kraeling, Bulletin of the American Schools of Oriental Research 67
(Oct.1937), pages 16-18)

As an enchantress she is often describes with long flowing red hair, pale skin and red lips and blushing cheeks. Sexually inviting, her beauty is unmatched and she is so captivating that she leads men to their own death. She is often adorned with ornaments as described in the passage below.

> *"Her ornaments for the seduction*
> *of the sons of man are:*
> *her hair is long and red like the rose,*
> *Her cheeks are white and red, from her ears hang six ornaments,*
> *Egyptian Cords and all ornaments*
> *of the land of the East hang from her nape,*
> *Her mouth is set like a narrow door, comely in its décor;*
> *her tongue is sharp like a sword,*
> *her words smooth like oil, her lips red like a rose*
> *and sweetened by all the sweetness of the world.*
> *She is dressed in scarlet and adorned with 40 ornaments less one."*

Raphael Patai's, The Hebrew Goddess, pg 233

Today Lilith is embraced by most modern day Pagans and witches as a Goddess of the Night and Sexual freedom, who initially debuted as a vilified, much feared She-Demon. Lilith is understandably the saboteur of patriarchy, the one who will NOT go with the flow, will not succumb nor lay down to be ruled over. She is the rebellious one who will create her own rules to live by. Demonized by a patriarchal society, Lilith represents the most frightening aspect of femininity. She represents what patriarchy wants to control, rule over and oppress. She can be seen as the hidden subconscious, as she's connected with night, the Moon, and the Moon is connected with waters, emotions, deep hidden emotions of the murky waters. In patriarchal writings, she is classified as a harlot, a vampire, a hag, a witch, an enchantress, seductress, barren one, child killer, insatiable, blood thirsty and most of all misunderstood. She is one with no milk upon her breasts as described in ancient texts and yet, she is also considered the mother of a race of Demons and equally referred to as a maiden in her epithet. She is a virgin archetype - for she belongs to no one and experiences life by her own rules.

Lilith and even Eve, perhaps share in the traits of another deity known as Blodeuwedd, as their most negative attributes seem to have been created by men's vision and fantasy, created to serve patriarchy; to be obedient, subordinate, unrealized, disempowered, sexually confined and restricted, only to serve the master. And yet, both (Lilith and Blodeuwedd) appear to be punished into Owl-hood, banished into the night for their divine awakening and refusal to play by the oppressor's rules. Representing the dark side of the unconscious, the night and the shadow, they become the scariest threat to patriarchy, and must then be ostracized, relegated, demonized into the night. How frightening must it be to a nation of self-proclaim masters to confront the true all-powerful strength of Goddess, reflected in the maiden, mother, crone, the bitch, the harlot, the warrior, the protectress mother, the seductress, sex loving, pleasure seeker, commanding, demanding, sea lover, compassionate, wise, strategic, intelligent, competent, beast lover, cave dweller, howler of the night......in each and every awakened Wombmyn upon this earth.

She is Goddess and she is a model for those who have opened themselves up to their autonomy, great beauty, sexuality and their self-reliant strength. For those who gladly surrender the suffocating chains of complacency and stereotypical female "nice-a-ties" of a life played under the thumbs of patriarchy, she is a powerful force to unearth. Yes, she is a She-Demon, just as todays' powerful, no nonsense, feminist is classified as "the bitch" and both are... in my opinion, **Goddess.** There is no debate, in my mind, whether she is a She-Demon or Goddess, for in Lilith we come to yet another sacred aspect of the Divine Feminine. A thunderstorm, with its massive pouring of rain, can neither be classified as good or bad for in the dry desert she is everything connected to good and in the marshland she is everything connected to bad. Thus, a thunderstorm, much like the Feminine Divine, and all of Nature, is neither good nor bad.... **it just is!!!** And to deny one aspect is to only embrace and comprehend half of Goddess. Hail to you most powerful beautiful Liliatu!!!!

****

LILITH BIBLICAL MUSING
Text Study From, "The King James, Holy Bible American Bible Society (1611)"

GENESIS - CHAPTER 1:26

".....And God said, Let **us** make man in our image, after **our** likeness: and let them have dominion over the fish of the sea, and over the cattle, and over the earth, and over the cattle..."

In these early Abrahamic scriptures we already see a conflicting statement that does not support a monotheistic view of the Divine. The translation states "**Our** image and after **Our** Likeness" suggesting the plural, that God implied more than one, perhaps a female and a male deity (one perplexingly long ignored), if we continue to look deeper at these passages.

GENESIS – CHAPTER 1:27

"So God created man in his own image, in the image of God created he him; **male and female created he them.**"

Again this is a contradictory statement, for woman, is also created and she most certainly is NOT in the image of a Male God...her obvious breast and genitalia makes this most apparent therefore how are we to understand that, in His image, this male God created both man and woman. It becomes clear that something important and logical is missing from this story.

GENESIS - CHAPTER 1:28

" And God blessed **Them** and God said unto **them**, Be fruitful and multiply and replenish the earth and subdue it..."

Two people are present here already; Adam and his partner but she is not Eve! Eve's creation comes later in these scriptures as you will see in Genesis 2:23.

GENESIS - CHAPTER 2:18 "And the Lord God said, It is not good that man should be alone; I will make him a help meet for him."

Yet early on, a reference was made to a woman already having been created by God in Genesis 1:27.

GENESIS - CHAPTER 2:21 "And the Lord God caused a deep sleep to fall upon Adam and he slept; and he took one of his ribs, and closed up the flesh instead thereof."

Adam is put into a deep sleep is not fully explained. We are not told why or how and it is as if there is a big chunk of the story missing, edited out here.

GENESIS - CHAPTER 2:22 "And the rib, which the Lord God had taken from man, made he a woman, and brought her unto the man."

Now we have probably the first reference to Eve, but it is not the first reference of a woman in the early writings of the bible.

GENESIS - CHAPTER 2:23 "And Adam said, This is now bone of my bones and flesh of my flesh; She shall be called woman, because she was taken out of man..."

GENESIS - CHAPTER 2:24 "Therefore shall a man leave his father and **mother** and shall cleave unto his wife; and they shall be one flesh..."

Evidence that early on there is a venerated concept of both father and mother...male and female, yin and yang, therefore where is this mother female figure in the early Abrahamic scriptures?

Isaiah Chapter 34:14-15 "The wild beasts of the desert shall also meet with the wild beasts of the island, and the satyr shall cry to his fellow; the **screech owl** also shall rest there, and find **herself** a place of rest. There shall **the great owl** make her nest, and lay, and hatch, and gather under her shadow: there shall the vultures also be gathered, every one with her mate." Perhaps one of the few allowed encrypted references to the Sumerian Goddess, Lilith.

LILITH GODDESS GATHERING DAY

Purpose: To journey to her cave by the red sea and unearth the wild one within. To awaken your rights to sexual freedom and pleasure, to break the chains of long ago. To escape from the oppression of the Garden of Eden and reclaim your whole autonomy! To reclaim yourself and your womanhood.

Check Ins: We gather around the Circle and introduce ourselves to one another, while also voicing our feelings on this month and our hope for the upcoming season.

Chants: Together we will join our voices to sing some commonly known Pagan chants, as well as new ones offered on the Chant sheet in the hand outs (see the last page of this chapter). Singing aloud is a wonderful way to raise energy effortlessly and it also sometimes helps in creating harmonious bonds.

Our Agreements bylaws and Pertinent group discussion... We go around the circle of women, reading a few lines each of our "Group Agreements" and add any new ones that seem necessary. Agreements are signed and submitted in confidence.

Drumming Grounding: A drumming musical CD track will be played, to give participants a chance to connect and ground to this very moment. Women are invited to find a comfortable seat or stand and add movement if they wish.

Conjuring Goddess via her Image: A photo image of Lilith, either from the Goddess oracle or a scuplture image of the Goddess will be shared around the circle, as each woman present will reflect on the image and state aloud what attributes and Divine messages need expression.

Lecture on the Sumerian Goddess, Lilith
Her myth and various folklores, her attributes and relevance for us today.

GODDESS WORKSHOPS
WORKSHOP I
Exploring her ancient symbols and their meaning
WORKSHOP II
The Snake and Owl as totem animals
WORKSHOP III
Today's Feminism, How do we exemplify our self-empowered self?
WORKSHOP IV
Barreness and fertility workings. Embracing our reproductive choices
WORKSHOP V
Sex Magick ethics and practices in ancient and modern times
WORKSHOP VI
Use of Blood Offerings and Sacrifices in Rituals
WORKSHOP VII
Contemporary and ancient Vampire & Goth Culture
WORKSHOP VIII
Rewriting her myths and reinstalling her in the ancient texts

LILITH GODDESS GATHERING RITUAL

Purpose: To journey to her cave by the red sea and unearth the wild one within. To awaken your rights to sexual freedom and pleasure, to break the chains of long long ago. To escape from the oppression and of the Garden of Eden and reclaim your whole autonomy!

Asperge: Feather and smudge, of sage and copal, at the entrance of our space.
Anointing & Welcoming: Special anointing oil will be offered to every participant upon their forehead as they are welcomed into the space. Drumming Music will playin the background throughout the ritual to set the tone for our day.

INTENT DECLARED: Today we gather to commemorate the season and invoke the liberating energy of the Sumerian Goddess, Lilith.

CIRCLE CASTING (*arms boldly out-stretched wide opens....*)
I cast this circle from my core,
From my spirit I call.. I call,
From above the light I use,
From below I see it bloom,
From the right it swirls across,
Windershin in blue sphere frost,
From the left it joins me now,
Feel the energy swirl around,
Feel the energy Go around (2X)
Go around, go around...

ELEMENTAL INVOCATION
EARTH
All Blessings and Salutations to the Guardians of the North, realm of the Earth.
Richest Black, Fertile and Ripe,
Mineral Rich, Pulsate tonight,
Awaken from my steps,
from my joyful dance to you,
Awaken prosperous Earth,
Come when called to this Sacred Room. **Hail and Welcome Earth!!!**
AIR
All Blessings and Salutations to the Guardians of the East, realm of the Air.
Air the Shifter,
Lightening my weight,
Lift me like the feather,
To fulfill my fate,
Fly me to the realms,
Of the Eagle on high,
Wise all seeing Gifts,
Come when called to my side. **Hail and Welcome Air!!!**
FIRE
All Blessings and Salutations to the Guardians of the South, realm of Fire.
Heat from the Cauldron,
That boils from my wish,
Sparks from Red Embers
Passions to fuel it.
Heat from the Cyclist,
From "Her" well engaged legs,
Heat from the drive
of a "will" to get ahead.
Come burning sphere,
Come when called to this place,

Come Fire's Gift,
Guard and hold our Sacred Space. **Hail and Welcome Fire!!!**
WATER
All Blessings and Salutations to the Guardians of the West, realm of Water.
In Thirst we seek you,
Oh womb waters from ancient times,
To quench us with knowledge,
And melodious rhymes,
To touch upon your wisdom,
And through your Waters, know,
The ebb and flow that brings us,
Your secrets of long ago.
Come when called Gentle flowing rain,
Water guard this Space we've made. **Hail and Welcome Water!!!**

CHANT: *"Mother of Darkness, Mother of Light"*

GODDESS INVOCATION

MEDITATION, TRANCE & RAISING ENERGY *(Drums, dance, cone of Power)*

CHANT: *"My Body is a Living Temple of Love..."*

SPELL WORKING

Lilith is a Goddess who represents Sexual liberation and our freedom from oppressors. In this working we will visit both of these themes, therefore forewarn participants just in case they harbor any serious hangs ups.

Snake crowns will be placed on women's head as they declare themselves daughters of Liliatu
She is the serpent and the screeching owl.
She is the climatic orgasm of sexually aggressive women on top.
We will tap into her energy by creating a collective **cone of power** in her screeching sound. Every participant is encouraged to screech until a high point is eventually felt (it will become very obvious as the room will vibrate). Then silence. Slowly, from deep within everyone's soul, we will go around the room with a murmur...like a primal growl. Then a groan develops and then more moans and sighs and then a full out moaning and giggles. The ritual space should vibrate by now with the sounds of women climaxing. We will move around the room in our own space, with eyes closed and re-create the sounds of woman climaxing, woman enjoying her sexual freedom. As we do this, the sound alone of our neighboring sisters might heat up and awaken our own root chakra, let it. Relish in the freedom, no judgment, as everyone's eyes should be shut. This should appear like an orgy, only without the actual act, just the sounds. Where it will lead? It's up to the participants and the actual energy level manifested,where this will lead, but allow space for this. When the energy begins to wane, Lilith or her Priestess will go to each woman individually speak;

"I offer you the fruit that will free you
of those who only want to oppress and chain you to illusions
and the Garden of Eden.
Bite of this apple /pomegranate if you are ready to
embark on this journey upon my wings..."
(women feed off the apple and then begin singing....)

Chant: *"Mother I feel you under my feet, Mother I feel your Heartbeat..."*

Final Check ins

<u>DEVOKING GODDESS</u>

DEVOKING ELEMENTS
WATER
Hail Guardians of the West, Realm of Water,
For Gratitude and the gifts we've received
Sacred Water the Quencher of our thirst,
In Peace, may you now leave....
Hail and Farewell Water!!!
FIRE
Hail Guardians of the South, Realm of Fire,
For Gratitude and the gifts we've received
Sacred Fire the Enflamer of our hearts
In Peace, may you now leave....
Hail and Farewell, Fire!!!
AIR
Hail Guardians of the East, Realm of Air,
For Gratitude and the gifts we've received
Sacred Air the Shifterof our realm
In Peace, may you now leave....
Hail and Farewell, Air!!!
EARTH
Hail Guardians of the North, Realm of Earth,
For Gratitude and the gifts we've received
Sacred Earth the Transformer in our lives
In Peace, may you now leave....
Hail and Farewell, Earth!!!

CHANT: *"We all come form the Goddess..."*

OPEN CIRCLE:
Our Circle is open but never unbroken,
may the love and peace of the Goddess
be forever in our hearts,
Merry meet, merry part
and merry meet again....

CAKES AND ALES/POTLUCK FEASTING

INVOCATION

INVOKING LILITH....

Temptress Snake, Eve Awakener,
Coiled inside every Womb.
Dark aspect unearth,
Deep within me, she must be searched,
She who makes up her own rules...

Because you would not lay underneath,
Refused to play the role of the weak
Angered Adam in pursuit of equality,
You garnered a reputation unfairly bequeath.

Misunderstood Lilith,
Labeled Demon and ill,
Goddess, You were first created
And your name is worshipped still.

First of the Feminist,
Demanding Equal respect,
Sexually free, fierce and strong,
Nocturnal and independent.

They said you thrived
on Blood of babes,
And Men, in dreams,
aroused with your gaze.

Oh Beautiful Lilith,
Insatiable and free,
Herein this ritual,
I call upon thee....

Hail and Welcome Lilith.....

SPELLS

PERSONAL CALL TO SUMERIAN DEMON GODDESS

Lilith, he's failed me, in frustration I cry.
He won't keep it up, long enough to satisfy.
He has purposefully frustrated and denied me my right...
As if to slowly drain the maiden joys from my sight,
"She" whom I once so cherished
And championed so close to my heart.
Slowly draining my youth, inner joys, self -esteem,
Unrecognizable worth, tearing me apart.

Lilith insatiable, strong one,
I have been treated unequally and wronged,
Starved of true love and intimacy,
Placed in this wretched realm of Complacency,
Whilst trapped, in a role I was assured would fit,
But it doesn't and extract me from my will and my gifts.
It strangles me and has cut off my divine Voice,
The constant loneliness, neglected hungry loins.

Dearest Goddess of the Anger and the Rage,
Can you see Eve needs you as the Awakener,
To rescue, balance and encircle her.
Wings of liberation, Claws to dig your heel,
Refusing mistreatment,
Breaking the oppressive Wheel.
Slithering Magick, Crown of the Night,
Hooting in Delight, for Retribution is your right.

Ancient Sumerian, First of the First,
Deep beautiful One, the awakener of what is fair,
Hear my stifled, nightly sobs,
And strip them of their quiet meekness,
Strip then and exposed them as the roars of a Lioness,
Fed up with wrongs done unto her for far too long,
Let these tears I cry silently,
Now become the roars and actions of Goddess,
Who will no longer take shit from the Adams of this world!!!
Help me climb over the Oppressive walls of this lie,
This dangerous illusion called Eden,
And awaken me to a vastly larger realm
Outside this sanctimonious jail.

Snake woman, offer me the Pomegranate,
That I may be enlightened to Your Divine truths,
YOURS and MINE...
Lilith, I call you,
Manifest and make the path from me to you,
For a better role, than the one I am in,
Never again, deceived into this prison den.
Awaken, she of action,
Seeker, finder, insatiable one, quencher,
Independent, courageous, joy awakener,

Pleasure, wellbeing and self- confidence are my rights,
As "Womyn" first created!!!
Let it Be So, onward from this Night!!!

LILITH'S VISIT IN A SNAKE DREAM

In this dream I remember seeing many different people on a line that was roped off, like a big Hollywood red carpet gala and I was among the many waiting on line. My friend G. was doing an academic study on pornography and I saw her taking notes on her clip board in a rather studious manner, while on this line. I stood there with her, among a group of people, just standing around waiting to get into this important event. I suppose we were all waiting for our turn to get admitted into this movie-like theater. I think there was a sort of mentor near me as well; talking and making light bawdy jokes. Then I noticed further down the line or in another room far off in the distance there was a snake in there. I sensed it and lo and behold it was true and I needed to see it for myself.

People nearby were being very helpful to me as I tried to grab the snake and I think the snake represented something troubling, unbalanced, not sure, but when I grabbed it, it was severed; missing its head and with lots of pieces of its skin torn. Snakes are about transformations, renewals, death and rebirth and thus, this image did not concern me as I considered the beautiful, regenerative attributes I love so much about snakes. It seemed normal to me at the time. In the Dream, I was not threatened by the snake and thus I had no fears or concern that it would hurt me, especially when in real life I loooooove snakes. Imagine my complete astonishment when I sat down carelessly carrying on a conversation, I turned to move her from one hand to the next without looking and this severed snake, without a head, still managed to attack me!!! I was so taken aback and her bite was so shockingly painful....even without a head. How???? I asked myself, stunned. How could that have happened to me?

Even without a head, severed body parts and in a state of presumed weakness, this snake was still able to inflict great pain on me and the most hurtful part is that I was just not expecting that reaction from one of my beloved totems. She bites me on my arm and it was harsh, both on an emotional and physical level. In the dream, my reaction to the bite was one of awakening and duly noting my personal error in this incident. I did not fault the snake, for she was being a primal animal in my opinion. I faulted myself for being so careless.

Afterwards, upon awakening, I spent hours meditating on this dream and the spiritual message it was offering me. As I started to have this emotional break through, I found myself crying. I knew... I understood.

The broken, the regenerative, can still impose much pain. Growth will cause you much pain but it is necessary to keep yourself awake and alert about your inner and outer environments. I was not alert at that pivotal moment when I got bit by the snake. I was talking to someone else and not paying any attention to the precious snake in my hands and I subconsciously assumed, that because it was broken and did not have a head, it did not have the power to hurt me ... but it did... it still did! I had my guards down and underestimated the power of its abilities to strike and yet, without a head, without a mouth, it still managed to inflict great pain on me.

Is it symbolic of me needing to not be complacent or naïve, but to be fully awake and realize that growth, and transformation is never painless. The snake, with its regenerative powers is warning me, Lilith is warning me. She is letting me know; *"....you are about to go through a transformation, a major re-birth. Do not enter this naively but be aware and alert to the attacks and the bites that will come your way as a result of your metamorphosis, as you begin shedding the old and growing new skin. You need to be more alert of the pain and conflict that might ensue as a result...."*

At the time, I was struggling with my role as wife and mother, author, artist and entrepreneur. I was finding it very challenging to tend to my personal needs, professional goals and spiritually growth, and yet... be true to myself and my family. I found myself resenting being a wife and for a brief moment, painfully questioning myself as a mother, as well. I was beginning to feel Lilith, scrawling within me, demanding that I abandoned the heavy chains of sacrifice, I felt so heavily placed upon me. I felt the Sumerian Goddess slithering, hissing with demands that I wake up, fiercely empowered to finally place myself, first and foremost before anyone, as a top priority and yet, this inner calling and demand, from my inner Goddess, conflicted with the role I was being forced to play in my household. The last eleven years found me as a stay at home mom, sacrificing myself and my personal ambitions all the while birthing and lovingly caring for my three beautiful boys but the tides were changing. The youngest now finally entering school inaugurated a different phase for me. I knew I was at a very delicate, pivotal cross-road in my life and I felt, not only scared but overwhelmed with the unknown journey before me. This dream clearly spoke to me of the transformation I would inevitably undergo and the pain and shocking discomfort it would bring, if I entered the journey complacently without vigilance and attentiveness.

When I woke up, I felt the loving embrace and guidance from my ancestors and spiritual teachers speak. Whether as a Deity or as a sacred totem like the snake, I listened fully with my heart. There was a powerful message that needed to get to me on this night and without fail my dreams always serve as an important vehicle for spiritual messages. I am blessed. In moments of doubt and insecurity, in the dream, as is in real life, I found comfort knowing that my spirit guides are never far from me and the snake is a most powerful totem and guide with much to teach me. Blessed Be!!!

EMBRACING ALL OF HER ASPECTS

A while back I came across a Goddess Chat group online in which the women that had gathered there had started a conversation regarding the prevalent modern day images of the Feminine Divine. And most of these women expressed great discomfort with, what they felt were, modern day images of the Goddess as being youth oriented, overly sexualized and to use their exact word, "bimbo-ish." A lot of the women voicing their strong opinions were admittedly older and they expressed a strong distaste for these new popular "sexy" images cropping up in various media genres. Many also confessed a lifelong connection to Crone archetypes and their complete aversion with their Goddess as young or overtly sexualized. I read the numerous posts that came in on the subject, some rather fervently expressing their personal truths. A lot of back and forth replies for weeks within this chat group, as these women were expressing their angst and frustrations, feeling as if their Goddess spirituality was being tainted. Some admitted the image that they have of themselves clashed with these new images being put out there by mainstream society. Many, feeling that these new images of Goddess conflicted with *"real life women"* and some explaining that most Goddess oriented women would **not** identify with these young, overly sexualized Goddess images.

The more I read each post, the more shockingly distressing I felt. I understood all too well the conflict among my Sisters in this chat group as I have witnessed and experienced, first hand, the pain felt when we are not embraced or when we feel marginalized. There are many various instances when we can experience this marginalization apart from this one present issue being discussed here. But what I saw and perceived in these posts was the ostracized, ostracizing, the misunderstood, not caring to understand and the hurt, inadvertently causing hurt.

Here was a group of women, my favorite kind; Goddess Women, and in their online bantering they were going against a very significant tenet in Women Spirituality; the belief in inclusivity, embracing all, empowering all women and encompassing, *"She of over Ten-thousand names."* I am writing about this experience because I sense it is not an issue exclusive to internet chat groups, but one I have observed and battled with among my Sisters, in real life. I am writing about this because it is a pertinent issue for those of us seeking to evolve, heal and advocate our gender's progress through Feminism and Goddess Spirituality.

What makes us different from mainstream religions likes Christianity, is our intolerance for patriarchal practices that, since the beginning of time, have been based on "dividing and conquering." Yet among this respected group of Goddess women I uncomfortably intuited a familiar form of prejudice that very much resembled the patriarchal practices we eschewed. The practice of championing one face or one aspect of Goddess and demeaning another is akin to patriarchal tenet of "conquering and diving..." To only embrace the aspect of Goddess you best understand, while degrading the other side you don't, is a disservice to our gender and our unique Spirituality. We are not fully embracing Goddess when we only champion our beloved, well understood parts of her. She is not meant to be loved fragmented, no more than you are.

In your most significant, fulfilling relationships you feel fully known, understood and embraced in all your many guises; when you are happy, depressed, when you are enraged or distress, when you are lusty or frigid, emotional or cerebral. Relationships in which we feel wholeheartedly embraced are the most cathartic for us and thus, this also carries into, not only our relationship with our human partners, but with our spiritual, and that includes the Feminine Divine. I certainly would not want to be in a relationship with someone who only expresses love for me when I am happy, skinny, stable or when I am being fully ambitious and succeeding. I would question the authenticity of my relationship and I suppose, in my rather protective nature of Goddess Spirituality, I shudder to think we are doing this as well. To embrace only one aspect of Goddess is to love only half of her and to do this has far reaching implications on how we also embrace ourselves and our sisters in community.

I think it perturbed me most because in Goddess Spirituality we're supposed to be accepting and embracing of ALL of her, not just bits and pieces or fragmented parts of her but the whole. And yet what I witness, ironically, was not uncommon to hear among groups of women. I have seen and heard it best when an athletic woman degrades and comments negatively on plus size women and just as often, when a curvaceous woman comments or degrades lean, skinny women but this is just one tiny example from the plethora of ways our gender contributes to painfully detrimental patriarchal practices. This exercise of demeaning or devaluing what seems foreign to us, or what appears vastly different, is a form of bullying that can rear its ugly head, yes, in blatant way, but also in the most subtle of ways that can be just as effectively detrimental. If I am a crone only embracing Hekate in my Goddess Spirituality, while degrading or devaluing the importance of the maiden huntress, Artemis, then I am essentially only worshipping half of the Divine, for she is **All**. If I, as a three hundred pound woman, cannot understand or connect with Lilith and I only declare Gaia as Goddess, then I am essentially only worshipping half of the Divine, for she is **All**. If I, as a Goddess woman, exalt the compassionate Kwan Yin but devalue and reproach the blood thirsty Kali or Sekhmet, then I am essentially only worshipping half of the Divine, for she is **All**. The very fact that most deities in my research exemplify multiple aspects within one Goddess is proof that she is multidimensional. She is not meant to be worshipped in bits and parts, she is meant to be fully integrated, embraced; both those aspects we know and love and those aspects of her we find challenging, mysterious and abhorrent.

Goddess is multidimensional. I think the Hindu culture represents it best when they exalt the Feminine Divine as being multi aspected and beholding all; the Mother, the wife, the maiden, the crone, the warrior, the light and dark, etc. For me to embrace one face of the Goddess (whether that face is Crone, Maiden or Mother, Light or Dark Deity) and not the other, is like cutting off one leg in favor of the other. Both legs are needed to stand in truth, to stand balanced. Just because you don't understand one aspect of Goddess and you refuse to acknowledge it in your spiritual practice, does not mean it has no validity. Even when we sadly make prejudicial decisions in life and choose to connect only with like-minded people, it does not eradicate the fact that we live in a world brimming with a diversity of human beings. Therefore our inability to accept Goddess fully, in her many guises, does not alter the fact that she exist in these numerous divergent, incomprehensible ways.

If there's anything I've learned in my research of the Feminine Divine is that she is not just one face, she encompasses all. And to view her as one dimension is to fail to fully see her. She is not just compassionate Buddhist deity, Kwan Yin, or Harvest Goddess Demeter, she is the old frightening bony Hag in Baba Yaga. She is not just frolicking maiden, Artemis, but also proliferating, multiplying, fertile mother earth, Gaia. She is not just crone, Hekate, but also pleasure seeking Aphrodite and Hathor. She is not just saintly Hestia but also overly sexualized, demon depicted, Lilith as well as bloodthirsty Kali Ma and Sekhmet. To embrace Goddess is to embrace **all** of her, not just snippets or an aspect of her you solely identify with. For she is not just that snippet that you can identify with, she is much more. And the problem begins when we try to make her into this "one" aspect and thrust, an injurious monotheistic tenet into an ancient, polytheistic view. In this very act we are not doing anything better than what the rest of society is doing with its patriarchal hues, we are adding to the problems our gender faces. When we do this, we are not only dividing and fragmenting Goddess but we are dividing and fragmenting ourselves.

The same way we fragment the Feminine Divine, we then subconsciously begin to fragment our own gender. When we only embrace one image of the Feminine Divine we sadly carry that belief into how we interact with our sisters. And it reveals itself when we only accept one type of woman as the true representation of our gender. As modern women, in particular, we are so much more multidimensional than our predecessors and this is thankfully, part of what Feminism birthed. Collectively we represent the many faces of the Goddess. In our modern day society we have a plethora of women that are tall, short, skinny, curvaceous, athletic.... Some that are reserved and some that are combative. Women in the military, huntresses, politicians, women raising families at home and some opting not to, women who choose to have children and some women who choose not to, married women and single ones by choice. Whether short haired or long, our gender in the 21ᵗʰ century is incredibly multidimensional and she reflects the Great Feminine Divine. When you champion one image of Goddess you are in a sense championing only one image of woman and that is a huge disservice to womankind.

There is a young aspect to the Goddess, the maiden, and she is just as significant as the crone. There is a dark aspect to Goddess and it is no less valuable than the light or sexually charged aspect of a Love Goddess. What I want to stress here is that Earth base religions advocate inclusivity. It is the one thing that makes us so different and more palatable for women than mainstream religions. When we reflect one aspect of the Goddess we are reflecting our preference for one aspect of woman. We must be ever mindful that how we view Goddess, is oftentimes how we view our sisters. If you are viewing Goddess as one dimension you are probably viewing our gender as one dimension as well. Our Goddess spirituality is not supposed to divide and conquer but unify. When we reject one aspect of Goddess, it is as if we're rejecting one aspect of woman and thus one aspect of ourselves...

What I had hoped to say to these women in the online Goddess chat group was that, it is better to find out why an aspect of Goddess is challenging you. It is better to ask yourself why you are opposed to one aspect and what does it have to teach you? I find it is always best to seek knowledge with regards to what irks us. The same is true about different cultures. The culture that you fear the most, the race or culture that turns your stomach is probably the one that in the end will bring you to the brink of enlightenment and growth. Learning and opening your heart to the unknown is the only way we can grow and be enlightened. The pool of ignorance, which is where prejudice and racism dwells in, is based in a refusal to learn and understand. A lot of women come to Goddess spirituality after many years of Christian conditioning and being indoctrinated in patriarchally based tenets. And many of the views, ideas and practices still permeate their lives. They've changed the name of their religion and affiliations but they are still, sadly, practicing the same prejudices and destructive ideologies against women kind. Goddess is all; what we embrace and understand and what we cannot, to disregard it has the stench of patriarchy. Just because we're not comfortable with one aspect of Goddess does not mean we can dismiss it as irrelevant. Most of us probably do not delight in the taste of blood, like Sekhmet and Kali, yet we cannot simply eradicate this aspect of the Goddess because we fail to comprehend it. This is as much a part of her as any other.

Claiming one aspect of Goddess while degrading another, in my humble opinion, is painfully damaging and plagues our gender and our spirituality with hints of patriarchy. When you claim one aspect and demean or trivialize the other it can, in a sense, have the potential to subtly, yet devastatingly, form itself as bullying and it is no different than the destructive tenets of Christianity. Our spirituality prides itself in being embracing, all inclusive, not dogmatic and rigid in its view of the Divine. When we claim one view or one aspect of her and not the other, we fail to see the brilliance of our multidimensional Goddess.

LILITH GODDESS GATHERING CHANT TEXT SHEET

SNAKE WOMAN By Michelle Mays from her music CD, "FireLeap, a Collection of Chants."
Snake woman, Beginning again,
Shaping, changing,
Renewing her skin
 Snake woman, Shedding her skin,
 Shaping, changing,
 Renewing, again.
The spiral of life keeps changing
It spins and turns rearranging.
 For everything there is a season,
 For everything there is a reason.

SPIRIT OF THE WIND (Traditional) From Music CD, "She Changes Moving Breath"
Spirit of the wind, carry me
Spirit of the wind, carry me home
Spirit of the wind, carry me home to myself.
Spirit of the ocean, depth of emotion
Spirit of the sea, set myself free
Spirit of the rain, wash away my pain
Spirit of the storm, help me be reborn
Spirit of the sun, warm light healing me,
Spirit of the sky spread my wings and fly.

*Mother of Darkness
Mother of Darkness
Mother of Light
Earth Beneath the Soul in flight
Songs of love and Love of life
Guide us to our heart.....

MY BODY
My Body is a living Temple of Love
My Body is a living Temple of Love
My Body is the Body of a Goddess (3X)
(lower)My Body is the Body of a Goddess

AFFIRMATIONS words by Valerie Girard From Music CD, "She Changes Moving Breath"
I am a powerful woman, I am- I am a powerful woman, I am
I connect with myself in everything
I am a powerful woman, I am
 I am a passionate woman, I am, I am a passionate woman, I am
 I express myself with power and love, I am a passionate woman, I am
I am a feeling woman, I am, I am a feeling woman, I am,
I accept all the things expressing through me,I am a feeling woman, I am,
 I am a loving woman, I am, I am a loving woman, I am,
 I love myself in everyone, I am a loving woman, I am,
I am divine woman, I am I am divine woman, I am,
The Goddess is fully awake in me, I am divine woman, I am...

MAIDEN MOTHER AND CRONE by Abbi Spinner
Smiling Virgin, shinning crescent,
Waxing fullness,
Luminescent
Sickle of Silver, reaper of Bones
Maiden Mother and Crone, Maiden Mother and Crone

CHAPTER EIGHT

Dantor

"I must not fear. Fear is the mind killer, fear is the little death that brings total obliteration. I will face my fears. I will permit it to pass over me and through me. And when it has gone pass, I will turn the inner eye to see its path where the fear has gone, there will be nothing, only I will remain…" *Frank Herbert, Dune, Bene Gesserit, Litany against Fear.*

DANTOR

DANTOR

Erzulie Dantor

Mama Dantor as Black Madonna of Czestochowa

"Each Time a Woman stands up for herself, without knowing it, without claiming it, she stands up for all women…" Maya Angelou

ERZULIE-DANTOR ALTAR SET UP
OUR ALTAR

__Altar cloth__: *Blue, plaid or Denim trimmed around the altar cloth is suggested for Erzulie-Dantor. As a Petwo Lwa, Red is her known color and thus, a red altar cloth is suggested but also dark blue, resembling denim.*

__Image:__ *The image of the dark Voodoo lwa, Erzulie-Dantor, is commonly viewed as the Black Madonna. Any sculpture of the African Santa Barbara, or the Black Madonna of Czestochowa is acceptable for an altar to Mama Dantor. You may also use a beautiful image or sculpture of a dark, African woman or warrior.*

__Always present on the altar__;
A silver pentacle, a cast iron cauldron, drums, speaking stick, wand, athame, elemental representations.....

__Air:__ *feather bundles, angel wings, bird, eagle or owl statuaries. Bell &, chimes, Incense type sticks, cones, charcoal brisket and fine powdered herbs; frankincense, myrrh.*
__Fire__: *pillar candles, glass enclosed candles in reds, gold and blues*
__Water:__ *Small glass bowl with Water and or chalice with Champagne, Cranberry Juice or Red wine.*
__Earth:__ *Incorporate lots of green fresh plants and flowers. Create a beautiful center piece and offer a small dish of soil or dry herbs can also be used*

Other items pertinent to this particular gathering
Red cord,
Handmade dolls
Daggers and machete,
Symbolisms of hearts
Heart veve illustration
Small wood box shrines that will be made into traveling altar boxes
Denim overalls
Head kerchief
Images of Mothers holding their children
Symbolism of black pigs
Sea Shells
Haiti's flag

__Sacred objects from members:__
__Notes:__

MONTH & SEASON

July

The astrological sign for the month of July is Cancer, the Crab. Cancer is ruled by the watery, feminine, intuitive powers of the Moon (June 21-July 20) and this is an energy that will be experienced throughout the month.   July is the seventh month of the Gregorian calendar, but in the Roman calendar, it was the fifth month and was known by its Latin name, "*Quintilis*," meaning fifth. Some speculate the month was probably named after the Roman ruler, Julius Ceasar around 46BC.

The Full moon was often called Blessing Moon, for indeed we feel the blessings of the Goddess, during this time of year, through the Earth's fertile transformation. Last month, we celebrated the height of the sun's power on the Summer Solstice at Midsummer and the solar energy of Fire continues to be prevalent this month. With this fiery, combustible energy felt everywhere, there are also the occasional lightning and massive thunderstorms. Together, we see how, fire and water influence the energy of July. According to the Farmer's Almanac, it is this reason why the Native Americans called June's full moon, the Thunder Moon.

The Chinese were the first to invent fireworks. With the combination of sulfur, charcoal and saltpeter, placed in bamboo pieces, and then set aflame, they created one of the most important ingredients to the customs of our U.S.A. holiday of Independence. Originally however, these colorful, loud fireworks were meant to drive evil away, but by the middle of the sixteenth century they were being used as a form of entertainment by many Europeans. It is therefore not surprising that upon migrating to the United States, many immigrants brought their traditions, like firework, with them to the new land.

With Independence Day celebrated through-out the U.S.A. on July 4th, this is undoubtedly a time of spectacular fireworks, both figuratively and literally and there is much warmth found among friends, family and community. Picnics and barbecues amongst loved ones are not that uncommon and travels to short and long distant locales are also prevalent. Romantic cavorting and liaisons permeate the warm breezes, perhaps indebted to the shorter outfits and the lack of heavy clothing covering us all up. There is a light casualness to July that encourages one to relax and enjoy all of nature.

July, is notorious for wrapping us in its warm bright light and conjuring up suppressed inner joys and childhood nostalgia. Warm days on sandy beaches, roller skating, bike riding, Frisbee playing, with so many of our activities taking us outdoor, nature indeed beckons you to stop, look and adore her at every angle. Much like November, there are a great many opportunities for lots of family gatherings and get together among friends. The warm sun during this month is inviting and because we find ourselves outdoors, we might seem to be more in tuned with the elements, fae and nature spirits. The waters at our beaches and lakes, the gentle breezes that inaugurates our cooler evening hours, all help to connect us more to the elements. And the moon and the stars garner our love and admiration, when we turn our attention towards the heavens to enjoy the fireworks on the 4th of July. Our connection to the earth is magnified even more, simply by sitting near a lush, full tree and as we survey the bright scenery of green grass and colorful flowers, which by now have bloomed everywhere.

In some parts of the world the heat is unquestionably strong now as we find ourselves smack in the middle of summer. The sun reminds us that fire is emanating from within and all around us. We are in the throes of the Summer season and the Goddess is adorned in her passionate, finest greenery. Enjoy this moment and the magick it affords to you as we are approaching the month of August, and, subsequently, our first Harvest.
This month, we will find ourselves inviting the Voodoo lwa, Goddess Erzulie-Dantor.

All Monthly intro text taken from author's first book,
"Gathering for Goddess, A Complete Manual for Priestessing Women's Circles"

DANTOR GODDESS LESSON

"As the spirit of light in darkness she comes to break the chains of those
who live in the prison of unconsciousness and
restores them to their true home...

"The Cult of the Black Virgin, by Ean Begg." Page 134,

DANTOR (ERZULIE-DANTOR)

Erzulie-Dantor is part of an assemblage of powerful iconic Voodoo Lwa, known as Erzulies. They are lwa, also known as Mysteres, that dedicate themselves to the realm of love, sex and the arts. There are numerous Erzulies in Haitian Voodoo but for the time being we will focus on Erzulie-Dantor and occasionally make mention of her sister Erzulie-Freda who is very much a part of her history and folklore.

In Voodoo, the Lwa, spirits, Gods, (and forgive me for I will tend to use these term interchangeably, as I address lwa as Gods and mean no disrespect by doing this. I understand the Lwa in Voodoo are viewed as mysteres and living spirits and since this too is my definition of Goddess and Gods I will often use the term in regards to lwa.) The lwa are divided into nanchons (nations) or groups. There are several Voodoo nanchons like the Ghede, Nago, Djab and the two we'll speak about here are the Rada Lwa and the Petwo or Petro Lwa. Some make the mistake of viewing these two nanchons as good and evil or light and dark but (according to author and Houngan, Kevin Filan) it is probably most effective to view them as Hot and Cold spirits or pantheons.

The Rada, which contains the lwa; Erzulie-Freda, La Sirene, Atibon Legba, Dambhala Wedo, Agwe Tawayo are considered cold, balanced, stable and beneficent. They are sometimes related to royalty and are familiar in nature. Their lineage is traced to West Africa; sometimes Dahomey, which is now considered Benin, Africa. The Petwo Lwa are considered hot, spicy, volatile, warrior-like, and become aggressive and quick to take actions. They are connected to military and also foreigners. Erzulie-Dantor, Ogou, Maynette and Ti-Jean lwa fall under this nanchons. Red is their color and there is no question of their mars-like intensity. They are even honored on a day ruled by Mars, Tuesday. The Petwo lwa's origins are found in some parts of Africa, like the Congo, and the New World (Americas), which is why so many of them retain some of their slavery attributes. Erzulie Dantor's origins would therefore be linked to Africa but more obvious is her connection to the new World, in Haiti.

Erzulie Dantor (Dantor, Danto, Ezili-Danthor, Ezili-Dantor etc...) is embraced as the Patron Lwa/Goddess of New Orleans and the one who protects the newly initiated Priest/Priestess (Mambo and Houngan) in Voodoo. She is also considered to be a part of the Orthodox practice of Voodoo. She is a Warrioress and fierce Mother and protectress of women and children. As a Lwa of the Petwo type, she is so strong and aggressive, sometimes even feared for her boldness, that some have even labeled her as a lwa from the "Djab", which translates as Devilish or connected with sorcery and magick. Others can view this reference to her as simply that she is a fierce lwa/Goddess, who exemplifies the "bitch" and is not one to be trifled with or approached haphazardly. She is known to exercise retribution when supplicated by her worshippers and she is a great defender of those women who have been abused or betrayed by their lover.

Erzulie Dantor's manifestation is linked and attributed to a very important historical period in Haitian history, as has been documented by numerous sources. It is believed that the Haitian Revolution began with Erzulie Dantor's manifestation at a Voodoo ceremony taking place in Bwa Cayman (Bois Cainman), Cainman Forest in 1871. There are some minor conflicting tales regarding the details of this night, for some say it was the spirit of Ogou that manifested, but a more popularly accepted belief among Voodoo practitioners is that Dantor was the spirit that made herself known on that fateful night.

At this particular time in Haiti there was much political unrest, resentment and anger among the citizens of the French Colony, known then as Saint-Domingue before the revolution. The land was one full of riches; producing sugar, coffee, cocoa, tobacco, indigo, cotton, sisal, fruits and vegetable to its mother land, France. Although it was a rich, fertile land, it was France and its greedy royalty that was benefitting distastefully due to Slavery. Citizens of Saint-Domingue were white, European, black African slaves, mulattoes, maroons (escaped slave blacks), free blacks, white slave owners as well as blacks and there was a lot of anguish and hostilities towards Europe's control on this rich land and its multi-raced people. It is important to note that the French Revolution (1789) and the dethroning of Marie Antoinette and Louis XVI must have also influenced this capricious, turbulent period in Haitian history.

These were unpredictably volatile and unstable times. Many Haitian slaves of African descent were being abused and even killed by their masters without any retribution or just consequence. There was mounting frustration, anger and resentment by the growing number of Blacks who were actually beginning to outnumber white citizens. It would not take much effort to push something that was clearly already on the edge of transpiring. Although the Haitian Revolution is documented as occurring from 1791 till 1804, its inception clearly began much earlier, but one particular documented event, catapulted Haiti's metamorphosis and eventual liberation.

Many disgruntled citizens; blacks, African descendants, slaves and maroons, were already gathering regularly trying to organize themselves but with little success. The evening of August 14, 1791, a Petwo lwa Voodoo ceremony was taking place at Bois Caiman, (Alligator woods) led by the maroon Houngan, Dutty Boukman. At this particular ceremony a priestess drew dawn the spirit of Erzulie-Dantor and as Dantor rode her serviteur she took her favorite form of offering, a Black pig, slit its throat and proceeded to have all participants drink of its blood, while simultaneously inciting courage and the warrior's confidence to these otherwise oppressed citizens of Saint-Domingue. Most present at this ceremony were of African descent, brutally suffering at the hands of European enslavement and Erzulie-Dantor ridding her serviteur rallied them to fight...fight for their freedom, fight for their humanity, banish the French and establish for themselves, the "Free Black Republic of Haiti." Thus, a week later, on August 21st, 1791, the Haitian Revolution had begun with unspeakable acts of courage and violence, massive killings, incineration of Haiti's lush land and a horrific revolution that would last for thirteen years before Haiti could declare itself the victor and finally free of France. It is only the second colony, next to the U.S.A. that was able to successfully free itself from the tyrannical, oppressive restraints and enslavement of a European country and its connection to Erzulie-Dantor is considerably monumental. Dantor can be seen as the liberator and mother of the "Free Black Republic of Haiti."

*"...Wisdom has always cried on the rooftops or at the street corners,
and the spirit of this world always punishes those who buy her wares.
The great age of the Black Virgin is the 12th century, but the legends about her
hark back to the dawn of Christianity, the dynasty of the Merovingians
and the age of Charlemagne..."*

The Cult of the Black Virgin, by Ean Begg" Page 133

www.webster.edu/-corbetre/haiti/history/revolution/revolution1.htm,

http://www.travelinghaiti.com/history_of_haiti/slave_rebellion.asp, http://wikipedia.org/wiki/Haitian_Revolution

The Revolution is also attributed to Dantor being mute. There are two different stories explaining how she became a mute. One claims that her own people cut out her tongue in fear that she would divulge their secrets if caught, captured and tortured to speak up by the enemy and it was a necessary sacrifice to protect and maintain their spiritual practices. Others say that she was indeed a victim of the Revolution and that the opposition caught her and she was brutally tortured by these soldiers. They mutilated her by chopping off her tongue for being a part of that ceremony and instigating this civil war. The "Ke, ke, ke, ke, ke, ke, ke," clicking of her tongue is the only sound you'll hear from her when she rides her serviteur nowadays in Voodoo rites. She is also known to spit out and vomit blood from her mouth, when she is in possession of her horse, her serviteur. This can be quite frightening for the uninitiated to witness but there is an explanation for it.

According to one Haitian Lore, Dantor was a savvy Business woman who actually sold Black Pigs (native to Haiti) at the marketplace in Port-Au-Prince. One day, she was attacked by a man and legend has it she was stabbed seven times, which is why you will find references to her being stabbed seven times in many of her songs, invocations and poetry. There is also a belief that her spitting or vomiting of blood is, again, related to the torture she underwent by the hands of the French. For each of the seven stabs she endured by the hands of her captors, she spat blood at them.

**Set kout kouto, set kout pwenya,
Prete m dedin a pou m al vomi sang mwen,
Set kout kouto, set kout pwenya,
Prete m dedin a pou m al vomi sang mwen,
Sang mwen ape koule.**

**Seven stabs of the knife, seven stabs of the dagger,
Lend me the basin, so I can vomit my blood,
Seven stabs of the knife, seven stabs of the dagger,
Lend me the basin, so I can vomit my blood,
My blood is pouring down...**

This very revealing and well known Haitian song is about the Petwo lwa, Dantor and it is included in VoodooMystic's website page created by Bon Mambo Racine Sans Bout Sa Te La Daginen as well as the Book, "Mama Lola: A Vodou Priestess in Brooklyn," by Karen McCarthy Brown, University of California, 2001

Despite the numerous tragedies surrounding her manifestation and her life, she is far from being a victim and instead is worshipped as someone who exemplifies strength and opens the gateway to our own inner strength and endurance capabilities. She awakens in us the fighter, the warrioress, the survivor that she herself is. In such an impoverished country, where daily living presents so many obstacles and challenges to ones very own precious livelihood, Erzulie-Dantor is a remarkable lwa/Goddess of fierce hope, determination and strength. Many say that she is a mystere who will fight for you with all her heart and soul and that she doesn't require much in exchange, unlike other lwa. She only requires that you not pity yourself and crawl away in fear but rather, to take action when action is needed and value yourself enough to fight... fight for what is yours... just as she incited Haitians to fight for their country and re-claim it as theirs. She want you to embrace your worth and take action. She is a fierce mother, a warrioress and protectress, who is particularly protective of all women and children; especially women who have been raped, violated and abused by men and single mothers trying to provide for their children.

Impoverished conditions in Haiti requires many men to travel far to find work, sometimes even forced to leave the country (going to U.S.A. and adjoining country Dominican Republic) to find ways to generate income. This creates a society brimming with numerous abandoned wives (or mates, as actual marriage ceremonies were not as popular, nor necessary in Haiti). This creates a society filled with single mothers left alone with their children, having to find a way to carry on and feed their kids during their father's absence. Erzulie-Dantor is therefore one who is very sympathetic to the struggles of woman, especially financial and she is quite moved to defend women and become invested in women's issues, especially those unique issues plaguing mothers and their children in today's day and age.

Erzulie-Dantor herself is known to have seven children. One of her daughter's "Anais," is her personal translator and interpreter since she is mute and Anais is revealed being carried in her mother's arms, holding a book, in a very popular Black Madonna depiction. Erzulie-Dantor also has a son, named Ti-Jan with one of her spouses, Ti-Jean. And some within Voodoo make her and her husband, Ti-Jean, the beloved respective mother and Father of the Petwo Lwa nation. She actually had two known husbands, however, they were Simbi Makaya (a Magician) and Ti-Jean (the Herbal magician). Baron Samedi the Lord of the dead and cemeteries and Ogou, the warrior, are also two other lovers, Erzulie-Dantor is often linked with.

Some say she is a Patron Goddess of Lesbians, though there is no mention of her being one, except that she is very bold, strong, aggressive and, again, exclusively very sympathetic to women's struggles and issues. I suppose these can be viewed as the perfect marker for a Goddess embraced by the Lesbian community, but certainly it is not a requirement to worship her.

In contrast to her sister Erzulie-Freda, Erzulie-Dantor is not as Frilly in pink, ultra feminine nor romantics of sorts. She is a warrior Goddess, lwa, mystere, who concerns herself with survival, strength, passion, sex , and the empowerment of women. You will find her dressed, not in the pink lace Chantilly that her Sister Erzulie-Freda donnes, but in the blue denim dresses (known as karabel in Haiti) of the common folks. She will also sport on her head a calico "moushwa" (headscarf) or a red handkerchief and always carries a dagger, as she has a great passion for knives, swords and daggers. Any altar dedicated to her would not be complete without displaying some sort of dagger for her.

Images of Erzulie-Dantor always reveal her cheeks scarred with two slashes, also known as "Twa mark" (three marks) even though only two slashes are visible. There are some conflicting stories behind these noticeable brutal scars on her face. Some say they are probably just indicative of the common sacred scarification that identifies certain African tribes and these scars might connect her to her roots in the Congo. Others note how similar these scars are to the warrior face painting that most indigenous tribes, like the Tainos, would wear prior to going into battle and since she is a warrioress this makes perfect sense. However, a more common explanation for these scars can be found in Haitian folklore that would also explain the rivalry between her sister, Erzulie-Freda.

According to one lore, Erzulie-Dantor and Erzulie-Freda both fell head over heels in love with the charismatic warrior Lwa, Ogou. These scars are the result of an intense fight where Erzulie-Dantor took her dagger and stabbed her sister through the heart (which explains Freda's popular image as the Mater Delarosa) and Erzulie-Freda in turn then took her dagger and slashed her sister's face a few times. This fight would also explain why many Voodoo Priest, Houngan/Mambo stress the importance of having separate peristyle (ritual spaces or rooms) for these two powerful lwa. It is not wise to serve or worship these two Sisters together, as they do not get along and your wanga (magick) will suffer as a result, according to Voodoo practitioners. Their respective Veve are also reflective of this connection with swords and daggers and the heart. One of Dantor's veve is a Heart with two daggers piercing through it.

Regarding the origins of the scars there is also a legend related to the original icon of the Black Madonna of Czestochowa, which is one of the most popular depictions of Erzulie-Dantor. It is alleged that a while back, in Poland, where this venerated icon was maintained, vandals caused damaged to the face of the painting of the Black Madonna and it resulted in these noticeable slashes upon the holy image of her right cheek. Despite numerous restorations the scars would always miraculously reappear and so to this day, when her image is reinterpreted and recreated authentically, those slashes are always revealed for they are a part of her lore and history.

While Erzulie Freda is often depicted as white or light skinned, Dantor, however, was often depicted darker; either as a mulatto woman or black, as in the numerous Black Madonnas, found scattered through-out history. Commonly accepted images of her can be found in the Mater Salvatoris, Our Lady of Perpetual Help, Santa Barbara Africana, Our Lady of Mount Carmel and Our Lady of Czestochowa. Erzulie Dantor as a patron Lwa of New Orleans is also connected to Our Lady of Lourdes, since she too, is patron saint of New Orleans in the U.S.A. There are some lore that also connects her to heavy rainstorms, hurricanes and natural disasters and this is slightly reminiscent of the Orisha, Oya, worshipped in Santeria.

The Black Madonna of Our Lady of Czestochowa is a beloved image often associated with Erzulie-Dantor. It reveals a dark skinned woman dressed in a dark blue robe, crowned as the Virgin Mary along with her child. She is holding her baby who has a book in her left arm. This image of the Virgin holding baby Jesus is believed to be Erzulie-Dantor with her daughter, not the baby Jesus so evangelized by Christians. And this image has been highly venerated in Poland since the late 1300's. Perhaps this holy image arrived to Haiti's shores when Polish soldiers came to fight with and against the French, alongside with the Haitians during the Revolution. Haitians immediately recognized in this image their beloved Lwa, mama Dantor.

*"It is, however, no longer shocking, to suggest that the images
represent a continuation of Pagan Goddess- worship,
and that some may have once been idol concentrated to Isis or other deities.
It is also undeniable that a remarkably high proportion
of Madonnas over 200 years old, that are credited
with miraculous powers, are Black,
as are the traditional patronesses of nations provinces and cities."*

"The Cult of The Black Virgin, by Ean Begg" Page 130

*August 15th is the Asumption day-The Virgin Mary is celebrated and
July 16th is Erzulie-Dantor's Feast Day
The Black Madonna of Czestochowa's feast day is on August 26th*

The origins of this famous icon are mysterious but according to several sources the Byzantine icon was originally painted by St. Luke the Evangelist, who lived during the same time period as the Christian, Virgin Mary. He painted her likeness on a cypress table top alleged to have been owned by the holy family and handcrafted by Jesus himself when he was a carpenter and an apprentice to St. Joseph.

Research reveals that the icon was kept hidden in Jerusalem by the disciples during the Roman's reign, fearing it would be destroyed but around 326 A.D. the icon was found again by St. Helena, mother of Constantine the Great, who took it to Constantinople. She then either gives it to her son or delivers it herself to Constantinople, where a special shrine is built for it among several other relics. It eventually went through various different owners and was housed by many, including the prince of Ladislaus of Opole. When his fortress was invaded by Tartars and their arrows had pierced and damaged the throat region of the painting, he sought to save and preserve it immediately. Some even claim he was guided by angels in dreams to have the precious icon safely sent to Czestochowa, Poland. He surrendered the painting to the Pauline monks and had it moved to Czestochowa, where it arrived in August of 1382 and remains to this day in Jasna Gora (translated as Bright hills). In 1383 the Jasna Gora monastery was created by Pauline monks, who had originally hailed from Hungary, and had been invited to create this special monastery by Wladyslaw, Duke of Opole.

In 1430, when the church of Czestochowa was invaded by looters, although many sources claims it was the Hussites that ransacked the Pauline monastery where the holy icon was being stored, the painting received more damage. The thieves ended up slashing the cheek region on this painting twice and there is a well- known folklore that tells of the severe punishment they experienced as they tried to steal this icon and further damage it with an unsuccessful third slash. According to popular folklore, the robbers fell to the ground, writhe in severe agony and quickly met their death. Another legend tells that the painting of the Madonna started to bleed actual blood at the place where the gashes had been executed. It was enough to scare the robbers and eventually spread the word of her great powers.

The icon, so often associated with Erzulie-Dantor, has garnered a reputation throughout the centuries for performing all kinds of miracles. To this day people make holy pilgrimages to visit and view this icon reputed to answer prayers and bring about all kinds of documented miracles.

In 1656, after frightening the Saracens from invading the land, Poland finally declared the Black Madonna as their Queen. In a ceremony held at the Cathedral of Lviv, the Black Madonna was there finally crowned and formally declared as Queen protectress of Poland, on April 1, 1656, by the King of Poland, Jan Kazimiertz.

(I don't know the original author of this poem to the Black Madonna but it fits perfectly for Dantor....It was attained from http://www.Marypages.com/Czestochowa)

The Song; Black Madonna,

There is a recess on this earth,
Where everybody wants to come back,
Where reigns Her face,
On the face – two cut scratches,
Eyesight has sorrowful, anxious,
Like She wanted to ask you,
You to entrust yourself to Her Protection.

Madonna, Black Madonna,
How it is good to be Your child,
O, allow, Black Madonna,
To be hidden in Your arms.

In Her arms you will find peace
And you will be protected from evil,
Because for all of Her children,
She has loving heart and she will protect you,
When you give Her your heart,
When you will repeat these words:

Madonna, Black Madonna,
How it is good to be Your child,
O allow, Black Madonna,
To be hidden in Your arms.

Today, when trouble is around us,
Where a person can hide herself,
Where a person should go,
If not to the Mother, who will give consolation.
So, we are beseeching , O, Madonna,
Direct eyesight on Your children
And hear, when we are singing , asking you:

Madonna, Black Madonna,
How it is good to be your child,
O allow, Black Madonna,
To be hidden in Your arms.

From; www.catholicculture.org/culture/library/view.cfm?recnun2996, www.marypages.com/czestochowa.htm, www.Czestochowa.pl/welcome and www.jasnagora.com,

www.enwikipedia.org/wiki/Black_Madonna _of Czestochowa.

Her Worship, Offerings and Altar Set Up

Serving Erzulie-Dantor is quite simple as she is a Lwa that welcomes her vodouisant/worshippers and, unlike her sister Ezulie-Freda, who loves all things pink, her preferred colors are Navy Blue and Gold or yellow. Sometimes red is added because, after all, she is a Petwo Lwa. Her colors reflect her beloved connection to the Revolution and to Haiti's independence and thus, she shares in their flag color of blue, red and gold. And because she is a hot Petwo lwa, it is suggested to first begin all workings for her with a goblet of cool water to keep her from getting too hot. An altar decorated with her sacred colors, via various altar cloths, flowers, candles, even the food (like the icing on a cake offering) can display her favorite colors. Practitioners of Voodoo spare no expense when it comes to their exquisite altars and rites and they really lay out ostentatious spreads for their lwas. Erzulie Dantor's altars should have daggers as these are sacred to her, as well as maraccas or calabash, dolls and silver jewelry, as this is her preferred metal of choice. She also enjoys the perfume Reve D'Or and Kleren or Aguardiente. And of course, no Voodoo altar would be complete without some Florida water on hand, as this is reputed to bring on spiritual possessions.

Food offerings, which are an important part of Voodoo rites, are also offered to Erzulie-Dantor. She is particularly fond of cane liquor, sweet potatoes and among her preferred offerings are the Griyo (fried pork). She loves unfiltered cigarettes grilled pork, rice, red or black beans. Cakes, with blue and yellow frostings, would also be appropriate on an altar dedicated to her. Black pigs are incorporated in rituals to her in Haiti, perhaps due to her folklore connection to this animal and the tales surrounding that infamous Voodoo Rite that started the Haitian Revolution. She is also noted for appreciating the offering of a spicy Haitian Dish made with marinated fried Pork cubes. Other common offerings to her are pan fried corn with pepper, fried bananas, black rice made with mushroom (also known as Riz Djon-Djon). And of course, serve her rum, red wine or honey with cinnamon and pepper, for as you can see, a hot Petwo lwa requires hot spicy food offerings. Brown Grain Breads can be used in place of animal offerings if you are a vegan and opposed to these meat offerings according author and Houngan, Kevin Filan and Sallie Ann Glassman but I feel it's best to respect the culture and their lore and serve the lwa what they would appreciate regardless of your own personal dietary preferences.

When preparing your food offerings for the Lwa it is suggested to first lift up the food (or food dish) over your head in a sign of offering, then lower it to your lips, breathe on the actual food, pouring your essences over it. Then elevate it to your forehead, then to your heart chakra and finally to your root chakra or pubic region to bless it. Next, one should pour three drops of crème de cacao on the ground and then place your food offerings to Erzulie-Dantor and verbalize your gift to her. Light your Voodoo candles around these food offerings. Allow your offering to surround your Voodoo candles and let it melt over it, burning all night if possible. The next day gather all remnants and these should be disposed of at a crossroad or wilderness, where hopefully it will not be disturbed by humans and will become compost for the earth.

Interesting to note, early Voodoo ceremonies allowed food offerings to be given to the animals whose blood would eventually be sacrificed to the Gods. This prepared and consecrated the animals for the Divine.

To begin your Voodoo rite to Erzulie-Dantor, begin by calling on your highest Divine deity. Most in Voodoo will begin by reciting the Lords'prayer (the Our Father) and the Hail Mary. Afterwards, as no lwa can cross the threshold into this realm without the help of Legba, the guardian of the Crossroads, you would be wise to invoke him and respectfully ask him to open the gates so that spiritual communion may take place. Be sincere in your petition and present an offering to him on the earth. Papa Legba will open the gates and allow for divine interaction to bless your rite from this moment onward.

The center of the peristyle (the Voodoo ritual room) holds a large erect pole at the very center. It is considered a Divine axis, the sacred pole, which is reminiscent of the ancient Canaanite Asherah, this center pole is the axis. It is through this pole that heaven and earth meet and we can begin to have access to the spirits/Lwa, for it is believed they travel through this pole to grace worshippers (vodouisants) with their presence. Spiritual possession, which is a common occurrence in Voodoo, is encouraged and very much a part of all Voodoo rites.

Erzulie Dantor, as a patron and protectress of those first initiated into Voodoo, is often invoked during a Kanzo, this is a special Petwo rite of initiation. She is also the patron of the "paket," which is a special power object made under the guidance of the Hougan/Mambo for the newly initiated Voodoo Priest/Priestess. "Bat guerre" or "Bat Ge" is the ceremony that comes before the initiation or Kanzo Ritual and it is the opening ceremony of a Voodoo initiation rite. All these rites fall under her domain as a Petwo Lwa and this also includes the creation of the "paket."

Other Rituals for Erzulie Dantor

For a Voodoo money ritual, a website called "Roots without End" suggests putting your candle within a boiled sweet potato, pour Crème de Cacao and let it burn. It is also suggested to offer frenetic dances to Dantor, as she greatly appreciates movement and dance as a form of worship. There is another simple ritual incorporating a request to the Warrioress lwa, written on a sheet of blue and gold decorated paper. Fold this paper with your written wishes and then, with your dagger or special knife, stab it seven times in her name and declare your wish done!

Musing

Erzulie-Dantor exemplifies for us the spirit of the true protectress and fierce warrior. She elevates the spirit of humanity with inspiration and confidence to go into battle, wherever those battles may be; whether in a country facing turmoil and fighting for its independence or in the privacy of ones' home, while asserting liberties and basic human rights. Her validity and importance for us today, is just as relevant as it was centuries ago and yet, her aggressive, "hot" energy is so often feared by women who have yet to unearth this aspect within themselves, electing to stay in a state of complacency.

Some may fear her but remember she is a fierce protective mother, first and foremost, to her vodouisant and worshippers, who so often even endearingly refer to her as Mama Dantor. Consider the nature of a Mama bear with her cub, consider your own interactions with those you most love and cherish, what wouldn't you do for them....?

Approach her with this view as a protectress mama bear and you will see your fears turn into reverence, great love and appreciation for someone so is lovingly invested in your own wellbeing. You are her cub. She would rather bestow to you magickal abilities and wealth but not the lavish, superfluous riches that her sister Freda is so often connected with. She rather bestow to those who serve her, the many opportunities to create riches of all kinds, through jobs and other means. Dantor opens the way to help you make your own fortunes and resolve challenges in unexpected fashion. In this way, she is lwa, and yes a Goddess, who opens the way to reveal opportunities, strength, courage and confidence to do more than survive but to thrive in pursuit of your most cherished goals.

"Our ancient, battered, much –loved, little –understood, Black Virgins
are a still-living archetypal image that lies at the heart
of our civilization and has a message for us.
The Feminine Principle is not a theory but real and it has a will of its
own which we ignore at our peril..."

The Cult of the Black Virgin, Ean Begg page 134

DANTOR GODDESS GATHERING DAY

Purpose: To unearth to mama bear within ourselves. To encounter mama Dantor, protectress of women and children and inspirer of great change. To awaken the spirit of the revolutionist and defender of our passionate cause. What requires our fierce commitment and determination now?

Check Ins: We gather around the Circle and introduce ourselves to one another, while also voicing our feelings on this month and our hope for the upcoming season.

Chants: Together we will join our voices to sing some commonly known Pagan chants, as well as new ones offered on the Chant sheet in the hand outs (see the last page of this chapter). Singing aloud is a wonderful way to raise energy effortlessly and it also sometimes helps in creating harmonious bonds.

Our Agreements bylaws and Pertinent group discussion... We go around the circle of women, reading a few lines each of our "Group Agreements" and add any new ones that seem necessary. Agreements are signed and submitted in confidence.

Drumming Grounding: A drumming musical CD track will be played, to give participants a chance to connect and ground to this very moment. Women are invited to find a comfortable seat or stand and add movement if they wish.

CHECK INS: Consider for a moment the Voodoo Lwa, Dantor. Reflect meditatively on her image found in the Goddess Oracle, Icon of the Black Madonna or any other images you have available and begin to invoke her by stating aloud the images that reveal themselves.

Lecture on the Voodoo Lwa, Erzulie Dantor
Her myth and various folklores, her attributes and relevance for us today.

GODDESS WORKSHOPS
WORKSHOP I
Cloth Voodoo Doll creation and an artistic rendering of her Heart Veve on canvas.
WORKSHOP II
Incorporating Denim and plaid in our magick creations; a blessed moushwa Headscarf
WORKSHOP III
Crafting a small shrine or Travel altar with a simple box and art supply
WORKSHOP IV
The occult practice and creation of Protection spells
WORKSHOP V
A discussion on Possession throughout religious history and a special aspecting workshop
WORKSHOP VI
Heart object Crafting; with clay, textile, paper mache or any other creative art medium.
WORKSHOP VII
Creating florida water or Spicy honey rum elixir
WORKSHOP VIII
Discussing Haitian history and political turbulence and committing ourselves to sending support in whichever way seems most appropriate.
WORKSHOP IX
Creating a special Women's shelter charity project, to contribute and help abused women.

DANTOR GODDESS GATHERING RITUAL

Purpose: To unearth mama bear within ourselves. To encounter mama Dantor, protectress of women and children and inspirer of great change. To awaken the spirit of the revolutionist and defender of our passionate cause. What requires our fierce commitment and determination now?

Asperge: sweep away negativity with a smudge bundle of sage and copal.
Anointing & Welcoming: use a CD track of African drumming to be heard throughout the entire rite
INTENT DECLARED: to honor the Voodoo Lwa Erzulie-Dantor and connect with her spirit

CIRCLE CASTING *(with Crystal wand and words....)*
From East to West this circle is Cast,
Below, above, only good can pass.
I call upon good spirits and Gods,
To shield this circle and be our Guard.

Invoking Elements
Earth
We call upon the spirit of the earth, honored realm of the north.
Listen to our words as we invite you to this rite.
Dark is the soil holding the mysteries of life and death. Earth the transformer holding bones of those no longer dead. Ancestors realm, breathing strong ever still...earth the transformer I call you by word and will. Guard and hold this sacred space. Keep us safe in this rite today. **Hail and Welcome Earth!!!**
Air
We call upon the spirit of air, honored realm of the east.
Listen to our words as we invite you to this rite
Air, the machetes, that cut through deceit, severing ties that no longer serve me. Air with its powers to pierce and defend, sharp as a razor, I call your element. Guard and hold this sacred space. Keep us safe in this rite today. **Hail and Welcome Air!!!**
Fire
We call upon the spirit of fire, honored realm of the south.
Listen to our words as we invite you to this rite
Fire that burns in a Warrior's heart, burn and inspire us to start. Scorching within, sparking our steps, dancing with spirits, in their fires we're safely kept. Guard and hold this sacred space. Keep us safe in this rite today. **Hail and Welcome Fire!!!**
Water
We call upon the spirit of water, honor the realm of the west.
Listen to our words as we invite you to this rite
Sacred Waters, I call you to this rite, lend your gifts of love and light. Healing gifts from tears and sighs, ebb and flow gently by my side. Guard and hold this sacred space. Keep us safe in this rite today. **Hail and Welcome Water!!!**

INVOKING PAPA LEGBA
LWA/GODDESS INVOCATION

CHANT: *"Mother of Darkness, Mother of Light"* and chanting simply her name....

MEDITATION, TRANCE & RAISING ENERGY *(Drums, dance, cone of Power)*

SPELL WORKING I
Every participant will create a special personal Heart Veve to the Voodoo Lwa Dantor. As it is being designed and painted we will collectively envision our ancestresses and all women and children being free and protected from harm.

SPELL WORKING II

The next part of our spell involves connecting with the technique of aspecting. To aspect is to embody the Divine and in this exercise each participant will reflect on the many aspects and attributes of Mama Dantor and relate it back to ourself. For example; one woman might stand up and say, *"I am a single mother, I am Erzulie-Dantor."* Another might say, *"I am a fighter for women's rights; I am Erzulie-Dantor,"* or *"I am a faithful sister, I am Erzulie-Dantor."* Someone else might say, *"I am a mother, fighting for my kids education, I am Erzulie-Dantor..."* Every person will state an attribute of Erzulie-Dantor they visibly can see and personally identify with. After each statement every person will put their dagger or athame through their Veve as a symbol of our pact. It is done! "So mote it be," is stated to end the working. We begin to sing around our veve.

CHANT: *"Eight Beads Chants"* & *"Voodoo Chant"*

Final Check Ins

DEVOKING LWA/GODDESS
DEVOKING PAPA LEGBA

DEVOKING QUARTERS
Water
Spirit of water honored realm of the west
we exalt you and give thanks to thee.
Water's gift felt by all today, guardian of our sacred space. Receive our gratitude as we bid thee adieu, hail and farewell to you. **Hail and Farewell, Water!**

Fire
Spirit of fire, honored realm of the south,
we exalt you and give thanks to thee.
Fire's gift felt by all today, guardian of our sacred space. Receive our gratitude as we bid thee adieu, hail and farewell to you. **Hail and Farewell, Fire!**

Air
Spirit of air, honored realm of the east,
we exalt you and give thanks to thee.
Air's gift felt by all today, guardian of our sacred space. Receive our gratitude as we bid thee adieu, hail and farewell to you. **Hail and Farewell, Air!**

Earth
Spirit of earth, honored realm of the north,
we exalt you and give thanks to thee.
Earth's gift felt by all today, guardian of our sacred space. Receive our gratitude as we bid thee adieu, hail and farewell to you. **Hail and Farewell, Earth!**
CHANT: *"Do you remember when God was a Woman...."*

OPEN CIRCLE:
Our Circle is open but never unbroken,
may the love and peace of the Goddess
rest forever in our hearts,
Merry meet, merry part
and merry meet again....

CAKES AND ALES/POTLUCK FEASTING

RELEASING THE OBSTRUCTING SHADOW MEDITATION

You are invited now to find a comfortable position. You may sit or lay down, whatever feels most appropriate for you at this moment. Take a deep breath, hold it for one second and then release it. Do this two more times, with each consecutive breath expanding your lungs more and more, as you take in more breath on your inhalation. With each inhalation feel your life force awaken and alive, survey your body and make note of how this feels. (pause)

Now exhale and continue to release stressors with each exhalation. Breathe and exhale audibly again (pause). With the sound of my voice breathe and again, release all worries or concerns with each exhalation. Follow my voice, if you will, and, rest assure, you are safe throughout this journey. You may go as far as you feel comfortable or simply stay put, follow your soul's calling as it will never lead you astray.

Turn around and in your mind's eyes see a glass enclosed room. See yourself in the middle of this room, inside. It could be a room you're familiar with or a completely brand new room, but nonetheless you are safe and comfortable here. Stand in the middle of this circular glass room; walk around it, no one is around you at this moment. Make note, if you can, the room's décor and what objects are near. These might be reflective of what's important to you at this moment, or the objects might represent different aspects of yourself. For example; a desk or a computer, if you're a writer; a large art canvas or paint brushes, if you're an artist; ballet slippers if you're a ballerina; photos of yourself when you felt most authentically at your best or a special outfit, if you're an aspiring designer...These are just some examples to help you journey easier into this place and into this special moment -for indeed, any time we pause to reflect and connect **it is** a special moment. Continue to look around the room, breathe and remember your newly charged awaken life force elevated with just your simple breath. Breathe and make note of what you see.... (pause)

Now walk around the room to find an entryway. Yes, you have been enclosed in this room, with glass walls but now you must find which one will lead you out. Press your hands on these special glass walls and feel which one will lead you outside. There is someplace you are obligated to go and see... (pause) Find the door, step outside of this doorway now. Leave your prized possessions. Leave the object that represents you in that room and walk away, walk away trusting that it will be safe in this room. (pause)

A pathway opens up to you and leads you out of this room and into a nearby clearing. Make note of the tall swaying trees, the verdant lush grass and the scattering pockets of colors from the local flowers in season. Breathe in this vision, as this is a calming, serene place for you. Allow yourself to get absorbed in the beauty of nature and the life force pulsating all around you. Breathe...

See butterflies swirling around you and feel the overall sense of peace emanating from you at this very moment. You have connected with your vision of this landscape; now engage your auditory senses. **What sounds are adding to your comfort level and what sounds are pleasing you at this moment? Do you detect the hint of any unusual sounds?** (pause)

A rustling is heard among the trees, possibly a bird but you're not entirely sure, follow it to discover its source. Follow the rustling sound and see if you can delineate what or who is disturbing your peace at this moment.... The rustling is getting louder and more distracting. Who is causing this rustling sound? Follow the disturbing rustling sound as it gets louder and louder, the sound seemingly bouncing from behind one tall large tree to the next. Let the source of this rustling be someone or something in your life causing you discomfort.... know that you are safe in pursuing the source of this disturbing sound and you are safe, if you should decide to confront it. For now, it is only a sound and you continue to follow it. Breathe (pause)

Unbeknownst to you, the sound leads you, via a different way, right back to the entryway of that glass room, the circular glass room that commenced this journey...the same room that holds a representation of you and what is most important to you at this time. You now can see the rustling sound is attached to a Shadow, a human form and it will not let you pass the entryway, inside the room.

Stand back calmly to witness this rustling turn fully into this shadow, the human form of someone or something that blocks you of your gifts. Remember you are safe and no harm can come to you during this meditation. Breathe....

You boldly step forward, but the shadow will not let you re-enter the room. It is blocking the entryway to this room. Breathe.... You explain why you must re-enter and what's so important awaiting you inside his glass room. The shadow appears uninterested in what you are saying and appears to almost make its noise louder. Breathe... (pause) Explain to it again why you must go back into this room and why you must reclaim **your gifts**.... Pause for a moment to assess and witness what it will do next? (pause)

Fatigued, you finally ask it, **"What do you want from me?" "Why do you block me from what is truly important to me?" "Why won't you let me through, to reclaim what is my very own unique gifts?" "Why do you block me?" "Why won't you let me just be...me..?"** Breathe... (Pause) wait for the ominous Shadow's answers if any are uttered.... Listen carefully. (pause)

Recollect now a time in your past when you most utilized your precious talents and gifts and make an energy medicine ball from these memories and present it as light to the obstructing black Shadow. Watch how this medicine ball of light, holding your memories, weakens the shadow. (pause)

Again, recollect another time in your past or present when you most utilized your precious talents and gifts. Remember how you felt then and every detail of this moment. Again, make an energy medicine ball from these memories and present it as light to the obstructing dark shadow. Watch how your memories weaken the obstructing shadow, as half of it seems like vapors now. (pause)

Now, envision your future, yes... look deep into the forth coming future... See yourself excited and best utilizing your most precious talents and gifts, tapping into your authentic YOU. **What are you engaged in?**
What talents are you displaying?
How do you feel? (pause)

Stay with this feeling if it's as positive as I suspect it will be and then, make another energy medicine ball from this projection and present it as piercing light to the obstructing shadow. This last medicine ball ERADICATES THE SHADOW

COMPLETELY, as it vaporizes into ether, unblocking your entryway. Breathe now... (pause) Exhale and breathe as you are now free to enter this room once more.

Walk around your glass room once more, make note, if you can, the room's décor again and locate your beloved objects. Locate reflections of what's important to you at this moment, the objects that represent different aspects of yourself, your Divine talented self. Walk back to what's important to you... (pause) back to parts of you, back to those things that best represent you.... (pause) Gather, if you can, all these representations and aspects of your divine self within your arms and take them into your hand, both hands, cup them tenderly and now place them carefully within your heart chakra... tuck them in safely. These are part of you. They are always within you. Your talents and gifts are a part of you and no one can take them away from you, not even obstructing black Shadow, no, not when you hold dear the memories, past experiences and future projections of utilizing them and connecting with your true self.

Hold tight to what makes you, You.... Hold dear all the opportunities; past , present and future that allows you to remember and engage your most important gifts and talents.... (pause) Breathe..... and exhale.... (pause) Now take your gifts and all parts of yourself and turn around. Follow my voice as you continue to breathe and exhale.... Close your eyes as you remember how good it felt to reclaim yourself and now watch the glass walls slowly disappear. One by one, the barriers disappear and this room no longer has walls, nor boundaries. It is open and free. Walk out now, liberated. Follow my voice as it leads you back to this room. Breathe...and exhale. Follow my voice as I count from ten to one, backwards to help you return to this room. Breathe... 10, 9 peace and content, remember, you. 8, 7 Breathe, happy and aware. 6,5 Breathe and exhale with gratitude hold your gifts. 4, 3 Breathe in peace and confidence 2, **You are.** ....1.

Welcome back. Join us back into this time and space, back to this room, slowly open your eyes. Breathe and exhale. Give your body a gentle stretch and slowly when you feel ready, rise up. If you need more time, that's okay and if you need some assistance, please raise your arms so that someone may come to assist you in grounding.

INVOCATION

LEGBA

Legba, Dearest Papa Legba,
Gate Opener,
I call you now
to make a path
for me and lwa to meet at last.
To converge and meet
And share this rite
Like old friends,
by your will, let us meet and unite.

DANTOR

Mama Dantor, beloved Petwo lwa,
Fighter of injustice
Protectress of all Mamas
Warrior Spirit,
Revolutionizing lives
Fierce defender, I call you by my side.

By the Blood of Black pigs
By the blood from your stabs
By the blood of Haiti's children,
Who were left without Dads...

For the strength of our gender
And the rise from our souls,
Dantor, I call you now,
accept my offerings in these bowls.

Silver and Knives
Black Dolls and hearts
I serve you Dantor
With these offerings,
may we start.

Hear this call
and stand by my side,
"Ke..Ke..Ke..! " songs from your lips
As Anais speaks for your mind.

Mother, protectress
Fuel me with your gifts
Help me attain
the wishes on my list.... _____*(write your request to her on a piece of paper)*

SPELLS

POPPET CASTING OUT MALADIES

Maladies that plague me,
Cease to be,
Exit from my body,
Illness and disease.

Lose their strength,
Now weakening,
Spirit of good health
Retrieved and stirring.

Fainting with the waning moon,
All disease and plaguing wounds,
I release you herein,
And say my goodbyes,
Let good health now,
Be by my side.

With this poppet of herb and blue,
I am reborn, healthy
And spiritually renewed...

> By powers of **Air-**
> I blow you away and release you
>
> By powers of **Fire** –
> I burn you maladies out of existence
>
> By powers of **Water** –
> I drown you and wash you away
>
> By powers of **Earth** –
> I bury you, illness, like a corpse, bury to your end
>
> By powers of **Air** –
> I fumigate you now, renewed, to good health.

And by all the elemental forces that exist
By the powers of magick and the ancestors, I enlist.
By the Fae and the spirit of immortal ones,
And by my will and word,
It is now completely done!!!!

BANISHMENTS OF ILLNESS

Into this black candle before me,
I banish and contain all maladies,
With waning moon and melted wax,
Lwa/Goddess tend to what I ask.

Herein lies the pain of solitude,
Illness,
Inertia,
A mind that's confused,

Stricken with all kinds of needs,
Plagued with senseless poverty,
Let this wick absorb these things,
So that new life may now begin.

Joys and money,
Energy and health,
Courage to embrace,
My transformative self.

Able to turn all wrongs into right,
Banish the obstacles,
That have plagued my sight,

And by the light of this burning flame,
I burn and banish these things I name;

      I banish_____
      I banish_____
      I banish_____(repeat)

DANTOR GODDESS GATHERING CHANT TEXT SHEET

EIGHT BEADS CHANTS by Carolyn Hillyer
Girlseed
Bloodflower
(dip it)Fruitmother
Spinmother,
(raise it) Midwoman
Earthcrone
Stonecrone
Bone

***Mother of Darkness
Mother of Darkness
Mother of Light
Earth Beneath the Soul in flight
Songs of love and Love of life
Guide us to our heart.....

THE RIVER IS FLOWING
The river is flowing, flowing and growing,
The river She is flowing, Down to the Sea.
Mother carry me; your child I will always be.
Mother carry me down to the Sea.
The Moon she is changing, waxing and waning,
The Moon She is changing, high, above me,
Sister, challenge me, your child I'll forever be,
Sister, wait for me, till I am free. *By Diana Hildebrand-Hull*

SYSTER RIVER, GIVER
From Victorian Christian's creation , Elijah The band of Light
Syster, River, Giver...Returning Whole,
Syster, River, Giver...Returning Whole
      Open up, To receive
      We are what we Believe. *(REPEAT)*
      Syster, River, Giver...Returning Whole (2X),
Growing Roots like the Trees,
Wee are planting seeds. *(REPEAT)*
Syster, River, Giver...Returning Whole (2X),
      Stored in Deep, Stories Sleep,
      Within Us, These Tales we Keep. *(REPEAT)*
      Syster, River, Giver...Returning Whole,
      Syster, River, Giver...Returning Whole,

MY BODY
My Body is a living Temple of Love
My Body is a living Temple of Love
My Body is the Body of a Goddess (3X)
(lower)My Body is the Body of a Goddess

BORN OF WATERS
Born of Waters,
Cleansing Powerful.
Healing , Changing,
We are...   *by Starhawk*

THE OCEAN
The Ocean is the beginning of the world
The Ocean is the beginning of the world
All life comes from the sea
All life comes from the sea.
By Delaney Johnson, Starhawk and Reclaiming collective

WE ALL COME FROM THE GODDESS
We all come from the Goddess
And to her we shall return,
Like a Drop of Rain,
Flowing to the Ocean *By Z. Budapest*

CHAPTER NINE

Sif

"The journey to financial freedom starts the minute you decide you were destined for prosperity, not scarcity- for abundance- not lack. Isn't there a part of you that has always known that? Can you see yourself living a bounteous life... a life of more than enough? It only takes one minute to decide. Decide now..." Mark Victor Hansen

SIF

"Your Sacred Space is where you can find yourself again and again..." Joseph Campbell

SIF ALTAR SET UP
OUR ALTAR

Altar cloth : *An altar to the golden haired Norse Goddess, Sif, should be in a yellow, ochre or Golden hue. If you happen to attain a fabric with grains, wheat stalks images or corn on the cob images, this would be most appropriate, as she is a Goddess of the Harvest.*

Image: *The image of the Blonde Norse Goddess, Sif, should decorate the center of your altar along with images of Harvest Grains; wheat and Corn on the cob. I have a Lunar Goddess, with long, flowing Blonde hair that I often use when creating my altar to Sif. Any sculpture of a beautiful Golden haired woman works just fine.*

Always present on the altar;
A silver pentacle, a cast iron cauldron, drums, speaking stick, wand, athame, elemental representations.....
Air: *feather bundles, angel wings, bird, eagle or owl statuaries. Bell &, chimes, Incense type sticks, cones, charcoal brisket and fine powdered herbs; frankincense , myrrh.*
Fire: *pillar candles, glass enclosed candles in yellow, gold, oranges*
Water: *Small glass bowl with Water and or chalice with Champagne, Cranberry Juice or Red wine.*
Earth: *At this time of the year I like to create a floral centerpiece with long stemmed Sunflowers and other golden colored blossoms, like yellow roses & daffodils. A small dish of soil or dry herbs can also be used.*

Other items pertinent to this particular gathering
Wheat stalks & Corn
Grains and seeds
Autumnal foliage
A large prominent Scissor
Hair clippings
A Chalice
A Cornucopia
Clear Glass bowl
Tarot or Goddess Oracle cards

Sacred objects from members:
Notes:

216

MONTH & SEASON

August

On the Roman calendar when March (the first month of Spring) was considered the first month of the year, August was better known by its Latin name, *Sextilis*, meaning sixth. August then, was the sixth month in the year but by around 700BC, it became the eighth month, thanks to King Numa Pompillius. By 8BC it was given the name August in honor of Augustus Caesar, who preferred to have his name sake bestowed on this month, rather than his birth month of February.

The Fiery sign of Leo is the month's astrological sign and its symbol is the fierce king of the jungle, the Lion. This sign is ruled by the sunny, jovial showman, ring leader, the Sun (July 21-August 20) and many of these attributes, and the deities that exemplify them, are celebrated in numerous festivals this month.

It's important to note that in some parts of the world, August brings oppressive heat, lazy, hazy, days of summer; heat so strong that it slows us down. It might appear that all we want to do is lounge around or escape the strong heat, in some air conditioned room somewhere. Much like Winter, nature, once again, shows us who is boss and forces us to slow down, just enough to make notice that these are the final days of the season of warm weather and we should relish the gifts of the earth, found in her bounty. For August is merely a pause before autumnal winds of change come through. Although outdoors we are subjected to the brightest and warmest Summer days, I often see this month as a time of preparing to bid Summer adieu, for we can begin to anticipate what is about to unfold in the coming months. The following month brings the season of Fall, a great shift in our cosmic atmosphere with the beginning of the school year for most children across America. Some students are preparing to go off to college and inaugurate a great change in their world and in August, most summer vacations are coming to a complete end. Life will return back to serious business after this month, but for now, we acknowledge the spin in the wheel of the year while lingering and enjoying the final days of Summer and honoring the bounty of the earth.

According to the Farmer's Almanac, the Full moon in August was known as Grain Moon. It was also known as Barley Moon and sometimes Corn Moon as these were, traditionally, the grains harvested during this month. Corn, rice, millet, rye, barley, oats wheat, were all commonly harvested during this season. The Native Americans would sometimes call this full moon, Green Corn Moon, in reference to the long rows of sweet corn stalk abundantly blessing the fields in August.

This is the time when the earth seems pulsating with vigor and life. It's bursting with succulent, ripe gifts and she appears in her grand role of Mother, nurturer and sustainer, as we are fed and nourish by her incredible bounty. Tomatoes ripen, rows of corn stalk grace the fields, apples (beginning to redden) abundantly grow in orchard and the Dionysian grapes, though still slightly green, begin to clusters and hang from the vines. All of nature and Mother Earth is alive, juicy and brimming with vitality. It is living, breathing via its creations, plants and animals, breeding abundantly with mouthwatering fruits and vegetables - offering her enormous bounty to her children.

Since ancient times, Grain has always been the staff of life for numerous cultures and for agrarian societies, the power of the Grain and the power of the Gods was closely interconnected. From Greece, to Egypt, to the Americas and for the Romans and the Celts alike, grain from the harvest provided sustenance for the people in various ways, most significantly the production of beer, rice, and bread. A good harvest was unquestionably imperative and assuring its fertile success was a matter of life and death for a people who lived so close to the land. Therefore various cultures from different parts of the world would offer numerous traditional rites and agricultural festivals to appease the Gods in the hopes of securing sound blessings upon their crops.

There was a common belief that harvest spirits, lived among the grain fields and performing certain rites would entreat them to bless the harvest. Sabbats and Festivals like Lughnassadh and Lammas are surviving ancient Celtic rites that were initially meant to honor the agricultural gods and beseech their continued blessings upon their crops. The Witches Sabbat of Lammas comes to us on the very first day of August and it commemorates the first harvest. The word Lammas, comes from the Anglo-Saxon word meaning "Loaf mass" and here again, reflected in its title, is the importance of the Grain.

In Ireland, the Celts celebrated the festival of Lughnassadh, which honored the ancient Sun God, Lugh and his foster mother Tailtiu. This Celtic God resembles the Greek Sun God, Apollo, as both were considered powerful Solar deities, patron gods of beauty, prophesies, medicine, music and the arts. Interesting to note, these are the fiery qualities found in the astrological sign of Leo which rules the month of August. In some parts of the Americas today, farmers have Harvest dances where a Harvest Queen is appointed, and music, eating, merriment and various fun competitions are incorporated in the festivities. They also hold county fairs, both of which resemble some of the earlier Pagan practices of our ancestors.

Grain has always been closely linked with the gifts of the Gods. Inherent in them is the sacred cycle of life, death and rebirth and the theme of sacrifice and gratitude. Every culture, from antiquity to our modern day, recognized the importance of the first harvest at this time of year, as it would determine the kind of livelihood we would face in the coming winter.

This month we call upon the Sacrificial Norse Goddess, Sif, who imparts her wisdom of sacrifices, forgiveness and severing for the greater good of all.

All Monthly intro text taken from author's first book,
"Gathering for Goddess, A Complete Manual for Priestessing Women's Circles"

SIF GODDESS LESSON

The beloved Norse Goddess with the long sun-kissed colored hair is known as Sif. Her long golden hair was reminiscent of the wheat, the yellow corn, the harvest she exemplifies. In Old Norse text she was also known as the Swan Maiden because she could easily shape-shift into this form. She is Goddess of abundance, prosperity, self-sacrifice and peace. Consummate wife and mother, she is a symbol of community, family, the clan and the protection of the whole, as oppose to the individual. Sif and her long Golden hair, is often considered the Harvest and the Earth itself. She represents the sacrificing of the individual for the greater good of all and as the guardian of the family she represents the importance of strengthening lineage, family bonds and community.

Sif is worshipped as a fertility deity, connected to the archetype of the Mother and very much like the Greek, Grain Goddess Demeter. She is worshipped as the Earth itself which is reminiscent of Gaia and most Earth fertility deities. But her numerous tales in Norse mythology reveal to me that she is indeed very reminiscent to the Aboriginal Goddesses of the Americas; Selu, Iyatiku and Corn Mother. This will be revealed when we delve further into the numerous examples that depict her role as a sacrificial Harvest Goddess who concerns herself with the wellbeing of her family and maintaining peace and harmony for all.

ETYMOLOGY

Perhaps it's best to start with the etymology of her name. The word, *"Sippe,"* in the German language means *"kin"*, *"kindred"* and or *"kith"* and the word *"sibling"* comes from the word *"sib"* which is very closely linked to this Norse Goddess. Scholar, Andy Orchard, believes her name means *"relation,"* while scholar, John Lindow, notes the meaning of Sif to be, *"in-law-relationship."* It becomes clear from numerous sources that her name is intimately linked with the idea of kinsmen, family, relationships and or related via a marriage. And these definitions are corroborated by her well known myths in Norse mythology. More precisely, her name is believed to be the singular form of the plural word "Sifjar," which is an Old Norse word, related to siblings, relations and again...connection via marriage. Some sources define the word "Sifjar" to mean, "to marry" and thus Sif connotes to a relationship via marriage and it aptly describes Sif, as she does become a highly venerated Norse Goddess exclusively via her union to the supreme God of Lightning, Thor.

HER ATTRIBUTES

Sif's ancestry is a mystery and sadly not much is known about her origins. We don't know who her mother and father are, nor if she had any brothers or sisters in her mythologies. We don't know where she exactly stemmed from but we can make some inference based on what little has been written about her and those she interacted with in her myths. She was believed to be part of the Elder race of Gods, possible a part of the Vanir, a second clan of Gods that existed before the Aesir and concerned themselves with cultivation, fertility, wisdom and prophecy. Sif was viewed as an Asa-Goddess that was later assimilated into the Aesir (newer clan of Gods that concerned themselves with power and wars) due to her marriage to Thor. Hence she is embraced as part of the modern race of Gods. Surprisingly not much is noted in the ancient text of the Viking period about this Goddess, thus what we do know about her comes from a few surviving poems, some fragmentary references to her and the few excerpts that have survived in the Elder Edda, the Prose Edda.

We do know that Sif is worshipped as Thor's wife and this very fact bestows on her a great position of importance among the Aesir Norse Gods, for Thor was highly revered as the beloved son of the King of the Gods, Odin. Thor's mother is the primordial earth mother Goddess, Jord, considered the last evidence of an earth deity who's position was later taken over by Frigga and Freyja, though some would argue that Sif herself was often mixed and amalgamated with these deities and might actually be the best representation of one generation or elder race, bequeathing her divine attributes to the next.

Sif garnered for herself a great position of power as the wife of the Great God of lightning and protection, Thor. He was liken to the Roman God, Jupiter and the Greek God, Zeus. And because marital unions in those days had less to do with romance or great love affairs and more to do with contractual business arrangements in an effort to preserve and strengthen the clan, we can only conjecture the dynamics of their marriage. She is actually his second wife and he is her second husband, as she was previously married to the Giant Orvandil. Interesting to note, this association with Orvandil also connects her even more to the Elder race of Norse Gods.

Sif comes into the union with her Divine second husband already with a child- a son named Ull or Ullr, the God of Snow & Archery. Ullr is associated with Winter, skiing and all things related to snow. His name means "the Magnificent." Known as a God of Archery, he later becomes the perfect consort for the Jotunheim Giantess, Snow Goddess, Skadi. The father of Sif's son is unknown or at least not mentioned in the text of this time period but we do know he is not considered Thor's child. He is not listed as one of Thor's children but Modi (which means Anger or the Brave one) and Magni (which means Might) are indeed listed as Thor's offspring and consequently, Sif's step children. They were conceived with his mistress and enemy of Sif, the giantess, Jarnsaxa, which means, "Iron Sword." Together, the Goddess Sif and her Aesir consort do give birth to one child; their daughter, Thrud (which means "Might"). Thrud becomes the Goddess of Storms and Clouds and one of the Valkyrie.

Our knowledge about the Golden haired Goddess comes from a compilation of the writings in Norse mythology. Deciphering, researching, compiling and putting all the little pieces together helps us get a better look at who Sif is and still remains to be, in the sacred realm of Asgard. It is through the writings found in The Prose Edda, written in the 13th century by Snorri Sturluson (c.1179-1241) and also the Poetic Edda, which is the oldest of the two and is considered a compilation of earlier traditional writings, that we are privileged to get a closer look at Norse deities. Sif is mentioned in both, though not with great frequency. Astonishingly enough, her name is not listed by Snorri Sturluson (c.1179-1241) in the Gylfaginning among the numerous other Norse Gods but her name does appear in numerous other tales. There are a combination of probably four different stories I will mention here that will help us learn, in greater detail about Sif, her lineage, her character, her important gifts and attributes and her vital role within the Norse pantheon. We will look at her presence in the Lokesenna, the book of Gylfaginning, the Skaldskaparmal and the story of the Giant Hrungnir.

SKALDSKAPARMAL

By far the most notable myth revealing a significant amount of information about this Norse Goddess is in the Skaldskaparmal tale in the Prose Edda.

One night while Thor was probably away, his stepbrother, the trickster god, Loki, also known as Loki Laufeyarson, decided to sneak into Sif's bedchamber and while the Goddess slept he crept, ever so sneakily and in his usual matter, and he cut off the beautiful golden hair of the Goddess while she slumbered. Now her beautiful golden long tresses had greater value than one would initially expect. Her hair was symbolic of her fertile powers and succinctly represented her as Goddess of the Harvest. A woman's hair in ancient times represented her powers of fecundity and often measured her beauty. Most ancient text, when describing a Goddess, do not frequently refer to physical bodies but will commonly make reference to the length of her hair, as a measure of her great beauty and fertile powers. And thus Loki, cutting off Sif's golden long hair was considered to be severely offensive, an act of monumental significance and detrimental to the Goddess herself. It was a symbol of her great sovereignty. When Thor returned home and discovered what his stepbrother had done and the pain and heartache it caused his wife, he became outraged. And when he got a hold of Loki, he proceeded to break every single bone of the scoundrel's body. In desperation, Loki begged Thor to spare him and promised he would make amends and rectify the situation.

When released from Thor's deadly grip, Loki then hurriedly arrives at the land of the Svartalheim, one of the nine sacred realms of Norse cosmology and here he connects with the Black dwarves to explain his plight and acquire their help. Some interpretation of the Norse text reveals he connected with dwarves or craftsmen-elves but a more common interpretation states that Loki connected with the sons of Ivaldi in this realm.

The dwarves came to the rescue and handcrafted a magickal wig that would grow hair made out of purely spun gold when placed upon the head of the Goddess, Sif. They truly outdid themselves with this magickal creation but they went even further by also crafting more gifts for the Aesir Gods. The sons of Ivaldi crafted powerful tools of magick for Odin and for Frey. Both Odin's Spear, known as the Gungnir and Frey's magic boat, known as the Skidbladnir, were manifested as an indirect result of Loki's mischievousness deed. Upon their completion, Loki was needless to say very pleased and relieved but... as was his nature he could not leave well enough alone...

On his way back to Thor and the Gods of Asgard, he ran into two more dwarves from the Elf-smith clan of Sidri; Brokk and Eitri. And he started to boast heavily about

221

what had happened and the great successful craftsmanship by the sons of Ivaldi. He showed off their impressive works and questioned the two dwarves before him and their own ability to do better. As was his mischievous nature, he presented an irresistible challenged to the two dwarves. Loki placed a wager with Brokk and Eitri that they could not surpass the artistry, skill and craftsmanship of the sons of Ivaldi. He challenged them with a bet that if they crafted something grandeur and far superior than the sons of Ivaldi had, he would offer them his own head on a platter. Well, this wager excited the Dwarves as they did not care much for Loki and they delighted in the possible conquest. Together they began crafting three additional tools that would prove to be most powerful for the Norse Gods. Loki watched in amazement and in his fear of losing to them, he shape-shifted into a horsefly to pester them while they diligently worked on the divine tools but it didn't stop the clever Dwarves from completing their grand masterpieces. Eventually, they won the competition by crafting; Frey's golden Boar, Gullinbursti, Odin's multiplying ring, Draupnir and Thor's revered Hammer, Mjollnin.

When proudly they presented their work to Loki, he refused to admit defeat and he would not surrender his head to the dwarves as promised, claiming that it was attached to his neck and he never promised his neck along with his head in the wager. The Norse Gods were called upon to decipher who indeed was the winner and when they gave their stamp of approval to Brokk and Eitri, it was Loki who had to eventually pay up. The Gods allowed the Dwarves to sew up Loki's mouth shut for his chaotic shenanigans and mischievous dealings and while the Dwarves took great pleasure in being declared the winners and finally punishing Loki by sewing up his mouth, it was the Norse Gods who were the ultimate winners, benefitting most by the exquisite magickal creations of the Dwarves.

PROLOGUE OF THE PROSE EDDA -REFERENCE AS A SYBIL
One thing is clear, the cutting off of Sif's locks by Loki resulted in the growth, extension and advancement of the Norse Gods, for her hair being chopped off, acted as a sacrificial rite that resulted in the manifestation of five of the most important Divine gifts and powerful tools of the Gods.

In the Prologue of the Prose Edda by Snori Sturluson, Sif is actually called a seer, a prophetess. She is described as a Sybil and thus someone with the gift of prophecy, powers of Divination and great psychic abilities. And in this prologue we learn of how she and Thor meet for the first time in the realm of Thrace or Thrudheim and then they later marry. Interesting to note, Thrace is the place that some scholars have claim Hekate, the Greek Goddess of the Underworld and Patroness of Witches and Seers, originates from. It is certainly thought-provoking to consider that Sif, with her gifts of prophecy, might have known and orchestrated this important, sacrificial rite in order for the Gods to grow in their powers. Of course, some would argue that many of the Norse Goddesses, like Freyja for example, had these inherent psychic abilities in varying degrees automatically as part of their numerous attributes, but it's interesting to note this ability in the Goddess Sif, paired with her role as a sacrificial harvest deity, who ultimately just seeks to create harmony and family unity.

Some would argue that perhaps the Goddess Sif, being attributed with psychic abilities, knew or had some psychic knowledge and premonition that this would need to occur for the advancement of the Gods. After all, this is her very nature, sacrificing for the greater good of all. These are parts of her known attributes and represented in her long flowing golden hair is the resemblance of the corn harvest. Upon closer inspection it would seem quite obvious that Sif and the cutting off of her long golden hair represents the first harvest pruning so often required in order to facilitate and help proliferate the subsequent harvest. As is her nature, she sacrifices for the harmony and greater good of all and thus her hair, which is so intrinsically a part of her, is shorn, sacrificed in the hands of the trickster God Loki, in order that the Norse Gods grow in power and strength. The end result is that the five powerful gifts to the Norse Gods; Frey's golden Boar- Gullinbursti, Odin's ring – Draupnir, Odin's Spear – Gungnir, Frey's magic boat – Skidbladnir and Thor's revered Hammer –Mjollnin, would never had manifested, had it not been for her golden tresses being cut off by Loki's mischievous deed.

LOKASENNA- CHALICE & PEACE MAKER

We get an even better glimpse into the Goddess, Sif, when we look at yet another powerful tale in the Prose Edda, which confirms and supports her established role as a peacemaker. In the Lokasenna, (Stanza 53-54), we meet Loki once again, only this time he arrives at the sacred banquet hall of the Gods to manifest yet another stage of cacophony and mayhem.

Prior to this moment, Loki had been banished by the Gods from the banquet hall for killing a host servant but he now returns with much to say. He stands in the middle of the sacred hall and with much malice and disgust, he begins to accuse the male Gods of being cowards and a fearful bunch. This is Loki's attempt to hit below the belt, so to speak. Then he proceeds to speak of the women present, the Goddesses; referring to them as flirts and "trampish," he even goes as far as making inappropriate claims about the Norse Virgin Chaste Goddess, Gefjion. Clearly in that moment, Loki is being very cantankerous, unstable and quite vulgar to the Norse Gods and in his usual manner, he's creating quite a scene, as he angers the Gods of Asgard. Yet, in the middle of this disruptive mayhem, it is the Goddess Sif who bravely steps forward to confront Loki and attempt to rectify the situation. Holding her sacred crystal chalice in hand, she approaches Loki and offers him the antique mead linked to the powers of her husband, Thor. In her efforts to calm his belligerent heart and bring peace and harmony to the banquet hall, she says to Loki, that as she is being cordial to him he should do likewise with her, but Loki has other plans. She mentions that she is blameless and his insults to the Goddesses do not reflect her own true character, but Loki appears to have some insightful knowledge that he elects to maliciously divulge before all the Gods, as if to try to embarrass her.

> *"Hail to thee, Loki, and take thou here,*
> *The Crystal Cup of Old Mead;*
> *For me at least, alone of the Gods,*
> *Blameless thou knowest to be..."*

Loki drinks down the Antique Mead given to him and afterwards begins to direct all his insults towards Sif, amongst the tribe; insinuating that she has not been as chaste, nor as pure and faithful as she claims. He goes on to reveal that the wife of the great Norse God, Thor, is not so innocent and has actually had intimate relations with him. Loki in his volatile, mischievous state actually makes the claim of infidelity with almost all the Goddesses throughout Norse mythology, so it is not clear how much truth there is in his statement. However, what is important to note in this poem is that Sif, again, has placed herself willingly in the middle of a very disruptive, uncomfortable and potentially dangerous situation, in her effort to manifest peace and harmony for the greater good of all and to protect the Gods from Loki's insults. Loki was being obnoxious and railing up the Gods in that banquet hall and it is Sif who decides to approach him to calm him down. Yet in the end, she again acts as the sacrificial one, for Loki diverts his attention now unto her and instead of continuing to insult all the Gods present, he turns to deliver his most venomous accusation and insults towards her. She makes herself available to circumvent a potential war and redirects his insults to spare her Divine community.

There is also an important connection between the chalice (cup, goblet and cauldron) regarding Sif, for she is considered the vessel or cornucopia that holds the essence of life. She is the Chalice, the feminine, the Yoni, the receptor and her consort, Thor as the masculine; is the mead, the fertilizer, the semen. In the Lokasenna she is thus, the cup bearer who is essentially offering herself when she offers the Crystal Chalice to Loki, filled with old mead. In this very significant act, she is also standing in her power as true representative of her husband's authority in his absence, which reflects her great sovereignty.

In the Lokasenna, we see a perfect example of her role as a peacemaker, as a Goddess who is looking out for the greater good of her community and as the one who steps forward to offer herself as the chalice, the sacrifice, to help diffuse the already volatile environment that Loki has created. In her efforts to make peace in that banquet hall among her family of deities, she is the one who ends up being trampled on because Loki begins to attack her, making inappropriate claims about her true nature and their past carnal history. It certainly leaves one more intrigued and wondering if there is any truth to Loki's claim, especially when we remember how he entered her bedchamber and cut off her hair in the Skaldskaparmal tale in the Prose Edda but none of this matters more than her consistent role as the one who self – sacrifices for the wellbeing of all.

This tale is yet again another example of how, Sif, in her effort to manifest peace puts herself in the mist of the chaos for the greater good of the Clan. But it's interesting because it turns your attention to yet another possible aspect of hers. And we don't know if there is any truth to Loki's claim but certainly there are other writings in theProse Edda that alludes to this beautiful Goddess as having many intimate relations apart from her husband, Thor.

GYLFAGINNING

In the Gylfaginning, it is Thor's father, the God Odin, who also makes a claim that Sif is entertaining lovers. In this tale, stanza 48, Odin, in disguise, meets his son and the two begin this sort of bantering, throwing jabs and insults at one another. One of the claims Odin makes, is that Thor's wife is back at home being unfaithful to him. Thor is not moved by this comment and neither does he appear angered or combative. He simply replies by accusing the masked Odin of lying.

We don't know all of the validity of these accusations or even if it merits further investigation. It makes me wonder if this was just a common way to teasingly insult and degrade a Goddess, especially one who was known for her great beauty and discriminatory gifts of inciting desire. But perhaps what becomes most obvious is that not much has been written about the Goddess Sif and this creates a kind of tugging at all hints of her nature, subjecting any mention of her in writings, through rigorous investigation, gravely analyzing every mention of her in ancient text; whether it was small or large, truth or fictional. Consequently, there is not enough written about her and thus every little bit of information we can discern from fragmentary comments, poems and excerpts, becomes weighted with great importance for those seeking to know her best.

It is important to note that marriages were contractual agreements that afforded greater power to tribes for the Norse and thus it becomes clear that infidelities were probably not such a big issue or concern among the Aesir.

GIANT HRUNGNIR

To say that she is a beautiful Goddess is an understatement, for almost every mentioned of Sif in the writings of the Viking and pre-Viking period reveals her as being exceptionally beautiful.

In the Hymir Poem we see how much she is valued and desired by one of the strongest Jotnar Giants. When the Giant Hrungir, in a drunken stupor, begins to berate the Gods and makes outlandish threats that he is going to destroy the Aesir Gods, he reveals his desires for the two most beautiful deities in all of Norse mythology. In this poem, Hrungir shares aloud his plans to destroy the Gods and take for himself the two most beautiful female deities; Freyja and Sif. This is very indicative of how important these two deities were. Eventually Thor kills off the Giant but it's interesting to note that these two Goddesses, lumped together, were the only two the Jotnar Giant wished to save for himself, as if they were the most valuable prize in all of Asgard. This becomes more intriguing because some scholars have even attempted to claim that both of these Goddesses are really one and the same, due to their many similarities. It is more likely however, that Sif, being from the Elder race of Gods, came before Freyja and while both share in similar attributes, especially their gift of prophecy and their reputed magnanimous great beauty, they are more than likely two different Goddesses that came to us from different periods and tribes, and are now equally embraced as two separate, powerful deities in modern Norse mythology.

SOME ADDITIONAL OBSERVATIONS

Sif is the fertile land; the yellow corn, the wheat, the Harvest. She is the Chalice that holds the essence of life and the mother archetype that protects and unifies the clan. Sif is a prophetess, beautiful beloved wife of Thor and a sacrificial fertility Goddess intrinsically linked with the prosperity and sustenance of her tribe. Like Selu, the indigenous Corn Mother deity of the Americas, there is a striking resemblance in their attributes and roles as Sacrificial Harvest deities, for both were considered representative of the land itself and both... willingly sacrificed themselves in an effort to save or sustain something bigger than the individual. Selu, whose very own body produced the harvest corn, allows her body to be cut up and scattered across the land so that when she is gone her children will survive, thrive and not be extinct from hunger. Sif, in a similar manner, allows her hair, which is the harvest corn itself, to be cut up, shorn, and as a result, the Gods are strengthen and their powers expanded upon, via the new tools they acquired from her sacrificed tresses.

It is through this sacrifice that she must surrender a part of herself, a valuable part of herself for the benefit of the greater good and the clan-which she and Thor are responsible for protecting. Her hair is what helps manifest the Divine gifts; Frey gets the golden Boar (Gullinbursti), the magic boat (Skidbladnir) and Odin gets his Spear (Gungnir), the ring (Draupnir), and Thor gets his Hammer (Mjollnin). Just as it is through the willing offering of Selu's spilt blood across the field, that the land then becomes fertilize to forever feed and sustain her people, in much the same way, Sif, as a prophetess, knows her role is to sacrifice, to strengthen the Norse Gods, facilitate their longevity, for she is their chalice and the fertile land.

Another example of her role as family protector, peace keeper and sacrificial Goddess is the way she takes on the two children (Modi and Magni) of her Husband and his mistress. Under most normal human circumstances, a wife would be conflicted to learn that her husband's mistress was birthing to life two children but Sif is a Goddess whose sole role is to create harmony and wellbeing for the clan and thus, the children of her enemy, Jarnsaxa, are embraced as her own. All are taken in by Sif and gathered, unified as one, to sit amidst the family dinner table. And any antagonistic emotions that would surface as a result of learning about this affair are relinquished for peace and the greater good of the whole family.

I find it titillating that she enters her union with Thor already possessing a child (paternal lineage undocumented) and both, She and Thor, come from starter marriages. Together they have a child, Thrud, but along with the two previously mention step-children; it appears Sif's familial situation is very similar to our Modern day, 21th century blended, nucleus family. In this day and age of unconventional unions, where divorce rates are at record high number and multiple marriages (unions) carry with them the potential for numerous step-children; combining households seems to be the norm. This ancient Norse Goddess is reflecting a modern condition affecting our growing society as a whole today. The grace in which she handles this sacrifice of herself, despite any pain or heartache she may deeply feel, for the benefit of the whole Divine Clan, is exemplary of a Goddess and one we can fully identify with in our modern day era.

SIF GODDESS GATHERING DAY

Purpose: To enter Asgard, the hall of the Norse Gods, and encounter the Golden Haired Goddess, Sif and her corn harvest. To courageously accept what needs to be pruned and sacrificed for the greater good of all. For my community, what do I willingly relinquish that will benefit all?

Check Ins: We gather around the Circle and introduce ourselves to one another, while also voicing our feelings on this month and our hope for the upcoming season.

Chants: Together we will join our voices to sing some commonly known Pagan chants, as well as new ones offered on the Chant sheet in the hand outs (see the last page of this chapter). Singing aloud is a wonderful way to raise energy effortlessly and it also sometimes helps in creating harmonious bonds.

Our Agreements bylaws and Pertinent group discussion... We go around the circle of women, reading a few lines each of our "Group Agreements" and add any new ones that seem necessary. Agreements are signed and submitted in confidence.

Drumming Grounding: A drumming musical CD track will be played, to give participants a chance to connect and ground to this very moment. Women are invited to find a comfortable seat or stand and add movement if they wish.

Conjuring Goddess via her Image: A photo image, Goddess oracle card or scuplture image of the Goddess, Sif, will be shared around the circle, as each woman present will reflect on the image and state aloud what attributes and Divine messages need expression.

Lecture on the Norse Goddess, Sif
Her myth and various folklores, her attributes and relevance for us today.

GODDESS WORKSHOPS
WORKSHOP I
Abundance and Prosperity Spell crafting
WORKSHOP II
Exploring the concept of Sacrifice as presented to us by Sif
WORKSHOP III
Exploring The Hangedman in the Tarot card
WORKSHOP IV
Different ways to incorporate Hair magick
WORKSHOP V
Manifesting Peace, finding resolutions to our inner and outer conflicts
WORKSHOP VI
Corn and wheat incorporated in our Harvest workings
WORKSHOP VII
Rune works with: Berkana and Inguz
WORKSHOP VII
Community and the StepMother's role and her powers to build the family unit
WORKSHOP VIII
The power of purging and pruning to promote accelerated growth.

SIF GODDESS GATHERING RITUAL

Purpose: To enter Asgard, the hall of the Norse Gods, and encounter the Golden Haired Goddess, Sif and her corn harvest. To courageously accept what needs to be pruned and sacrificed for the greater good of all. For my community, what do I willingly relinquish that will benefit all?

Asperge: with a smudge bundle of sage & copal
Anointing & Welcoming: With a small bowl grains, participants are invited to anoint their third eye with a handful of harvest grains.

INTENT DECLARED: We gather to commemorate the first Harvest and attune ourselves with the Norse Goddess, Sif.

CIRCLE CASTING
We cast this circle, May love abound,
From our feet below,
To the top of our crown,
We cast this circle,
Make sacred space,
Create this shield,
To keep all Herein safe.!!!
The circle is cast!

Elemental Invocation
Earth
Hail and welcome powers of the **earth**, realm of the **north**
Earth the cornucopia, our provider, our meal. Earth the nurturer with each corn-ear. Earth bringer of Harvest in its blanket of golden hair, we invoke the Fertile Mother in the golden grains she now wears. Come splendid riches to guard our rites today, Hail to you earth, we bid thee to stay. **Hail and welcome Earth!!!**
Air
Hail and welcome powers of **air,** realm of the **east**
Air Spinning leaves, as they fall to the ground, whispering winds growing stronger as they alter their sound. Song of the sparrow, autumn's melody I hear, Air's gentle stirring bringing music to my ears. Whispers from the wind in foreign tunes and tongues, come and guard this space and let our magick be done. **Hail and welcome Air!!!**
Fire
Hail and welcome powers of **fire**, realm of the **south**
Fire's powers in the Blacksmith's art, hands of the elves and their sacred forge. Blessed creations that emerge from thy realm, Hail to you Fires and the gifts you have held. We invoke your fires of divine creativity and ask that you keep us safe in our rites, so mote it be. **Hail and welcome Fire!!!**
Water
Hail and welcome powers of **water,** realm of the **west**
Consecrated Water, the Elixir of Life, desired by the Gods and mortal alike. Held in her chalice, remover of all thirst, a sip of her brew will enlighten our way. Healed from all infirmities as we dwell in this place, Hail to you Waters, in our rites keep us safe. **Hail and welcome Water!!!**

CHANT: *"In the earth, deep within there is a magick..."*

GODDESS INVOCATION

RAISING ENERGY *(Drums, dance, cone of Power)*

SPELL WORKING I

Reflecting now on the first Harvest and the lesson of pruning and sacrifices.
Consider for a moment, what needs to be surrendered in your life for the greater good. What
needs to be cut and pruned to allow for greater growth?
At the sound of her bell each person around the circle will say aloud what they surrender and
sacrifice, as they cut a snippet of their own hair.
Each snippet of hair will be placed upon a communal clear glass bowl of rain water.
This water will then be offered to the earth for nurturance.
ALTERNATELY: you may use yellow ribbons to symbolize her golden stresses and cut these as
you would your hair. These can either be placed in the clear bowl of water
or burned upon the cauldron.

SPELL WORKING II

We will gather to communally bake a loaf of Bread, imbuing it with visions of prosperity and offer
a big chunk, as a sacrifice to the land...the rest we eat and enjoy.

CHANT: *"Mother I feel you under my feet, Mother I feel your heart beat"*
Final Check ins

DEVOKING GODDESS

*DEVOKING ELEMENTS
Water
Hail powers of **water** with gratitude we say goodbye. Water's gift felt by all today, guardian
of our sacred space. Receive our gratitude as we bid thee adieu, hail and farewell to you.
Hail and Farewell, Water!

Fire
Hail powers of fire with gratitude we say goodbye. Fire's gift felt by all today, guardian of our
sacred space. Receive our gratitude as we bid thee adieu, hail and farewell to you.
Hail and Farewell, Fire!

Air
Hail powers of air with gratitude we say goodbye. Air's gift felt by all today, guardian of our
sacred space. Receive our gratitude as we bid thee adieu, hail and farewell to you.
Hail and Farewell, Air!

Earth
Hail powers of earth with gratitude we say goodbye. Earth's gift felt by all today, guardian of
our sacred space. Receive our gratitude as we bid thee adieu, hail and farewell to you.
Hail and Farewell, Earth!

CHANT: *"We all come from the Goddess"*

OPENING CIRCLE:

Our Circle is open but never unbroken,
may the love and peace of the Goddess
rest forever in our hearts,
Merry meet, merry part
and merry meet again....

CAKES AND ALES/POTLUCK FEASTING

FIRST HARVEST MUSING

Lammas – The first Harvest has arrived and though as a modern woman, I don't live an Agrarian life, attuned to a farm's cycle... I am a witch, in tuned with the cycles of the seasons; the sun, the moon, the waters, the air, death, rebirth, the sacred cycles of life.

The Sun reached its Zenith last sabbat on the Summer Solstice/ Litha and here, at Lughnasadh/Lammas, on August 1st, we begin to sense the slow start of the waning year, the Sun, declining ever so faintly, unperceptively surrendering to the tides.

The Sun wanes as it enjoys its final few weeks of Summer, burning to a crisp our flesh, our land, our once blooming Spring flowers and even some of our crops, before the long days of Summer begin to give way to the dark, Autumnal breezes. Night will soon dominate our days, but for now....we celebrate the last month of Summer, the last pause before the shift in the Sacred Wheel of life begins once more.

The First Harvest is upon us. So much has happened to bring us to this moment in time. Many memorable moments and unique, inner and outer, experiences, that have masterfully forged for us this journey and this moment in time. Reflecting now on the last two months, going back to Beltane and observing our journey since then.... (pause)
What can we be most grateful for manifesting since then?

Going back even further, like five months ago, to the Spring Equinox and considering all those tiny seeds that we held ever so tenderly in our hearts... in our hands and in full excitement and anticipation for what they might bring. **Can you hold this hope and see how you've nurtured it, especially the last few months? Do you remember that sensation of newness, potential and hope?** (pause)

It is the first Harvest and before us is our initial first banquet. Whether full or slim in its offering, it is a moment of much gratitude and my own heart swells in appreciation for all that has manifested and all that I have been blessed to experience. I pause and invite you to do likewise... Pause in this sacred moment to connect with this stage upon the Sacred Wheel of the Year. Contemplate on this auspicious sabbat as our ancestors have done for many year before us. Honor them and the Gods that still live on in our reverence. I give thanks....

1.

2.

3.

4.

5.

Lighting this flame, I look to manifest in the coming months of Autumn these goals written and stated aloud....

1.

2.

3.

4.

5.

May it be so...in the Name of the Fertile Harvest Goddesses Sif, Demeter, Selu, Gaia,

_____, _____, _____, _____

May the Goddess watch, protect and guide me as I endeavor to fulfill these said goals listed now on this sacred sabbat of the Harvest....

1.

2.

3.

Upon the next two months, it is Done!!!!
By all the Powers that be,
I envision, I manifest,
These things or Better,
And for the greater good,
So Mote it Be!!!!

INVOCATION

INVOKING SIF

Beautiful Sif,
Teacher of sacrifice,
Bringer of Harmony,
We invoke you tonight.

Seer Beauty,
Prophetess and Queen,
Thor's Second Wife,
Harvest Deity.

You of the Golden Tresses,
Loki's mischievous deed,
Shorn for the Harvest,
And the God's Longevity.

Seeing the Bigger picture,
Sacrificing for the greater good,
Peacemaker Creator,
Invested in our Livelihood.

Mother of Ulr & Thrud
Tend to our Call
Pour forth abundance,
As we honor you this Fall.

Lead us to Release,
Make space for prosperity to grow,
Honored Norse Goddess,
We invite you to our homes.

Hail and Welcome Sif!!!!!

SPELLS

GROWING INSIGHT

Goddess of Love,
Goddess of light,
Bless me with a
Warrior's might.

Wisdom and strength
To stand as I am,
Growing each day
With my Craft clan.

Protect me and guide me,
Surround me with your light,
Open my soul to greater insight.

The Sun, the Moon,
I embrace within me,
This spell has been cast,
So mote it be!

A DEDICATION RITE

Magick reveal itself to me,
Let my life be exemplary.
The Goddess is alive,
And magick is afoot,
And ALL I will,
Manifest like a book...

Luck and fortune,
Good health and great things,
Bless me, Your Priestess,
With thy Goddess wings.

To soar to the Heights,
Of all that's I've dreamed,
To rise to fulfill
And, with courage, Achieve

To soar to the depth of
All that can be,
Connect to the Goddess
And her immortal energy,

I dedicate myself now
on this sacred night
Blessed Goddess,
Receive me in this Rite.....

SIF GODDESS GATHERING CHANT TEXT SHEET

HARVEST CHANT by T. Thorn Coyle From music CD, Reclaiming, Second Chants
Our hands will work for peace and Justice
Our hands will work to heal the land
Gather around the harvest table
Let us feast and bless the land...

AFFIRMATIONS words by Valerie Girard From Music CD, "She Changes Moving Breath"
I am a powerful woman, I am- I am a powerful woman, I am
I connect with myself in everything, I am a powerful woman, I am

I am a passionate woman, I am, I am a passionate woman, I am
I express myself with power and love, I am a passionate woman, I am

I am a feeling woman, I am, I am a feeling woman, I am,
I accept all the things expressing through me, I am a feeling woman, I am,

I am a loving woman, I am, I am a loving woman, I am,
I love myself in everyone,I am a loving woman, I am,

I am divine woman, I am I am divine woman, I am,
The Goddess is fully awake in me, I am divine woman, I am...

EARTH, MOON,MAGICK
by B. Melusine Mihaltses
In the Earth, deep within,
There is A Magick,, I draw it in.
      In her Caves, in the Trees
      Hear her Heartbeat, Pulsing thru me.
When I Rise, I feel her Love
With feet Grounded, I'm soaring high above,
      In the Earth, deep within,
      There is A Magick, I draw it in
Ancient Moon, my Soul reveres
With my Singing, I call you here.
      When this flame, ignites tonight,
      Priestess dancing, Under the moonlit night....
In the Earth, deep within,
There is A Magick
I draw it in.... There is A Magick, I draw it in }3x

Mother I feel you under my feet
*Mother I feel you under my feet, Mother I feel your Heart Beat 2X
Heya Heya Heya, Heya Heya Ho 2X
Mother I hear you in the Rivers Sound, Eternal Waters going on and on 2X
Heya heya heya heya heya ho 2X
Mother I see you in when the Eagles fly, Flight of the Spirit gonna take our time 2X
Heya Heya Heya, Heya Heya Ho   By: Unknown source

Elemental Chant
*The Earth, The Air
The Fire, The Water
Return, Return, Return
Below, Above
the Center is Love
Return, Return, Return By: Robin Rose Bennet -addy, Origins unknown...

CHAPTER TEN

Sri Lakshmi

"...Expect your every need to be met, expect the answer to every problem, expect abundance on every level..." Eileen Caddy

"Beginning with audacity is the very great part of the art of painting...." Winston Churchill

SRI LAKSHMI

SRI LAKSHMI ALTAR SET UP
OUR ALTAR

Altar cloth : *An altar cloth for the Prosperity, Hindu Goddess, Lakshmi should be golden and this also relates to the natural colors of the second Harvest. She is often depicted wearing red so you might consider a red accompanying altar cloth as well. If you dare be more creative and if your rituals pertain to financial prosperity, you may also wish to acquire a textile with images of prosperity like; your country's currency, or green USA dollar bills and golden coins.*

Image: *The image of the richly adorned Hindu Goddess, Lakshmi should be most prominent on your altar. Also the Divine elephant God, Ganesh, who is so often linked with Lakshmi can be displayed. Sometimes she is paired with her consort Vishnu and that's fine to offer this for an altar dedicated to her.*

Always present on the altar;
A silver pentacle, a cast iron cauldron, drums, speaking stick, wand, athame, elemental representations.....

Air: *feather bundles, angel wings, bird, eagle or owl statuaries. Bell &, chimes, Incense type sticks, cones, charcoal brisket and fine powdered herbs; frankincense , myrrh.*
Fire: *pillar candles, glass enclosed candles in yellow, gold, oranges*
Water: *Small glass bowl with Water and or chalice with Champagne, Cranberry Juice or Red wine.*
Earth: *At this time of the year I like to use blooming branches and create a beautiful center piece of long stemmed flowers. Cornucopia is appropriate, as well as a small dish of soil or dry herbs can also be used.*

Other items pertinent to this particular gathering
Gemstones
Coins and dollar bills
Shiny Jewelry and mala beads
A representation of chakras
A cornucopia
Lots of food offerings like Bread, Rice and Honey
A bowl of Milk
Images of elephants
Head Crown
Personal Symbols of prosperity, like U.S.A. dollar bills

Sacred objects from members:
Notes:

MONTH & SEASON

September

The name of this month is derived from the Latin word *"Septum,"* meaning seventh, as this was the seventh month in the Roman calendar. The astrological sign for September is Virgo, the maiden, ruled by the crafty, messenger of the gods, Mercury (August 21- Sept 20). Virgo is considered an earth sign and as we approach the second harvest with Mabon, it's easy to see how its energy will influence the entire month.

September has always been a month about getting back to business and adjusting to this seasonal change. The cosmic atmosphere is really about re-adjusting to changes in our climate, our roles and our routine. Sometimes it literally feels like the start of a new year as everything seems to shift- this holds even more weight for school age children, as they prepare for a new school year with new school supplies, shoes and scholastic wardrobe. The summer days have clearly ended -gone are the hot, sweaty days of August. For most of us, our vacations are over, our chances to visit and sunbathe on sandy beaches, in some parts of the world, are gone and family barbecues or picnic opportunities have lessen. Perhaps stemming from childhood and the educational system, this month always beholds that energy of returning back to work. Our ancestors, who lived so close to the land, would've also experienced this urgency to work, prepare diligently for winter and gather the harvest.

Now we return to our learning institutions or our employment and life just has that busy feeling once more. It is a time to take stock of your accomplishments and assess where you might need to make up for lost time. Even among the critters in nature, there is busy work being done, as they prepare to stock up, before the arrival of winter.

September, for most agrarian cultures, brings the second Harvest, only this time we are much closer to the cold, dark winter season. While we might want to rest and celebrate the new crops, we realize we can't stop there. We can't avoid the work load before us any longer and it is time, once more, to harvest and prepare for the changing wheel of the year. In ancient times, the effort and hard work at this point would assure a more pleasant viable winter. Harvesting and storing food was obviously imperative and downright crucial in order to survive the cold months.

The Full moon of this month was sometimes known as the Harvest Moon but it was also known as Wine Moon, as this was the time to harvest grapes for wine making. This commemoration also reveals the sacredness of wines and spirits, especially during the cold winter months. Alcohol had many uses, but an important one, was helping our bodies feel warm in the midst of frigid low temperatures. The Wine Gods, Bacchus and Dionysius, were often the two Deities honored in Greece and Rome during this time of year and many Pagans today continue to revere them for the Sabbat of Mabon because of this connection.

Mabon (around September 20-22nd) celebrates the Autumnal Equinox of this month and honors the waning sun during this time of harvest. Day and Night stand in equal balance on the Equinox. Balancing work and play becomes a challenge, as we endeavor to leave the summer behind us and enter the fecundities of Fall. Did you play all summer long or did you take the time, every now and then, to work and put some efforts into future projects? As the air gets cooler you sense the changes in Mother Nature and it is this change that motivates our very own souls to go forward, find balance, work and plan ahead. If you've paced yourself during those summer months, this will be smooth sailing for you. If you played all summer long, then you have much work ahead of you before the dark season approaches.

This month we connect with the Hindu Matriarchal Goddess of Prosperity, Sri Lakshmi, to help us connect with the energy of the harvest.

All Monthly intro text taken from author's first book, "Gathering for Goddess, A Complete Manual for Priestessing Women's Circles"

SRI LAKSHMI GODDESS LESSON

The name Lakshmi in the Hindu language denotes "Good luck." In Sanskrit text it comes from the word, "Laksya" which loosely means "a goal" or "an aim." In yet another text, the name Lakshmi has been interpreted to mean; a sign, an omen (good or bad). The first part of her name, "Lakh" means, a "hundred thousand," that is to say, a multitude and this supports the understanding that Lakshmi is a Goddess who bestows abundance, a multitude of blessings and prosperity.

Lakshmi or Sri Lakshmi, as she is best known in later Vedict text, is the Hindu Goddess of wealth, well-being and prosperity. Known by over one hundred eight different names, she is the radiant, golden one. She is known as Padma, Kamala in this role as the beautiful one who bestows riches, great fame and beauty. She is also the embodiment of the ideal wife in Hindu culture, as she exemplifies; chastity, truth and righteousness.

It is believed that Sri Lakshmi is actually the amalgamation of two Goddesses, for in the early Hindu sacred text we learn only of the Goddess Sri and this name, later in the Vedas, becomes appended to the name Lakshmi, evolving to Sri Lakshmi. These two respective Hindu deities hold numerous identical attributes that makes it nearly impossible to separate the two. To get a clearer insight into who we worship today as Lakshmi, it helps us to begin, by first taking a closer look and researching further this earlier version or aspect of her.

Scholars note that we don't even begin to see the name Sri Lakshmi in early Vedic text but we do find the isolated name Sri. Later, during the Upanishad period, we begin to unearth the acknowledgement and amalgamation of Sri Lakshmi as the supreme Hindu Goddess of wealth.

Sri is possibly a Pre-Vedic fertility Goddess possessing many of the same attributes as Lakshmi. A bringer of wealth, fortune, fertility, power and beauty, she was sought after by many, including those pursuing positions within royalty. According to author Carl Olson in his book, *"The Book of the Goddess, Past and Present"*, Sri might have been a pre-Aryan Goddess and possibly considered a Yakshinis, which were the feminine aspect of the Yakshas. Yakshas were semi-divine chthonic spirits and known to be guardians of wealth. In particular, Yakshinis, as feminine spirits, were guardians of the root of trees, as one can surmise the roots of trees and its overall good health and wellbeing, determine the potentiality for fruits, sustenance and richness upon the land and its inhabitants. It is the source for humanities nurturance and prosperity and a logical place for these beloved prosperity spirits to tend to. Yakshas were also known to be shape-shifters and they were attendants to another great, well known Hindu god of wealth, Kubera. Interesting to note, much like Lakshmi, the Yakshinis were often linked with the waters of life.

"I invoke Sri Lakshmi who has a line of horses in her front, a series of chariots in the middle, who is being awakened by the trumpeting elephants, who is divinely resplendent. May that divine Lakshmi grace me. I hereby invoke Sri Lakshmi who is embodiment of absolute bliss; Lakshmi who is of pleasant smile on her face; whose luster is that of burnished gold; who is wet as it were, (just from the milky ocean) who is blazing with splendor and is the embodiment of the fulfillment of all wishes; who satisfied the desire of her votaries; who is seated on the Lotus and is beautiful like the Lotus..."

(a excerpt from the Hymn to Sri in the Sri Sukta,)

More can be learned of Lakshmi through Sri when we look at early Hindu text. There is an appendix to the later Rig Veda text, which is the Sri-Sukuta hymn of praise to Sri. She is considered bountiful, giver of fame; abundance, gold, cattle, horses, food, prosperity and riches of all kinds. And she is said to eradicate her sister, Alakshmi, who is bringer of misfortune. Sri is described as radiant as gold, illustrious as the moon and wearer of both gold and silver necklaces. She is depicted as shinning like the sun; like fire, which is a most sacred, divine element for Hindu Spirituality. The Hymn of the Sri-Sukuta which pre-dates Buddhism, reveals her powers of fertility in the description of her scented moistness and as dwelling (as described) amidst cow dung and bringing an abundant harvest, for she was also associated with the plentitude of grains and rice. She is even attributed for having a son called, Kardama and this name translates as; mud, mire, slime. This links her closely to the rich soil of the dark, moist earth. Ancient worshippers of Sri Lakshmi are known to even anoint their foreheads with cow dung as well, during the Nilamata Purana festival. Another example of her fertile, moist attribute can be found in the Pancaratra text. There is a Lakshmi tantra in the Pancaratra, in which she is quoted saying, *"Like the fat that keeps a lamp burning, I lubricate the senses of living beings, with my own sap of consciousness (50:110)"*

In the Mahabhrata (300 B.C.E. and 300 C.E.) Sri Lakshmi is considered the daughter of Brahma, though the God Brahma is often associated with another great Hindu Matriarch, the Goddess Saraswati. In one tale she has two brothers; Dhatr and Vidhatr and she is one of ten daughters of Daksha. In this particular myth she is given in marriage to the God, Dharma. Later, Sri Lakshmi becomes associated with the special attribute of Dharma (righteousness) as one of her many aspects and names.

In the Vaishnava texts, of the late fifth to sixth century C.E., Sri Lakshmi appears as the creative power of the God, Vishnu and she is the prakriti (life force) of the Universe itself.

In the Mahabhrarata, it is stated that she is born out of the sacred golden lotus that came forth from the brow or forehead of the God Vishnu, the preserver. And here again we have what appears to be a common tenet in Hindu mythology, that of the Goddess being both bride and daughter, much like Saraswati is considered daughter and bride to the God, Brahma. It wasn't until late 400 C.E. that we see a consistent connection to Sri Lakshmi and her steadfastness devotion and inseparability to the God Vishnu, whom she lives with in Vai Kuntha.

Some of Sri Lakshmi's symbols are the lotus, pouring water, vessels, gold, the owl, elephants and the colors; pink, dark gold, yellow, white. Sometimes she appears as golden as the sun or as yellow as the corn, which was an important food stable for Hindus. As a symbol of purity, the moon, the milky waters she is born from and her Divine righteousness, she might appear glowing white. In her aspect as the dutiful loving wife she would appear in pink and rose hues. In the Mahabharata she is shown as wearing white robes and white clothing, emerging from the churning white, milky sea. When she is shown with her four hands she is holding;
1. Padma,
2. Sankha,
3. Amrtakalasa,
4. Bilva, a Fruit or a more citrusy fruit, Mahalinga.

When Sri Lakshmi is shown with eight hands it is a reference to the supreme Hindu Mother Goddess, Durga. In this aspect, she usually holds in her hands; a discus, mace, bow and arrow and the additional attributes of;

5.Dharma –righteousness,

6.Artha –wealth,

7.Kama- pleasure of flesh,

8.Moksa –beautitude.

One popular image of Sri Lakshmi is of her rising from a vessel, or also, rising from a lotus flower that is in a vessel. Like the Japanese Sun Goddess, Amatersu's association with the mirror, Lakshmi is distinctly linked with vessels. They are known for their receptacle, womblike quality, succinctly resembling the Yoni and their feminine qualities of containment, openness and universal receptivity. The Goddess of wealth is the ultimate sacred vessel and the Divine cornucopia; with its food association of nurturance and its open shape, it is a perfect example of her many gifts and relevance to women.

The Lotus is an extremely powerful ancient symbol in Hindu mythology. Often Sri Lakshmi is shown holding a lotus in each hand or sometimes holding her sacred fruit, the Bilva. The Bilva, much like the pomegranate, was a citrusy, sometimes bitter fruit associated with longevity and the removal of illusion (Maya) and misfortune. Lakshmi was known as, Mahamaya, as the Goddess who removed illusions and blessed women's womb.

According to the Brihadharma Purana, Lakshmi in her devout worship offered one thousand lotuses to the God Shiva daily. When one day she noticed she was missing one, she quickly offered, in its place, her breast and this was transformed into the sacred Bilva fruit.

Lakshmi is almost always adorned with lotus garlands and some text describes her adorned with gold and silver necklaces around her neck. Standing or sitting on a lotus, Lakshmi is often in yellow to represent her association with Gold and even the yellow nurturing corn. She was sometimes known as Gauri, linking her to these essential foods and grains in Hindu culture.

Another popular image of the Goddess Lakshmi can even be seen in the royal coinage of ancient times. One image found in the early coins of India, reveals Sri Lakshmi being showered by two elephants, one on her left and one on her right and these elephants are holding her sacred vessels, pouring or spraying her with water, as a sign of her fecundity. This popular image, known as Gaja Lakshmi, represents her fertilization gifts of wellbeing and earthly Goddess attributes.

There are eight known forms of Lakshmi and they are known as the Astamahalaksmi. Some of her most popular forms are mentioned below.

- Gaja Lakshmi -this most popular image of her found on door frames, and royal coinage, shows her seated on an eight petal lotus. She has four hands and a conch, framed by two elephants. They are shown pouring water over her.
- SamanyaLakshmi or Indra Laksmi, Here she is depicted with two hands in this role.

- Varalaksmi, holding two lotus in two hands and mudras in her other two hands she is known as Varalaksmi.

Other Sacred Names Sri Lakshmi is known by are:

1. Adi Lakshmi - here in this aspect known as Rama (bringer of happiness to humanity), and also known here as Indira (holder of lotus of purity) servant of the whole of creation via her consort. She resides with Lord Narayana/Vishnu in Vaikuntha. She is Shakti, energy and the source and power of Narayana.
2. Dhanya Lakshmi – Harvest aspect as Dhanya means grains. In this aspect she is the guarantor of good Harvest.
3. Dhairya Lakshmi – infinite Courage and strength are her gifts in this aspect. She grants patience and inner stability.
4. Gaja Lakshmi – daughter of the Ocean-a most common depiction of the Goddess being born from the churning ocean like the Greek Goddess Aphrodite. She is seated or standing from a Lotus flower, surrounded by two elephants on either side of her pouring water on her, from her sacred vessels. This most popular aspect of Lakshmi is even captured in the coinage of the time and can even be seen on entryways carvings and temples.
5. Santan Lakshmi -children and family blessings, in this aspect she blesses your family with many desirable healthy children and long life.
6. Vijay Lakshmi – Vijay is Victory and in this aspect Lakshmi presents the victory in all areas of your life.
7. Dhana Lakshmi – Dhana means wealth. In this aspect she imparts wealth in its numerous guises; love, health, intellect, prosperity, food, land etc...
8. Vidya Lakshmi - Vidya means education, thus in this aspect she imparts the numerous blessing that come from education including but not limited to sincerity, equanimity, adaptability, tenacity, generosity, purity, humility etc..

MORE OF HER SACRED SYMBOLS

Sri Lakshmi has a strong association with elephants, who are also sacred to the remover of obstacles, the God Ganesh. It makes sense that a Goddess so attached to the manifestation of prosperity would also be linked to the elephant God who removes obstacles and thus elephants would play an important part in her own mythologies.

Long ago, it was believed that elephants had wings, and lived in the sky. Ancient Hindu mythology reveals that elephants were the clouds themselves, regulating rain showers upon the earth. The elephants lost their flying privileges and cloud connection when, according to one Hindu folklore, a Sage, one day, meditating under a tree was disrupted by the fall of one elephant. He cursed all elephants as a result, stripping them all of their wings and flying capabilities, but they still retain their great value to the Hindu culture, as we see them so often incorporated in marriage nuptials and other important Hindu ceremonies.

In ancient times, elephants were extremely important to Hindu Culture, as war artillery. They were considered weapons in wars, as valuable vehicles for the King to ride and as a sacred symbol of Royalty. The King always owned several of them and, as royalty, he was only fit to ride on the massive regal looking, elephants. Even the

Rajasuya, a royal consecration ceremony, involved the abhisekha ritual in which the king would be blessed with the pouring waters from elephants to validate his Divine rights. This royal ritual mimicked the popular image of the Goddess herself being divinely showered by the elephant's pouring waters in the Gaja Lakshmi portrayals.

"There is a Goddess who possesses eyes like a Lotus flower (Padma, Kamala), her thighs are like the Lotus, she possesses a Lotus face and her skin is the color of the lotus. She dwells in this aquatic flower, sometimes envisioned as standing erect on the lotus and often holding the lovely flower in her hands. Once upon a time she was born from the lotus, her ears delighting to the trumpeting sounds of elephants...."

"The Book of the Goddess, Past and Present" by Carl Olsom, Chapt 10 page 125.

The Lotus is an aquatic, sacred flower born and rooted in the muddy waters, yet miraculously able to blossom and shine in its exquisite beauty, uncontaminated by the mud. It is one of the most recognized, venerated symbols of transcendence for Hindu and Buddhists, as it connotes spiritual authority. In this flower's wholeness and its ability to hold, nurture and water its own seeds, there is a divine reflection of the Universe itself and this links it to the Gods of the Hindu pantheon. We see the Lotus associated with many other deities, like Saraswati. It is also shown growing from Vishnu's navel as well as his forehead, where it is believed to have birthed the Goddess Lakshmi herself. Thus, the symbols of Divine source, purity, spiritual authority and the nectar of all creations, is represented in the Goddess Lakshmi through the Lotus flower.

Of all the creatures to be associated with the Goddess Lakshmi, it seems, at first glance, odd that the Owl would be one of them. The Owl, however, has often been associated with various deities from different pantheons; like the Greek Goddess of Wisdom, Athena, the Sumerian ancient Goddess, Lilith and the Welsh Flower-born Goddess, Blodeuwedd. The Owl is a sacred symbol of wisdom and divine insight and in Hindu mythology it is depicted as Lakshmi's vehicle. Known as an Uluka, in the Hindu language, the owl was also another name for Indra, the King of the Gods. One can only surmise that Lakshmi ridding an owl, or the King of the Gods, is a reference to her powers over anything connected with Kings and royalty. It is Sri Lakshmi who can bestow fame and fortune, fertility, longevity and success and thus, her blessings are sought after by all, especially those seeking sovereignty.

ROYALTY & COINAGE

We first see images of Sri Lakshmi appearing in coins during the Gupta Dynasty (320-540 C.E.) During the Samudragupta (ca.335-376), her image in the coinage is now seen on a throne with a lotus to hold her divine feet. And in the Chandragupta II (ca. 376-415) period we begin to see the King now portrayed on the opposite side of the coin holding a lotus in his hand, while Sri Lakshmi's image, an exact pose with the lotus, is revealed in support of the king, on the other side of the coin. By the Skandagupta period (ca. 454-467) Lakshmi is shown on the same side of the coin, standing right next to the King, who is holding a bowl. This is remarkable evidence of the King's Divine right to rule and Lakshmi's blessings on his kingdom. It was believed that only through her blessings of wealth, fame, longevity and wellbeing, could any King rule with much success and thus it is Lakshmi who blesses and ordains sovereignty. Sri was so valuable to a King that it was considered the actual cushion which the King must sit upon, for she bestowed not only prosperity and success but also physical health, longevity, beauty, and special blessings to the ruling Kingdom.

HER BIRTH

The Hindu Holy book of Srimad Bhaganata tells the story of her birth, known as Samudra Manthan. According to this sacred text, one day there was a battle between Demons and the Devas (minor Gods), and they both wanted the nectar of immortality, also known as Amrit. *(This story already sounds familiar, reminding me of the Norse tales of the Goddess, Idunna and the Apple of immortality for the Gods of Asgard, but I digress.....)* Desperate, the Devas consulted the God, Vishnu, who was now in the form of Kurma, the wise tortoise. Vishnu instructed them to churn the ocean floor; churn it and while they churned, the wise tortoise would endeavor to maintained and hold up the mount of Mandara on his back. Thus the Devas churned the ocean into a frothy milk and there unearthed Amrit, the Elixir of immortality, in the birth of Sri Lakshmi herself. Then as she appeared, Sri Lakshmi elected to reside in Vishnu's chest, his heart, making this her beloved dwelling place.

HER CONSORT

Most of Hindu mythology connects Sri Lakshmi to the God, Vishnu, also known as Narayana, among his numerous incarnations. She is inseparable from her consort and the sacred text of ancient times reveals that however Vishnu incarnates, Lakshmi is always there by his side; whether he appears as human or as creature; she too, almost always appears in a complimentary aspect to her consort. Theirs is a relationship of supreme, tender love and for Hindus, an aspiring model of an ideal marriage. Lakshmi is viewed as the ideal dutiful wife, always tending to her partner's needs and comfort. She exemplifies devotion and self-surrendering to her husband and the embodiment of "Prema," an ideal love that rises above carnal desire. One common depiction of the Goddess by the feet of her reclining consort expresses their relationship best. In this image, Vishnu has one foot resting on the Divine Serpent, Sesha, and the other foot is upon his adoring dutiful wife, who appears to be massaging his foot, catering to his comfort.

Sri Lakshmi is held in high esteem as the model of a Hindu devoted wife, exemplifying chastity, beauty and controlled proper sexuality. Their marriage appears to be the personification of pure love, tenderness and profound fondness for one another, according to Hindu culture. The numerous depictions of the two together, gazing lovingly into each other's eyes, supports this conclusion, as well as the images of the two deities exchanging lower body parts, revealing their supreme unity.

Lakshmi is considered to be the energy or shakti of Vishnu. Sometimes Vishnu is depicted with other wives like Sri and Pusti (prosperity) or Sri and Bhu (earth Goddess) but Sri Lakshmi herself always appears on his right side, denoting supremacy.

Interesting to note, when depicted with her husband, Sri Lakshmi only appears to have two arms, unlike the four arms she is typically attributed with, when depicted alone. She also sometimes appears diminutive in size compared to Vishnu and some believe this is yet another representation of her subordination to her husband. I would like to

244

think that perhaps with a loving strong spouse by her side the need for four hands becomes superfluous –maybe... or maybe her powers are so great that displaying them all at once on the table could threaten the patriarch, represented by the God Vishnu. Despite some of the interpretations of Hindu sacred text I've encountered, it is hard for me to view a Goddess, especially one of her great caliber, to be subordinate to anyone, let alone her mate but perhaps what we as humans interpret as lowly or subordination is really, in actuality, something effable and completely beyond our understanding in relation to ancient deities and spiritual beings.

She is the dispenser of grace, grants all desires and salvation and she is the bestower of liberation. Lakshmi's worship has withstood the test of time. She is a Goddess still worshipped today much like in ancient times but it's important to note here her worship in relation to her consort, as she was widely worshipped both alone and in succinct connection to her husband. In the Maharashtra region of India, in the city of Pandharpur, there is a temple dedicated to the Divine Couple but interestingly enough, the shrine for Lakshmi is found in the Southern region of this temple, which, according to some Hindu scholars, was typically considered the region associated with dark, demonic forces and the dead. Some view this shrine's positioning, again, as a reflection of Lakshmi's subordination but remember, she was called upon to remove evil with her golden light, as well as to keep the dead at bay, so this placement makes perfect sense not as a place of subordination but as a critically compulsory and valuable for any temple.

As protecting powers of Vishnu, Lakshmi is known as;

- Sridevi- Goddess of wealth and fortune
- Bhudevi – earth representation
- Sridevi – again but as junior sort of consort Vishnu, symbol of sovereignty over the earth
- Saraswati- Mother of Learning
- Priti – Love personified
- Kriti and Santi – Fame and peace
- Tusti and Pusti – grants pleasure and strength
- When propitiated, she can dispel evil and bring prosperity –She eradicates Alaksmi, the opposite of Laksmi, a goddess of misfortune...

RELATING TO OTHER GODS

In some sacred text Sri Lakshmi is the wife of Dharma and her father is Daksa, the Virtuous conductor. Some other Hindu text reveals that she resided in Prahlada with the Demon God, Bali, when he succeeded in defeating the God Indra. And here we have a reflection of her attraction to the energy of Success and Victory, for she only draws near him due to his great achievement. Later on she withdraws from him when Vishnu intercedes on behalf of Indra to reclaim his power.

To the male rain God of Indra, who becomes the King of the Gods, she bestows Royal authority and powers. And there are images of the Goddess ridding Indra as an Owl. She appears and blesses the God Soma; Lord of plants, vegetation, associated with saps, when he performs a sacrifice in her honor. And as already mentioned, she is often associated with the God of Wealth, Kubera. Kubera is known as the Lord of Yakshas, the race of supernatural beings who dwell in uncivilized areas; like the wilderness and forest. They are guardians and distributors of wealth, and are linked with her early incarnation as the Goddess Sri. In Prajapati, it states that all the gods having witness Sri and her gifts of fortune, fame and prosperity, desired with all their heart to be blessed by her presence. The Gods, seeking the Elixir of Immortality, found it in her and thus, sought after her continuous blessings forever more, thereafter.

FESTIVALS

Lakshmi is a Goddess who has transcended all time as she is very much venerated today as in ages past. Her known month is October and coincidentally, her festival Dipavali (Diwali) is usually held in late autumn. Lakshmi's birth and wedding day are commemorated at this time, for three days, during Navarathri. And Friday is also a very special day for Lakshmi's celebrations. The Friday before the Full moon, of the month of Sraavan, is of great significance to her worship. Known as a festival of light, lamps are lit in her honor and there is merry making and lots of great celebratory noises to drive out any maladies or signs of her sister, Alaksmi. Merchants use this time to bless their financial documents, accounting logs and businesses plans. Sheep and goats are sacrificed and offered to the Goddess during some festival ceremonies and there is also cow dung veneration, for this is how the ancient sacred text depicts her; as the moist, fertileness of her sacred animal's dung. Her close associated with cows, due to their nurturing attributes, is very reminiscent of the Egyptian Divine Bovine, the Goddess Hathor.

Lakshmi Puja is celebrated, again, on the Full moon night of the Kojagari Purnima. At this time of the year, in late autumn, she is also called upon to keep the ghost of the dead away from the living. It is not surprising that this festival coincides with the ancient Pagan/Druid holiday of Samhain and the themes of the final harvest, surviving the darkness and the propitiating of the dead, as these are the prevalent theme at this time of year.

Kaumundi Purnima Festival -In this festival, women honor her in the mounds of seeds and grains and together they recollect the ancient tales, quite similar to the Greek Goddess Demeter, in which Lakshmi had temporarily disappeared from the Earth taking away her gifts of prosperity from the land. They pay homage to her gifts in the hopes of never experiencing her devastating withdrawal from the world.

Caitra-Gauri Festval -Held during the second month of spring. Here in this festival Lakshmi is celebrated for her vegetative attributes to the land.

Durga Puja-Here in this festival, Lakshmi is also celebrated as another aspect of the divine mother and in her agricultural association. She is supplicated to bring back the crops, make them abundant and fertile and this festival takes place at the Full-Moon following the Durga Puja.

Pujabi Festival-In this festival Lakshmi is exalted with gratitude for her fertile, womb blessings. Women celebrated her with colored cord representing each child they were able to conceive and offering these cords in gratitude to Sri Lakshmi's blessings.

There is also a festival in the **Summer** time that honors both Sri Lakshmi and Vishnu in their role as the ideal Divine couple. In this festival sometimes Vishnu is known to take on a second wife or he is believed to hibernate and fall asleep for a long period, either way, he will not be available to his beloved Lakshmi. At this time, worshippers call upon the Goddess and her gifts of steadfastness, loyalty, truthfulness, and strength within all relationships.

Gobardhan Puja - In this festival Lakshmi is celebrated as the fertile, prosperous giving mother and exalted as an incarnate Bovine.

The Goddess of abundance, beauty, royalty and prosperity is very much alive and worshipped today as she was in years past. She has transcended time and has remained a beloved immortal Hindu Goddess that speaks to our gender on the exclusively unique gifts of the Feminine Divine. She introduces yet another important aspect of the sacred feminine, one that is sought after by both men and women who seek to know success, victory, beauty and abundance.

Lakshmi's 108 Names

1. Sri
2. Bhuvaneshwarya
3. Trikalagyanasampanna
4. Brahma-Vishnu-Shivatmika
5. Mahakali
6. Navadurga
7. Sarvapradavanivarini
8. Devi
9. Daridrya Dhwamsini
10. Narayana Samashrita
11. Prasannakshi
12. Vishnupayni
13. Vishnuvakshah
14. Devi
15. Mangala
16. Jaya
17. Samudratanaya
18. Hiranyapraka
19. Shubha
20. Vasuprada
21. Varalakshmi
22. Nrupaveshvagathananda
23. Shuhaprada
24. Straina Soumya
25. Siddhi
26. Dhanadhanyaki
27. Hemamalini
28. Harini
29. Udaranga
30. Vasundhara
31. Yashawini
32. Vararoha
33. Bilvanilaya
34. Bhaskari
35. Shuklamalambara
36. Shanta
37. Preeta Pushkarini
38. Vaalakyaaashinii
39. Pushti
40. Vimala
41. Satya
42. Shivakari
43. Shiva
44. Pushti
45. Ahladajanani
46. Indussheetala
47. Indira
48. Chandrarupa
49. Chaturbhuja
50. Chandrasahodari
51. Chanda
52. Chandravadana
53. Prabha
54. Prasadabhimukhi
55. Suprasanna
56. Punyagandha
57. Padmagandhini
58. Padmini
59. Devi
60. Padmamaladhara
61. Ramaa
62. Padmanabhapriya
63. Padmamukhi
64. Padmodbhava
65. Padmasundari
66. Padmakshya
67. Padmahasta
68. Padmapriya
69. Lokamatri
70. Karuna
71. Dharmamilaya
72. Lakashokavinashini
73. Deepa
74. Amrutha
75. Ashoka
76. Harivallabhi
77. Anagha
78. Buddhi
79. Anugrahaprada
80. Kamalasambhava
81. Kamakshi
82. Kantha
83. Kamala
84. Vasudharini
85. Vasudha
86. Deepta
87. Deetya
88. Aditi
89. Vibha
90. NityaPushta
91. Lakshmi
92. Hiranmayi
93. Dhanya
94. Sudha
95. Swaha
96. Swadha
97. Shuchi
98. Padma
99. Padmalaya
100. Vachi
101. Paramatmika
102. Surabhi
103. Vibhuti
104. Shraddha
105. Sarvabhootahitaprada
106. Vidya
107. Vikruti
108. Prakruti-------------------

See website www.saisathyasai.com

SOME MANTRAS DEDICATED TO LAKSHMI AND MANIFESTING ABUNDANCE

1. Om Shreem Mahalakshmiyei Namaha
Salutations to that heart centered and great Lakshmi....

2. Kubera Yantra, for the Banker of Heaven
Chant:
Om Brezee Namaha (108x)
27, 20, 25
22, 24, 26
23, 28, 21

3. Om Brzee Namaha Dattatreya

4. Om Shreem brezee namaha

5. Om Shreem, Om Hreem, Shreem, Hreem,
Kleem, Shreem, Kleem, Vitteswarei (continuous repetition of her seed mantra)

6. Shreem, Shreem, Shreem.....
Reciting her seed chant 108x daily also is very effective.

7.Om Shreem Hreem Shreem Kamale Kamalaleyi
Praseed Praseed, om Shreem Hreem Shreem MahaLaxmiyei Namaha....

Translation: Underlying vibration of all creation, abundance please, cherishing your lotus feet, be pleased Great Lakshmi Goddess, I bow to You. *Youtube, Lilasakura, Recording sung by Shri Anandi Ma's group and Dileepji, from CD "Mantra for Abundance." Published by Sounds True also see Youtube by Lilasakura*

8. Om Kleem, Shreem Lakshmi (another popular mantra exalting the Goddess, Lakshmi)

9.Om Hrim Shri Lakshmi Bhyo Namaha
Check out, Youtube by Sainath459

10.Om Shreem MahaLakshmiyei Swaha

Om seed sound for the 6th chakra that commences most mantras,
where the masculine and the feminine meet in the brow.

Shrim second seed sound for the principle of abundance

Maha means "great all" referring to quality and quantity

Lakshmi is Sanskrit word meaning the energy of abundance

Swaha new levels of energy rise uttering this simple principle of abundance.
For more info see, Youtube by wealthful

11.Lakshmi Gayatri:
"Om Mahalakshmyaye cha Vidmahe, Vishnu patnyai cha dhi-Mahi, Tanno Lakshmihi prachodayat.."
Translation: Om. Let us meditate on the Great Goddess Sri Lakshmi, the consort of Sri Maha Vishnu. May that effulgent Maha Lakshmi Devi, inspire and illuminate our minds with understanding.

12.Om Hreem, Shreem, Lakshmi Bhyo Namaha...
Translation: Om, Goddess Lakshmi, resides in me and bestow sthy abundance on all aspects of my existence...

Source: www.freemeditationinfo.com

SRI LAKSHMI GODDESS GATHERING DAY

Purpose: To bathe in Lakshmi's churning foaming milk and honor the Great Hindu Goddess of wealth, beauty, success and prosperity.

Check Ins: We gather around the Circle and introduce ourselves to one another, while also voicing our feelings on this month and our hope for the upcoming season.

Chants: Together we will join our voices to sing some commonly known Pagan chants, as well as new ones offered on the Chant sheet in the hand outs (see the last page of this chapter). Singing aloud is a wonderful way to raise energy effortlessly and it also sometimes helps in creating harmonious bonds.

Our Agreements bylaws and Pertinent group discussion... We go around the circle of women, reading a few lines each of our "Group Agreements" and add any new ones that seem necessary. Agreements are signed and submitted in confidence.

Drumming Grounding: A drumming musical CD track will be played, to give participants a chance to connect and ground to this very moment. Women are invited to find a comfortable seat or stand and add movement if they wish.

Check Ins: Consider for a moment the Goddess Lakshmi. Reflect meditatively on her images, found in the Goddess Oracle or Goddess tarot, sculpture or any other image you have available and begin to invoke her by stating aloud the images we see in her.

Lecture on the Hindu Goddess, Sri Lakshmi
Her myth and various folklores, her attributes and relevance for us today.

GODDESS WORKSHOPS
WORKSHOP I
Mantras. Incorporating and reciting aloud her traditional mantras, but also creating new ones with her numerous sacred names.

WORKSHOP II
Communal baking with milk and honey a special Ritual, offering Cakes; incorporating her sacred ingredients; honey, fruits and rice.

WORKSHOP III
Pyramid creation with paper using one of her important names, "Sri".

WORKSHOP IV
Anointing scented Oil Creations and crafting a special spellworking with Tumeric Paste

WORKSHOP V
Connecting to her powerful totems; Elephant, Cow and Owl. Unearthing their personal meaning for us.

WORKSHOP VI
The Lotus and her spiritual meaning

WORKSHOP VII
Yantra and Mandala designs and artistic creations. Meditating on these sacred designs

WORKSHOP VIII
Prosperity wishing and getting serious about our business plans - communal strategizing.

WORKSHOP IX
Incorporating her sacred waters/milk in our craft workings. A special water blessing!

WORKSHOP X
Discusion on "Wifehood/Partnership," and how to find empowerment in this role that is so often typified as subordinate or oppressive to feminist/empowered women. Finding balance.

WORKSHOP XI
She is a Goddess of great radiance and beauty. In this workshop we gather to share what is beautiful to us personally.

WORKSHOP XII
Leadership, discussion on soreignty and being a prosperous trailblazer

SRI LAKSHMI GODDESS GATHERING RITUAL

Purpose: To bathe in Lakshmi's churning foaming milk and honor the Great Hindu Goddess of wealth, beauty, success and prosperity. To honor the second harvest and find ways to manifest prosperity, love and abundance for the coming dark season.

Asperge: with sweet scented incense

Anointing & Welcoming: Blessed Tumeric paste will be offered unto the third eye of participants as they enter the space. Hindu Music and mantras can be played throughout the ritual.

INTENT DECLARED: To commemorate the second Harvest and honor the Hindu Goddess of Prosperity and Abundance.

CASTING CIRCLE

I make this consecrated space,
To hold our circle,
In love's embrace.

I build and make this magic land,
By will and word and bright blue sphere,
Let only good enter, as I will
And block the rest from passage here.

Preserve and guard our sacred rites,
And welcome Deities, I call tonight,
Outside of time, outside of space
We stand here now,
In love's embrace-
The circle is cast!!!

ELEMENTAL INVOCATION

Spirit of the earth, from the sacred North. Come as we call you!
The sacred Bovine, we now call,
Her heaps of nurturing Dung
Fertilizing this astral Hall.
Guardian of this place,
Earth's Rich Blessings,
Come now into this circle space. Hail to you, Earth!

Spirit of air, from the sacred East, Come as we call you!
Wise Ukula, Sacred Chariot of our Queen
Owl, fly to us, Guard our space,
Bring your Wisdom and Blessings
Come as her Chariot,
Ancient Wise One,
Realm of the East,
We are blessed when you come... Hail to you, Air!

Spirit of fire, from the sacred South, Come as we call you
Fires Energy...
Held in her Diwali Lamps
Come eradicate all darkness here,
Where we stand.
Your radiance and Golden Jewels,
We invoke you from the warmth of the South,
Thy Fires gift, we feel,
As your name is uttered from our mouths. Hail to you Fire!

Spirit of water, from the sacred West. Come as we call you!
Churn... Churn...

Waters of Immortality...
Churn in the Frothy nurturance of thy milk.
Awaken the Supreme Mother,
To rise above thy deep oceans,
And float effortlessly to us, like silk. Hail to you, Water!

CHANT: *"Born of Water, Cleansing Powerful..."*
GODDESS INVOCATION

MANTRA CHANTING: *"Om Shreem Mahalakshmiyei Namaha"*
***MEDITATION OFFERING ***
TRANCE AND RAISING ENERGY *(Drums, dance, cone of Power)*

SPELL WORKING I
This is the Season of Balance and Thanksgiving. Lakshmi or her Priestess will pass slips of scented paper and ask you, **"What makes you rich?"** List and give thanks for all things you already possess that makes you very prosperous, these can be actual, tangible things or personal attributes you acknowledge.
****
As each person recites aloud what makes them rich, a third eye will be drawn over each participant (be creative, you can use henna or oil or simply a blue eyeliner) Lovely **music** will play in the background for this part of our ritual.
SPELL WORKING II
Writing her name, **"Sri,"** over and over again unto a green, triangle shaped paper while envisioning more prosperity and success. When all are done, we begin singing,
until all have joined in song and dance.
CHANT: *"We are Opening up in Sweet Surrender..."*

Final Check ins
DEVOKING GODDESS

DEVOKING QUARTERS
Hail to you Waters from the Sacred Western Realm,
Waters of Immortality guarding our rites,
We thank you for your presence here today.
As ye was called and arrived in peace, depart in peace.
With Gratitude we bid thee Adieu, **Hail and Farewell, Water!**

Hail to you Fires from the Sacred Southern Realm,
Fires from the Diwali Lamps guarding our rites,
We thank you for your presence here today.
As ye was called and arrived in peace, depart in peace.
With Gratitude we bid thee Adieu, **Hail and Farewell Fire!**

Hail to you Air from the Sacred Eastern Realm,
Ancient wise Owl guarding our rites,
We thank you for your presence here today.
As ye was called and arrived in peace, depart in peace.
With Gratitude we bid thee Adieu, **Hail and Farewell Air!**

Hail to you Earth from the Sacred Northern Realm,
Earth's fertile Bovine guarding our rites,
We thank you for your presence here today.
As ye was called and arrived in peace, depart in peace.
With Gratitude we bid thee Adieu, **Hail and Farewell Earth!**

CHANT: *"We all come from the Goddess..."*

OPENING CIRCLE:
Our Circle is open but never unbroken, may the love and peace of the Goddess
rest forever in our hearts, Merry meet, merry part and merry meet again....

Potluck feasting to folllow

HARVEST MEDITATION MEETING SRI LAKSHMI

Welcome to the season of Harvest. I invite you to find a comfortable spot to sit or lie down upon and if you will, join me in this special journey to meet the Goddess of fecundity and prosperity. Begin by first taking a deep cleansing breath, hold for one second then release. Again take a deep breath and this time let it fill your whole body. Feel this breath course through every cell inside of you. Now exhale and release any concerns or stress from your week and simply be. Relax into this moment. This is a moment of reflection and divine connection. It is your time and it is a gift to yourself. Continue to breathe and exhale with the intention of creating space... creating space for this journey to manifest itself. Breathe and make space within your body, mind and spirit for this moment in time. Exhale and breathe. Follow your breath as it leads you deep into relaxation. Let it guide you to the place between your eyebrows, your third eye, the sixth chakra. It is here where you will have sight, from this moment forward. It is through this divine eye that you will see in this journey. Breathe and look through your third eye, open it with confidence to see.

Look around you now with your third eye. You stand on a brightly colored vast landscape. Look out into the fields of yellow, sun kissed tall stalks of wheat. There are rows upon rows of silk like, golden hairs, swaying in the gentle autumnal breeze. There is a sense of serenity and calmness among the tall golden grains. Let the breeze also sway you gently. Feel the sun's waning strength caress your cheeks now with its warmth. This is the Harvest! This is the result of all your work this year, especially the last few months. Reflect now on what, in particular, you have done to manifest this great Harvest. What has been your greatest achievement this year and thus far? (pause)

Feel the sense of achievement. Feel good about yourself. You've done well and you should feel proud of yourself. It was no easy feat but you envisioned it, pursued it, committed and fought to see it through and finally now attained it. This is a moment of great celebration and recognition of your hard work. This is your harvest....But at this particular time of the year, this harvest must be gathered and prepared and stored for the coming dark season. Ah... you know now that in a few months, darkness will prevail and nothing will grow upon the earth. All will be quite and still. The bright hues that ornament our landscape now will be but a distant memory in the dark cold season of winter. (pause)

You begin to notice others on the field, beginning to gather stalks of wheat among other grains and you now sense their urgency in contrast to the calm sense of accomplishment you just experienced while reflecting on your Harvest. Begin now to contribute to your community by helping to also gather the stalks of wheat, placing them in your nearby rust colored weaved basket. One by one, methodically pick each stalk while reflecting on the upcoming winter months and consider what else is required of you, in preparation for the dark season. (pause)

Now take this bundle of wheat and walk with it to the nearby temple; a brightly colored red house with its blinding gold leaf, double doors to welcome you in. Your harvested wheat will be used as an offering and the Goddess will be most pleased with your visit to her Temple. See the temple's entryway. Stand before these luminous, large golden temple doors for a brief moment, while holding your wheat stalks. Be mindful of where you're entering. Be mindful of the sacredness of this very moment (pause)

Om Ein Shreem Lakshmiyei namaha...

You detect whispers and then more distinct voices. Listen to the chanting that is growing stronger in volume, emanating from the holy temple...Hear them call her with this chant;

Om Ein Shreem Lakshmiyei namaha...Om Ein Shreem Lakshmiyei namaha...

Om Ein Shreem Lakshmiyei namaha...

Instinctively you too begin to chant her mantra... You hear yourself chanting;
Om Ein Shreem Lakshmiyei namaha... And now go through these temple doors.
Make note immediately of your surroundings with your third eye. Make note of all the many
worshippers as they make supplications and offerings to the Goddess. Note her many highly
bedecked altars and begin to approach the one with her largest image, prominently displayed .
And when you can, walk courageously towards this altar and present your harvest to her. (Pause)

Reflect once more on your journey to create this harvest and consider again what the
winter months will require of you. Reflect once more on the upcoming season and the final
preparations needed to ensure a prosperous winter. Are you confident your harvest will last
through the cold hungry, winter months? Is there anything else you need to do to prepare better?
What do you hope to manifest now? What requires her gift of abundance now in your life? As you
stand before her altar, reflect on these questions. Allow yourself to hear the collective mantra,
continuously invoking Lakshmi now in this temple. Join in the chanting to invoke her blessings
now. (pause)

Om Ein Shreem Lakshmiyei namaha...

You watch as many make offerings of flowers, rice, honey, sweet cakes, breads, beans,
corn, barley and many other grains to the Goddess. You watch as many devotees make
supplication and wishes known to her on leaves of parchment paper... You notice now the crowd
of worshippers begin to move collectively towards what appears to be a pool in the back of the
temple. Follow the crowd of worshippers, as you endeavor to also invoke her.

Again with your third eye, watch as each worshipper jumps and dives into this pool. But
as you get closer you notice the pool is not filled with clear water, instead it is white. It is a
whirling swirling, twirling pool of Opalescent creamy white milk. It is the same substance she is
known to have been born from. It is the "Elixir of life" from which the great royal Hindu Goddess
of prosperity and abundance manifested. At the bottom of this pool of milk she was believed to
have risen. It is deep down, in the bottom of this pool of her immortal divine nectar, where you
see each worshipper dive now, to touch upon the Goddess and invoke her blessings. Approach the
pool now and gaze deeply into this creamy rich white elixir and when you are ready, dive into it.

Let yourself revel in her thick creamy substance, let your body swim playfully in her
divine immortal juices... (pause)Feel the weight of your body floating effortlessly on her creamy
rich essence, her immortal "Elixir of life." (pause) When you are ready, dive down deeper, deeper
into her milky nectar to visit with the Great Goddess Lakshmi, where she is waiting for you. See
her brilliant crown upon her head and the golden rays emanating from her body. See her
beautiful face and gaze upon her translucent brown eyes. In this pivotal moment speak to
Lakshmi of your hopes for the coming dark season. Ask her to bless you and help prepare you for
the coming winter months. (pause) Hear her words of wisdom, as she counsels you on how to
achieve these goals. Listen to Sri Lakshmi, the Queen of prosperity and abundance, as she shares
her wisdom with you. (pause)

When all has been said and you hear only the silence of the moving waves of milk, give
your gratitude for her love and guidance. Bid her adieu, as you begin to feel the current of the
pool's milky substance begin to agitate and splash heavily. The current of her juices begin to pull
you in a different direction after you have said your goodbyes. Begin to feel the current and the
energy of the whirlpool change; spiraling now, twirling ever faster as it begins to appear to drain

itself down a hole. You are also a part of this twirling and you feel yourself go round and round now, with the pool's fluids. Slowly the opaque white of the milk begins to transform itself into translucent water and you feel it begin to twirl faster, like a whirlpool, twirling round and round as it hurries down the drains. You also twirl around in this transforming divine water, as it begins to go round and round.... And around and around down the drain. This drain acts like a sacred portal now to bring you back to this room.

As you and the water now begin to drain from the pool, make note of my voice as it gently guides you back to this room, back to this time and place. Turn your attention to my voice as it gently guides you back to where this journey began. Feel yourself going down this drain ridding her liquid wave. Go down this drain along with the pearlescent milk that has now become translucent pool water. Feel yourself being pulled down, through this drain, through this tunnel. And as I count from ten to one, backwards feel yourself traveling back, traveling back to where this journey commenced. You are journeying now back to this time and place, bring your attention to my voice and let it guide you back to this room.

Ten, nine, eight; feel the weight of your body passing through this drain, passing through this sacred portal. **Seven, six, five;** breathe and exhale as you connect with your breath and your physical form. **Four, three,** detect a light coming through this special entryway, enter this doorway as it will lead you back to this room...**Two**; breathe and release with your exhalation. **One**; You are here! Welcome!

Open your eyes and gently stretch out your body. Let the palms of your hands touch the ground. Make sure you continue to breathe in and exhale. Gently rotate your head on your relaxed, limbered neck. If you find yourself feeling dizzy or in need of extra help grounding, raise one hand up in the air and someone will be with you shortly to offer additional help. When you feel ready, please stand or sit up so that we may begin to do a proper check in.
Thank you...and welcome!

INVOCATION

LAKSHMI ELEMENTAL INVOCATION

The sacred Bovine, we now call,
Her heaps of nurturing Dung
Fertilizing this astral Hall.
Guardian of this place,
Earth's Rich Blessings,
Come now into this circle space.

Wise Ukula, Sacred Chariot of our Queen
Owl, fly to us, Guard our space
Bring your Wisdom and Blessings
Come as her Chariot,
Ancient Wise One,
Realm of the East,
We are blessed when you come...

Fires Energy...
Held in her Diwali Lamps
Come eradicate all darkness here,
Where we stand.
Your radiance and Golden Jewels,
We invoke from the warmth of the South,
Thy Fires gift, we feel,
As your name is uttered from our mouths.

Churn... Churn...
Waters of Immortality...
Churn in the Frothy nurturance of thy milk.
Awaken the Supreme Mother,
To rise above thy deep oceans,
And float effortlessly to us, like silk.

SPELLS

A CALL FOR PROSPERITY
From unknown source,
I trust in thee,
To bring about
prosperity.

From flaming wick of candle green,
This spell is cast to draw money.
And on this night of waxing moon,
I call for money to come soon.

To pay my bills and pay my debts,
To live with riches and abundance,
Easy money that come to me,
Quickly bringing prosperity.

The gates now open
For money to flow
With rhyme and word,
I make it so.

In Harmony with the Universe
And for the greater good,
Harming none,
This spell is understood...

Money comes from below and above
From the left and the right
And from all around
Sprouting money, I manifest now,
In Magick's fertile sacred ground.

MANIFESTING PROSPERITY

Money overflows, scarcity goes,
Opportunities arrive,
Salaried or Grand Prize,

Prosperity multiplies
And arrives to our home,
For me and my children
And all that we grow...

Money to clear,
All tiring debt,
Money to pay off loans,
Cars and mortgages.

Money to travel,
For vacation and school,
Money for good health, joy,
Wellbeing and creative tools

Money to overflow,
From bosses and patrons
Money shifts now,
Into my exact location.

Door now open
And a clear path appears,
Prosperity and opportunities,
I call you now here!!!!

GANESH DREAM

This is a powerful dream I had and documented on November 7th, 2011, it is from my chicken-scratched writings from my dream journal and it is written in a very loose, non-academic way, so I will apologize in advance if its style offends anyone's esthetic as I sincerely tried to capture and share every detail of my dream.
******

So strange... so eerie!!! I don't even know if I'll be able to fully describe it here in a way that will even make sense to anyone that would read this but I will try anyway to paint, to the best of my knowledge, these nocturnal images that beg to be understood in the light of day.

Last night (I must note- for I believe it to be of great significance) was the real Samhain, according to those who observe astrological configurations as oppose to just noting our hanging, printed calendars. And the dream I had was quite revealing of the thinning veil at this auspicious time of the year.

I was dead in this dream. I'm almost sure of it now, though in the dream, I'm not entirely confident that I was fully aware of this fact. It felt as if I was embodying the maiden Greek Goddess, Persephone, as I journeyed throughout different dream scenes. She is the Maiden Goddess of Spring but, also at this time of year, she is linked with her consort, Hades and becomes the Queen of the underworld. And it felt as if I was traveling through various halls, eras, traveling through inner and outer quirky realms, between life and death and all the while, encountering people...all sorts of strange characters. To say it felt very hazy and nebulous would be an understatement but indeed the dream felt watery in its hue, almost Neptunian in nature. Oh dear....I can't believe I just described it in this way, as I just realized the planet Neptune goes direct tomorrow but I digress, back to the dream.

I found myself standing in the middle of this funky looking Pizza parlor, I think that was John I saw there as well. There were a few people, not many and I was buying the large pizza pie-the mozzarella slice, you know the ones I use to loooove in my old home of New York City. He was ordering some slices for himself and I don't know, but I think we were trying to decipher what to get or how many slices, etc... All of a sudden a criminal or someone that was up to no good, and made everyone cautious and scared, appeared. This man appeared in a very sneaky, kind of illegal way and I could see him on the right hand side, trying to sneak into this other room within the Pizza Parlor. I caught this person's presence, shadow formation, with the corner of my eyes. It was someone who you had to watch out for and he was sneakily entering the children's Bowling alley room that was on the right side, within this colorful Pizza parlor, as many of us cautiously watched in the dream. A woman who looked like my real life friend G. appeared next to me, probably also ordering pizza but also among the many engrossed by the scene. I could not really see my dear friend in precise details in the dream but I could only identify her by the feeling she created, by her form, and how I felt in her presence. Strange... it was as if I did not need to see her to know it was her. I simply opened my heart to identify and experience her and this is one of many typical phenomenons when I dream; boundaries are erased, forms and precise details on a face can sometimes be obscured and replaced by simply a feeling, and an attached emotion.

She started talking to me about her personal rehab experiences and we were talking confidentially and then I started to share my life experiences and people I've met along the way and she listened. We continued to talk while we stood on this line waiting for our ordered pizzas. Then all of a sudden, the dream scene switched as if by my words and recollection I moved the scene to images linked to my past. I was now in a vehicle with a few other people and we were now driving to my old apartment in New York City, the last one I had, before marriage.

In the dream I was considering contacting my old landlord- lady, at the apartment on Broadway, to see if I could somehow retrieve my old apartment and lease back and plead the case that I was always a good tenant and deserving of this second chance. In the car, I think there were three people with me, as we were driving back to this apartment. They were young too but I suspect they might have been people in my past. I was like the front driver or the front passenger, talking to them about possibly moving back to New York City and having them as roommates to help me out with the finances. They all seemed very interested in coming along for the ride. I now strangely wonder if they were different aspects of myself. It just seemed like, in my mind, I was trying to correct or amend something in my past that went awry. Something that was supposed to happen, didn't have a chance to and yet here, in this dream, I was lamenting and scheming of a way to get it back, make it work, the way it was supposed to.

In my head I started to calculate and figure out what life may have been like, if we had unified, shared or had become roommates. I spoke to the people sharing this car ride with me in the present tense as we began to consider sharing the apartment and becoming roommates. In the car, there was a young girl, a guy and someone else on the left. Again, I couldn't really see their faces in this dream and only identified them according to the feeling they conjured in me.

Seamlessly, it appeared we flew to my old apartment. I saw it there and entered every room. I walked through it nostalgically, tracing my fingers across the lines of my old stove, the unused oven. I tenderly touched all the different things from my old apartment and considered for a moment what it would be like if I could go back to this time and place, only now with caring friends and a vital support system.

The dream now changed. I was in this strange castle, a palace that Persephone herself lived in. Making note here that I have dreamt of castles many times before and their massive, brick by brick structure always makes a significant impression on me, in dreams. Anyway, here it was again, a castle, Persephone's to be exact, and the first person I see is a young girl I know by the name of Ash. In the dream, I see her fly right through these palatial brick walls. It appeared she had just learned to fly and was somehow experimenting with her newly acquired skill. Knowledge was being passed on to me for somehow, I did not know yet, what I could do in this new place. Suddenly I too was experimenting with my formlessness. I flew through the walls and the doors and felt my formless body and expansiveness, like I had no boundaries. It was like I was becoming familiar with this new realm and with my new capabilities.

The scene switched again and there was an old lady, gathering people. Maybe she was the landlady, hum...don't recall, but she was formulating a line, as she organized us, one by one. She was like a headmistress and she was gathering everyone in a procession. *"We're going to walk,"* she said, or was it, *"fly"*. *"We are going to fly over to another place, a very important place and almost necessary place..."* I heard her say. In a straight line everyone gathered and reached this entry way before jumping through into the dark abyss, like an elevator shaft. I was scared and unsure, I mean.... after all, it was dark down there past the threshold and I didn't know what awaited me. I watched and let others go before me as they would reach the threshold and disappear. I was hesitant to go but it was now my turn and so I followed through. It was not clear then in the dream, but now I am sure, here I was in the underworld or one level of the afterlife.

It led me to the next scene, where I arrived upon a sandy desert, like the Middle East, with numerous large mountain tops scattered in the background. Everyone that had been on that processional line made it there too but we had one more hurdle to overcome it seemed. I discovered in the middle of this desert landscape this big, mammoth size grey blob. It just lay there, blocking any access from the rest of the land. It was like this strange, bigger than life road block...and it was grey and formless. I studied it with much intrigue and this massive grey blob began to slowly reveal itself in my mind, attaching itself to mental associations. And it was only after inspecting it and closely seeing its distinct ridges, its distinct trunk features that I knew. I knew then what this huge grey blob was, no one else seemed to know but I was able to detect that it was indeed a gargantuan elephant.

I could see in the distant the tall mountaintops and on the low flat land, sand and yet, there was this "hugamongous" elephant taking up the whole space with its massive grey flesh. It took me a few seconds but I had this epiphany right then and there. I realize then this giant elephant was the Hindu God, Ganesh.

I dreamt about Ganesh a few nights ago and so in this dream it didn't take me long to finally recognize his monumental presences. Now here's a strange part of that particular moment, for in this dream, the line of people from the old lady's procession, had to walk through that grey blob, yes... pass through Ganesh. There was no other way around it. We had to walk through the God Ganesh in order to reach the other side, for the landscape was divided. And at that very moment it was clear we were not living human forms but actual spirits. I noticed we were so small, so miniscule compared to him. We were tiny, like ants, next to this massive Divine being. We looked like tiny dots or a line of ants in comparison to Ganesh, as we walk forward, through his resting legs.

On the other side were Indians, Hindi people nearby, as we all managed to pass through this sort of rite of passage, the elephant threshold. And then I saw, all of a sudden... there were beads, multiple strands of colored beads; I felt them around my neck. Yes, all of a sudden my neck was lined with the most precious colored glass beads strung up like tiny exquisite mala beads, the sacred beads so often used in prayers and Hindu mantras. I can remember seeing others holding; red, green, yellow beads, of all kinds of bright color and people surrounding me with curiosity. They looked at me and asked, where I had acquired my beads because mine were the specific work of Ganesh and they studied me and those coveted beads with wonderment. I did not know how they came to be around my neck but passing through Ganesh bestowed this precious gift for all to see.

Then at this point I now started walking around the area with my prized necklace beads. It appeared we had all completed our rite of passage through Ganesh, and now we scattered about exploring this new divine terrain. I started to walk past an area that looked like a deep bowl of sorts, like sunken land. The Elder woman there had some gadget, like a back to the future(or present) machine or something. Now I can't really remember what followed with this gadget when it was connected to me but it revealed something grand about my life journey and the lessons I was required to master. Magickally this gadget revealed.... Oh dear... its coming back to me now....I think it revealed where my soul had been initially fragmented or where I went wrong in my life. Perhaps this was going to be my life review, with this Elder woman. Not sure of it now, but at that very moment, I felt my parents... I didn't see them, again unable to see precise detail of people's faces but identifying people only through the sensations they conjured in me. I just felt their presence, I felt my deceased parents at that very pivotal moment in this dream. I woke up soon after that and felt the stream of bright images return back to me, as I tried to recollect and document every single detail I saw and experienced in this spiritual dream. I recognized quite instantaneously that this was not an ordinary dream but one with a very powerful message for me and I had to open myself up to receiving this gift.

The entire dream felt Lunar, very watery and lucid and so full of encrypted, detailed symbolisms. And I didn't know if I was dead or alive most of the time... I didn't know if it was night or day or if I was flesh or spirit. Although many scenes in my dream reveal that I had to have been in spirit form, for how could I fly through walls or do the number of strange things I was doing in this dream that I couldn't do before. And it seemed I was reviewing my life or at least the important parts in my life. I also saw the numbers 11:11 which helped to confirm the importance of this dream.

The most significant part of the dream was finally seeing this huge massive form of an elephant and discovering that this was a Divine being I had to go through. There was no other way to arrive at nirvana/ heaven/ paradise. I was required to pass through the Divine Hindu God, Ganesh (the obstacle remover) and then discover that, in passing, I was gifted with these precious Ganesh Mala Beads. This was so very important in the dream! Everyone wanted them and yet they were around my neck, magickal placed there by some unknown great power as a result of my rite of passage...... I was awestruck in tears when woke up this morning.
11/7/11

GANESH DREAM II

This is a powerful dream I had and documented on November 4th, 2011, it is from my chicken-scratched writings from my dream journal and it is written in a very loose, non-academic way, so I will apologize in advance if its style offends anyone's esthetic as I sincerely tried to capture and share every detail of my dream.

******Oh my Goddess!!! Oh Divine Being!!!! Thank you…thank you…thank you, Ganesh!!!! Beloved Ganesh, I received your message loud and clear in this dream and my heart is swelling in complete gratitude.

I dreamt I was on some sort of journey. I saw a highway, only it was as if I was a car, a human car, not a person but I was traveling and I could feel my spouse near me. We were arguing over which direction to take. I wanted to go one way and he wanted to go another and because I was in the driver's seat and he was just a passenger, he was trying not to get angered and frustrated at my choices and direction. I had elected to take the upper region or left side of this highway and he did not approve of that direction and there was so much tension and animosity coming from him because of it.

Finally we reach an area, like a type of border patrol. It seemed like a port and there were other people standing around waiting to be let through. Again, I believe I was a vehicle, not in human form. Now there were other people waiting around. It had the feeling of a bus terminal or a boat ferry port. At this important intersection there was a border barricade, the type you hear about in Mexico and we were stopped there just waiting for the others to join us, for there was an entire tour group and an operator expected to come to drive us over this great border bridge. I suppose a lot of things happen during that waiting period, things I can't recall now.

Again my spouse and I were not seeing, eye to eye on certain things as we waited there and the conflict and stress between us was growing. I noticed then, among the people joining us was an Adonis looking, very muscular man, seemingly trying to command the attention of every single person around him, especially other men. And I watched as it appeared he was succeeding at captivating my husband's admiration. Oh, yes… here we go again, with spouse's sexual ambiguity, a strange recurring, annoying theme that seems to always creep into my dreams. Anyway, I watched from the corner of my eyes as these events unfolded and slowly, I tried distancing myself from my spouse but in the dream he just kept following me around.

Then the scene turned to this lake area, it was more like a small, man-made pond where you could walk effortlessly around the perimeters. There was like a tiny trail around this insignificant pool of water and I stood there and gazed deeply into the water and it was cloudy, not clear - marshy almost, and that's when I noticed the two hockey sticks. Floating in this cloudy pond were two large, very obvious Hockey sticks and as my husband is a big hockey fanatic I knew they belonged to him. And to my astonishment, the hockey sticks looked like they were slowly drowning in this murky water. Being a woman of action, I quickly yelled for my husband to come closer and help retrieve these hockey sticks. I tried to get him to respond swiftly with the same passion and fervor that I was expressing to retrieve his drowning hockey sticks. With great effort, I manage to get one of them out and this was very significant in the dream because, I remember reaching out…struggling… placing myself at great risk but successfully being able to grab it and feeling the distinct form of this hockey stick, retrieved in my hand. I yelled to him to make him aware of the importance of him grabbing his other stick, that I would not be able to get it for him. I could not reach and I stressed to get him to do something about it, but he wouldn't. And I yelled at him to go around the pond to grab the other hockey stick, as I feared he would lose it. I could see his hockey stick going all the way down, drowning, sadly sinking further and further down, in the dream, and it was such a powerful, yet painful imagery to witness. It wasn't the hockey stick, but what it represented, that hurt so much to lose.

I was so disappointed after this incident and I think I started cursing at him because I was so miffed and mad that he, yet again, was being complacent and lazy about things that should matter to him. They were his.... they were HIS hockey sticks and yet... he was not heavily invested in salvaging them, the way I was. It was an insightfully painful moment for me in the dream because I saw clearly what I sometimes negate in real life and I felt hopeless and drained.

The truth is, in awakened life, **I am** the one who salvages. I am always the one invested in fixing things, saving things, putting much effort to do what is right and being proactive about my life but that is not who I married. I had managed to save one of his hockey sticks but it was too late to salvage the other and in my anger, I realize he would never change. Disappointed, I started to walk away from the murky pond and as was the theme of this particular dream, he continued to simply follow me; like an annoying, pathetic shadow, incapable of claiming his own life, unwilling to embrace his own power to make things happen for himself.

Despite my obvious disgust with him, he, of course, continued to follow me and was very adamant about being a nuisance; constantly bickering with me, while following me around. It almost felt like he was deriving pleasure from playing the role of the pest. And so...I walked around until I came upon another sort of waiting area. I entered what appeared to be a bus terminal. Again the recurrent bus, ferry port and port waiting areas cannot be denied in this dream. This was yet another kind of port waiting area, it looked like an airport or bus terminal and I entered it on my own, though I could sense my spouse soon following nearby. I arrived at this room, which had a few people scattered about also waiting, and I felt disgusted and resigned about my marriage at this point in the dream. Quietly, I reflected on the monumental symbolism of those hockey sticks in the dirty pond water and the sad meaning of that one stick, unsalvageable by him, drowning. I saw the symbolism of what just happened as a reflection of our life together and the pain I would be forced to endure.

Then I noticed one lady to my left, waiting, like the rest of the people. And we were all there very quiet, enduring the awkward silence of most sterile waiting areas. On the metal bench there was an envelope, or a kind of pouch and it was mine. Apparently I had left this pouch at an earlier time and there it was, still awaiting me on this public, bus terminal bench. I had left my savings of seven hundred dollars in this envelope and in the dream, I guess I had already spent three to four hundred but to my surprise the reminder of the money was still there, untouched and ready for me to reclaim it. It was safe and no one had touched it, nor even tried to steal it. In my mind it felt like a miracle and affirmed that whatever treasure I saved and put away, had not been lost but was easily retrievable and still available for me to utilize and enjoy. Finding my old money at this pivotal time in my dream, was such a shock especially when, as a city girl, I tend to be skeptical about people's honesty. To add to the mix of emotions I was experiencing, I noticed there was a woman near it too (possibly resembling my deceased mother) and I could feel her, having no desire to steal my saved money, instead it was as if she was guarding it for me, to my surprise.

So... there was the remainder of my money, something old, clearly left behind, that I was now able to retrieve because it had not been stolen. Something remained and it was not completely lost. At this moment I felt my husband now following in after me and my immediate gut reaction was to grab my money as quickly as possible and conceal it from him and then... here is the most amazing part of the dream...... I guess I was trying to figure out how much money I had already spent and how much still remained in the dream and all of a sudden, statues appeared, elephant statues.

There were these images in the form of small statues before me, like a tiny Ferris-wheel, going round and round, displaying all of these strange images of elephants. And they weren't just average images of elephants; no... they were the most unusual, unique images of elephants I had ever seen. These images or elephant statues were coming towards me with greater frequency and I noticed how beautifully ornamented and highly adorned they were. I mean I had never seen such bejeweled elephants; all different kinds, dressed like royalty in different poses, so elaborate, each one more beautiful than the next. The elephants appeared before me like a collection found in one of those scholastic slide shows, revealing all of its different elaborate guises, first in what I thought were photo images, then in actual highly ornamented sculptures. And I looked at them adoringly with curiosity and intrigue. I even noted the long elegant playful eyelashes of one of the feminine elephant images, so enchanting, as it continued to pose before me and that's when it dawned on me.... "WAIT A MINUTE!!!!" These were not just elephants; these were images of the Hindu God, Ganesh, paying me a special visit.

It took me a few minutes to realize I was being visited by the great obstacle remover, the beloved Hindu God, Ganesh and I found myself saying WOW!!! I felt so overwhelmed and astonished at this auspicious blessing. Then in the dream, I heard myself saying, *"I need one of those. I don't think I own any images of Ganesh...."* Well, the reality is that I do have numerous images and sculptures of this beloved Elephant God. I love Ganesh and recently I have been consistently working with Lakshmi and Ganesh in my spiritual practice. I guess it shouldn't surprise me then, that they are making themselves intimately known and visiting in my dreams.

In this Dream, I had an epiphany, almost like an awakening to the very obvious spiritual messages being channeled to me at this pivotal stage in my life. This was Ganesh, lovingly confronting me, assuring me of his power and presence in my life despite my struggles. I was looking at all of these various images of the great God and he was blessing me, assuring me that obstacles would be removed and that opportunities would soon come. Blessed be!!!! I woke up in a state of complete awe and jubilation, trying desperately to remember every single detail of this incredible dream. And so.... here it is, documented for reference. Blessed be to Lakshmi and to the Hindu God Ganesh, the divine obstacle remover has made himself known to me. Blessed Be!!!!!
11/4/11

LAKSHMI GODDESS GATHERING CHANT TEXT SHEET

WE ALL COME FROM THE GODDESS
We all come from the Goddess
And to her we shall return,
Like a Drop of Rain,
Flowing to the Ocean,
By Z. Budapest

BORN OF WATERS
Born of Water
Cleansing Powerful.
Healing , Changing,
We are...   *by Starhawk*

THE RIVER IS FLOWING
The river is flowing, flowing and growing,
The river She is flowing, Down to the Sea.
Mother carry me; your child I will always be.
Mother carry me down to the Sea.
The Moon she is changing, waxing and waning,
The Moon She is changing, high, above me,
Sister, challenge me, your child I'll forever be,
Sister, wait for me, till I am free. *By Diana Hildebrand-Hull*

SYSTER RIVER, GIVER
From Victorian Christian's creation , Elijah The band of Light
Syster, River, Giver...Returning Whole,
Syster, River, Giver...Returning Whole
        Open up, To receive
        We are what we Believe. *(REPEAT)*
        Syster, River, Giver...Returning Whole (2X),
Growing Roots like the Trees,
We are planting seeds. *(REPEAT)*
Syster, River, Giver...Returning Whole (2X),
        Stored in Deep, Stories Sleep,
        Within Us, These Tales we Keep. *(REPEAT)*
        Syster, River, Giver...Returning Whole,
        Syster, River, Giver...Returning Whole,

MY BODY
My Body is a living Temple of Love
My Body is a living Temple of Love
My Body is the Body of a Goddess (3X)
(lower)My Body is the Body of a Goddess

THE OCEAN
The Ocean is the beginning of the world
The Ocean is the beginning of the world
All life comes from the sea
All life comes from the sea.
By Delaney Johnson, Starhawk and Reclaiming collective

SWEET SURRENDER
We are opening up,
in sweet surrender,
to the luminance
Love light of the one, (Repeat)
        We are opening ....We are Opening (z2X) *by Gladys Gray*

CHAPTER ELEVEN

Baba Yaga

"Women need real moments of solitude, and self-reflection to balance out how much of ourselves we give away..." Barbara De Angelis

BABA YAGA

BABA YAGA

"Thinking will not overcome fear, but Action will..." Clement Stone

"...Fear makes the wolf bigger than he is..." German Proverb

BABA YAGA ALTAR SET UP

OUR ALTAR

Altar cloth : A Black altar cloth is most appropriate for the Slovenian Crone Goddess, Baba Yaga, as a symbol, not only of the Goddess, but also of the Dark season. I'd like to also suggest an accompanying altar cloth decorated with images of skulls and bones, as Baba Yaga was known to possess many bones in her hut. At this of year you will find a plethora of available textile with Halloween and skeletal images perfect for an altar to the Crone.

Image: The sculptured image of an old lady and Crone, can be utilized. There are many types of statuary at this time of year of witches and old hags and thus, you may find with great ease, an image that speaks to you personally of Baba Yaga. Placed this representation of the Crone on your altar.

Always present on the altar;
A silver pentacle, a cast iron cauldron, drums, speaking stick, wand, athame, elemental representations.....

Air: feather bundles, angel wings, bird, eagle or owl statuaries. Bell &, chimes, Incense type sticks, cones, charcoal brisket and fine powdered herbs; frankincense , myrrh.

Fire: pillar candles, glass enclosed candles in black

Water: Small glass bowl with Water and or chalice with Champagne, Cranberry Juice or Red wine.

Earth: At this time of the year I like to use bare branches and create a beautiful center piece of these long, arm-like branches. A small dish of soil or dry herbs can also be used

Other items pertinent to this particular gathering

Mortar and Pestle
Poppy seeds
A lantern
Skulls and skeletons & Bones of various kinds
Handmade dolls or wooden figurine
Bare branches
A small wooden box to make into a hut, to represent where she lives
Images of the woods and forest
Tarot or Goddess Oracle cards
Representation of Chicken legs
Horses to symbolize Dawnsunrise and sunset,

Sacred objects from members:
Notes:

MONTH & SEASON

October

    This month is believed to receive its name from the Latin word *"Octo,"* meaning "eight," as it was the eighth month in the Roman calendar. The astrological sign for the month is Libra, the balancing scales, ruled by beautifully, harmonious Venus (Sept 21-Oct 20). The Full Moon of this month was more commonly known as the Blood Moon. According to the Farmer's Almanac the Native Americans named it Hunter'sMoon.

    Reds, Oranges and Yellows, are the prominent colors surrounding us in the Earth's landscape, and the beautiful foliage, in some parts of the world. Pumpkins and gourds are everywhere. Much like February, there is a sense of mystery in the air. A time when in the darkness and deep beneath the earth, you know that nature is working her magick once more. The Goddess, in her Crone aspect, is heavily invested in her work. In the air you begin to feel the change that inevitably takes us into a time of introspection. Change, is stirring the cauldron all around us. In the air and our climate; our inner and outer landscapes announces, to those of us connected to nature, that the season of darkness is clearly upon us now.

    For Wiccans, this is the final harvest. Our work is considered done. And here, as the last harvest, is the reaping or the regretting, for what we sowed or forgot to sow. This month we are aware of the physical and spiritual planes. The Wiccan year comes to an end and we celebrate the weight of this in the Celtic holiday known as Samhain, an ancient Celtic word that translates as *"Summer's end."*

    For non-pagan, this holiday is better known as Halloween, but interestingly enough, its name derives from a mixture of Pagan and Christian Lore. Saints and Christian Martyrs, who died for their faith, were honored on "All Saints Day" and the eve of this day was known as "All Hallows eve". Also known as "Hallowmas", this holy day literally translates as, *"Mass of the Holy Ones"* and it is directly connected to our modern day, Pagan sabbat - Samhain.

    For Witches, this is considered the end of Celtic year. It stands between the balance of the old and the new, the living and the dead, autumn and the coming of winter. The end of the old year. For our ancestors living so close to the land, they would have stocked up their food pantries and welcomed their farm animals inside their home for this time in the season, in preparation for the cold winter. As indoor hibernation replaces the customary outdoor activities of the summer, it lends itself to the feeling of an annual cycle ending and the anticipation for the birth of the Sun, at the Winter Sols-tice. These are all influencing themes of this month. It is the quiet before the storms, as the subsequent months, for most people in our modern era, will bring a fair amount of stress, whether you are a farmer or a city dweller. With the mainstream holidays a few months away there will be a resurgence of excessive activities we won't be able to escape from and much of it, goes against what our bodies naturally wants to do in the winter.

    Samhain and Halloween is the time to remember and honor those who have passed away, more specifically those who died during the year. We honor the dead and thus the spiritual realm commands our attention at this time. As is evident in all the Halloween costumes and ghostly stories, psychic related activities and haunting phenomenons, it truly is the time to remember the underworld and those who have crossed over to "Summerlands." We can honor the dead in the traditional dumb supper, in elaborate altars, in prayers, visits to graveyards and churches, in our own special rituals or even in just a single candle prayer. Some opt, at this time, to connect with the dead, via the talents of psychic mediums and oracle readings, but just admiring a simple photo of a lost loved one, can be the most profoundly, powerful remembrance ritual. At this time of year, the Cosmos will support any effort to contact your deceased loved ones, making it easier to connect.

    This month we bravely connect with the Slovenian Goddess, Baba Yaga, journeying to our fears and discomforts, while communing with the Crone.

All Monthly intro text taken from author's first book, "Gathering for Goddess, A Complete Manual for Priestessing Women's Circles"

BABA YAGA GODDESS LESSON

"But Baba Yaga does not merely stand for the end of the cycle;
She is the Cycle, the black earth that closes over dead bones yet also is the fertile womb for
seedlings in Spring. Her hut turning on its chicken legs is the turning of seasons,
the endless motion of the Universe..."

Rebecca Vassey, writer for SageWoman Magazine

Her imageries conjure up all sorts of frightening stereotypical, old images of the Witch, the Hag, the decrepit wicked and the near dead. With her long bony fingers and limbs, and her oversized long nose with hairy warts decorating its edge, she can appear quite frightful to our inner child. Her hunched back and the appearance of her menacing gnawing iron clad black teeth is enough to make you run for the hills. She triggers our earliest memories and terrors of heart stopping childhood fairytales that warned us about the unknown and kept us from going into secluded, distant places, like the woods. We didn't ever want to meet the child-eating witch out there and so these infantile fairy tales, with their ghastly painted pictures, certainly made us cognizant of the possible dangers in the worlds but also fed our consciousness, tenacious prejudices and negative views on the unknown, the different and the old.

Baba Yaga is the Slavic Crone. Her origins come from the Baltic region but there are hints of her in Ukrainian and Polish folklore as well. She is found in numerous fairy tales as the wicked terror-striking Hag and although there is some conflict regarding her deity status, many myth scholars and Goddess worshippers exalt her as the quintessential, and misunderstood, Crone. She is elevated from this fairytale folklore dark fearsome character, to the Black Goddess we unearth her to be, after years of patriarchal suppression. Baba Yaga, like many powerful, ancient female deities that can threaten patriarchal growing societies, has been vilified and pushed out into the outskirts of civilization, far out into the uncultivated woods. Those who are researching "herstory," connecting to the Divine in her numerous guises and seeking to reclaim lost forgotten heritage are finding it in the tales orally passed down and later documented; patriarchally altered and revised and modified to hide the sacred feminine. We are finding her again and Baba Yaga is yet another reflection of Goddess in her Crone aspect; as Grandmother Moon, as Dark Mother, as the Black Goddess. And again I must stress, as I have in my previous books, that the color Black is not viewed as negative, at least not in Goddess Spirituality. Black, the Crone and Dark Goddesses in general are not viewed as negative or something evil or bad, on the contrary, they are very strong and powerful... and necessary. Black connotes the mysteries yet discovered, like our dark womb, it is a term used to define the hidden, the shadow, that which is misunderstood, what is prime and awaiting fertilization, There is much power in this.

Baba Yaga is a Goddess of death, and regeneration. She is a Goddess of monumental transformations and courageously facing our biggest fears. As her myths will reveal, she is a Goddess of initiatory characteristics, for she inaugurates for us, change that comes from knowledge and facing our truths. She is the Grandmother archetype, the wise, all knowing Crone. A Deity of prophecy and bringer of psychic and intuitive gifts, she is Goddess of our intuition and the primordial mysteries found in nature and her cyclical continuous patterns. Though her image might be frightening and at times down right gruesome, she beckons us to take courage and lift the façade, to unveil considerable wisdom and power that can positively transform our lives.

Perhaps it is best to begin by examining her name. In Russia the word for Grandmother is Babushka. Not surprising, some believed the name "Baba Yaga" originates from this sweet affectionate appellation. However when we look at the word "Baba" it has not only a different feel but also a slightly different meaning. In Russia the term "Baba" was used to describe an old woman, more specifically it was a term meant to describe a woman who is or was married and therefore non-virginal. Listening to the sound of the word "Baba," it has a harsher phonetic feel, as this was a deprecating term, meant to infer the whining wife. Baba meant the complaining, constant yelling and nagging woman. It is a word to connote that women, once they become wives or mothers, are witch-like, hags, complainers and naggers. Therefore, the first part of her name in our modern language suggests a rather whining, bothersome, unpleasant woman and old, certainly not virginal or maiden-like. Another indication of her association as a crone deity is her nicknames. Baba Yaga was also called "Blue-nosed" and "Bony-legged" Her full name was accepted as, "Baba Yaga Kostianaya Noga," which means "Baba Yaga Boney Legs" and this confirms even further her elderly status.

Connected as a Goddess of Cycles and Life and Death, it is not surprising she is Goddess of Bones but also a Goddess very much linked with the Harvest. For it is believed she plants us, fertilizes us, then prunes us and through-out the cold, Winter months, keeps us safe until we are ready to be replanted again, to bloom in the spring. Baba Yaga is the cycles of nature and the cycles of birth, life and death and rebirth, we personally experience at various points in our lives.

Described as a bony, hunchback, with numerous warts covering her face, disheveled silver hair and a bent crooked, long nose, that could reach the underside of her chin, she was meant to conjure fear in you. Baba Yaga was a frightening sight. As frail and bony as she appeared, she was a ferociously strong force to be reckoned with and she delighted in the nightly rides inside her spinning iron mortar and pestle. She would steer her pestle across the sky and make the howling sound of the fierce nightly breeze and if you listened closely enough you could hear her cackles amidst the orchestra of night. Yet it is important to note that it is our fears of the unknown; of death, of the old, that makes Baba Yaga so fearsome and ugly in our collective consciousness.

Gruesomely depicted as an ogre and known as a Hag, it is very important to understand that the term Hag had a very different meaning in olden times than it does today. In the Middle-Ages, the word Hag was often associated with nature Fairies. The word Hag often connoted something holy. It is derived from the Greek word Hadia or Hagiolatry, which means the worship of Saints. Considering this definition and

Baba Yaga so often being referred to as a hag, her numerous names and titles already begin to reflect a different perception of this Dark Goddess, when we endeavor to study her more closely.

To be sent to Baba Yaga was to be sent on a journey to death but courageously facing this fact manifested into an unfathomable freedom and liberation from all things fearsome. As a Goddess of death she was known to be the Guardian of the Waters of life and death. It was believed, corpses were brought back to life with a mere sprinkled of these waters, of life-powers, to be reborn again. Baba Yaga is best viewed as a Goddess of initiation and transitions. As the midwife of death she is the sacred portals we must all bravely pass through.

The brick oven, which plays a prominent role in her Baltic myths as the place where she lures and bakes her victims before devouring them, has often long been associated with the sacred womb. In its capacity to heat up and transform grains into nurturing bread, it is reminiscent of the pregnant Mother/Goddess birthing new life. In this same manner we are invited to consider that Baba Yaga's myth reveals her powers of actually taking us through this process of womb-like transformation, as we face our biggest fears, allow them to be devoured, buried, then transformed and reborn again. She is thus, in this way, a midwife of death and powerful initiations.

Often we think of three archetypal stages for women but really one may consider there to be four and the fourth one can be viewed as the afterlife or what appears after death. Baba Yaga precedes this stage and prepares us for the next, whether it does come to pass or whether a slight of hands changes our fate unexpectedly. As the Maiden precedes the Mother and the Mother precedes the Crone, it seems likely that the crone prepares and precedes what comes next, until the cycle is repeated once more. This is Baba Yaga's domain. They say she eats humans, especially children but it is really our inner child that she devours and transmutes in preparation for the next stage of life. In this way she is indeed the perpetual alchemist who transforms our fears and pain into our ultimate strengths. She leads women into transformational states, into this sort of *The Third Age of Woman,*" one in which she is no longer suffocatingly bonded to the role of maiden (daughter to her parents) nor mother to her offspring. In this new stage of her life, her new role affords her to taste freedom and this allows her to better serve her community and herself.

The crone is ultimately the one who births herself and, as a wise-woman, she offers the opportunity to receive and re-view the world through different eyes; wiser, all knowing eyes, that can reflect back to a long life filled with experiences and monumental reference points that shed invaluable spirit filled wisdom. Yes, she is indeed a midwife and the real labor unfolds as she reflects back at the culmination of her life experiences and looks forward to birthing the space for this new era as she enters into herself and the archetype of the Crone.

More of Baba Yaga and her Dark Goddess stature is memorialized in the famous popular Russian tale of "**Vasilisa the Beautiful**" There are numerous versions of this Russian tale that introduces us to Vasilisa and Baba Yaga. The story of Hansel and Gretel also comes to mind as well as a Spanish folktale named, "Don Octavio" and "Pedro and the Witch," coming from the Philippines. Below I will try to capture one version of the famous Russian tale as best I can.

"Vasilisa the Beautiful"

Most of the various versions of her tale begin in the same way...

There was once a man and his lovely wife who lived together in a home with their exquisite child, named Vasilisa but one day the wife became very ill and unexpectedly died leaving the man a mournful widower. On her death bed, right before dying, the mother asked to see her daughter. She handed her daughter a tiny wooden magickal doll. She spoke to her daughter about the importance of this doll imbued with love and how it had been passed down to her from her mother. She instructed Vasilisa that the doll would protect and help her in times of need and that she should keep it safe and hidden. In times of distress, she should feed the doll and heed its counsel. The crying Vasilisa took the doll with both hands, trying to logically comprehend her mother's last words. She then embraced her dying mother for the last time before death snatched her away. Many mournful years passed for her before Vasilisa even remembered the doll and its purpose.

Life without his wife became very difficult for Vasilisa's father. He was required to make numerous business trips and eventually he realized he needed to find a new wife to help with the maintenance of his home and rearing his beloved only daughter. At the time, there weren't too many available women in their village and thus he took on a widower who already had two daughters and they were older than Vasilisa. The news of her father's engagement was dreadful to Vasilisa, especially because he would be marrying the well-known village's shrew, named Lilya, but she tried to accept this turn of events. In time her father remarried Lilya and brought the daughters along with his new bride to move into their home with Vasilisa. Life changed drastically for Vasilisa as a result of this marriage. This new wife did not look too kindly to her stepdaughter, as Vasilisa was beautiful and well-loved by everyone in the community. It was hard to find potential suitors for Lilya's aging daughters, as every young man that came by the home only wished to see and court the young and beautiful Vasilisa. As time progressed the stepmother grew more frustrated, resentful and intolerable of her stepdaughter. Daily she showed preference for her own children while slowly denying her stepdaughter a mother's care and affection. Often she would yell at her and order her around the house to do various harsh and laborious chores but Vasilisa, with her blessed wooden doll, was well protected. This doll, when petitioned with a small morsel of food, would often comfort her and magickally do the entire chores for Vasilisa. When Vasilisa felt alone and mistreated, she often found comfort in the little wooden doll her mother gave her. It repeatedly made things right and assured her she was truly still loved.

Resentment and disdain for her stepdaughter grew as Lilya could not compete with Vasilisa's beauty and popularity. The thought of getting rid of her became ever more prevalent in Lilya's wicked heart and one day she crafted a plan that would surely get rid of the child.

Vasilisa's father was often absent from the household, away on long business trips and one day he had to take an exceptionally long trip away from home. When Vasilisa was told of this impending trip she begged her father to stay and tried to convince him of the cruelty she was experiencing in the hands of her stepmother and stepsisters but the father had to meet his work obligations. He assured his beautiful daughter that all would be right and perhaps it was all in her mind and that she needed to try to get along with everyone. Despondently, she accepted her father's request and watched as he left. As one would have expected, the abusive cruelty towards Vasilisa escalated as soon as her father left. Even the nosy neighbors now made notice of how cruel Lilya and her daughters were treating the beautiful Vasilisa. And though they tried to intervene to help the young maiden it only made matters worse as the stepmother began to lie and publicize that Vasilisa's father had abandoned them and would never returned.

Unbeknownst to anyone, the stepmother decided that they would move to the countryside in the middle of the night. She had hoped they would move close enough to the forest, where the infamous old hag, who loved to kidnap and eat children, would surely catch and devour the young Vasilisa. Lilya's plan was revealing itself, as she had hoped to feed her to the old Hag of the Forest, Baba Yaga.

Vasilisa during this painfully abysmal time relied on her magick wooden doll and it reassured her that her father loved her and had not abandoned her at all and thus she stayed hopeful and happy. Although she was sent often to work and fetch things in the deep frightening forest, she always returned safe and sound, much to her stepfamily's chagrin. Unbeknownst to anyone, the wooden doll her mother gave her, kept her well protected and safe during these frightening sojourns. One night however, the wicked stepmother and stepsisters orchestrated a plan to get Vasilisa eaten by the ill-reputed Baba Yaga once and for all. Late at night, when the last candle had been blown out in the household, the sisters sent Vasilisa out to the nearest neighbor, to Baby Yaga's hut, claiming a need for a source of light (candle) so that they may fulfill their mother's wishes and chores. Vasilisa was frightened but as always, she found comfort and strength in her mother's wooden doll. Close to her heart she carried it and asked for its counsel and guidance. She was assured that all would be well on the journey, so she continued onward towards the forest.

Vasilisa headed out into the deep dark forest and she walked for what seemed like eternity until she felt hopeless and lost. There was nothing in sight, except for darkness and she began to feel a gripping terror. She walked further deep into the forest and then discovered the house, passed a clearing. It was a wooden hut strangely elevated on chicken legs with eyes for windows and a mouth as its door. It was a house strangely animated; appearing as if it had its very own personal soul and entity. The frightened Vasilisa looked around and spied a plethora of scary bones and bright red eyed skulls all around the property and the fence that was made up of corpses. There were animals too; a black cat, vicious geese-swan and a hungry looking dog. Then all of a sudden, she heard the thundering hooves of a horse approaching, it was getting louder, flying above her, as it went passed Baba Yaga's entryway. She saw the Black Horseman disappearing into thin air as he entered the hut. Eventually she would also see a Red Horseman flying through Baba Yaga's entryway and in the morning she would again hear the hooves of horsemen and watch as a White Horseman would appear to fly into her hut and disappeared into thin air. Vasilisa would later learn that these were Baba Yaga's servants. They were her brightest Dawn, her Red Sun and her Black Dark Night. Vasilisa would also learn that Baba Yaga shared her home with her "Soul friends" and "trusty servants," the herdsman named Koshchey and three magickal hands that would grind the grain for her breads and press the oil from her Poppy seeds.

Standing in the dark of night, Vasilisa finally encounters the bony, hideous looking Baba Yaga as she flew in her spinning mortar and pestle, back to the elevated chicken leg held hut. She utters an incantation to make the hut turned to her, lowered itself and welcome the hag inside but not before smelling the scent of a Russian nearby. Baba Yaga smelled the child near and confronted her. Terrified at the numerous ghastly sights before her, Vasilisa finds the strength to speak to Baba Yaga and tells her why she is there. Baba Yaga immediately puts the child to work, telling her she will get what she needs and will not get devoured by her, if she completes a number of tasks. With her doll in hand, Vasilisa is again comforted and protected by her mother's blessing, as all the daunting tasks the hag had demanded from her were magickally completed by nightfall. Baba Yaga returned from her daily rides on her spinning mortar and pestle to find her house had been cleaned and a large meal prepared for her by the young girl. The old Hag devoured the meal, fit for ten men and laid herself out, dissatisfied that she had nothing to complain about. She gave Vasilisa another series of task for the next day with the same threat, that if she wanted to survive in her hut, she needed to complete these tasks. Baba Yaga indicated that her Poppy seeds needed to be cleared of any signs of the earth and Vasilisa was again required to complete some of the most hideously daunting tasks to gain her freedom. With her wooden doll however, she was able to magickally complete these demands. The poppy seeds were cleaned and now pressed by Baba Yaga's trusty servants, the three magickal hands that had prepared the grain for bread the night before.

When all was done and Baba Yaga had finished her colossal feast she asked the child to finally speak. Vasilisa asked the crone about the three different horsemen she had seen outside. Then Baba Yaga asked how she managed to get these impossible tasks done and the intimidated girl replied simply, with her mother's blessing. This revelation of Vasilisa's mother's blessing sent Baba Yaga into a tiff. *"I cannot have a child blessed by her Mother in my home, away with you..."* I imagine her saying. Baba Yaga claimed that Vasilisa's mother's blessing was actually hurting her bones and she needed to swiftly get out of her hut. Vasilisa hastily tried to get out of the house as quickly as possible but she had not yet received the source of light she was obligated to bring back home. Quickly Baba Yaga pulled one of her red-eyed glowing skulls, propped it on a stick and gave it to the child to give to her stepmother and stepsister for light. Then swiftly the young girl proceeded to get herself out of there and find her way back to the house.

Vasilisa tried to hurry as fast as she could but the journey was long and arduous. She walked for eternity it seemed without any clue or evidence if she was even on the right path but she persevered. The red glowing eyes of the skull, given to her by Baba Yaga, helped shine a light for her but its light went out a few time throughout the long journey, only to come back on as she finally arrived to the doorsteps of the house. When she arrived back home, she found her stepmother and stepsisters looking rather sickly, crouched in a corner in the dark. They had not eaten nor had any form of light since Vasilisa had first left on her journey. Somehow they were unable to maintain a consistent source of light in their house in her absence and they looked horrible. When Vasilisa presented them with Baba Yaga's gift they dismissed and ridiculed it. They poked fun at the maiden for taking so long to return. Then the red eyes of the eerie looking skull began to glow brightly and it stared right back at the ungrateful women. Within minutes Lilya and her two daughters caught sight of the skull's enchanted stare and they quickly burned, disintegrating into ashes. Vasilisa, with her pure heart and protected by her mother's love was unscathed by Baba Yaga's final tool of enchantment.

The Russian tale ends with Vasilisa returning to her old home in the village and happily finding her father there awaiting her return. Some claim she would become the love target of the Tzar and later agree to become his loving bride but that goes into yet another fascinating Russian folk tale.

BABA YAGA MUSING & MEDITATION

"...She has a way of showing certain mountains up
for the relatively insignificant molehills they often are..."

Rebecca Vassey, writer for SageWoman Magazine

The Dark Goddess, Baba Yaga, is the shadowy, hidden ugliness that one must admit to before arriving at our destination. She is the test! The painful confrontation of all that paralyzes and scares you is encapsulated in her frightful cackles. She is a mirror to our deepest fears and reluctancies. In the end, she reveals and exemplifies a fearlessness and courage based on simply her truths, for she doesn't sugar coat the battle scars we are expected to courageously endure, if we dare. She is the old crone who has earned the right to tell it like it is without any filters, fears or concerns and this is very scary for most in our society, as the unpleasant is always disguised and relegated to the far off regions of mainstream society. Our fears of the unknown; of death, monstrocities, the sick and the old, is what makes Baba Yaga so fearsome and ugly in our collective consciousness. Her ways are viewed as harshly abrasive or negative, even evil, to those uninitiated, because she doesn't have to make her message pretty, nor acceptable to our esthetic. Our modern day society, that so often likes messages to be delivered neatly in veiled illusions, is ill-equipped to handle the uncensored power of the bold, fearless Crone, who is untamed and immuned to societal manipulations. She stands in her truth, unadorned, alone and sovereign, for she has lived a long life that has garnered her unfathomable gifts. Her eyes pierce through all realms and her lips reveal truths marinated in her oozing rawness and timelessness. She does not need to be ornamented, laced up in pretty pinks or enchanting youthfulness, for those days of endured entrapment have long gone.

Baba Yaga has lived, it seems many lives and played many conventional and unconventional roles and I bet she has also sacrificed a lot in her lifetime in order to survive for so long. And Baba Yaga has seen, experienced and witnessed much in her unnaturally long life. Unnatural...for how many people are able to live many years and outlive their families, communities and even survive being marginalized and relegated to the irrelevant and invisible realm of the near silence.

Her bony, disheveled, hunchback physique is a testament to all she has endured in her lifetime and her frightfully mangled body reflects numerous wounds (emotional, mental, spiritual and physical) as well as the years of battle scars that have rewarded her with wisdom. She has earned the right to be...simply be, in her truth; whether nice or gruesome, clean or disheveled, unadorned, alone and in rags. She is not invested in impressing you or society at large. She simply is and this state of being intimidates many who are unaware, unconsciously living, and many who dare not dream of unearthing their own authentic voice.

You need to meet her to confront that which appears ugly, threatening and downright frightening.... Let the rest of the world stay in sad states of delusions, self-deceptions, states of unconsciousness, complacency and ignorance and paralyzing fears.... You know your life is a Soul journey, cyclical and ever evolving. You have embraced that your life is approaching a major turning point and these are the fires you must now confront to proceed forward. This is the dark forest you must travel through. She is your test and passage of initiation, for you have arrived at the sacred threshold, the edge of her forest. You are ready to be free of all hindrance. And in her spinning mortar and pestle you will find the liberation to just be and fly. Her wisdom expands far beyond your self-imposed limited reality and she will not save you, nor spare you of the truth. Heed her tasks, heed her counsel and she will lead you though the labyrinth of darkness, pain, destruction, rebirth and ultimately into the conquerable. Be prepared to know, what it is you seek and why you must stand before her now.

The journey to her chicken leg elevated, wooden hut is monumental. Beginning the journey alone through this dark forest is an admirable feat, in and of itself, but it is not enough. Arriving at her door steps and courageously demanding to be let in, to face her and your deep rooted fears, is only the beginning of this journey. Come face to face with Baba Yaga and bring your purest of hearts encased within. Come with your sincerest endeavor to know, to heal, to unearth truth, her wisdom, to be guided and to somehow find the spark of light within the darkness. Meet her eye to eye and come with reverence for the one who has immeasurable wisdom and insight to guide you through even the darkest of Labyrinths. Come and confront the archetype of the Crone and welcome Baba Yaga's ancient wisdom.

"Why do you come here?
What do you seek to know from me?" you hear her ask.

I begin; *"..... Baba Yaga, I am scared... I am scared of failing but most of all, I am scared of succeeding. Oh my... oh dear...I am scared of actually succeeding, it hadn't dawned on me but I am scared of actually achieving my biggest brightest childhood dreams. I am scared of being fully fulfilled, happy and completed. I am scared of meeting myself as this brilliant, talented, well-loved being. It has been such a long time on this expansive, self-defeating road. I've gotten so accustomed to feeling loneliness and failure that they have become comforting familiar friends. Anything else to feel and experience would send me to a frightful place and awaken the intense anxiety so entangled in my self-worth. And I fear the self-sabotaging entity that always seems to creep up at the most expertly orchestrated moments. I need to say goodbye to past failures and ideals that no longer serve me and release the comfort of the painfully outworn. I wish to singe the scripts of the past so that I may be liberated to rewrite new ones..."*

*"How do you prepare your bones for death, most holy, old wise one? I fear I will die...I will surely die. I know I will... She who has placed herself in the hermitage coffin, the orphaned, the isolated island, the frightened, secluded, lonely one will die and I fear her death. I fear the consequences of her death. I fear the metamorphosis in her absence... I fear what she will demand of me next...I will have nothing to hold on to, nothing to blame for this life and the choices I've made and the ones I was too scared to make. I will have nothing holding me back....no more excuses, for the wings will be exposed and Baba Yaga will say...."Fly!!!!" And I will say, "**but...I, I have no wings**" and she will point to the ones that have always been on my shoulders; dusty, neglected, abandoned so long ago. "FLY!!!!!" she commands, as she pushes me off her spinning mortar and cackles away..."* **"Fly...."**

BABA YAGA GODDESS GATHERING DAY

Purpose: To journey deep in the recesses of the scary woods and meet the frightful one, the intimidating Baba Yaga, to learn her wisdom and mysteries. Travel to the Slavic Crone to receive her counsel and face our biggest fears, represented in her. Moving past our paralysis into courage and action.

Check Ins: We gather around the Circle and introduce ourselves to one another, while also voicing our feelings on this month and our hope for the upcoming season.

Chants: Together we will join our voices to sing some commonly known Pagan chants, as well as new ones offered on the Chant sheet in the hand outs (see the last page of this chapter). Singing aloud is a wonderful way to raise energy effortlessly and it also sometimes helps in creating harmonious bonds.

Our Agreements bylaws and Pertinent group discussion... We go around the circle of women, reading a few lines each of our "Group Agreements" and add any new ones that seem necessary. Agreements are signed and submitted in confidence.

Drumming Grounding: A drumming musical CD track will be played, to give participants a chance to connect and ground to this very moment. Women are invited to find a comfortable seat or stand and add movement if they wish.

Conjuring Goddess via her Image: Using a photo image of the Crone or a Goddess oracle card or a scuplture image of the Goddess, Baba Yaga, we will share around the circle, as each woman present will reflect on the images and attributes they intuit.

Lecture on the Slovic Crone Goddess, Baba Yaga
Her myth and various folklores, her attributes and relevance for us today.

GODDESS WORKSHOPS
WORKSHOP I
The Crone, connecting with her energy as Grandmother Spirit
WORKSHOP II
The Hag, confronting the ugliness. The light and beauty inherent in the dark.
WORKSHOP III
Forest & Nature workings in our Spirituality
WORKSHOP IV
Solitude and the gift of the Hermit, exploring the Hermit and Death Tarot card
WORKSHOP V
Aging & Growing Old. A discussion on Aging in our modern society, especially in our country, at this pivotal time in history.
WORKSHOP VI
Baking Magick and the Kitchen Witch. Mortar & Pestle and the sacredness of the Oven, Communally baking a meal.
WORKSHOP VII
Bone Crafting and the sacredness of our Bones.
WORKSHOP VIII
Crafting a special magick doll like Vasilisa owned.

BABA YAGA GODDESS GATHERING RITUAL

Purpose: To journey deep in the recesses of the scary woods and meet the Crone, the frightful one, the intimidating Baba Yaga, to learn her wisdom and mysteries. Travel to the Slavic Goddess to receive her counsel and face our biggest fears, represented in her. Moving past our paralysis into courage and action.

Asperge: with a smudge bundle of sage and copal and Rue anointing oil on the forehead.
Anointing & Welcoming: Tribal deep drumming music can be played throughout this ritual to set the tone for this rite.

INTENT DECLARED: With the dark season upon us, we endeavor to travel deeply into her fields of bones. Connect with Goddess, Baba Yaga, and the wise, old crone.

Circle Casting:
With my will and word,
I conjure thee,
Ancient Circle of power.
Be thou a safe meeting place,
Between the realms for Humanity
and Spiritual forces.
Be thou a place of protection and safety,
A barrier against all evil,
And a sealant to protect those present here.
The Soil for our energy,
The sphere of our protection.

Be thou a place where the North, South, East, West
And the Center can be honored,
And worked in harmony with our energy,
To perform our Sacred rites.

Be thou a place held sacred to the ones invoked
And worshipped here today,
By my will and word.
I conjure thee,
The circle is cast,
So Mote it be!!!

Elemental Invocation
Hail to you Earth from the realm of the North.
Deep in the forest, where the gnomes make their home, where the wise old crone, finds her place among the sacred, where all is transformed, given and taken. **Hail and Welcome to you, Earth!**

Hail to you Air from the realm of the East.
Spinning, fierce breezes that howl as she speaks. Air that announces that change has begun, breezes that shift us, prepares us for what's to come. **Hail and Welcome to you, Air!**

Hail to you Fires from the realm of the South.
From the flames of our hearth, from the passions of our heart. From the welcoming warmth, on a chilly autumn night. Hail to you fires as you brightly burn through this night. **Hail and Welcome to you, Fire!**

Hail to you Waters from the realm of the West.
From the waters of tears that lives only to express. From the dew on the flowers, resting lightly in the morn'. Hail to you waters as our feelings take form. **Hail and Welcome to you, Water!**

CHANT: *"Mother of Darkness, Mother of Light"*
GODDESS INVOCATION

ASPECTING PROSE
TRANCE RAISING ENERGY *(Drums, dance, cone of Power)*
CHANT: *"Bones, come Dance with me"*

SPELL WORKING
Raising energy, around the circle we state aloud what we fear,
we'll state individually while holding our bone as its symbol;
"I fear _____"

Confronting our fears represented in BabaYaga, in skulls and bones, we will grind our fears in her mortar and pestle. We take this sacred moment to visit with the crone and face our biggest fears; facing those things that may appear ugly and full of complexities. Gather our bones (the ones we carried into the ritual). Let the bones you hold in your hands represent what you fear, then one by one, in her mortar and pestle, which will be passed around the circle so that each person will have a chance to grind them, we will pulverize our fears and then feed it to the earth far away from our homes or bury it into a coffin-shaped paper box and bury it far away.

Holding a bone we say;
"This bone represents my fear of _____
I will face it, pulverize you and feed you to the Crone"
****

ALTERNATELY SPELL II: Crafting a doll like Vasilisa to help strengthen you when you face your doubts and fears. While thinking of someone who has expressed great love for you, create this poppet, fill it with herbs and anything you wish to include inside of it. When you are ready sew it shut.

CHANT: *"Old woman wrap your cloak around me..."*
Final Check in

CHANT: *"Going Down in the Cauldron..."*
DEVOKING GODDESS

DEVOKING ELEMENTS
WATER
Hail to you Water, receive our Gratitude.
Sacred Waters that birth us anew, you came when called to guard our sacred space. As we bid thee adieu, receive our Gratitude for your presence here today. Hail and Farewell, Guardian of the West, Realm of Water!
FIRE
Hail to you Fire, receive our Gratitude.
Fires from the hearth that makes our nurturing foods, passionate flame awakened from within, you came when called to guard our sacred space. As we bid thee adieu, receive our Gratitude for your presence here today. Hail and Farewell, Guardian of the South, Realm of Fire!
AIR
Hail to you Air, receive our Gratitude.
With its Howling breeze and its message to start a new, your presence was felt as you guarded our rites. Receive our Thanks as we bid thee adieu, with Gratitude for your presence here today. Hail and Farewell, Guardian of the East, Realm of Air!
EARTH
Hail to you Earth, receive our Gratitude.
From deep in the forest you came to share your embrace, held us safely as we invoked you to guard our space. As we bid thee adieu, receive our Gratitude for your presence here today.
Hail and Farewell, Guardian of the North, Realm of Earth!

CHANT: *"We all come from the Goddess..."*
OPENING CIRCLE:
Our Circle is open but never unbroken,
may the love and peace of the Goddess rest forever in our hearts,
Merry meet, merry part and merry meet again....

*****POTLUCK FEASTING*

INVOCATION

BABA YAGA
Stirring, spinning,
Baba Crone,
Deep in the Forest,
Gathering the Bones.

Ridding her Mortar,
Cackling with the Breeze
Baba Yaga,
Do not eat me...

I have come
To know your ways,
Bravely read
The lines on your face,

Conquer fears
Of the hideous and unknown,
Garner wisdom,
From those who've lived long ago.

Grandmother Spirit
I come to you
Respectfully honoring,
The magick you do...

Your mysteries,
Your counsel,
I request on this night,
I stand before you,
For answers, despite the fright.

Cackling Crone,
Baba Yaga hear me,
I invoke you in this ritual,
Bring thy presence and blessings.

SPELLS

AWAKENING THE WITCH

I am Witch today,
As I've been in the past,
Gathering, reclaiming,
As this Circle is cast.

Ability to Enchant,
Whomever I will,
Ability to hex
And when needed,
To heal,

To call on my ancestors,
The elements, Fae, and spirits
Priestessing for the Goddess,
Knowing her love has no limit.

Traveling all realms,
And unlocking all doors,
Knowledge of invocations
To worship "Her" even more.

Blessed and guarded
By my elders of the Craft,
Akashic knowledge I manifest
From future, present and past.

I declare myself Witch,
As my lineage has deemed,
By the power of the ancient ones,
And by all that is felt and seen.

The Moon and the Stars,
I am daughter of the light,
I reclaim here now
My Witch Birth right!

From this day forward
And forever more,
Awakening the powers
Once so foreign to my core....

I am Witch, awaken on a count of three
This I make true,
So Mote it be!!!

BABA YAGA'S NOCTURNAL VISIT

In this dream I entered a huge crowded room, like a school hall cafeteria and I walked around this room very humbly, quietly looking for a familiar face or a friendly smile that would ease my discomfort and erase my social awkwardness, but no luck. I felt alone and uncomfortable as I walked around this cafeteria. Finally I settled on a small round table alone. Eventually two women joined me there, one of them looked like the woman named Kandee, from one of the Housewives Reality television shows and she started to talk to me about music, a common interest we both actually share. Anyway, I continued to look around, when my eyes finally rested on the Priestess in front of the room, as she began to prepare herself and the altar for a special ritual. I watched her with great interest as she prepared the various food offerings; there were many fruits and vegetables like a big Harvest Banquet. I watched as she also organized the people who were there with the intention of partaking of this ritual. I walked pass the Priestess and her beautifully crafted altar and all those exquisite offerings on the floor. Then my vision looked upwards and I saw an Elderly lady sitting, almost elevated, like on a small throne. She was very wrinkled and dark, resembling the Yoda from Star Wars or my High School Choral conductor, music teacher, Mrs. W.

This woman appeared to be a respected Elder and she gestured to me to come over, be near her, sit by her and so I did. I sat by this crone who appeared to be my longstanding ancestral guide, my spiritual teacher. There was something so special about her and she radiated in a way I could not describe. Together we sat side by side and watched the preparations taking place for the ritual and the various attendants as they appeared slightly below us because we were elevated. I watched as offerings were being given and taken, and humbly, I allowed everyone to go ahead before me. I was either not in a hurry or was too scared of over stepping my boundary but I recall the old lady telling me it was okay, again, with a simple gesture and smile.

Then to my surprise, I sat there and within a few minutes I noticed the Priestess caught sight of us and she started walking towards us with offerings in her arms. All the while I had let everyone go before me, feeling unprepared and unworthy of the offerings and here was the Priestess herself, actually hand delivering it to me personally, as if I was royalty. I guess sitting by the elderly woman made me her honored guest, her apprentice and I was thus treated as so. The Priestess approached us and lovingly extended her hands with two offerings; a Ham sandwich and a special kind of Corn or Bean (Grain) dish, contained in a bowl. Since I am a vegetarian I refused the Ham sandwich but humbly accepted the Bean dish. My spiritual teacher next to me encouraged me to go ahead take a bite of the offering and as I reached for a tiny morsel of the bean dish and placed it in my mouth, something magickal happened. The room twirled around instantaneously. I heard her cackles and I felt her fly away with laughter and joy, like the Slovic Goddess, BabaYaga. And I felt the whole energy of the room switch suddenly. The whole room was spiraling, dizzying and the echoes from her cackles sent shivers up my spine. My Elders are a long list of strong empowered women in my lineage, that keep watch over me and take pleasure in guiding me throughout this journey and I am most grateful for their love, protection and guidance. I am strengthened in the presence of the wise, old Crone. Blessed Be!!!

BABA YAGA GODDESS GATHERING CHANT TEXT SHEET

EARTH, MOON,MAGICK
In the Earth, deep within,
There is A Magick, I draw it in.
          In her Caves, in the Trees
          Hear her Heartbeat, Pulsing thru me.
When I Rise, I feel her Love
With feet Grounded, I'm soaring high above,
          In the Earth, deep within,
          There is A Magick, I draw it in
Ancient Moon, my Soul reveres
With my Singing, I call you here.
When this flame, ignites tonight,
Priestess dancing, Under the moonlit night....
In the Earth, deep within,
There is A Magick
I draw it in.... There is A Magick, I draw it in }3x
By B. Melusine Mihaltses

BONES, *By "Flight of the Hawk"*
Bones, come Dance with me,(3x rept)
Dancing in the desert, in the desert tonight (2Xrept)
Bones, Come Sing with me, (3X rept)
Dancing in the desert, in the desert tonight (2Xrept)
Bone dance know the Shaman dance
Bone dance hear the Raven cry
Bone dance see the Ancestors,
Dancing in the desert, in the desert tonight (2xrept)
Bones, Come fly with me, (3x rept)
Dancing in the desert, in the desert tonight (2Xrept)
Bones come die with me, (3Xrept)
Dancing in the desert, in the desert tonight (2X)*start*

Mother of Darkness
Mother of Darkness,
Mother of Light ,
Earth beneath the Soul in Flight
Songs of Love
and Love of Light,
Guide us to our heart...

In the Caudron
I am going down in the Cauldron,
Don't you worry and don't you moan,
I am going to lay my body down,
In the Cauldron,
Crones are calling,
Gonna be reborn.... (Rpt)

Mother I feel you under my feet
*Mother I feel you under my feet, Mother I feel your Heart Beat 2X
Heya Heya Heya, Heya Heya Ho 2X
Mother I hear you in the Rivers Sound, Eternal Waters going on and on 2X
Heya heya heya heya heya ho 2X
Mother I see you in when the Eagles fly, Flight of the Spirit gonna take our time 2X
Heya Heya Heya, Heya Heya Ho   By: Unknown source

WE ARE A CIRCLE by Rick Hamouris
We are a Circle, within a Circle, with no Beginning and never ending....
You hear us Sing, You hear us Cry,
Now hear us Call you, Spirits of Earth and Sky
Within our Hearts, there goes a spark
Love and Desire, a burning Fire...
We are a Circle, within a Circle,   with no Beginning and never ending...(chorus)

RATTLE MY BONE
Old Woman Wrap your cloak around me, Death Bringer rattle my Bones,
Old Woman Wrap your cloak around me,Death Bringer rattle my Bones,
Rattle my Bone, Rattle my Bones, Death bringer rattle my Bones.

ANCIENT MOTHER
Ancient Mother, I hear you calling,
Ancient Mother, I hear your sound,
Ancient Mother, I hear your laughter,
Ancient Mother, I taste your tears... (rpt)*by Deena Metzger & Charlie Murphy*

Elemental Chant
*The Earth, The Air
The Fire, The Water
Return, Return, Return
Below, Above
the Center is Love
Return, Return, Return By: Robin Rose Bennet -addy, Origins unknown

CHAPTER TWELVE

Ma'at

"Truth is always in harmony with herself and is not concerned chiefly to reveal the justice that may consist with wrong-doing..." Henry David Thoreau

MA'AT

MA'AT

"Justice turns the scale, bringing to some, learning through suffering" Aeschylus

MA'AT ALTAR SET UP

OUR ALTAR

Altar cloth : *A blue or purple altar cloth to the Egyptian Goddess, Ma'at is highly suggested, as purple is related to sovereignty and blue is often connected with the law. Some might also feel comfortable utilizing a white or black altar cloth since she is connected to the afterlife and her judgment hall. If you can obtain an altar cloth with images of scales or feathers, in particular, ostrich feathers, this would be ideal but not essential.*

Image: *The image of the Egyptian winged Goddess, Ma'at should be prominently displayed upon your altar to her. She can also be represented simply with a weighting scale. An image of the blind lady of justice can also be displayed.*

Always present on the altar;
A silver pentacle, a cast iron cauldron, drums, speaking stick, wand, athame, elemental representations.....

Air: *feather bundles, angel wings, bird, eagle or owl statuaries. Bell &, chimes, Incense type sticks, cones, charcoal brisket and fine powdered herbs; frankincense , myrrh.*
Fire: *pillar candles, glass enclosed candles in yellow, gold, white, blue or purple*
Water: *Small glass bowl with Water and or chalice with Champagne, Cranberry Juice or Red wine.*
Earth: *At this time of the year I like to use bare branches and create a beautiful center piece of these long, arm-like branches. A small dish of soil or dry herbs can also be used*

Other items pertinent to this particular gathering
A weighting scale
Feathers, in particular Ostrich feathers
Image of an eagle
Images that connote the judicial system
A symbolism of a Heart made out of clay or papier-mâché or a balloon shaped heart
Papyrus and scrolls with her invocations
Pen and paper
A tiny image of a boat
Tarot or Goddess Oracle cards

Sacred objects from members:
Notes:

MONTH AND THE SEASON

November

November is the Eleventh month in the Gregorian calendar, yet this month probably attained its name after the Latin word *"novem"*, meaning "nine," as it was traditionally the ninth month in the Roman calendar. The astrological sign for November is intense, passionate Scorpio and the venomous scorpion is its symbol. Scorpio is ruled by fiery, aggressive Mars, but also by transformative, regenerative, dark Pluto (Oct 21-Nov 20). It is these significant elements that influence the energy of the month of November.

The Full moon of this month is sometimes called Frost Moon, as the first Frost usually arrives at this time, in some parts of the world. According to the Farmer's Almanac it was also known as Wind Moon, Oak Moon and Beaver Moon because, for the Native Americans, this was the best time to hunt for Beavers, as their fur was quite desired during the cold winter months. The swamps would not have been frozen yet and hunting for beavers would have proven successful.

The Anglo-Saxon often referred to this month's Full moon as Blood Moon because this was typically the time when animals were slaughtered and their blood spilled upon the earth. Keep in mind, that for our ancestors, the last Harvest would've been at the end of October, nothing will grow on the land from this point onward until the coming of spring. In preparation for the anticipated long Winter, food, including animal meat, would've been chopped up and prepared for storage. Food that they stored away now needed to last them for the entire winter season.

November's Full moon was also often known as the Mourning Moon and there are many obvious reasons for this name. At the end of October we traditionally honor our ancestors during one of the major witches sabbat- Samhain, but for other cultures, like Mexicans and South-Westerns, the season of honoring the dead continues right into the first week of November. November 2nd finds many Mexicans, non-Pagans and Pagan alike celebrating, *"El Dia de los Muertos,"* Day of the Dead. Interesting to note that the celebrations take on a much more festive, humorous hue, as people often dress up their skulls in bright colors or as celebrities. Parades (of both adults and children dressed up in skeletal outfits) are not that uncommon in Mexico. Their altars (to honor their beloved deceased) would typically have bright orange and yellow marigolds, sugar and elaborately painted skulls and beautifully dressed female skeletal figures called Katrinas. Altars to the dead would also include platters of their favorite tasty foods, along with the photos of the departed. You might also find many Mexicans, as well as Catholics, spending the days and nights at their local cemeteries with their beloved deceased. The Spanish Catholics observed this time to mourn the dead and pray for the departed souls on their traditional "All Souls Day" on November the 2nd.

Towards the end of the month many celebrate the U.S.A. holiday of Thanksgiving, which was originally conceived as the first harvest of Indian corn by the Pilgrims in 1621. Pilgrims and Native Americans sat down together and shared in the bounty of the Earth by feasting on all kinds of foods in the young, new land of America. The festivities lasted for three whole days and was originally commemorated sometime in the summer months, but the U.S.A. government later changed the date and today we honor this historical event by re-enacting it, with our own festivities, the fourth Thursday of the month.

Inherent in Thanksgiving are family gatherings, dinners, pumpkin pies, red and orange autumnal leaves, turkeys, corn and a cornucopia of all sorts of edibles. Towards the end of the month, this is the dominate theme. It has become, however, a peculiar time of overindulgences, whether its shopping too much and hoarding or being swayed by all the astronomical, unbeatable sales everywhere. A variety of indulgences at parties and dinners temps us all. In general, this marks the beginning of the holiday season and all that it entails; lots of gatherings, long and short voyages to family and friends, elated and stressful spirits, Dining room tables spread with decadence, football games and sweet nostalgic parades, and did I mention, shopping..... In the U.S.A., towards the end of November we are inducted into the Christmas shopping season, with the traditional 'Black Friday', massive insane sales offered the day after Thanksgiving.

Amidst all the chaotic and blurry festivities, it is a good time to contemplate on our own personal blessings. A time to truly look at what we have to be grateful for and set aside quietude, sanctuaries, creating moments of deep reflection and Gratitude.

This month we call upon the Egyptian Goddess of the underworld and Judgment hall, Ma'at.

All Monthly intro text taken from author's first book,
"Gathering for Goddess, A Complete Manual for Priestessing Women's Circles"

MA'AT GODDESS LESSON

Ma'at is probably one of the oldest, most recognized deities in the Egyptian pantheon. She stems from the Old Kingdom (c.2680-2190BCE) and the earliest mention of this Goddess can be found on the Pyramid text of King Unas in the 5th Dynasty (around CA 2375 BCE- 2345 BCE). *"Egyptian religion" by Siegfried Morenz, translated by Ann E. Keep page 275, 1992 Cornell University Press.*

Most of what we know about Ma'at is derived from the Egyptian *"Book of the Dead,"* a collection of funerary text, religious and magickal rites. Composed mostly in hieroglyphics or hieratic script, it's original Egyptian title translated as, *"Book of Coming Forth by Day"* or *"Book Emerging Forth into the Light."* Its origins come from the Egyptian city of Thebes and can be traced to the first pyramid text of the 5th Dynasty (around 2400 BC). Kings and Pharaohs would often commission their own personal version of *"The Book of the Dead,"* later this practice was taken over by nobilities and those with status and the financial means to commission a personal funerary text rite. This text served as a guide for the dead transitioning into the afterlife via the journey through the Duat (the underworld). The numerous spells found in these writings were often painted and engraved on coffins, tomb walls, pyramids, and sarcophagi. Some of these funerary text, the more traditional ones, date as far back as the 3rd millennium BC but new Egyptian spells and writings were created as time went by and it was not uncommon to also reuse well established older, funerary text from this period. *"The Book of the Dead"* is an extremely invaluable source for those seeking to understand funerary practices and beliefs, related to death and the afterlife in ancient Egyptian culture. In early times it was a text well consulted by many and today continues to provide much insight on a mysteries subject that still eludes so many of us.

Ma'at, or Mayet as she is endearingly called, is the Goddess of Truth, Justice, the Law and Divine Order. She is Goddess of Moral Integrity and a primordial Goddess of Righteousness. She is the judge of the dead in the halls of Duat, in the underworld. She is the personification of order and the law. Because she is considered a primeval deity, some debate whether she is an actual human formed Goddess or simply the concept or female principle of order in the universe. She epitomizes the importance of justice for a thriving society, the importance of proper behavior, and fairness for the disadvantaged. She is in essence, truth embodied but she is more than the legislative; she is the cosmic law of the universe.

Her name in Egypt is synonymous with the word truth. Some scholars translate her name as literally meaning, *"that which is straight,"* a reference to her abilities to create order from chaos and provide the straight foundations necessary for the world to be built upon and exist in harmony. Even her hieroglyphics, an Ostrich feather, depicts this important aspect of the Goddess, with its straight lines, the hieroglyphics represents the Goddess of Justice.

Lady of Heaven, Mistress of the Underworld, Ma'at was often depicted with wings and this connected her to the pre-dynastic vulture deity of Upper Egypt; Nekhbet.

Whether sitting, kneeling or standing, she is often shown dressed in the traditional Egyptian close fitted dress, in the color red or gold with a feather protruding from her head of solid black straight stresses. On one hand she holds the Ankhs, a symbol of peace and on the other hand she holds a scepter, a symbol of power. Though many Egyptian Gods are often linked with animals and are sometimes even depicted with an animal's head form, you will not find this to be the case for Ma'at. She is often represented as a beautiful woman, an Ostrich feather or the very scales she would employed as she judged the dead.

As with most ancient deities there is some confusion regarding her parentage but we do know, from the ancient texts, her strong connection to Ra. The Egyptian Sun God, Ra, originally had two known daughters; Hathor-Sekhmet and Tefnut-Ma'at. The beloved Ma'at was considered the eye of Ra but also the heart, for it is the heart where moral judgment is made and this was her domain. Today, she continues to be the one who steers his boat, as he flies across the sky. It is Ma'at who guides the sun to set at night and rise every morning. She is the Goddess who controls the motions and patterns of nature in the Universe. She regulates the seasons, the stars, the planets and the waters upon the earth. Even the inundation of the Nile River, which was so important for Egyptians, falls under her domain. Ancient Egypt and its prosperous growth was heavily dependent on the water of the Nile river and naturally a Goddess who rules over the progression of the season and its sacred patterns found in the universe, would be responsible for these vital waters as well.

Ma'at existed since the beginning of time according to Egyptian mythos and cosmology. In the beginning there was darkness, the void, formlessness and chaos, as numerous cultures confirm and support in agreement in their respective folklores. In this chaotic, abysmal, boundlessness, which is found in so many varying myths explaining the earth's beginnings, there was also water and a cosmic egg floating upon the shapeless world. In the cosmic egg was the Kephera, the light, which remained hidden inside the darkness of the egg, until one day it was cracked open and unleashed upon the formless universe. In that very moment the world began to take shape; Shu, the atmosphere, manifested and soon thereafter Tefnut, as moisture, emerged and through the space between these two, emerged the Sun God, Ra. According to Egyptian writings one of the first deities to manifest was the Sun God, Ra. Ra emerged from the Nun, the primordial waters and subsequently right then, the straightness to set the orderly foundation of the world was immediately necessary and thus the Goddess Ma'at was called upon and she too emerged with Ra. Some scholars believe Ma'at gave birth to Ra, making her his mother, but more often she is considered one of his beloved daughters. Upon creation she is the one who organizes chaos and brings cosmic order into the universe. In her presence the natural laws of the universe exist and are enforced. She rules the movement of the stars and planets, the rising and setting of sun and the ebb and flow of the waters.

According to Egyptian cosmology, at this auspicious moment in the creation of the universe, there existed three Gods alone on the Solar Barque; the Sun God, Ra,

Ma'at, Goddess of Divine order and her consort, the God of Wisdom, Throth. Ma'at was to replace the God of Chaos and destruction, Set, and she becomes his antithesis. And this reminds me of the Japanese myth related to Amaterasu, the Sun Goddess, and her struggles to eradicate the chaos of her brother, Susano-o, but I digress. These three primordial Egyptian Gods emerged and rode on the sacred *"Boat of a Million Years"* and together they helped to tame "Chaos," organize the universe, bring balance, cosmic harmony, order and form into the world.

On a coffin inscription it states: *"Tefnut is my living daughter and she shall be together with her brother, Shu; his name is life and her name is Ma'at...."*

Ma'at is sometimes associated with other Goddesses and Gods. She was considered as aspect of the parthenogenetically birthed Tefnut, the lion headed Goddess of Moisture, Dew and Rain. Tefnut was linked with Throth as his partner but so was Ma'at. The God of Wisdom and Knowledge, Throth, or Tehuti as he is also known, was considered Ma'at's consort. It is important to look at her spouse because in understanding him we can begin to understand parts of her. Some say they share similar attributes and they complement one another, as can be expected when two powerful deities are joined. Lord of Time, Throth was a Lunar Egyptian deity, attributed for inventing speech and writing. He reflects Ma'at's ideals and her finest qualities. In the Papyrus Nebseni, he is quoted as declaring that he brings Ma'at and her gifts to those who love her. His role as "bequeather" of Ma'at's most precious gifts becomes indisputable. It's important to note that Throth, the Lord of Wisdom, is also the patron God of Scribes. In ancient Egypt, scribes were exceptionally important. They were the ones that documented in writing; religious, political and social events of great significance to world history. In the *"Instruction of Amenemope,"* Egyptian scribes are encouraged to follow the ways of their Goddess, Ma'at, in their work but also in their personal lives.

The Ibis headed, Throth, who is credited for having invented Hieroglyphics, and also rules over learning and sciences (involving measuring and counting) reflects the best of her laws. She becomes known as his counterpart. In their unified light all darkness is eradicated. Together they were credited for creating eight children, Amon, being the most famous of all of them. These offspring became known as the Chief Gods and Goddesses of Hermopolis. Thus, Maat and Throth became known as the ancestor Gods of Hermopolis and respectively mother and father of the Ogdoad.

"She adorns the breast of Throth"

Just as it is stated, Throth carries her on his chest with great love, the Kings and the Pharaohs of Egypt also held the Goddess Ma'at with the highest esteem. The Pharaohs were known as priest of Ma'at, she was their mystic sister and they too wore emblems, and personal symbols of the Goddess. They also carried with them ostrich feathers, to symbolize their commitment to represent her cosmic laws when asked to judge. Everyone from the lowest of slaves, to the Pharaohs and Kings, all were considered, by the Goddess Ma'at, instrumental for cosmic order and harmony. For Egyptians, there was a particularly strong belief that, lack of integrity caused disharmony not just in their personal lives but they also believed it had the power to reverberate into the cosmos; directly affecting nature, potentially causing global disasters; like plagues, earthquakes, droughts and famine upon the land.

Egyptian Kings were also zealously devoted to Ma'at and her tenets of truth and justice. Some would even add her name to their title to suggest an even stronger allegiance and devotion to the great Goddess, Ma'at. A King's decision always rested on Ma'at and her Divine righteousness and laws. In Egyptian theology there is a belief in a reciprocal relationship to deity, that as they give and provided to you, the devotee, so must you also give back to them, via offerings, worship, ritual, and songs etc.. Humans and the Divine cooperate and help one another exist in the universe and this is the balance and harmony of Ma'at.

"Lady of Heaven, Queen of the Earth, Mistress of the Underworld" E.A. Wallis Budge....

Another very important function of the Goddess Ma'at is to judge the dead. The *"Egyptian Book of the Dead"* reveals the Goddess Ma'at is met by every person who has transitioned to death. She waits at Duat, the underworld, where the Jackal headed God, Annubis, leads the dead to meet their fate on her scales. In Ma'at's Hall it will be determined if the deceased person's soul may continue onward to meet the God Osiris and join the other Gods and Spirits into eternity.

With Throth by her side and the 42 Assessors of Ma'at, a life review for the deceased is inevitable in her Judgment hall. This is the moment of her truth, when the true heart of a person will be examined and weight. Ma'at, sometimes known as the scale herself, will weight a person's heart against her sacred Ostrich feather. A scale is presented and on one side rest Ma'at's ostrich feather and on the other side the deceased person's heart. All in Ma'at's Hall will watch as the scale will go back and forth trying to find its equilibrium and then in the end, reveal the deceased person's fate in the afterlife. If it is a balanced scale or if the heart appears lighter then Ma'at's ostrich feather then that person will be met and embraced into the Hall of the Gods and immortality. They will go on to meet with Osiris, the Egyptian God of the Dead and the Afterlife. However, if the heart of the deceased person is heavy and out weights the feather, then the deceased person will have much explaining to do, for this will reveal a life lived poorly and sins, much too many, to be welcomed into the Hall of the Gods. The God, Ammit, the devourer, will ghastly lick her choppers in anticipation for what's to come next, as the deceased person will be sent to the deep recesses of the underworld, while its heavy heart gets hungrily devoured by hideously looking Ammit. Ammit, who was a smorgasbord grisly looking deity beholding the menacing snout of a crocodile, the mane of a lion and the body of a Hippopotamus, fed on those heavy sinful hearts of man. But before giving Ammit the satisfaction of a juicy meal, the deceased person will have a chance to come before the 42 deities of Duat, known as the "Assessors of Ma'at," to plead their case and recite the "42 Denials of Sins," also known as the "Negative Confessions." These writings derived from the Papyrus Ani found in chapter 125 , of the *Book of the Dead."* Below they are listed taken from Wikipedia.com

The"Forty Two Declarations Of Purity" or "Negative Confessions"

1. I have not committed sin.
2. I have not committed robbery with violence.
3. I have not stolen.
4. I have not slain men or women.
5. I have not stolen grain.
6. I have not purloined offerings.
7. I have not stolen the property of the Gods.
8. I have not uttered lies.
9. I have not carried away food.
10. I have not uttered curses.
11. I have not committed adultery; I have not lain with men.
12. I have made none weep.
13. I have not eaten the heart.
14. I have not attacked any man.
15. I am not a man of deceit.
16. I have not stolen cultivated land.
17. I have not been an eavesdropper.
18. I have not slandered no man.
19. I have not been angry without just cause.
20. I have not been debauched the wife of any man, or God.
21. I have not debauched the wife of any man,(repeated addressed a god)
22. I have not polluted myself.
23. I have terrorized none
24. I have not transgressed the law.
25. I have not been wroth.
26. I have not shut my ears to the words of truth.
27. I have not blasphemed.
28. I am not a man of violence.
29. I am not a stirrer up of strife or disturber of peace
30. I have not acted or judged with undue haste
31. I have not pried into matters.
32. I have not multiplied my words in speaking.
33. I have wronged none, and done no evil.
34. I have not worked witchcraft against the King nor blaspheme.
35. I have never stopped the flow of water.
36. I have never raised my voice, spoken arrogantly or in anger.
37. I have not cursed or blasphemed the Gods.
38. I have not acted with evil rage.
39. I have not stolen the bread of the Gods.
40. I have not carried away the Khenfu cakes from the spirit of the dead.
41. I have not snatched away the bread of the child, nor treated with contempt the God of my City.
42. I have not slain the cattle belonging to the Gods.

From http://en.wikepedia.org/wiki/Maat--

Before Throth, Ma'at and the 42 deities, known as the "Assessors of Maat," (Their names listed in the Papyrus of Nebseni), the deceased person will have a chance to address his or her sins and hopefully, save himself from remaining in the darkest place of the underworld, tragically ending his journey in the afterlife.

From the earliest of dynasties it was the Goddess, Ma'at who was well worshipped and today continues to reign powerful in our collective consciousness. Ma'at is the standard by which we measure ourselves from. The heart must be free of weight for you to enter the hall of the Gods in the afterlife and living by her laws of truth and justice helped manifest an orderly thriving universe.

Though some compare Ma'at to the Hindu concept of Karma this is erroneous, as Karma implies that negativity is simply punishment for something done in a previous life. Early Egyptian doctrines would not have agreed in this belief, instead viewing the exact same negativity as proof of Ma'at's absence and indicating the need to supplicate her presence in order to make things fair and right. Early Egyptians and worshippers of Ma'at viewed misfortunes and catastrophic disasters as being caused by demons or spirits of the dead or being a direct result of falsities and inauthentic, unbalanced living, not by Ma'at herself. She was not viewed as a vindictive Goddess but rather as one who made things right, straight, fair and just, and so in this case she does not resemble the Hindu concept of Karma.

Recognized from the middle of the third millennium even earlier, Ma'at had many known Temples dedicated to her worship but today only one still survives. Her Temple in the city of Thebes, in Karnak (Carnac) lies in ruins as an open air museum in Egypt today. Some parts of it were believed to be originally built by the pharaoh, Queen Hatsheput. Later when it had been destroyed by invaders it was commissioned to be rebuilt again by Amenhotpe. Many Egyptian Pharaohs had a part in constructing this Temple throughout the years and part of its renowned reputation comes from the fact that it was started in the Middle Kingdom and continued to be rebuild and expanded upon through into the Ptolemaic period.

Over three millennia, whether as a concept or an actual Goddess in human form, Ma'at, the Goddess of Truth, Justice and Divine Order has reign in our lives, making herself and her laws and principles prevalent in our lives. Invoke her when you are facing anything related to the law, our judicial system or when trying to correct a wrong done unto you. Before invoking her in your workings, be sure you examine your motives and assess your own life, to make sure you are living in the most authentic, righteous and Ma'at pleasing way. She is also a powerful Goddess to connect with when you are approaching death (whether literal or figuratively). She will help you dig deep to intimately connect with you, the genuine you, and offer memories of those times when you best exemplified her attributes of truth, order and justice. She will force you to be honest with yourself and look at the many ways you can lighten your heart and come closer to weighing as little as her sacred ostrich feather, then lead you to a blissful afterlife.

MA'AT GODDESS GATHERING DAY

Purpose: To meet the Egyptian Goddess, Ma'at at her judgment hall in the underworld. To offer our hearts to be weighed against her ostrich feather, upon her sacred scales of justice. To review and assess our lives, recommit ourselves and determine how to make our hearts lighter and healthier to meet Ma'at's approval.

Check Ins: We gather around the Circle and introduce ourselves to one another, while also voicing our feelings on this month and our hope for the upcoming season.

Chants: Together we will join our voices to sing some commonly known Pagan chants, as well as new ones offered on the Chant sheet in the hand outs (see the last page of this chapter). Singing aloud is a wonderful way to raise energy effortlessly and it also sometimes helps in creating harmonious bonds.

Our Agreements bylaws and Pertinent group discussion... We go around the circle of women, reading a few lines each of our "Group Agreements" and add any new ones that seem necessary. Agreements are signed and submitted in confidence.

Drumming Grounding: A drumming musical CD track will be played, to give participants a chance to connect and ground to this very moment. Women are invited to find a comfortable seat or stand and add movement if they wish.

CHECK INS: Consider for a moment the Goddess Ma'at. Reflect meditatively on her image, found in the Goddess Oracle or Goddess tarot or any other sculpture and images you have available and begin to invoke her by stating aloud the images we see in her.

Lecture on the Egyptian Goddess, Ma'at
Her myth and various folklores, her attributes and relevance for us today.

GODDESS WORKSHOPS
WORKSHOP I
Crafting with Ostrich feathers which are considered sacred to Ma'at

WORKSHOP II
Learning Hieroglyphic and how to best incorporate them into our magick.

WORKSHOP III
The sacredness of the scepter and the anks; creating our tools of magick.

WORKSHOP IV
Exploring common Egyptian spiritual beliefs and practices

WORKSHOP V
Heart crafting with paper mache.
Creating an open heart sculpture, that we can incorporate into our ritual and spellworkings.

WORKSHOP VI
Discussing and exploring The Death and Judgment Tarot card.

WORKSHOP VII
Exploration of after life concepts and Past-life Regression

WORKSHOP VIII
A personal Life Review, writing a eulogy and or our personal obituary

WORKSHOP IX
Crafting with the weighting Scale which was also a very important symbol for the Goddess Ma'at.

WORKSHOP X
The archetype of the Judge and Truth seeker. Exploring her personal message to us.

MA'AT GODDESS GATHERING RITUAL

PURPOSE: To meet the Egyptian Goddess, Ma'at at her judgment hall in the underworld. To offer our hearts to be weighed against her ostrich feather upon her sacred scales of justice. To review and assess our lives.

ASPERGE/ANOINTING: Sweet scented incense will fumigate the ritual space and participants are welcomed with a hand-crafted, special anointing oil on the forehead.

WELCOMING: Egyptian Music lightly playing in the background welcomes participants throughout the ritual

INTENT SPOKEN: Today we endeavor to travel to Duat and offer our hearts to be weighted upon her sacred scale.

CIRCLE CASTING:
From earth to sky,
And elements around,
Keep safe this circle,
And all here on ground,

Container, preserver,
This circle shall be,
And only allow good energy.

Through portals of light,
We bless this task
By will and by word
This Circle is now cast.....

ELEMENTAL INVOCATION

Hail to you Sacred Guardian of the NORTH, Realm of EARTH,
Earth that wraps us in its embrace as our bones sink down to its sacred space. Earth the transformer that opens its wide doors transmuting our flesh to reveal our true core.

Hail to you Sacred Guardian of the EAST, Realm of AIR,
Winged creatures that fly, liberated with ease, lightly to your destination you go as you please. Lightly with no anchors, just your heart and mind to lead, air hail to you, the creator of new beginnings

Hail to you Sacred Guardian of the SOUTH, Realm of FIRE,
Flames that pierced through the darkest of night. Flames that give us perfect sight. Burning through illusions and deceit, hail to you fires, the throne our Heart seeks.

Hail to you Sacred Guardian of the WEST, Realm of WATER,
In primordial waters we came to be, ebbing and flowing through divine creativity. Powers of water that births all new life, we call you forth on this sacred night.

GODDESS INVOCATION

CHANT: *"I Honor what is sacred...."*
Raising energy with a Cone of Power; *Ma...Ma... Ma...*
Meditation offering***

SPELL WORKING
At the altar, Ma'at or her Prietsess will offer you an open heart made of papier-mâché and it will be filled with lots of blank pieces of paper. It will be your task to empty out the heart of these papers and write on each one, what weight you down. What are you ready to surrender and

release now? Then place these slips of paper in the communal cauldron where later it will be burned. Your liberated heart will now be weighted against her feather.

In the end a scroll (with her invocation) will be given to you as a sign of her approval.

CHANT: *"She's been waiting waiting..."*

Final Check ins
Begin Devoking Goddess

DEVOKING ELEMENTS

Thank you sacred element of **Water** for birthing us anew; your presence felt as we invoked you here today to guard our rites. Receive our Thanks as we bid thee Adieu. Hail and Farewell to the realm of Water. **Hail and Farewell Water!!!**

Thank you sacred element of **Fire**; burner of illusion, giver of Divine sight. Your presence felt as we invoked you here today to guard our rites. Receive our Thanks as we bid thee Adieu. Hail and Farewell to the realm of Fire. **Hail and Farewell Fire!!!**

Thank you sacred element of **Air**; liberated and free, flying to and from with ease. Your presence felt as we invoked you here today to guard our rites. Receive our Thanks as we bid thee Adieu. Hail and Farewell to the realm of Air. **Hail and Farewell Air!!!**

Thank you sacred element of **Earth**; transformer and holder of our flesh and bones. Your presence felt as we invoked you here today to guard our rites. Receive our Thanks as we bid thee Adieu. Hail and Farewell to the realm of Earth. **Hail and Farewell Earth!!!**

CHANT: *"The earth, the air, the fire, the water, return, return, return return...."*

OPENING CIRCLE:
Our Circle is open but never unbroken,
may the love and peace of the Goddess rest forever in our hearts,
Merry meet, merry part and merry meet again....

TRADITIONAL POTLUCK TO FOLLOW

"The heart of the person before you is a mirror. See there your own form..." anonymous

MA'AT MUSING

I heard a whisper say, *"We are many beautiful people with such wounded souls...."* Everyone I see seems to carry these palpable wounds and it appears to impair our living capabilities and the quality of our lives here on this planet. Our choices and how we interpret and experience life is enmeshed in these unresolved wounds. How we interact with others and how we treat ourselves is directly affected by the deep lacerations of our neglected hearts, whether conscious or unconscious.

Many of us are walking around in states of slumber, in complete denial and downright unconsciousness with only a bloody trail of our unresolved wounds rearing itself prominently in the most unsuspecting places. We carry these heavy hearts, oozing with crimson pulsing blood from these old, large open gashes as if there was nothing to be concerned about. As if acknowledgment would be the ultimate death of all (I suppose the "all" would be the ego and its life experience). We walk around pretending to be functional when nothing could be further from the truth; carrying what requires stitches, wearing what necessitates healing but never having a chance to take on the task in states of denial and neglect. Forsaking the most important thing that directly alters and influences everything in our lives and the lives of those we come across - our core soul, our heart.

I heard the whisper continue, *"Love is cyclical."* There is no straight line or destination in the experience of true love and yet, most of us practice (and rather unconsciously, I must note) this very detrimental, unfulfilling form of artificial love. This practice of external loving is evident when we say; *"I love my house, I love this book, I love this person, etc..."* It is a deceptively, placating practice that exalts, popular, society defined love, declaring everything outside of itself as beloved but never once considering its fuel and source. The source of this declared love, we never once trace it to consider its capacity, ability and health within ourselves first and foremost. How can you claim to love anything outside of you when you have no love for yourself? It is not possible, for love is cyclical. Love for myself is what allows me to know love for you, for we are all connected. In every you, there is a me, and in every me, there is a you. And thus, when I love myself I have the capacity to love you; formless, boundless, no separation, no beginning, no end....**cyclical.** And that love, reveals itself as infinite, timeless and returning, always returning again to source, to me, to all in my presence.

> *"The fundamental delusion of humanity is to suppose*
> *that I am here and you are out there..." Yasutani Roshi, Zen Master (1885-1973)*

When I don't love myself this reveals itself in my interactions and experiences with people. It also shows up in my interpretation of people's actions, everything and all, is obscured by that lack of love. When I watch horrific news stories of the day I am always most struck by this sad realization. The abused, abuses, the unloved, hates, the murdered soul inexplicably and without conscious murders in vastly different ways, the robbed and deceived, lies and steals and each one is contributing to this cyclical motion of life and death in painful ways.

> *"We need to feel our way into the future and unite with others...*
> *Our evolution is contingent upon our ability to connect and*
> *realize ourselves through others..."* Tom Lescher; Astrologer on the Pele Reports

I had reached a very obvious pinnacle point in my marriage of late and found myself in a strange sort of threshold regarding all of my relationships. If our human capacity to grow and evolve is directly linked with the relationships that manifest in our lives, then I had some serious work to do.

Recently, I found myself trying to figure out what was/is the personal spiritual lesson I can detract from my often painfully challenging relation with my husband. Last night I felt the lightning bolt of illumination hit my threshold, the one I had been so impatiently sitting upon while scrutinizing every fiber of the thinning threads in our marriage. And finally, while waiting there on this uncomfortable volcanic threshold answers were given to me in a moment of profound inexplicable breakthroughs. By the end of our four hour conversation not only was I given an invaluable spiritual gift but I felt used; like the gauze that had soaked up the blood, like the tissue that had wiped away the child's tears. I was simultaneously, the child and the tissue.

There was a tangible eeriness to the start of this conversation with him, like I was entering the center of the storm, Oya's earth shattering, *"let me crumble your presumably strong edifices,"* storms. I experienced the eye of this storm as myself and I remained as both a witness and participant. I remember distinctly putting down my guards and assumptions, the ones I typically carry so proudly with me into battles. And I simply stood there before him... spacious, very spacious from a new place of inquiry and acceptance, ready to receive whatever answers came through. For a brief moment I realized I could not enter this ground without first releasing old anger, resentments and the back-breaking baggage of disappointment I had been lugging around for years. The accusatory tone that exposed and weight both of our hearts in most of our previous conversations had no power at this pivotal moment in time. I opened myself up and allowed Spirit to use me as a vehicle to receive and deliver important messages to one another and I experienced the direct link between offering myself compassion via the offering I made to someone else in this monumental moment.

My spiritual practice of late had been taking me to this realm of divine compassion and the challenging exercise of seeing parts of myself in everything and everyone I encountered, even in those I initially might despise, not fully understand or be utterly repulsed by, as was becoming the case in my marriage. It is a practice that suppresses my raging ego and forces me to see the oneness of our spirit. Ego want to be individualize, it is what motivates racism, degradation, manipulation and power. It is what constantly separates and states, *"I am"..* instead of *"We are."* It is what constantly says *"You are"* instead of *"we."* It lives in a realm of separation and thus, rooted in loneliness and incomprehension. It does not want, nor need to **know**, it simply feels from one dimension, the "You," and this is exactly why it also leads into frustrations, relationship failures; failure to touch and know the divine and genuine Love. It is the obstacle for an evolving human race.

It was becoming clearer that Love is indeed cyclical. This is why we never stop loving someone, even when they are physically gone; whether they are gone for a day, a month, through break-ups or in an actual physical death... Those that have passed through the veil have informed me, Love is cyclical and it originates within you for your birth required it to be so and you are composed of it. It is where there is a joining from me to you and you to me, until there is no you and me and there is simply love. This is where our spirit journeys to when we are no longer in physical form. It is where we journey to in moments of ecstasy, when we look into the mirrored eyes of our beloved. This realm of love, is formless, with no boundaries, no separation from source. It is the experience of what I do to you, I do first to myself and thus, what I do to myself, I do to you. It is felt in death, for in death we have no extraneous artifices that hinder this truth, like we so often do in life. It is this ego and thus separation, which keeps us in a state of wounded and wounding. It keeps us in this cycle of pain that stubbornly clings to every karmic life we endeavor to live. And our lives are severely influence, as we carry this, not as a backpack on our shoulder, but in the infinite veins that hold our soul... our soul, which is never ending and impossible to dismiss.

At a pivotal moment in our conversation, I realized that I have been shielding a lot in his presence; loving with heavy pre-conditions, wearing clanking iron armors around my heart. He naturally sensed this and having his own childhood traumas, responded with heavy clinging and suppression of the emptiness in his own heart. The more he would cling, the more I shielded and backed away, fueling the repulsion ever more. The more I sense his desperation and encroachment on my physical space, the more I detached. As we continued to talk and unravel the fraying threads of our marriage, I listened and in his language I unearth his lack of love and self-esteem for himself. He said he could not put into words why he loved me (something he has said many time before) and in this statement I spied the codependency and sadly, his need to cling to an external source of love to falsely give him back what he lacked within and I saw my equal prominent part in this cycle. The more I pulled away, the more I had been affirming his disappearing self-worth...and the more he needed to be with me as a result. Because surely it is a guaranteed, *"he'll feel good about himself only when external artifices, like* **she***, out there, in the form of wife, is expressing love to him. All validation of his self-worth would be confirmed then, right?," I note sarcastically.* But, that is not how it works, is it? The more I sensed these energies, the more it made me run, as it reminded me of my own suppressed childhood issues of self worth. For a while now, I felt something about him increasingly repulsing me, making me hide and forcing me to shield from him and yes, separate emotionally. It revealed itself to me last night as I found myself confessing my deep truths in this heart opening, spirit filled experience we both shared.

I realized, only when I practiced this act of compassion, after seeing myself in him, that he is mirroring the part of myself that is internally struggling to maintain self-worth and self-esteem. As human beings on this planet, I think we all are struggling, in varying degrees, with our self-love and self-worth and it has a lot to do with external elements, our upbringing and our human/physical experiences, as well as karmic. As humans we fail to realize that we are indeed spirit in physical form and not the other way around. Our dominant physical form, so often, becomes a hindrance and blocks this truth, of us being spirit first and foremost and approaching life and issues with this in mind. So, I looked at myself in this man sitting before me, this man that, up to that point, had elicited so many negative emotions, conflict and confusion, and I saw me in what I despised and it was then that spirit spoke. In his own lack of self-worth and self-love, he has been mirroring for me my own shadows and personal struggles with this, though it's not something I was willing to confront on a daily basis. I simply have become better at masking these issues while he wears them on his sleeve for me to see. I have made it my goal to uplift and love myself and stay in a positive state for the most part, despite all the sad and unexpected devastation that had befallen by my feet but it has always been a constant work in progress to keep myself strong, autonomous and motivated. On the exterior I carry an obvious strength and light that is alluring but, deep within, in the shadow realm, I am plagued by the constant fight with my self-worth and sometimes it seeps out exposing itself in subtle ways. The strength and light that emanates from me is an attracting feature for him, though time and time and again, he cannot verbalize this. But upon closer inspection during our conversation, we realized our strange dance. I do constantly struggle with my own self-worth though I am better at concealing these daily battles. In subtle ways it is what has kept me from singing Opera professionally, or what sometimes blocks me from marketing my books now after writing them. It is what keeps all of my art creations locked away in closets, along with so many of my numerous creations, hidden from other people's eyes and judgment. That is my issue – OUR issue- in the most subtle, unsuspecting ways, he, who I have grown to despise, is abstractedly mirroring that ugly part of myself. And lo and behold, this *"aha"* moment dawned on me as I saw myself in everything I criticized in this man.

Everything I despise within myself but am too proud to admit aloud. My wretched insides, the ones I cleverly disguise before the world, he displays outwardly, shamelessly before me, in his clinginess, fear, codependency, paralysis, self-destruction and parasitic behavior.Parts of me I try to kill off daily, he dangles and flaunts them, pestering and infuriating me with them. To a certain degree he is mirroring and revealing the importance of self-worth and self-love, which I have managed to convince him I have gained but deep within have not been fully able to sustain. It is not something I want presented to me daily, the issue of self-worth, and yet, in this challenging relationship, it is presenting itself to me, as his self-worth lies in shambles in relationship with me. I see an aspect of myself that I dislike and want to shut away, hence the repulsion and the constant shielding. Weak attributes that I need to suppress, he is unconsciously presenting them to me daily, just as I am presenting to him the, *"strong autonomous exterior, who doesn't need anyone,"* an open aspect of myself that is lodged and shadowy within him. He can't quite get to these attributes that I am displaying for him, in his psyche, at least not yet, so he clings to the external face of it, in me, hoping to acquire it or get a taste of it, but he never does because it is not meant to be tasted from the outside, it is meant to be unearthed from within.

There were many issues we discussed late into the night; shedding tears, misunderstandings. Laughing and centered in those moments of pure enlightenment, I understood the symbol of the yin and yang as it was being presented to me in this pivotal relationship. I understood the heaviness of one's heart and how it has the capacity to attract and catapult us into the most challenging relationships of our lives. And how, if we don't take up the challenge to learn what we are supposed to master within the relationship, it will become increasingly more painful until eventually it deteriorates and a new one comes along to replace it with the **exact** same crude lesson.

> *"Nothing ever goes away until it teaches us what we need to know..."*
> ***Pema Chodrom***

There are some lessons we are here to learn that will simply not go away just because we are stubborn or dense. Situations of a similar nature will consistently have a way of manifesting itself over and over again via the relationships we attract, until we've addressed and mastered our life lesson. Simple as that! Whatever was exhausted in one relationship and could not be learned will transmogrify itself into the next and the next and the next, until the soul lesson is learned. I really don't know the future of our relationship but I understand the work that is required of me, through us, and the importance of this spiritual work as it will continue to show itself in other people if I don't honor it now.

I am holding true to living and communing with spirit and understanding what needs to be understood to bring healing to myself and those I am in contact with. I made a deliberate choice the night I opened myself up to this critical conversation with my spouse. I made a conscious decision that I was going to spiritually allow myself to evolve and figure out the life lesson I needed to learn within this marriage, in this lifetime, for I had no intention of repeating this pain, disguised in the pretty package of a new relationship. Clearly our heart needed some stitching and our bloody wounds had become much too cumbrous and complicated to be ignored. That night we made a pact to awaken to our inner and outer dynamics, become more aware of these pertinent issues and how they can strangulate our relationship if left unchecked. We also agreed to strive for love, genuine love, which begins first and foremost within our selves and ejects flowingly to our mate in the most authentic way. We agreed to come from a place of love and wholeness when interacting with one another and acknowledge the mirror that spirit so often places before two people within a significant relationship. It is important that we do this for ourselves and for our children and the generation that follows. As for me, I also reflect on my deceased parents and the memories of their tumultuous relationship and the unresolved pain they have carried with them into the afterlife, a heavy pain bequeathed to me, one I have had the misfortune of also shouldering. I do not wish for my heart to be so cumbersome as I flow from this life to the next.

May Ma'at allow me the chance to lighten this precious gem upon her sacred scales and may I have a chance to embrace love and the infinite divine in this life and the next.

> *"When our focus is toward a principle of relatedness and oneness, and away from fragmentation and isolation, health ensues..."* **Larry Dossey**

INVOCATIONS

<u>MA'AT</u>
Ra's beloved daughter,
Keeper of the law,
Born to mend Chaos,
Unhinged its evil jaw.

Creator of Cosmic Order,
Upholder of Divine Truth,
I search deep in my heart,
To unearth aspects of you.

Light as a feather,
May my Heart be viewed,
At Duat, on your scales,
May my soul be renewed.

42 Assesors,
Goddess look to me,
Guide me from this Judgment Hall,
Straight to eternity.

Shield my desperate heart,
From Ammit's devouring fangs,
As my heart and your feather
On thy holy scale now hangs.

Justice Seeker, Mayet,
Throth consort and Queen,
With your Scepter and sacred Ankh,
I kneel before thee.

I state the, ***"Negative Confessions"***
As the *"Book of the Dead"* instructs,
Holy Ma'at, Goddess,
Hail to you who is Just.....

SPELLS

MA'AT SPELL FOR CLEARING

For wrongs of my past,
For all mistakes done,
I clear the way now,
With the power of the sun.

With its bright healing rays,
And sincerity of my heart
I seek to create
a better, new start.

To ease my journey
From here to "Her" hall,
To weight on her scale,
Much lighter, this fall.

To rise like the feather,
Surrendering the weight,
Releasing all wrongs,
And the consequences they make.

I make amend now,
And vow to make peace,
This spell bound round,
In the name of the Goddess,
So Mote it Be!!!

REVERSAL

Evil wisher, evil eye,
May the three fold law,
Judge right by my side,
You who wished me ill and wrong,
With this spell the curse is gone.

I reverse your ill intent.
Dissolve away any evil you've sent,
Return it back,
With a powerful force,
Plague your life,
With guilt and remorse.

Unknown culprit,
Who wished me ill,
You have no power,
Over my will,

My strength and power,
Increases with each day,
As negativity and misfortune
Are kept at bay.

This spellbound round
And it shall be,
To reverse the curse,
That was sent to me.

To keep me safe,
And free of harm,
To bless my family,
And correct all wrongs.
So mote it be!

HEX REMOVER

I am free of all that plagues my soul,
I cleanse and purge
to make myself whole.
      Those parts held shattered,
      by what you did to me,
      Herein this spell,
      I release it to be free...
I call on water,
in images of rain
to wash it all
and ease my pain.
      I feel the earth,
      contain my weight
      as it compost,
      the anger and the hate.
I sense the air,
brush by my cheeks
To dry the tears,
of all that reeks.
      I call on Fire,
      held in my heart,
      Alchemical magick,
      with this spell it starts....

MA'AT'S MEDITATION

You awake from deep mysterious and veiled slumbers. It is unbeknownst to you how long you've been asleep but the touch of someone's hands has awakened you and now you must stand. Look around this place, if you will. Your eyes are gone and so is your flesh but you learn quickly how to employ your intuition in this place. Feel the essence of the you, that has remained and connect with your energy in this new realm. (pause) Look around and notice who is holding your hand now. Who has made himself your guide at this point. (pause)

The Jackal headed Egyptian God, Annubis, steps closer and asks you to join him in this monumental journey. You dare not question him as he pulls you by the hand down the corridor. It is a narrow space, increasingly getting darker with each step you take. Trust that Annubis will take you to your next destination. Trust that every step you take in this dark place will lead you closer to your afterlife destiny. You feel yourself getting dizzy as each step winds down further into the Duat. Spiraling down you go, as you get closer and closer to the deep layers of the underworld. Continue to follow Annubis as he takes you with every step deeper into the spiral. Spiraling down with every step you take, feeling the spin where your head would be. Spiraling down there, where there is void, no light in sight. Continue to spiral down feeling each step in front of the other. Amidst this darkness a sliver of light all of a sudden can be detected. It appears you are being led to it. As you get closer, you notice a lit entryway...

The Guide Speaks:
"Enter this Hall, for only within will you learn of your fate. You've waited and lingered long enough, hidden in darkness. Your heart seeks to be known now, either way, Ma'at awaits you inside..."

When you are ready, open the door to Ma'at's Hall. Immediately upon entering, you are bathed with an inexplicably warm, strong light. Take a moment to adjust your energy and spirit to this space and make note of all that you see now before you. (pause) Gently step further out into the room. This grand hall made of the most brilliant gemstones, glistens with the precious metal of gold. Look around you. Annubis has found his seat by the Ibis headed, God, Throth, and that's when you notice a most hideous looking creature coming towards you with speed. With the mane of a lion, the large body of a hippopotamus and the ghastly snout of a crocodile, Ammit waste no time making herself known to you. With her monstrous appearance and intimidating gaze, she is known as the Devourer and she greets you with sniffs, snorts and a salivating mouth. She hungrily licks her chops already imagining what your juicy heart meat would taste like in her mouth. The Egyptian God, Throth, majestically arrives quickly to brush off and dismiss, Ammit away from you. He beckons you to enter Mayet's Hall and come closer. You're invited to stand before The Goddess, Ma'at....but try as you may, you do not see her anywhere in the brilliant hall. All that you see before you is a large luminescent Golden weighting scale. (pause)

Throth, the God of Wisdom and Knowledge, holds a papyrus scroll with hieroglyphics and he ceremoniously opens it as you approach the scale. You step closer to find a feather, an ostrich feather, upon one side of the scale, while the other side stands empty.

Throth speaks;
"State your name_____,
How and what brings you to Ma'at's Judgment Hall today?"

The first part of the question is easy to answer, the second part is not... and so you take a moment now to consider carefully your answer to the highly venerated Gods of Egypt. As his question reverberates in your mind, you start to reflect on your last days, perhaps hours, on earth and you strangely find yourself reliving those final moments that manifested in your death. The images and memory form in an unclear, blurry haze, but the emotions you felt are still very much with you at this moment, to your astonishment. While the exact detail of what happen might not be very clear, the emotions of what you experienced are. You remember the sobs and painful weeping at the funeral. You remember the sorrowful heartache and lament, both from you and the ones you left behind. You remember and it invites the sound of their voices. Their pain arrives instantaneously; liquefied in a pool that now you must descend upon....a pool of their tears you must drown upon as you journey deeper into the experience of the underworld.

As if it was just yesterday...was it? Was it just yesterday? You are not sure as time seems so irrelevant here, almost non-existent... Reflect on those who mourn for you, reflect on those you have left behind. Think upon those who are missing you the most now. Enter this pool of their tears, journey here to this sacred Hall and now in the realm of your heart.(pause)

Instinctively you reach inside your heart-chakra and search for your encased organ. You pull out your vital, slow thumping heart. See its pulsating sponge-like, crimson red, spewing contractions and expansions in the palm of your hands now. See the thin threads of blue- black veins as it wraps around itself commanding your scrutiny. Feel its multi-valve, strange round form calling your attention to its weight upon your hands. (pause)

Offer your effervescent, blood filled, soul organ to the sacred scale of Ma'at now. Make note of the ostrich feather on the right and carefully place your heart on the left. Now watch as her sacred, omnipotent scale goes up and down, up and down, battling to find its secure equilibrium. Watch as it tries to decipher who will win this battle of truth and gaze hypnotically as the scale struggles to endeavors to be fair and just, with its final verdict.

You continue to watch the scale holding your heart and the ostrich feather, going up and down, in a trance and then you notice the reputed Forty-two Assessors of Ma'at, also watching assiduously, waiting for the results. Your heart is losing this battle as it appears to slowly tilt the scale with its weight. Hopelessness and desperation seizes your entire being as you watch your heart sink further and you feel your tears begin to stream down your cheeks, as you don't know what to do now. You begin to panic at the thought of what this might mean. And now you feel the weight of your death even more profoundly, regretting the things you never said or had the chance to do, lamenting those you left behind to mourn for you. The more your thoughts dwell on those you hurt with your life and death, the heavier your heart becomes on the scale. You begin to notice the direct correlation between your piercing sorrow and the weight of your heart. It is then that you hear a voice...

You detect a woman's voice but just as quickly it disappears, drowning into the minutia of other voices; whispers doubling, multiplying in speed now...multitude of whispers traveling in oceanic waves to confront and overwhelm you. It is then that you hear again a woman's voice speak gently but just as quickly you hear her voice drown into the myriad of voices heard speaking simultaneously, whispering incessantly, creating a cacophony of sounds. You search desperately with your intuit hearing to detect and grasped once more the sound of that woman's voice. Search for it. Search for her voice amidst the dissonant orchestra of whispers from the Forty-two assessors. Search to hear her voice again. (pause)

Ma'at Speaks:

"....But you have loved... and you have been kind. There is at least one person whose life was positively transformed because of your heart's gift of love. And many were the times when you exemplified my tenets of truths, order and justice... Think upon who still maintains your gift of love within their heart?"

When have you given of your heart? When have you given the true substance within your heart to another, it is the memory of these times that will lighten your heart now. Can you see with your soul? Can you feel who keeps you alive at this very moment in your death? Whose love magickally lifts the weight from your heart now? What memory and positive experience from your past has the power to lighten and save your heart from Ammit's ferocious, gnawing teeth? Think.... Reflect upon those times. Hold onto those memories. Look at your entire life span now from birth to death and gather up all those memories, for only in them will you find salvation. Only in them can you lighten your heart. Only those precious, unique memories can save you now. (pause)

313

Feel who eradicates the burden and heaviness of your heart now? Watch Ma'at's golden sacred scale as it begins to struggle to **again** find its new equilibrium, as you joyfully remember...continue to remember. (pause) Hold on to these memories and watch as the omnipotent scale reflects your heart much lighter now. Watch as it sways against the ostrich feather in perfect balance, finally revealing its truth.

The judgmental voices from the Forty-two assessors now also becomes clearer as they begin to speak all around you, the ultimate judge however is Ma'at, but you have yet to see her... Call her now and invoke her as best as you can. Call her and asked her to judge your heart in truth so that you may attain ever lasting peace. (pause)

As you gaze upon your crimson muscular organ, hanging delicately in balance on the sacred scale before you, begin to note a slight change as the scale mutates into the Goddess herself. Her arms and wings outstretched, triumphantly holding up your heart and her sacred symbol, the Ostrich feather. She magickally appears before you and to your surprise, she hands your heart back to you. You notice its obvious weightlessness now. Take your heart in your hand and place it back into your chest.

While the devourer, Ammit regrets not being able to dine on your heart, Annubis, the jackal headed God wishes to guide you back now. Let Annubis take you by the hand and walk out of Ma'at's Golden Hall, retracing your steps. Bid the highly venerated Egyptian deities adieu and retrace your steps now, back through the golden entryway, back through the dark corridor. Continue to walk now through the dark underworld, begin to spiral upward now with the God, Annubis as your guide. Let your steps guide you as you walk up, spiraling upward now with peace and love. Breathe and exhale, as you begin to move closer to the sacred threshold. Follow my voice, and spiral back to this room. Breathe as you follow my voice, let it lead you back to this room, back to the onset of this journey. You are asked now to return to this room.... As I count from seven to one backwards allow yourself to sink back into your body, back to this time and space. 7, 6, breathe and release into this moment with your exhalation. 5, 4 and follow my voice back to this room. 3, 2 1, welcome back. Open your eyes, gently stretch your body, breathe and welcome.

MA'AT GODDESS GATHERING CHANT TEXT SHEET

WE ARE A CIRCLE by Rick Hamouris
We are a Circle, within a Circle, with no Beginning and never ending....
You hear us Sing, You hear us Cry,
Now hear us Call you, Spirits of Earth and Sky
Within our Hearts, there goes a spark
Love and Desire, a burning Fire...
We are a Circle, within a Circle,   with no Beginning and never ending...(chorus)

ELEMENTAL INVITATIONby B.Melusine Mihaltses
East of the Winds,
That stirs and inspire,
Come Eagle's gift
Guard and hold me like this.
      Fire with your spark
      Passion's in my heart
      Come with the Jaguar
      In this circle stand on guard.
Hail to you Waters,
Realm of all tears,
Womb of all wommin,
Come approach my dear...
      Earth that transforms,
      Making Visions to form,
      Realm of my seedlings,
      Guard our space as we're born.....
Earth, Air, Fire, Water,
I am the Witches' daughter....(Goddess daughter etc...) raise energy

FREE THE HEART by Starhawk and Reclaiming community, From music CD, Reclaiming, Second Chants
Free the heart and let it go
What we reap is what we sow...

SHE'S BEEN WAITING - by Paula Walowitz
She's been waiting, waiting
She's been waiting so long,
She's been waiting for her children
to remember to return (repeat)
Blessed be and blessed are the Lovers of the Lady,
Blessed be and blessed are, Maiden , Mother, Crone,
Blessed be and blessed are, The ones who dance together
Blessed be and blessed are, The ones who dance alone.......

HARVEST CHANT by T. Thorn Coyle From music CD, Reclaiming, Second Chants
Our hands will work for peace and Justice
Our hands will work to heal the land
Gather around the harvest table
Let us feast and bless the land...

DREAM WEAVERS
Dreaming, Weaving
We are the Magick weavers,
As above so below,
Within us and without,
We are the dream weaver.

We are the weavers, we are the woven ones
We are the dreamers, we are the dream.
By Michelle Mays from her music CD, "FireLeap, a Collection of Chants."

PRISTESSING & DEDICATIONS

"Be faithful to that which exist within yourself..." Andre Gide (1869-1951)

Ways of Connecting to Divine

When we first encounter the Goddess and Feminine spirituality we open ourselves up to all types of new, unique experiences. It is not unusual to also unearth many strong emotions and spiritual callings; some very subtle, but others very startling and life altering.

The appearance of a particular Goddess might pierce through your realm, making herself known in your life through dreams, whispers, images, strange coincidences and even via friends and perfect strangers. Ordinary people and even animals might be among the numerous spiritual vehicles utilize by spirit, to get you to take notice of "Her" Divine call. If you find yourself being called to one particular deity or if you develop a persistent curiosity about a particular Goddess heed this as a sign to connect. Below are some suggestions on the various ways to link ourselves to Goddess, establish a positive respectful relationship to the Divine Feminine and connect even further to the particular Goddess tugging at your soul. Partaking in some of these suggestions will also facilitated easier connection for aspecting the Goddess, if you wish, in Sacred Rituals.

Prayer
A simple prayer or supplication, as has been practiced by all religions since the beginning of time, can begin to open up the channels of communications between you and spirit. Simply carve out a moment to speak in whispers or aloud about your intentions and believe that indeed you are being heard.

Imagery, Visual, Art
Acquire an image of the Goddess calling you and spend some time reflecting on her image and nuances. Allow yourself to even scry and trance while gazing deeply upon "Her." How does it speak to you? What is the message "She" is trying to convey to you personally? Does the image match with the message? In time you might want to keep your eyes open for anything that remind you of "Her" and maybe even acquire a sculpted statue. You can also handcraft one yourself and see how this, by its very nature, links you even further to her energy.

Meditation
Trance and Meditation, either experienced within a group or on your own, via a pre-recorded soundtrack or even by reading a script, can also begin to open up your consciousness. Be mindful of what transpires and document your experience (s).

Prose, Words stated, Invocations
After spending sometime meditating and in communion with the Divine you might feel inspire to pen a Prose or an Invocation to the "Her" as an offering, commitment or a pact of your union with "Her".

Historical Context/Cultural knowledge
It goes without saying, that learning as much as you can about the deity that is calling on you, is one of the first things you should engage in. Although some ancient deities have fragmented historical research, limited scholarly information and sometimes even conflicting stories, it is a good starting point for the new devotee. I would also suggest opening yourself up to any new, sometimes unorthodox, information spirit wants you to further look into, as a way to connect further into her Divine essence.

Sound, Music, Song, Melody creations and Rhythm
Music is another highly sacred language that can, not only reveal a lot about our deity, but keep us entranced and connected to her energy. Every Culture has its distinct sound; melodies, rhythms and favorable chosen musical instrument. We have a lot of historical information on the Goddess because of music, songs and prose, written in her honor and as special offerings to her in ancient times. Creating your own personal song in devotion to the Goddess is a wonderful, most cherished reflection, to honor her and even today it is well appreciated by Goddess. It will link

and endear you to her, in much the same way as it did in Ancient times.

Culinary Foods/ Offering
What is "She" known for liking? Does "She" have a particular favorite meal, or fruit or vegetable, or a culinary preference with her offerings. Does her documented mythologies reveal a preference in food? As a devotee it will only behoove you to familiarize yourself with her taste in everything, including food and food can be used, not only as an offering but also to connect you even closer to a particular Goddess.

Language
Learning her native tongue or at least a few significant words in her language will endear you to her as well, in the same way that we are endeared and connected to someone upon learning they can speak our language, when we are traveling abroad.

Clothing Attire, Physical Body and Her Attributes
How does "She" appear to you? What is "She" wearing, when she comes to you in dreams and during meditations? In her mythologies, what did she often elect to wear? Consider if you can, what that felt like and how it directly affects her duties. If you can, acquire or sew an outfit that is similar to help you identify with this Goddess, even further. Consider what Her known attributes are and her distinct physical appearance, as they will help create a clearer image of "Her."

Activities beloved by that Deity
Familiarizing yourself with the activities your Goddess is known to love to partake in, can add another dimension to your sacred relationship. If your Goddess is a runner and likes to hunt in the forest, or if she loves swimming and lounging in the Oceans, or if she is known as an ecstatic dancer , taking an interest in her activities will open a better understanding of this deity and bond you to her, in the same way it so often bonds people into close relationships. Learning that she delights in growing a harvest, or surrounding herself with animals or that she is one who loves climbing mountaintops; all of these activities are a gateway to enhance your relationship with Goddess and further help your connection to "Her".

Totem/Animal
Sometimes Goddesses are known to have a strong affiliation with an animal and unearthing this connection will lead you to much valuable, hidden wisdom. Make every effort to connect with this sacred animal and they will reflect another important, yet often overlooked, aspect of "Her" essence.

Finally, I would encourage you to create a special journal, or utilize your Book of shadows, to document these thought-provoking findings and unique experiences with Goddess.

Blessings on your journey to "Her."

SOLITARY PRIESTESS DEDICATION

Purify smudge self with Copal and Sage. A special cleansing ritual bath should take place prior to this work.

Oil anointing with specially made Priestess Oil (see suggestion in book)

Casting Circle & Quarter Call (see suggestions but since this is a solitary ritual, do what feels best.)

Chant: *"Mother I call you," "Don't you know, you and I are both Divine..." "I align my Desire.."*

Music: Play a spirited drumming CD track to raise energy and dance.

When you have raised the energy, approach your altar, begin by lighting your Goddess candle...

Invocation

Here do I stand,
Dear Ancestors, Spirits, Deities of old,
Goddess and the great Feminine Divine...
Here do I stand to take up thy work,
to dedicate myself to you, now as always.
In this ritual, I dedicate myself as your Divine daughter,
always in thy service,
in the role of Priestess of the Goddess,
teaching womyn your sacred mysteries,
as they are revealed to me,
and sharing with them the expansive love,
that you've imbued in me, for magick, the craft
and the Goddess, the Sacred Feminine.
I dedicate myself to the advancement,
enrichment and fulfillment of this
newly formed Goddess study group called:

*Grove of the Feminine Divine....

(Light your second candle)

I do so dedicate myself to being Priestess to this Goddess Group of Womyn
and I ask that you bless my role and journey
in the sacred name of Aradia, Hekate & Artemis,
I ask that you help me attract the right members for this group.
I ask that you present, good honest sincere, positive wommin,
that will fit into our newly formed coven family,
...for it is indeed a family I'm birthing here
in the sacred name of Gaia, Athena, Oya and Brid,
I ask that there will be loyalty,
enthusiasm, harmony and
effortless commitment from all members.
Bless, guide and protect herein this Goddess group (*)
that it may flourish and strive,
with success and become an anchor
in the greater community of
Feminist Pagans -Dianics -Wiccans.
This I make true, by the law of three
and in the name of the Goddess,
these things or better, So mote it be!!!

*Herbal Placket Spell Working...

Consecrate tools of Magick that will be used; Athame, wand, cauldron, grimoire, jewelry, crown circlet, statues etc... and bless them by all the elements via incense, oil, herbs and the heat of your hands .

Meditate with Music/ Future Visualization
Grounding, Thanking Goddess,
Devoking quarters, Opening Circle, Tidy up.....

PRIESTESS DEDICATION
FOR OUR GROUP MEMBERS-GROVE OF THE FEMININE DIVINE

Purpose: To formally dedicate ourselves to the Goddess path and our Sisterhood.
Music will play in the background the entire time as we set up our communal Altar

Purification/Asperge: With smudge of copal and sage
Welcoming & anointing: Eye connections (our windows to the soul), Priestess Oil anointing for heart chakra and third eye -Ask them to anoint their sister next to them with a long, sisterly gaze of love, and a welcoming into the sacred space.... Connect with the spirit of love and sisterhood and open yourself up to gifting this energy to the womyn before you.

Cast Circle; Bell chimes vibrating tone as circle is cast with Athame
From earth to sky and elements around
keep safe this circle and all here on ground
Container, preserver this circle shall be,
And only allow good energy.
Through portals of light we bless this task
by will and by word
This Circle is now cast.....

Calling Quarters
*(see suggestions in appendix, though each participant should be encouraged to formulate **their own** personal invocation now to the elements)*
Elemental Chant: *"Air I am...fire I am, water, earth and spirit I am.."*

Intent spoken: *We have gathered today for the purpose of dedicating ourselves to the Goddess and to this Sisterhood....*

Priestess Invocation (light Goddess Altar Candle)
Great Goddess; Gaia, Aradia, Hekate, Oya,
Aphrodite, Artemis and a multitude of many more.
She of Ten Thousand Names revered since the beginning of time,
We call you, we lovingly invoke you to our sacred rites.
As we dedicate ourselves to our Sisterhood
and the Feminine Divine. *(light first candle)*

In the name of Themis, Skadi, Athena and Maat,
Bear witness to our vows and sacred rites
We call you Goddess as we link with you tonight. *(light second candle)*

We, your daughters come before you on this day__(date)___
Come- Lend us your wisdom,
your strength, your beauty and power...
We invoke you and call you on this holy hour,
to bear witness to this sacred rite,
as we dedicate ourselves to each other,
this group, further learning, to our craft and to you..
*Dear Goddess, Welcome and blessed be,
All Hails with Gratitude, Bless your daughters and Priestesses!
So mote it be!!! **Wommin repeat:** *"So mote it be"* (light third candle)
was facing altar now turn face them
Participant all together recite **Charge of the Goddess ***

Priestess will Declare
This rite formalizes our intent to work together as "Grove of the Feminine Divine"
as we follow the path of the Goddess and the Sacred Feminine and practice our craft to the best of our abilities. We state our intention to work together by our free will, in perfect love and perfect trust, for betterment of all...Are we all here so agreed?

All say: **We are**

(Signature with our witchname are collected on ritual parchment paper as candles are given in exchange.)

The Working: *Instructions are given to inscribe name on candle and anoint the candle all the while quietly visualizing yourself on this new path. When all are done begin spirited singing...*

Chanting: *"...Do you remember when God was a woman..."*

*Now priestesses, one by one, will approach the altar candle and incense stick to light their individual candles from it....Each womyn will light her candle from the center Goddess candle and state aloud **her personal dedication piece**. Each participant should have a few words prepared (personal invocation is fine) about their own hopes and vision as a newly dedicated priestess to this sisterhood.*
All support by saying: **So Mote it be!!!**

When candle are lit....
Together Recite Agreement created*
We are dedicants of the ancient, immortal Goddess
Worshipped since the beginning of time.
Seeking to work magick with her divine energy
Seeking higher knowledge and spiritual growth.
Tapping into our inherited Goddess given rights
And tapping into our own personal Womyn Power.
(each womyn will snip a piece of her hair to add to the Group's Cauldron as this is being recited)

From this moment on
We will not walk alone,
From this moment on
we will learn and grow.

Practicing our craft,
together we will worship
Build community
Rejoicing in the Divine
Celebrating ourselves as reflections of her light.

We vow to work from this day forward
in perfect love and perfect trust
According to the free will of all
and for the greater good.

Love is the law and the law is the bond.
In the name of the Goddess
and the Feminine Divine, we make it so...
With vows to thee
We are her Priestess,
So mote it be...!!!

Chant: *"We all come from the Goddess"*

Allow for a moment of silence, then begin humming and raising the Cone of power as our tone leads to an open mouth call to her, "Ma" and then ground this and begin to devoke.

Devoking Goddess
Great Goddess... We thank you for your presence in this special ritual of dedication to you. May your magick continue to guide and protect us, when we are together and when we are apart. Hail and farewell!!!

Devoking Quarters
Sacred Earth, the transformer, manifesting the fertile creatress, We thank you for guarding our sacred space. As ye arrived in peace, depart in peace. **Hail and Farewell Earth.**

<u>Sacred Water,</u> the flow of balance and harmony in our expression, We thank you for guarding our sacred space. As ye arrived in peace, depart in peace. **Hail and Farewell Water.**

<u>Sacred Fire</u>, truth seeker, the drive and passion, We thank you for guarding our sacred space. As ye arrived in peace, depart in peace. **Hail and Farewell Fire.**

<u>Sacred Air</u>, wisdom and insight, divine vision and the gift of the mind, We thank you for guarding our sacred space. As ye arrived in peace, depart in peace. **Hail and Farewell Air.**

Open Circle, holding hands...
"...From hand to hand I open this space",
Chant:*"The circle is open but never unbroken... merry meet merry part and merry meet again"*

A short Blessing on the **Cakes & Ales** before distribution of moon cakes. As we are passing it, eating the food, we can go around make announcements or share anything we'd like to...

Final Thoughts: *Wommin are encouraged to create a more private moment for themselves at the communal altar if they wish to continue their working... The collection of hair offering will be kept in a Green or silver felt placket, which will be present for each and every sabbat, esbat and Goddess gathering to represent our Sisterhood. As more wommin join the group you may establish this Dedication ritually annually.*

Helpful Tips and Observations When Gathering

Transparency and Clear Goals
One of the most important components when first preparing for a group gathering is having a clearly defined goal and purpose for the day. After all, wommin are carving out a precious moment from their extremely busy lives for fellowship and placing much faith in you, that it will be worthwhile. Reward them for their efforts to be present by, at the very least, having a concise objective for the day. Speak aloud what the purpose of this gathering is so that everyone's conscious, focus and intent can help contribute to its very own manifestation. In being transparent and open, it allows all participant to be on the same page, present and actively contributing to our mutual goal; namely and quite often, to connect with a particular deity, the seasonal sabbat and form sacred community.

Intimacy and Immediate Connection
In gatherings, it's to be expected that not everyone will know one another. In fact, you will have a larger percentage of the people attending being complete strangers, perhaps with vastly different personalities and lifestyle. Still, it is our similarities and common goal, to connect with the Divine, that becomes what we should ultimately hone into, as facilitators. The awkwardness of standing in a room full people you don't know can be daunting, both as a participant and as a facilitator and yet the kind of work and journey we are endeavoring to embark on together, at a Goddess gathering, is saturated and nursed in the arms of intimacy. Needless to say, it is incumbent on us to take on the challenge of building intimacy rather quickly in any group gathering. Many of the techniques below will aid in its ultimate fruition.

Removal of Barriers, Coziness and intimacy
Never underestimate the magickal effects of physical proximity and its ability to break (both, conscious and unconscious) psychological, emotional and physical barriers. Large rooms can be deathly cold, sterile and rather stalwart, inhospitable to intimacy. I have attended gatherings in large fancy rooms that made my jaw dropped in awe at their initial beauty but after and through-out the day-feeling cold, alone and uncomfortable, unsure if I even connected with anyone. On the contrary, I have attended gatherings in tiny closet like spaces, that initially made me cringe and worry if there was even enough room for all, and yet quite surprisingly, found myself feeling the warmth of kinship, love and yes....immediate intimacy, among those who were strangers just hours beforehand. The important lesson here is to prepare and plan accordingly. As we can't always elect the size of our gathering place, but we can be mindful of the potential pitfalls and how to make them work in the most positive way. In large rooms, I try to invite participants to stand or sit closer together and it invariably always forms a tight knit comfortable circle. The result? People soon find themselves at arms left, ready to receive or give a hug as needed and their initial reservations begins to slowly wane as the seeds of intimacy root themselves.

Atmosphere
Entering into an altered state of being, for some, can be more challenging than for others and while I like to think of the sacred permeating everything around us (including the mundane) I know that it helps when my environment supports and reflect images of the Divine. It is precisely why I take great care in decorating and altering the mundane environment to reflect "Her" Holy temple. To encourage and help shift wommin's consciousness as they enter the space of a Goddess gathering, I suggest bringing into the room many images from nature, statuaries, silken fabrics and tapestries. I also offer pillows, mats, rocks and crystals, lots of candles and incense and various colorful objects, like fruits and flowers to help set the tone of our day.

Remember every time you gather you are erecting an ancient practice and a sacred sanctuary, and transcending the mundane by visually changing the space with appropriate Temple décor, will help participants tune out the stressful mundane and tune into the sacred.

Windows of Our Soul
In our fast paced, technologically driven world, we are sacrificing something of utmost importance and that is the power of human connection. Computerized customer service, online

shopping, take-out meals ordered through machines, cell-phones and emails ruling all forms of communications, computerized social network and so many other inventions that are meant to improve the quality of our lives and yet they divert us away from one of our most basic human need.... intimacy, human eye to eye connection.

I will say that personally this has always been a tough one for me to admit to, especially coming from New York City, where it appears in the mad rush and chaos of city life, no one ever looks at you. As a matter of fact, looking directly at someone for too long in the city is an invitation for trouble, so you grow up avoiding people's eyes and you learn from an early age not to invite trouble with your gaze.

However, I have discovered that there is something quite powerful and yes, magickal, about letting someone gaze deeply into your eyes and you in turn, doing the same. It is inherently vulnerable and yet, it the course and path of intimacy, one not traveled upon often enough in our so called "advanced" modern day society.

In our effort to create immediate intimacy within a group of wommin be sure to allow for a brief moment of connection through the eyes, for indeed, they are the windows to the Soul. When someone takes the time to look deeply into my own eyes, I feel affirmed as a human being. I feel recognized, supported, acknowledged and strangely...I feel valued, no longer just an invisible entity walking the earth in this carcass, but with the deep gaze upon me, I feel my soul is recognized, vouched by another fellow human being.... that is a powerful state of being and it births intimacy.

Loquacious, Garrulous, Chatty Gifts

There is no denying that as wommin one of our greatest gift is our ability to talk, empathize and gladly share everything that is going on in our lives. When we, wommin, get together it is only natural to want to talk up a storm and it's quite a powerful phenomenon to stand back and witness the intensity of our chatter. With this in mind, it is crucial that you honor and make the space for such a wonderful expression of womynhood. For gatherings, I like to offer a speaking stick which allows for each womyn holding it to take her turn speaking and also allows for others to practice fully listening in the most respectful, meditative way-without censoring or inter-ruption. As long as she is holding the speaking stick, she is expressing a need to be heard and thus the space to be heard is created and we circumvent the potential for chatter chaos.

I also suggest offering a sort of icebreaker question, at the onset of every gathering so that wommin can begin to get to know one another better by sharing something more precisely about themselves. Depending on the question, this can also help in creating bonds and immediate intimacy among participants.

Awakening and Engaging the Body in our Journey

Honoring our physical body is just as important as our spiritual and in our gatherings it's always good to engage our heart, mind, spirit and body. In our quest to spend our day in fellowship and connecting with the Divine it's good to incorporate some type of movement and acknowledgement of that which houses our soul- the sacred body. I suggest incorporating an activity like; breathing exercises, stretching, yoga, tai-chi, mudras, handicrafts, even belly dancing to name just a few effective ways to engage our body in a Goddess gatherings.

Silence is Golden

You have planned your day with lecture talks, many workshops and a flurry of activities and all seems to be going well, but unexpectedly, there might be one or two moments when the awkwardness of silence rears its less than ideal, ugly head, into your gathering. Instinctively, you want to fill this, seemingly empty space with sound, **please don't**. There is something significant about the ebb and flow of a group gathering and silence is a part of that sacred cycle, even on this microcosmic level. Moments of silence are almost mandatory when endeavoring to connect with the Divine. Embrace all the ingredients of group gatherings, including this undervalued component amidst our journey to Goddess.

Silence and stillness is not something many of us excel at in our fast paced world and quite often, might make us feel very uncomfortable, even reaching to fix or eradicate it, but this is precisely where we are to find that much needed water fountain that quenches our dry throat before going on to the next leg of our journey. This is indeed a special aspect of the Divine, it is in a sense, a threshold. Between the talks, prayers, laughter, activities and chatter of wommin there will be some moments of silence... trust, that like all cycles, it will come and go and like all stages in our journey, it deserves our utmost respect and reverence. Allow silence to come and go as it pleases through out the day, sharing its gem of invaluable wisdom for all in the group to personally experience, for indeed silence is golden.

The Five Senses Must Always be Engaged in Any Group Gathering

The sense of touch, taste, sight, smell, and hearing, when honored and incorporated into our day, can truly have a most powerful effect and contribute greatly to a wonderful memorable Goddess gathering.

With the varying, sweet scents of burning incense and smudge bundles you can incorporate the sense of **smell.** Also living flower arrangements, herbs and scented oils can help connect us by way of our nose. Be sure to inquire if anyone has an aversion or allergies to any particular scents.

The sense of **taste** is incorporated rather easily with the inevitable tasty potluck held at the end of a ritual, cakes and ales or in a buffet, set out to be enjoyed throughout the day. Also, as part of our ritual, there are a number of food offerings like; honey, dark chocolate, fruits, water and or wine offerings that connect us by way of our taste buds.

The sense of **hearing** is activated with the appropriate, well thought out sequence of music, whether it is music offered on a CD sound track or music offered in a chant workshops at the beginning of our day together. When gathering, our sense of hearing should be actively scintillated with an assortment of pleasing sounds and that includes; the sound of our chatter and laughter, the sounds of drums and bells, the sound of a beautifully executed invocation to the Goddess, the sound of silence and meditations, the sound our beautiful voices weaving in and out fluidly and all coming together in **"Her"** honor.

Engaging the sense of **sight** with a feast of beautiful imagery that correlates to the Deity and season we are respectfully honoring, is quite easy to do and yet undervalued. While some in Wicca prefer to work without tools and eschew the use of elaborate paraphernalia and fancy accoutrements, I quite like to greatly engorge and arouse this sense the most.

With colorful ornate altar cloths (one or two) pedants and flags, Goddess sculptures or statues as representation of our beloved deities and various photographs and artwork, the sense of sight is engaged throughout our day and the images live on in wommin's mind, long after they have left the temple. Participants are encouraged to contribute to the visual feast by adding their own sacred tools and images, and the traditional tools of the trade like; our cauldron, athame, wands, flowers, bowls and chalices also grace our communal altar with their presence.

Lastly, the sense of **touch** is honored and incorporated with our various activities and handicraft creations. Yet most effective, the sense of touch is awaken, when the, scented anointing oil touches our skin, as we welcome one another into our sanctuary. It is also awaken when our hands join together as Sisters to cast the circle and when at the end of our day we embrace one another in the hopes that our exuberant, warm hugs will long last us, until we merry meet again.

Energy and the Art form of the Facilitator

One of the most important roles of a facilitator, besides disseminating important information on the Goddess, is managing and directing energy. In any given monthly, group gathering, you will find an array of different personalities, that come from all different walks of life and with various degrees of skills, regarding energy. Some womyn can be very quiet, low leveled energy, some can be, attention grabbers, very highly elevated, while still others, can drain and zap a room of vital energy within minutes. It's important, as a facilitator, to be aware of this and oversee the equal distribution of time and energy among ALL present in a group. That means if you sense someone is shy and not being heard, you need to make the way for them...a gentle platform for them, to get their needs met and be heard. If someone is rambunctiously being an obvious distraction, disrespectful or requiring an unusual amount attention, you'll need to divert it and find a way to shift the energy, gently, away from them, so that everyone in the group will feel more comfortable. If someone is standing distant, with their body language shielded and not saying much, you need to somehow pull them gently, energetically, into the orb of the group.

After a lecture or a certain group activity, sometimes one participant might display agitation and while another might even express fatigue, here too as a facilitator, you'll need to look for ways to neutralize, raise up the vibration in the room so that, the "one" person, doesn't bring everyone else spiraling down into that negative state of being. Spontaneous chanting or drumming might help, movement is also a great way to shake and shift the energy in a group, as is the act of simply addressing it to yourself and making your intention to remedy the situation.

When you stand as a facilitator, you have a vastly different perspective than as a participant and you have the wonderful advantage of looking out for the group's general well-being. Sort of like being in the driver's seat, redirecting energy when necessary will require you to be aware of energy at all times -your very own, the room's, nearby spirits and entities and the energy of all those around you.

Handling Trolls and Vampires Energy zappers and Manipulators

And speaking about energy, I need to briefly make note of the distasteful phenomenon of group trolls, vampires and troublemakers.

Occasionally, much to your surprise, you'll find yourself amidst one of these disruptive entities and perhaps (like I did) you'll ignore it, excuse it or simply try to dismiss it as just a figment of your imagination. **Don't!!!** These personalities are indeed real, and if left to go rampage, can cause a lot of unnecessary trouble within the group.

Be ever mindful of the power of energy and how easily manipulated it can be by maligned individuals; troll, vampires, sociopath and those with less than honorable intentions. Renowned and beloved witch, Z. Budapest, coined it as the *"Goddess of Discord,"* rest assure, there will invariably, always be someone who will, willingly, offer themselves in this nasty role, as the one who will attempt to throw off the balance and energy of the group. A lot of it has to do with power hungry, emotionally unbalanced individuals, who crave constant adoration and attention even at the unfortunate expense of everyone around them.

There are numerous books on the subject of psychic vampires, socio paths, malign people and trolls... how to recognize them, how to handle and banish them etc, etc... I will not go into these assorted, lengthy details here, for that is a book all unto itself, but I will strongly advocate being aware of them and taking necessary precautions when necessary.

If a regular participant in your group appears to balk, complain, whine and make more than your average negative comments, you might have a troll in your midst. If you have someone who appears to go out of their way to disagree with you publicly, appears indifferent to other's plight, gossips incessantly about many - be leery, this could be just the beginning tactics of a group troll. If you encounter a person in your group who appears to always have personal drama, takes every opportunity to voice their woes openly, often leaves early or arrives late - that might very well be a troll. If you meet a person that eagerly and often expresses an exorbitant amount of problems and yet when numerous solutions are offered by group members, they refuse to consider possible solutions, yes that just might be a troll, trying to monopolize the entire group's time and energy. Make a special note of how the energy of the room shifts when that particular person speaks aloud and note if you witness a low depressed or compressed drop in energy, a sort of sapping of vitality. If all of a sudden everyone around you begins to express melancholy, this is the pathetic work of a troll and psychic vampire in your midst. So what can you do, as a facilitator being subjected to this madness?

The first thing is to nip it in the bud as soon as you see it and this might require addressing the person in private, reminding them of our rules, group's modality and our efforts to look out for the group's best interest. In your conversation with them, make them aware of how they are coming across and ask if they are aware of this problem. If this doesn't help, the next step is to suggest that perhaps another group would suit them better and that they should not return. I would also suggest facilitators to follow this up with personal protection spells to shield themselves, the group as a whole, and its members. Early on, in the formation of Goddess gatherings, I strongly suggest crafting a spell to shield your temple's land, room and space from any and all troll, vampires or malign energy and, if necessary, adding a banishing spell, as both will lessen the likelihood of encountering one of these entities amidst your sacred Goddess group.

Extra curriculum activities and bonds

It is quite lovely when wommin start regularly attending these Goddess gatherings and begin connecting with one another on a more personal level. The bonds of true sisterhood and friendship begin to sprout even deeper when we start involving each other in our more private parts of our lives. Thus arranging for outside events, non- Goddess related, social get-togethers, at other times throughout the year, is perfectly natural and actually encouraged. As a facilitator I suggest having the occasional field trips scheduled like; visiting crystal shops, botanical gardens, bookstores, wine tasting, coffee shops, performances and variety shows, and natural trail hikes to name a few way to nurture stronger bonds with our Goddess systers.

Dependability, Reliability and Consistence

Just like when we begin any important courtship or relationship there is an initial period when we might not trust wholeheartedly and need reassurance that we're on the right track. Being present and available helps, but even more effective is being dependable, and every time you, as a leader, honor your commitment to host a Goddess gathering you are affirming this fact.

As a facilitator you might on occasion waver and question when and where to host gatherings. If the number of attendees unexpectedly fluctuates drastically, however, you might also get discouraged and carelessly even consider cancelling a date or two without much thought for its greater ramification. Let me, at this point, strongly advise against this choice of action.

People generally want to know and be assured that what they've invested their time and energy into, is going to stand the test of time and have longevity. Cancelling promised gatherings and or changing dates, place and time can be quite disturbing and deviates from the intimate, supportive, trustworthy and dependable group dynamic, you're trying to give birth to. To alternate these scheduled gatherings too often will promotes a feeling of insecurity and non-trustworthiness, so despite the occasional unexpected ebb and flow of attendance, you as a facilitator, must try to remain true and committed, if you expect wommin to do the same.

There are times when unforeseen circumstances prevent you from honoring your commitment, let it be obvious to the group the reasons why and do not under estimate the importance of making it up to them as well. Honoring the Divine and the Sisterhood is important work and missing it, just as hosting it, is not to be taken casually. Offering regular meetings at the same time each month as planned, reflects your true commitment to the group, its members and the Feminine Divine and you will find participants will soon eventually exemplify your model commitment.

This last "Priestessing & Dedication" Chapter is from author's first book,
"Gathering for Goddess, A Complete Manual for Priestessing Women's Circles"

INVOCATIONS

GROUP DEDICATION RECITE TOGETHER *

We are dedicants of the ancient, immortal Goddess
Worshipped since the beginning of time.
Seeking to work magick with her divine energy
Seeking higher knowledge and spiritual growth.
Tapping into our inherited Goddess given rights
And tapping into our own personal Womyn Power.
> From this moment on
> We will not walk alone,
> From this moment on
> we will learn and grow.
Practicing our craft,
together we will worship,
Build community
Rejoicing in the Divine
Celebrating ourselves as reflections of her light.
> We vow to work from this day forward
> in perfect love and perfect trust,
> According to the free will of all
> and for the greater good.
Love is the law and the law is the bond.
In the name of the Goddess
and the Feminine Divine, we make it so...
With vows to thee
We are her Priestess, So mote it be...!!!

PRIESTESS DEDICATION PROSE

Great Goddess as in ancient times,
Immortal ones,
Come as invoked here today.
We, your Daughters seek to know you,
To embrace you from within.
> Awaken now our slumbered parts,
> Those yet to be enlightened,
> And let your love, light the dark corners,
> So that they will be hidden no more.
Come sacred Maiden, Mother and Crone
Come Creatrix, life giver and keeper of Bones
Come Virgin, Amazon and Sacred whore
Come now as in ancient times before.
> Come brightest star and darkest Moon
> By air, by fire and earth's eternal tomb
> By watery gifts found in our womb
> Come Goddess we seek to worship you!!!
Lend us your wisdom, Your strength,
Your beauty and power...
We invoke you Dearest Goddess,
On this Sacred Hour.
> We dedicate ourselves
> To this ancient path,
> Working as a sisterhood
> Practicing our Craft.
We invoke you and call you,
To bear witness to our rite,
Hail and Welcome Goddess,
On this Lunar Night...

GROVE GODDESS GATHERING CHANTS

DO YOU REMEMBER
Do you remember, When God was a woman she had many, many names. (2X)
They called her Isis, Astarte, Diana, Hecate, Demeter, Kali, Innana.... *repeat*

EARTH, MOON, MAGICK by B.M.M.
In the Earth, deep within,
There is A Magick, I draw it in.
In her Caves, in the Trees
Hear her Heartbeat, Pulsing thru me.
When I Rise, I feel her Love
With feet Grounded, I'm soaring high above,
In the Earth, deep within,
There is A Magick, I draw it in
Ancient Moon, my Soul reveres
With my Singing, I call you here.
When this flame, ignites tonight,
Priestess dancing, Under the moonlit night....
In the Earth, deep within,
There is A Magick, I draw it in.... There is A Magick, I draw it in }3x

LISTEN TO MY HEART SONG
Listen, Listen, Listen to my heart Song
Listen, Listen, Listen to my heart Song
I will never forget you
I will never forsake you
I will never forget you,
I will never Forsake you ..... *by Susun Weed*

(CREATING A CIRCLE) WE ARE A CIRCLE by Rick Hamouris
We are a Circle, within a Circle, with no Beginning and never ending....
You hear us Sing, You hear us Cry,
Now hear us Call you, Spirits of Earth and Sky
Within our Hearts, there goes a spark
Love and Desire, a burning Fire...
We are a Circle, within a Circle, with no Beginning and never ending...(chorus)

(FACING NORTH) MOTHER I FEEL YOU UNDER MY FEET
Mother I feel you under my feet, Mother I feel your Heart Beat 2X
Heya Heya Heya, Heya Heya Ho 2X
Mother I hear you in the Rivers Sound, Eternal Waters going on and on 2X
Heya heya heya heya heya ho 2X
Mother I see you in when the Eagles fly, Flight of the Spirit gonna take our time 2X
Heya Heya Heya, Heya Heya Ho By: Unknown source

(FACING EAST) ARAPAHO SONG
I circle around, I circle around, The boundaries of the Earth
I circle around, I circle around, The boundaries of the Earth
Heyana Heyana, Heyana Heyana
Wearing my long wing feathers as I fly
Wearing my long winged feathers as I fly. *(repeat) by Arapaho Ghost Dance Song*

(FACING SOUTH) SPIRITS OF FIRE
Spirits of Fire come to us
we will kindle the Fire,
Spirits of Fire come to us
we will kindle the Fire,
We will kindle the Fire
dance the magic circle round
We will kindle the fire dance the circle around

(FACING WEST) SISTER RIVER- *From Victorian Christian's creation , Elijah The band of Light*
Sister, River, Giver...Returning Whole,Sister, River, Giver...Returning Whole
Open up, To receive
We are what we Believe. *(REPEAT)*
Sister, River, Giver...Returning Whole,
Sister, River, Giver...Returning Whole
Growing Roots like the Trees,
Wee are planting seeds. *(REPEAT)*
Sister, River, Giver...Returning Whole,, Sister, River, Giver...Returning Whole,
Stored in Deep, Stories Sleep,
Within Us, These Tales we Keep. *(REPEAT)*
Sister, River, Giver...Returning Whole,
Sister, River, Giver...Returning Whole....

REFERENCES & BIBLIOGRAPHY

RHIANNON

Ancient Mirrors of Womanhood, a Treasure of Goddess and Heroine Lore from around the World, by Merlin Stone, Beacon Press,Boston, Massachusetts, 1979

Goddesses in World Mythology, a Biographical Dictionary, Martha Ann and Dorothy Myers Imel, Oxford University Press, New York 1993

365 Goddess, a Daily Guide to the Magic and Inspiration of the Goddess by Patricia Telesco, HarperSanFrancisco, a Division of Harper Collins Publishing, 1998

The Goddess Oracle, a Way to Wholeness through the Goddess and Ritual, by Amy Sophia Marashinsky, Massachusetts, Element Books, 1997

The (Mabignon) Mabinogi translated by Patrick K. Ford, Berkeley: University of California Press. 1977

Internet: www.mabinogion.info/Rhiannon.htm

Internet: www.paganwiccan.about.com

Internet: www.goddessgift.com/goddessgallery/Rhiannon.html

Sagewoman Magazine, Issue 73. Rhiannon the Mare Mother, One of Ten Thousand: Goddess Lore and Ritual regular Column by Diana Paxson (pages 25-33)

NU-KUA

Chinese Mythology, Irene Dea Collier, Enslow Publishers, Inc. 2001

Chinese Mythology: An Introduction by Anne Birrell

Goddesses in World Mythology, a Biographical Dictionary, Martha Ann and Dorothy Myers Imel, Oxford University Press, New York 1993

Handbook of Chinese Mythology (Handbook of World Mythology) Lihui Yang, Deming An, with Jessica Anderson Turner,   Oxford University Press, 2005

The Goddess Oracle, a Way to Wholeness Through the Goddess and Ritual, Amy Sophia Marashinsky, Illustrated by Hrana Janto,Element Books, Inc, Rockport, MA, 1997

365 Goddesses, a Daily guide to the magic and inspiration of the Goddess, Patricia Telesco, Harper SanFrancisco,1998, Nu Kwa- Feb 13

Internet: www.Mysticwicks.com

Internet: www.Wikipedia.org/wiki/N%C3BCwa

Internet: www.chinavoc.com/history/ancient/myth_nw.htm

Internet: www.squidoo.com/nukuagoddess

Internet: From WIKI http://en.wikipedia.org/wiki/N%C3%BCwa

Internet: http://www.Chinavoc.com/history/ancient/myth-nw.htm

Internet: http://www.thaliatook.com/AMGG/nukua.html)

DURGA

Goddess Grimoire Journal, a Collection of Simple Prose and Spells, by B. Melusine Mihaltses, Publisher; Feminine Divine Works, Schertz, Texas, 2012

Hindu Goddesses, Visions of the Divine Feminine in the Hindu Religious Tradition, by David R. Kinsley,University of California Press, Berkeley and Los Angeles California, 1988

Hindu Gods and Goddesses by Swami Harshananda, The President, Sri Ramakrishna Math, Mylapore, Madras

Pagan Anger Magic, Positive Transformations from Negative Energiesby Tammy Sullivan, Citadel Press, Kensington Publishing Corp. New York, NY 2005

The Book of the Goddess Past and Present, An introduction to Her Religion, edited by Carl Olson, The Crossroad Publishing Company, New York NY, 1987

The Goddesses' Mirror, Visions of the Divine from East and West, by David R. Kinsley, State University of New York Press, Albany New York, 1989

Twenty-Four Aspects of Mother Kali by Babaji Bob Kindler, SEV Associations, Honoka'a, Hawaii, 1996

Internet: www.philhine.org/uk/wrting

Internet: www.Dollsofindia.com

Internet: lotussculpture.com/Durga.htm

Internet: www.Womeninworldhistory.com

Internet: www.srimatham.com/storage/docs/arjunas-hymn-to-durga

Internet: www.dipika.org.za/index.php?option...hymn...durga

Internet: www.shivashakti.com/durga.htm

Internet: www.hinduism.com

UZUME

Ancient Mirror of Womanhood, a Treasury of Goddess and Heroine Lore from around the World, by Merlin Stone, Beacon Press, Boston 1984 edition

Gathering for Goddess, a Manual for Priestessing Women's Circles, by B. Melusine Mihaltses.Publisher; Feminine Divine Works, Schertz, Texas, 2012

Handbook of Today's Religions- by Josh McDowell & Don Stewart

The Book of The Goddess Past and Present, an Introduction to Her Religion Edited by Carl Olson, The Crossroad Publishing Company, New York 1987

The Goddess Oracle, a Way to Wholeness Through the Goddess and Ritual, Amy Sophia Marashinsky, Illustrated by Hrana Janto,Element Books, Inc, Rockport, MA, 1997

365 Goddesses, a Daily guide to the magic and inspiration of the Goddess, Patricia Telesco, Harper SanFrancisco,1998, Nu Kwa- Feb 13

Shinto, a Celebration of Life by Aidan Rankin, OBooks, Winchester UK, Washington, USA, 2010

Internet: www.uwec,edu/philrel/shimbutsudo/uzume.html

Internet: www.greenshinto.com

Internet: Kojiki Records of Ancient Matters transl. B.H. Chamberlain

Internet: Religion in Japanese History, Joseph M. Kitagawa

Internet: www.1000questions.net/en/religion/shinto.html

Internet: en.wikipedia.org/wiki/Ame-no-Uzume-no-Mikoto

Internet: www.Goddessgift.com/goddess/Japanese_goddess_Amaterasu.htm

Internet: www.Pantheon.org.>Areas>Mythology>Asia>Japanese mythology

Internet: www.Bukisa.comReligion & Spirituality

Internet: www.Ancient history.about.com/od/uzumemyth/

Internet: www.Land of wisdom.com

ASHERAH

Ancient Mirrors of Womanhood, a Treasure of Goddess and Heroine Lore from around the World, by Merlin Stone, Beacon Press, Boston, Massachusetts, 1979

Goddesses in World Mythology, a Biographical Dictionary, Martha Ann and Dorothy Myers Imel, Oxford University Press, New York 1993

The Book of the Goddess Past and Present, an introduction to Her Religion edited Carl Olson, The Cross Road Publishing Company, New York, New York, 1987

The Hebrew Goddess by Raphael Patai, Wayne State University Press, Detroit Michigan,1990-third enlarged Edition

Internet: http://en.wikipedia.org/wiki/Asherah

Internet: "Asherah, the Tree of Life and the Menorah" http://wwww.asphodel-long.com/htm1/Asherah.htm1

Internet: The Goddess in Judaism www.asphodel-long.com/htm4goddess

Internet: "Asherah, the tree of Life" http://www.asphodel-long.com/htm1/asherah.html

Internet: Classical Hebrew.com - http://blog-en.classicalhebrew.com/tag/asherah

BLODEUWEDD

Goddess Afoot, practicing Magic with Celtic and Norse Goddesses by Michelle Skye, Llewellyn Worldwide Publishing, Woodbury, Minnesota, 2008

Goddesses in World Mythology, a Biographical Dictionary, Martha Ann and Dorothy Myers Imel, Oxford University Press, New York 1993

The Goddess Oracle, a Way to Wholeness through the Goddess and Ritual, by Amy Sophia Marashinsky, Massachusetts, Element Books, 1997

The White Goddess, a Historical grammar of Poetic myth, by Robert Graves, International Authors, N.V. Farrar, Straus And Giroux, New York1948

365 Goddess, a Daily Guide to the Magic and Inspiration of the Goddess by Patricia Telesco, HarperSanFrancisco, a Division of Harper Collins Publishing, 1998

Internet: www.orderwhitemoon.org/goddess/Blodeuwedd2.html

Internet: www.goddessrealm.com/goddess-of-the-moment/16

Internet:: www.mysticwicks.com

Internet:www.paganpages.org/contenttag/blodeuwedd

LILITH

Ancient Mirrors of Womanhood, a Treasure of Goddess and Heroine Lore from around the World, by Merlin Stone, Beacon Press, Boston, Massachusetts, 1979

Goddess Grimoire Journal, a Collection of Simple Prose and Spells, by B. Melusine Mihaltses, Publisher; Feminine Divine Works, Schertz, Texas, 2012

Inanna Queen of Heaven and Earth, Her Stories and Hymns from Sumer, by Diane Wolstein and Samuel Noah Kramer, Harper and Row Publishers, New York, New York, 1983

Pagan Anger Magic, positive Transformations from Negative Energies, by Tammy Sullivan, Citadel Press, Kensington Publishing Corp. New York, New York, 2005

The Case of Lilith, 23 Biblical Evidences, identifying the Serpent as Adam's first failed wife in Genesis, by Mark Wayne Biggs, Published by ReligionBookMix, 2012

The Cult of the Black Virgin, by Ean Begg Chiron Publishing, Wilmette, Illinois 2006

The Goddess Oracle, a Way to Wholeness through the Goddess and Ritual, by Amy Sophia Marashinsky, Massachusetts, Element Books, 1997

The Hebrew Goddess by Raphael Patai, Wayne State University Press, Detroit Michigan,1990, -third enlarged Edition

The Witches' Goddess, the Principle of Divinity by Janet and Stewart Farrar, Phoenix Publishing Inc. Custer Washington, 1987

Internet:Embracing the Dark Goddess by Dominae

Internet:www.flutterbywings.com/goddess /Lilith.htm, "I am Goddess, Worship me" Nov. 2008

Internet:Sumerian Legend of Lilith, translated by Charles Alexander Moffat from The Lilith Gallery

Internet:An Order of the White Moon, "Lilith —Child of Light, Daughter of Darkness

Internet:Lilith; A Romance by George MacDonald, 1985

Internet:The Lilith Shrine by Dante Gabriel Rosetti, "Collected Poems," London 1906

DANTOR (ERZULIE-DANTOR)

Gathering for Goddess, a Manual for Priestessing Women's Circles, by B. Melusine Mihaltses.Publisher; Feminine Divine Works, Schertz, Texas, 2012

Mama Lola: A Vodou Priestess in Brooklyn, by Karen McCarthy Brown, University of California, 2001

Secrets of Voodoo by Milo Rigaud, City Lights Books, San Francisco, CA 1969, 1985

The Cult of the Black Virgin, by Ean Begg Chiron Publishing, Wilmette, Illinois 2006

The Haitian Vodou Handbook, Protocols for Ridding with the Lwa by Kenaz Filan (Houngan Coquille du Mer), Destiny Books, Rochester, Vermont, 2007

Vodou Love Magic, A Practical Guide to Love, Sex, and Relationships by Kenaz Filan), Destiny Books, Rochester, Vermont, 2009

Internet:www.Voodoomystic.com, website page created by Bon Mambo Racine Sans Bout Sa Te La Daginen

Internet:www.squidoo.com

Internet:www.widdershins.org

Internet:www.Mysticvoodoo.com

Internet:www.rootswithoutend.com

Internet:www.vodoureligion.com

Internet:www.Qualiafolk.com

Internet:www.webster.edu/-corbetre/haiti/history/revolution/revolution1.htm,

Internet:http://www.travelinghaiti.com/history_of_haiti/slave_rebellion.asp,

Internet:http://wikipedia.org/wiki/Haitian_Revolution

Internet:www.catholicculture.org/culture/library/view.cfm?recnun2996,

Internet:www.marypages.com/czestochowa.htm, www.Czestochowa.pl/welcome

Internet:www.jasnagora.com, www.enwikipedia.org/wiki/Black_Madonna_of Czestochowa,

SIF

Dictionary of Northern Mythology, byRudolf Simek

Goddess Afoot, practicing Magic with Celtic and Norse Goddesses by Michelle Skye, Llewellyn Worldwide Publishing, Woodbury, Minnesota, 2008

Myth and Religion of the North, by Turville-Petre

Norse Magic by D.J. Conway, Llewellyn Publications, St. Paul Minnesota, 1997

Northern Mysteries and Magick: Runes and Feminine Powers by Freya Aswynn, published in 1998 by Llewellyn

Poems of the Elder Edda, Trans. P Terry

Poetic Edda, Snorri Sturluson, Trans A. Faulkes

Sagewoman Magazine, Issue 62, Courage, A Circle is Cast, Column, by Sage women readers. Autumn Equinox Ritual by Gallina Krasskova page 73-76
Scandinavian Mythology, by H R Ellis Davidson

The Cassell Dictionary of Norse Myth and Legend by Andy Orchard

The Goddess Oracle, a Way to Wholeness through the Goddess and Ritual, by Amy Sophia Marashinsky, Massachusetts, Element Books, 1997
The Rites of Odin by Ed Fitch 1990, Llewellyn

365 Goddess, a Daily Guide to the Magic and Inspiration of the Goddess by Patricia Telesco, HarperSanFrancisco, a Division of Harper Collins Publishing, 1998
Internet: http://www.sodahead.com/unitedstates/sif-norse-goddess-of-the-grain/question-1596261

Internet: http://www.mysticwicks.com

Internet: http://www.thorshof.org/sif.htm.

Internet: http://ancienthistory.about.com/od/norsemyth/a/aa081799Norse.htm

Internet: en.wikipedia.org/wiki/sif

Internet: http://www.Valkyrie tower.html.com/sif

Internet: http://www.Mistress of EnchantmentBlog.com:Sif- 2010

LAKSHMI

Healing Mantras, Using Sound Affirmations for Personal Power, Creativity and Healing, by Thomas Ashley-Farrand, A Ballantine Wellspring Book- The Ballantine Publishing Group, New York, New York, 1999

Hindu Gods and Goddess by Swami Harshananda, printed in India; Sri Ramakrishna Math Printing Press, Mylapore, Madras

The Book of Goddesses, Invoke the Powers of the Goddess to Improve Your Life by Roni Jay, A Quarto Book, Baron's Educational Series, Inc. Hauppauge, New York, 2000

The Book of the Goddess Past and Present, an introduction to Her Religion edited Carl Olson, The Cross Road Publishing Company, New York, New York 1987

The Goddesses' Mirror, Visions of the Divine from East to West by David Kinsley, State University of New York Press, Albany, New York 1989
The Goddess Oracle, a Way to Wholeness through the Goddess and Ritual, by Amy Sophia Marashinsky, Massachusetts, Element Books, 1997
Internet: Goddess Lakshmi by Bansi Pandit at wwwkousa.org/Gods/God6.html
Internet: Lakshmi Goddess of Wealth and Beauty, by Subhamoy Das, About.com
Internet: www.freemeditationinfo.com

BABA YAGA

Baba Yaga — The Ambiguous Mother of the Russian Folktale by Andreas John ($28) 2004, Isbn#13-9780820467696

Balkan Traditional Witchcraft by Radomir Ristic

The Goddess Oracle, a Way to Wholeness Through the Goddess and Ritual, Amy Sophia Marashinsky, Illustrated by Hrana Janto, Element Books, Inc, Rockport, MA, 1997
365 Goddess, a Daily Guide to the Magic and Inspiration of the Goddess by Patricia Telesco, HarperSanFrancisco, a Division of Harper Collins Publishing, 1998
Internet: www.realmagick.com/700 BabaYaga article by Freya

Internet: www.examiner.com/article by Juliet Friette

Internet: www.matrifocus.com/ SAMO/BabaYaga,Susun Weed Article

Internet: www.orderwhitemoon.org

Internet: www.healingwayofrabbit/BabaYaga Part I and Part II

Internet: www.helium.com

Internet: wwww.Blueroebuck.com

Internet: www.7yearoldwitch.blogspot, BabaYaga 2009

Internet: www.Mythling.com

MA'AT

Ancient Mirrors of Womanhood, a Treasure of Goddess and Heroine Lore from around the World, by Merlin Stone, Beacon Press,Boston, Massachusetts, 1979

Egyptian Paganism for Beginners, bring the Gods and Goddesses of Ancient Egypt into Daily Life by Jocelyn Almond and Keith Seddon, Llewellyn Publications, St.Paul, Minnesota, 2004
The Book of Goddesses, Invoke the Powers of the Goddess to Improve Your Life by Roni Jay, A Quarto Book, Baron's Educational Series, Inc. Hauppauge, New York, 2000

The Gods of the Egyptians; studies in Egyptian mythology- Vol.I, by E.A. Wallis Budge, Dover publication 1969

The Goddess Oracle, a Way to Wholeness through the Goddess and Ritual, by Amy Sophia Marashinsky, Massachusetts, Element Books, 1997
The Witches' Goddess, the Principle of Divinity by Janet and Stewart Farrar, Phoenix Publishing Inc. Custer Washington, 1987

365 Goddess, a Daily Guide to the Magic and Inspiration of the Goddess by Patricia Telesco, HarperSanFrancisco, a Division of Harper Collins Publishing, 1998
Internet: Themystica.org/mythical-folk/articles/maat.html

Internet: From http://en.wikipedia.org/wiki/Maat

Internet: Egypt.idolhands/maat/intro.html

Internet: Crystalvaults.com/pages/goddess_maat.php

Internet: Paganwicca.about.com/od/egyptiandeities/p/maatprofile.htn

Internet: www.Daughterofmaat.hubpage

Internet: www.touregypt.net/godsofegypt/maat2.htmCaroline Seawright

Internet: ancient-egypt.info/2012/03/maat-egyptian-goddess-and-blinding-of.htm

Internet: In existence since the old kingdom, pyramid text of Unas (CA2375 BCE and2345 BCE)

Egyptian religion by Siegfried Morenz, translated by Ann E. Keep page 275, 1992

Cornell University Press, I

SageWoman Magazine no. #78, Spring 2010- Finding our Balance,

"One of Ten Thousand: Goddess Lore and Ritual' by Diana L. Paxson page 36-42

**** *For a more comprehensive Reference and Bibliography of helpful Goddess books check out the author's first book;*
"Gathering for Goddess, A Complete Manual for Priestessing Women's Circles," -Isbn#978-0-9851384-4-8

ABOUT THE AUTHOR

About the Author...

...She's supported by her ancestral lineage of strong, magickal, high priestesses'...

Great grand-daughter of a small town's renowned priestess, healer and advisor, B. Melusine was born and raised into a magickal, spiritual household. Her mother was an astrologer, dream analysis consultant, spiritualists and social worker, who dabbled in occult studies and B. Melusine was the recipient of the pool of spiritual knowledge shared by her ancestry. Her interest in the occult were nurtured and cultivated early on by extended family members and by those she surrounded herself with. By age 15, however, she faced the tragic unexpected loss of her mother and even more devastatingly, four years later, she would find herself mourning her father's death too, as he struggled and lost his battle with a liver disease. In the midst of tragedy, spiritual studies enlightened, comforted and guided her during this most difficult time of her life and her connection to spirit grew.

Music also, had always played a very important part in her life and, by its own accord, held a great deal of magick in her own self- healing. Continuing her education after High School, despite the grave loss of her parents, was compulsory and proved to be the right choice for her. In college she devoted herself to her music conservatory studies but continued her tarot and spiritual practice on her own. Her music conservatory disciplined garnered her a Bachelor's in Music, with summa cum laude distinction, from Westminster Choir College in Princeton, New Jersey. Pursuing her Master's Degree brought her back to her birthplace in New York City and in two years, she completed her Master's in Music in Voice Performance, at the prestigious Manhattan School of Music.

Time in New York City exposed her to numerous learning venues and greater opportunities to further her occult studies. At the New York Open Center she studied tarot with renowned psychic/tarot reader Patti Canova. She also participated in numerous lectures, seminars on spiritual matters, drumming circles and rituals. She participated in open Sabbat rituals held by thealogian Susan Marie Hellerer, DMIV. She also partook in lectures by Margot Adler, author of "Drawing Down the Moon" and Phyllis Currott, author of "Book of Shadows", "The Love Spell", "Witch Crafting" and HP of Temple of Ara, in New York City. Attending seminars by Kaitlynn, introduced her to the Fey Wiccan tradition, at The Source of Life in NYC. At the Learning Annex she took classes on traditional magick, tarot practice and participated in lectures and rituals held by Donna Limoge, co-author of "Sexual Bewitchery and other Ancient Feminine Wiles". Around this time B.Melusine had also joined a yearlong Pagan grove study with High Priest, Joe A. Zuchowski and his partner, distinguish High Priestess, Jezibell Anat, at New York City's emblematic "Enchantments, Inc.", where she learned the various disciplines of Witchcraft and Thelematic Wicca. She was later also handfasted in 1999, at this prestigious New York City Landmark.

At the Zodiac Lounge on the upper Westside in New York City, she was a member of The Zodiac Lounge Women's Circle -an all-female Goddess centered group led by High Priestess Jezibell. This, along with the numerous female centered Goddess literature she was being exposed to like; Z. Budapest,

Shekhinah Mountainwater, Marion Weinstein, Ffiona Morgan, Diane Stein, all sparked a greater interest in Women's spirituality. B. Melusine, then added another spiritual women's group, when she learned of "Crystal Quilt Inc." in Manhattan, N.Y. They offered a weekly, all female circle, advocating the tradition of – "Wise-Woman Healing Ways" and it was facilitated by Robin Rose Bennett. Robin Rose Bennett is a well-known Herbologist , student of Susun Weed, Green-Witch and author of "Healing Magic; A Greenwitch's Guide Book" and it is in these numerous wommin circles that B. Melusine unearth great magick, empowerment, healing, sisterhood and an ancient way of being that resonated so close to her own ancestry. It was in these precious Wommin's circles, amongst some of the most amazing powerful sisters (*"all of us were hungry for wisdom, healing and knowledge,"* she remembers) that her life started to shift in ways she had not anticipated. These Goddess and wommin centered groups enriched her life greatly and in the presence of such great teachers, facilitators and priestesses, she was privileged to learn a great deal about the art-form and how to formulate groups and circles that nurture Women's spirituality.

Upon jumping the broom with her husband, she moved to Levittown, New York, in Long Island, where she continued her Goddess centered Wiccan practice, more now as a solitary, due to her new role as wife and mother. She immersed herself in informative books, the occasional Open group sabbat rituals and worked on creating her own Grimoires and invocations. She expanded on her artistry with numerous arts and craft projects and continued to raise her family. At this time also, she added Hinduism, mantra and yoga studies to her list of passions.

A change in climate and lifestyle lured her, and her family, to the South-West, in Texas, where she now resides with her three young boys, husband, two Boston Terriers, Luna- the malti-poo and a, rather aloof, mystical black cat. Just recently she was claimed by the newest member of her clan, a vivacious Corn snake affectionately called Nymphy-Lilith. Now in Schertz, Texas, she continues her eclectic Goddess spirituality practice and has included pagan art song compositions, spiritual crafting, intuitive arts, Goddess paintings, trance work and creative writing. Her first year in Texas found her immediately involved, facilitating and priestessing Goddess rituals for one of the few (at the time) established Goddess groups in the area. Seeing a need for more wommin centered sacred space and wanting to re-create the enriching sisterhood experiences from her past, in New York City, she started to consider formulating a Goddess group. It was only after a powerful series of visions, dreams and coincidences that she bravely took on the task. Being new to the area and not knowing many people was daunting at first, but her devotion to Goddess and Women Spirituality remained true and in that effort, she founded, **"Grove of the Feminine Divine,"** an all womyn's monthly Goddess Gathering group. Her first book, **"Gatherings for Goddess, a Complete Manual for Priestessing Women's Circles",** holds her priestessing journey, invaluable lessons and precious experiences through-out the creation, nurturance and sustenance of this group. It is a treasure trove of insight for any dedicant heeding the call to promote community, wommin's Circles and Goddess Spirituality. It was also around this time she partook of several Goddess Gatherings sojourns, traveling to San Jose California, to attend the 2008 Goddess Gathering, where she finally met and was initiated by beloved founder of the feminist Wiccan Dianic tradition, Z. Budapest. The following year, she traveled to Madison, Wisconsin to attend yet another important Dianic event. This time, B. Melusine partook of Dianic Author and songstress, Ruth Barrett's Daughter of Diana, annual Goddess Gathering and here, she continued to expand her ritual experiences and knowledge of Goddess and Women Spirituality.

"Living Goddess Spirituality, a Feminine Divine Priestessing Handbook, " **"Gatherings for Goddess, a Complete Manual for Priestessing Women's Circles",** and **"Goddess Grimoire Journal, a collection of Simple Prose and Spells,"** are now available on Amazon.com and at http://www.createspace.com /4002824, 3795965 and 3799105 or directly from the author 's **website at http://www.Femininedivineworks.com.**

"...As if you were on Fire from within... The moon lives in the lining of your skin..." Pablo Neruda

ISBN#: 978-0-985138479 LCCN: 2012950223

Dear friends,

Thank you for your interest in our growing company and our various tools that facilitate spiritual growth. We have many more helpful products available for our wonderful patrons. Below we have provided an order form with some of our current offerings for sale. Please feel free to utilize this form to place orders or contact us; either by email, social networks, our blog or website, mailing address or Phone. Thank you again for your support, we look forward to being of service to you.

ORDER FORM:

	Price	Qty	Amount
1. Living Goddess Spirituality, 18.99			
2. Goddess Grimoire Journal, 15.99			
3. Gathering for Goddess Manual, 25.99			
4. Goddess Gathering T-Shirts (s, m, l) 11.99			
5. Artwork by the Author *(Please contact price varies accordingly)*			
6. Meditation Recordings by author 11.99			
7. Goddess Songs Music CD Recording, 11.99			

Subtotal:

20% discount for purchases of 3 or more:
State Tax:
Shipping and Handling (2.95 per bk):
Total:

Enclosed Payment and this Order form in an envelope and Mail to:

FEMININE DIVINE WORKS,
B. MELUSINE MIHALTSES
P.O. Box 114
Schertz, Texas 78154-0114
Femininedivineworks@gmail.com
Groveofthefemininedivine@yahoo.com
Visit our WEBSITE at: http://www.Femininedivineworks.com

Your Name_____

Mailing Address _____

_____

Telephone _____
Payment Information: Check___ Money Order _____

Please allow 2-4 weeks for delivery

FEMININE DIVINE WORKS

FEMININE DIVINE WORKS, P.O.BOX 114, SCHERTZ, TEXAS 78154
www.Femininedivineworks.com

www.ingramcontent.com/pod-product-compliance
Lightning Source LLC
Chambersburg PA
CBHW080811280326
41926CB00091B/4183